TYNDALE NEW T COMMENTARIES

VOLUME 14

TNTC

THE PASTORAL EPISTLES

Tyndale New Testament Commentaries

Volume 14

SERIES EDITOR: ECKHARD J. SCHNABEL
CONSULTING EDITOR: NICHOLAS PERRIN

The Pastoral Epistles

An Introduction and Commentary

Osvaldo Padilla

Academic

An imprint of InterVarsity Press
Downers Grove, Illinois

InterVarsity Press
P.O. Box 1400 | Downers Grove, IL 60515-1426
ivpress.com | email@ivpress.com

Inter-Varsity Press, England
36 Causton Street | London SW1P 4ST, England
ivpbooks.com | ivp@ivpbooks.com

InterVarsity Press® is the publishing division of InterVarsity Christian Fellowship/USA®. For more information, visit intervarsity.org.

Inter-Varsity Press, England, originated within the Inter-Varsity Fellowship, now the Universities and Colleges Christian Fellowship, a student movement connecting Christian Unions in universities and colleges throughout Great Britain, and a member movement of the International Fellowship of Evangelical Students. That historic association is maintained, and all senior IVP staff and committee members subscribe to the UCCF Basis of Faith. Website: www.uccf.org.uk.

First published 2022

USA ISBN 978-1-5140-0673-3 (print) | USA ISBN 978-1-5140-0674-0 (digital)

UK ISBN 978-1-78974-404-0 (print) | UK ISBN 978-1-78974-405-7 (digital)

Typeset in Great Britain by Avocet Typeset, Bideford, Devon

Printed in the United States of America ♾

Library of Congress Cataloging-in-Publication Data
A catalog record for this book is available from the Library of Congress.

British Library Cataloguing-in-Publication Data
A catalogue record for this book is available from the British Library.

30 29 28 27 26 25 24 23 22 | 12 11 10 9 8 7 6 5 4 3 2 1

CONTENTS

GENERAL PREFACE

The Tyndale Commentaries have been a flagship series for evangelical readers of the Bible for over sixty years. Both the original New Testament volumes (1956–1974) as well as the new commentaries (1983–2003) rightly established themselves as a point of first reference for those who wanted more than is usually offered in a one-volume Bible commentary, without requiring the technical skills in Greek and in Jewish and Greco-Roman studies of the more detailed series, with the advantage of being shorter than the volumes of intermediate commentary series. The appearance of new popular commentary series demonstrates that there is a continuing demand for commentaries that appeal to Bible study leaders in churches and at universities. The publisher, editors and authors of the Tyndale Commentaries believe that the series continues to meet an important need in the Christian community, not the least in what we call today the Global South with its immense growth of churches and the corresponding need for a thorough understanding of the Bible by Christian believers.

In the light of new knowledge, new critical questions, new revisions of Bible translations, and the need to provide specific guidance on the literary context and the genre of the individual passages as well as on theological emphases, it was time to publish new commentaries in the series. Four authors will revise their commentary from the second series. The original aim remains. The new commentaries are neither too short nor unduly long. They are exegetical and thus root the interpretation of the text in its historical context. They do not aim to solve all critical questions, but they are written with an awareness of major scholarly debates, which may be treated in the Introduction, in Additional Notes, or in the commentary itself. While not specifically homiletic in aim, they want to help readers to understand the passage under consideration in such a way that they begin to see points of relevance and application, even though the commentary does not explicitly offer these. The authors base their exegesis on the Greek text, but they write for readers who do not know Greek; Hebrew and Greek terms that are discussed are transliterated. The English translation used for the first series was the Authorized (King James) Version, the volumes of the second series mostly used the Revised Standard Version; the volumes of the third series use either the New International Version (2011) or the New Revised Standard Version as primary versions, unless otherwise indicated by the author.

The first and second series of the Tyndale Commentaries owed an immense debt of gratitude to R. V. G. Tasker and L. Morris who each wrote four of the commentaries themselves. The recruitment of new authors for the third series proved to be effortless, as colleagues were enthusiastic about becoming involved in this project, a testimony both to the larger number of New Testament scholars capable and willing to write commentaries, to the wider ethnic identity of contributors, and to the role that the Tyndale Commentaries has played in the church worldwide. It continues to be the hope of all those concerned with this series that God will graciously use the new commentaries to help readers understand as fully and clearly as possible the meaning of the New Testament.

Eckhard J. Schnabel, Series Editor
Nicholas Perrin, Consulting Editor

AUTHOR'S PREFACE

This is the first time I have written in the 'genre' of the commentary. This experience has made me aware that, although I have been wanting to say something fresh and possibly original at times, we really do stand on the shoulders of those who came before us. Some of the shoulders upon which I stood were the following. In French, the commentary by C. Spicq, although published in 1947, continues to be an authoritative piece of work. I have consulted this commentary often, refreshed by the sound exegesis and theology of the author. In English, I have found the commentary by I. H. Marshall in the ICC series difficult to disagree with. Although Marshall ultimately opted for non-Pauline authorship of the letters (a disappointment), his exegesis is thorough and his theology evangelical in the best sense of that word. I have also benefited from the commentaries by P. H. Towner and L. T. Johnson. Unfortunately, the commentary by R. Yarbrough appeared after the bulk of research was completed. I could only use his commentary for the Introduction. In German, the multivolume work by L. Oberlinner was helpful in making me rethink a number of areas. This is a very detailed commentary that often surprises with nuanced interpretations that I had not considered before. Lastly, although not a commentary proper, the reader will note that I have benefited greatly from the writings of A. Malherbe. His profound grasp of the primary sources, particularly of the moral philosophers of the Greco-Roman period, constitutes a treasure trove for anyone studying Paul's letters. Within the purview of this commentary series,

I have attempted to make a contribution to the understanding of the Pastoral Epistles in two ways. First, I have consulted the primary sources as often as possible in order to shed new light on the biblical text. Second, I have attempted to theologize seriously from the Pastorals, with the belief that these letters can enrich considerably the life of the church. Thus, in the Theology sections the reader will often find reflections that interact with Christian dogmatics.

I thank Eckhard Schnabel for the invitation to contribute this commentary to the TNTC series and for his many helpful suggestions to improve the work. Any remaining mistakes are mine.

I thank my students at Beeson Divinity School, Samford University. Together we have explored these letters for the past few years. It has been a pleasure to study God's Word with these men and women who are committed to God's call on their lives. They have often encouraged me more than they realize.

I thank the founding dean of Beeson Divinity School, Timothy George, for all his support and hospitality throughout the years. He suggested a visit to the Pontifical Biblical Institute (Biblicum) in Rome. I followed his advice and I was glad I did. My family and I spent part of a summer in *bella* Roma: I would spend the morning and early afternoon at the library of the Biblicum while they walked through the streets of Rome and my son Philip (I was told) ate gelatos at what seemed every corner! In the late afternoon we would go out and have dinner together and then walk through the city. This arrangement could have lasted for years, as far as I was concerned.

I thank the current dean at Beeson, Douglas Sweeney, for his friendship and commitment to the institution. He suggested that I visit Emory University for my sabbatical in the autumn of 2021. I followed his advice and I was glad I did. Emory University and Candler School of Theology were very hospitable in welcoming me as a Visiting Scholar. The Pitts Theological Library at Candler must be one of the top theological libraries in North America. I thank in particular Drs Anthony Briggman, Jonathan Strom and Richard (Bo) Adams. I also thank Robyn Pollette for helping me with efficiency and warmth in my temporary move to Atlanta.

These research trips would not have been possible without the generosity of Beeson Divinity School and Samford University.

I thank the board of trustees and the office of the provost for ample provision for both the trip to Rome and the sabbatical expenses at Emory. I also received an anonymous gift from a friend of Beeson. Without this gift, I could not have visited these wonderful libraries that made the writing of the commentary such a pleasurable experience.

I thank God, whose grace makes us sufficient when we are not. And finally, I am extremely grateful to my family: Kristen and Philip. Kristen has read just about every page of this commentary, making helpful comments along the way. During our walks we have also gone back and forth on a number of theological problems raised by the Pastoral Epistles. I am blessed to have such a patient and intelligent wife, who takes time from her own busy ministry to help a husband who often forgets what day of the week it is! Philip was very little when I received the commission for this commentary. As I write, he is a growing adolescent: intelligent, gentle, curious and God-fearing. He is also a very good basketball and even better tennis player. We have enjoyed reading *The Lord of the Rings* together before bed for the past year.

And so, this book too I dedicate to Kristen, and now also Philip. *Con todo mi amor.*

Osvaldo Padilla

ABBREVIATIONS

General

AB	Anchor Bible
ABD	*Anchor Bible Dictionary*, ed. D. N. Freedman (New York: Doubleday, 1972)
BBR	*Bulletin for Biblical Research*
BDAG	*A Greek-English Lexicon of the New Testament and Other Early Christian Literature*, ed. W. Bauer, F. W. Danker, W. F. Arndt and F. W. Gingric, 3rd edn (Chicago: University of Chicago Press, 2000)
BECNT	Baker Exegetical Commentary on the New Testament
BMSEC	Baylor-Mohr Siebeck Studies in Early Christianity
BNP	*Brill's New Pauly*, ed. H. Cancik and H. Schneider (Leiden: Brill, 2002–2012)
BNTC	Black's New Testament Commentary
BSac	*Bibliotheca Sacra*
BTCB	Brazos Theological Commentary of the Bible
BWANT	Beiträge zur Wissenschaft vom Alten und Neuen Testament
BZNW	Beihefte zur Zeitschrift für die neutestamentliche Wissenschaft
CBQ	*Catholic Biblical Quarterly*
CH	*Church History*
CIJ	*Corpus inscriptionum judaicarum*. ed. Jean-Baptiste

	Frey (Rome: Pontificio Istituto di Christiana, 1936–1952)
EDNT	*Exegetical Dictionary of the New Testament*, ed. H. Balz and G. Schneider (Grand Rapids: Eerdmans, 1990–1993)
EKK	Evangelisch-Katholischer Kommentar
ÉBib	Études bibliques
FRLANT	Forschungen zur Religion und Literatur des Alten und Neuen Testaments
FS	Festschrift
GELS	*A Greek-English Lexicon of the Septuagint*, ed. T. Muraoka (Leuven: Brill, 2009)
HTA	Historisch Theologische Auslegung
HThK	Herders Theologischer Kommentar zum Neuen Testament
HTR	*Harvard Theological Review*
ICC	International Critical Commentary
JBL	*Journal of Biblical Literature*
JETS	*Journal of the Evangelical Theological Society*
JR	*Journal of Religion*
JSNT	*Journal for the Study of the New Testament*
JSNTSup	Journal for the Study of the New Testament Supplement Series
KEK	Kritisch-exegetischer Kommentar über das Neue Testament
LEC	Library of Early Christianity
LGPN	Lexicon of Greek Personal Names
LNTS	Library of New Testament Studies
LSJ	*A Greek-English Lexikon*, ed. H. G. Liddell, R. Scott and H. S. Jones, 9th edn, with rev. supplement by P. G. W. Glare (Oxford: Oxford University Press, 1996)
LXX	Septuagint; English translations of LXX passages are taken from Albert Pietersma and Benjamin G. Wright, eds. A New English Translation of the Septuagint (Oxford: Oxford University Press, 2007)
Maj	Majority Text
MM	*The Vocabulary of the Greek Testament Illustrated*

	from the Papyri and Other Non-Literary Sources, ed. J. H. Moulton and G. Milligan (Grand Rapids: Eerdmans, 1930; reprint 1982)
NA²⁸	*Novum Testamentum Graece*. Nestle-Aland 28th rev. edn, by B. Aland, K. Aland, J. Karavidopoulos, C. M. Martini, B. M. Metzger and the Institut für Neutestamentliche Textforschung (Stuttgart: Deutsche Bibelgesellschaft, 2012)
NICNT	New International Commentary on the New Testament
NIGTC	New International Greek Testament Commentary
NovT	*Novum Testamentum*
NovTSup	Novum Testamentum Supplements Series
NTD	Das Neue Testament Deutsch
NTL	New Testament Library
NTOA	Novum Testamentum et Orbis Antiquus
NTS	*New Testament Studies*
NW	*Neuer Wettstein. Texte zum Neuen Testament aus Griechentum und Hellenismus*, ed. G. Strecker and U. Schnelle (Berlin: de Gruyter, 1996–2013)
OCD	*The Oxford Classical Dictionary*, ed. S. Hornblower and A. Spawforth, 4th edn (Oxford: Oxford University Press, 2012)
ODCC	*The Oxford Dictionary of the Christian Church*, ed. F. L. Cross and E. A. Livingstone, 3rd edn (Oxford: Oxford University Press, 2005)
PL	*Patrologia Latina*
PNTC	Pillar New Testament Commentary
ProEccl	*Pro ecclesia*
RB	*Revue Biblique*
SBLDS	Society of Biblical Literature Dissertation Series
SNTSMS	Society of New Testament Studies Monograph Series
SNTW	Studies in the New Testament World
StUNT	Studien zur Umwelt des Neuen Testaments
TDNT	*Theological Dictionary of the New Testament*, ed. G. Kittel and G. Friedrich (Grand Rapids: Eerdmans, 1964–1976)

TGST	Tesi Gregoriana Serie Teologia
ThHK	Theologischer Handkommentar zum Neuen Testament
TLNT	*Theological Lexicon of the New Testament*, ed. C. Spicq (Peabody: Hendricksen, 1995)
TNTC	Tyndale New Testament Commentary
TSAJ	Texte und Studien zum antiken Judentum
TynBul	*Tyndale Bulletin*
WBC	Word Biblical Commentary
WMANT	Wissenschaftliche Monographien zum Alten und Neuen Testament
WUNT	Wissenschaftliche Untersuchungen zum Neuen Testament

Ancient texts

	1–4 Macc	1–4 Maccabees
Aeschylus	*Sept.*	*Septem contra Thebas*
Aesop	*Fab.*	*Fabulae*
Apuleius	*Metam.*	*Metamorphoses*
Aristotle	*Eth. nic.*	*Ethica nicomachea*
	Oec.	*Oeconomica*
	Pol.	*Politica*
	Rhet.	*Rhetorica*
Arrian	*Anab.*	*Anabasis*
Athanaeus	*Deipn.*	*Deipnosophistae*
Athanasius	*Ep. Fest.*	*Epistulae festales*
Augustine	*Doctr. chr.*	*De doctrine christiana*
	Fund.	*Contra epistulam Manichaeum quam vocant Fundamenti*
Cicero	*Cael.*	*Pro Caelio*
	Sen.	*De senectute*
Clement of	*Protr.*	*Protrepticus*
Alexandria	*Strom.*	*Stromata*
Demosthenes	*Cor.*	*Corinthiaca (Or. 37)*
	Mid.	*In Midiam*
Dio Chrysostom	*Or.*	*Orationes*

Diodorus Siculus	*Hist.*	*Bibliotheca historica*
Diogenes		
Laertius	*Vit. phil.*	*Vita philosophorum*
Dionysius		
of Halicarnassus	*Ant. Rom.*	*Antiquitates romanae*
	Din.	*De Dinorcho*
	Is.	*De Isaeo*
Epictetus	*Diatr.*	*Diatribai*
	Enc.	*Enchiridion*
Euripides	*Heracl.*	*Heraclidae*
	Orest.	*Orestes*
Eusebius	*E.H.*	*Historia ecclesiastica*
Galen	*PHP*	*De Placitis Hippocratis et Platonis*
	Tum. Pr. Nat.	*De tumoribus praeter naturam*
Herodotus	*Hist.*	*Historia*
Hesiod	*Theog.*	*Theogonia*
Homer	*Il.*	*Ilias*
	Od.	*Odyssea*
Ignatius	*Eph.*	*To the Ephesians*
	Mag.	*To the Magnesians*
	Trall.	*To the Trallians*
Irenaeus	*A.H.*	*Adversus haereses*
Isocrates	*Bus.*	*Busiris (Or. 11)*
	De pace	*De pace (Or. 8)*
	Demon.	*Ad Demonicium (Or. 1)*
	Hel. enc.	*Helenae encomium (Or. 10)*
John		
Chrysostom	*Hom. 1 Tim.*	*Homiliae in epistulam i ad Timotheum*
Josephus	*Ag. Ap.*	*Contra Apionem*
	Ant.	*Antiquitates judaicae*
	J.W.	*Bellum judaicum*
	Vita	*Vita*
Justin Martyr	*Dial.*	*Dialogus cum Tryphone*
Juvenal	*Sat.*	*Satirae*
Lucian	*Alex.*	*Alexander*

	Anach.	*Anacharsis*
	Cal.	*Calumniae non temere credendum*
	Fug.	*Fugitivi*
	Merc. cond.	*De mercedi conductis*
	Philops.	*Philopseudes*
	Salt.	*De saltatione*
	Tim.	*Timon*
	Tox.	*Toxaris*
Marcus		
Aurelius	*Med.*	*Meditationes*
Musonius Rufus	*Diatr.*	*Diatribai*
Ovid	*Am.*	*Amores*
	Ars.	*Ars amatoria*
Philo	*Abr.*	*De Abrahamo*
	Agr.	*De agricultura*
	Conf.	*De confusione linguarum*
	Contempl.	*De vita contemplativa*
	Decal.	*De decalogo*
	Flacc.	*In Flaccum*
	Fug.	*De fuga et inventione*
	Hypoth.	*Hypothetica*
	Ios.	*De Iosepho*
	Leg.	*Legum allegoriae*
	Legat.	*Legatio ad Gaium*
	Migr.	*De migratione Abrahami*
	Mos.	*De vita Mosis*
	Praem.	*De praemiis et poenis*
	QE	*Quaestiones et solutiones in Exodum*
	QG	*Quaestiones et solutiones in Genesin*
	Sacr.	*De sacrificiis Abelis et Caini*
	Spec.	*De specialibus legibus*
Philodemus	*Oec.*	*Oeconomicus*
	Vit.	*De vitiis X*
Philostratus	*Vit. Apoll.*	*Vita Apollonii*
Plato	*Ap.*	*Apologia*

	Def.	*Definitiones*
	Euthyd.	*Euthydemus*
	Gorg.	*Gorgias*
	Leg.	*Leges*
	Phaed.	*Phaedo*
	Phaedr.	*Phaedrus*
	Prot.	*Protagoras*
	Resp.	*Respublica*
	Symp.	*Symposium*
	Tim.	*Timaeus*
Pliny the Elder	*Nat.*	*Naturalis historia*
Plutarch	*Ag. Cleom.*	*Agis et Cleomenes*
	Alex.	*Alexander*
	Amat.	*Amatorius*
	An. virt. doc.	*An virtus doceri possit*
	Apoph. lac.	*Apophthegmata laconica*
	Cat. Min.	*Cato Minor*
	Comp.	
	per Fab.	*Comparatio Periclis et Fabii Maximi*
	Conj. praec.	*Conjugalia Praecepta*
	De Laude	*De laude ipsius*
	Garr.	*De garrulitate*
	Lib. ed.	*De liberis educandis*
	Lyc.	*Lycurgus*
	Mar.	*Marius*
	Mor.	*Moralia*
	Per.	*Pericles*
	Praec. ger.	
	rei publ.	*Pracepta gerendae rei publicae*
	Tranq. an.	*De tranquillitate animi*
	Virt. prof.	*Quomodo quis suos in virtutes sentiat profectus*
Porphyry	*Abst.*	*De abstinentia*
Posidonius	*Frag.*	*Fragmenta*
Seneca	*Ben.*	*De beneficiis*
	Ep.	*Epistulae morales*
Sophocles	*Aj.*	*Ajax*

Strabo	*Geogr.*	*Geographica*
Tacitus	*Hist.*	*Historiae*
Tertullian	*adv. Marc.*	*Adversus Marcionem*
Theophrastus	*Char.*	*Characteres*
Thucydides	*Hist.*	*Historia belli peloponnesiaci*
Xenophon	*Oec.*	*Oeconomicus*

Bible versions

ESV   Scripture quotations are taken from the ESV Bible (The Holy Bible, English Standard Version), copyright © 2001 by Crossway, a publishing ministry of Good News Publishers. Used by permission. All rights reserved.

KJV   Extracts from the Authorized Version of the Bible (The King James Bible), the rights in which are vested in the Crown, are reproduced by permission of the Crown's Patentee, Cambridge University Press.

The Message   Scripture quotations are taken from *THE MESSAGE*. Copyright © by Eugene H. Peterson 1993, 1994, 1995, 1996, 2000, 2001, 2002. Used by permission of NavPress Publishing Group.

NIV   Scripture quotations are taken from The Holy Bible, New International Version (Anglicized edition). Copyright © 1979, 1984, 2011 by Biblica. Used by permission of Hodder & Stoughton Ltd, an Hachette UK company. All rights reserved. 'NIV' is a registered trademark of Biblica. UK trademark number 1448790.

NRSV   Scripture quotations are taken from the New Revised Standard Version of the Bible, Anglicized Edition, copyright © 1989, 1995 by the Division of Christian Education of the National Council of the Churches of Christ in the USA. Used by permission. All rights reserved.

SELECT BIBLIOGRAPHY

Commentaries on 1 Timothy, 2 Timothy and Titus

Bray, Gerald (2019), *The Pastoral Epistles*, International Theological Commentary (London: T&T Clark).

Collins, Raymond F. (2002), *1 & 2 Timothy and Titus*, NTL (Louisville: Westminster John Knox Press).

Dibelius, M. and H. Conzelmann. (1972), *The Pastoral Epistles*, trans. Philip Buttolph and Adela Yarbro, Hermeneia (Philadelphia: Fortress Press).

Guthrie, Donald (1990), *The Pastoral Epistles*, TNTC, rev. edn (Leicester: InterVarsity Press).

Hutson, Christopher R. (2019), *First and Second Timothy and Titus*, Paideia (Grand Rapids: Baker Academic).

Jeremias, Joachim (1963), *Die Briefe an Timotheus und Titus*, NTD (Göttingen: Vandenhoeck & Ruprecht).

Johnson, Luke Timothy (2001), *The First and Second Letters to Timothy*, AB (Garden City: Doubleday).

Kelly, J. N. D. (1963), *A Commentary on the Pastoral Epistles*, BNTC (London: A. & C. Black).

Knight, George W. (1992), *The Pastoral Epistles*, NIGTC (Grand Rapids: Eerdmans).

Köstenberger, Andreas (2017), *1-2 Timothy & Titus*, Biblical Theology for Christian Proclamation (Nashville: Holman).

Marshall, I. Howard (1999), *The Pastoral Epistles*, ICC (London: T&T Clark).

Merkel, Helmut (1991), *Die Pastoralbriefe*, NTD (Göttingen: Vandenhoeck & Ruprecht).

Neudorfer, Heinz-Werner (2012), *Der Brief des Apostels Paulus an Titus*, HTA (Witten: SCM R. Brockhaus).

Oberlinner, Lorenz (1994), *Die Pastoralbriefe. Erste Folge. Kommentar zum Ersten Timotheusbrief*, HThK (Freiburg: Herder).

—— (1995), *Die Pastoralbriefe. Zweite Folge. Kommentar zum Zweiten Timotheusbrief*, HThK (Freiburg: Herder).

—— (1996), *Die Pastoralbriefe. Dritte Folge. Kommentar zum Titusbrief*, HThK (Freiburg: Herder).

Roloff, Jürgen (1988), *Der Erste Brief an Timotheus*, EKK (Neukirchen-Vluyn: Benziger/Neukirchener).

Saarinen, Risto (2008), *The Pastoral Epistles with Philemon & Jude*, BTCB (Grand Rapids: Baker).

Schnabel, Eckhard (2006), *Der erste Brief des Paulus an die Korinther*, HTA (Witten: SCM R. Brockhaus).

Spicq, C. (1947), *Les Épitres Pastorales*, EB (Paris: J. Gabalda).

Towner, Philip H. (2006), *The Letters to Timothy and Titus*, NICNT (Grand Rapids: Eerdmans).

Weiser, Alfons (2003), *Der Zweite Brief an Timotheus*, EKK (Düsseldorf: Benziger/Neukirchener).

Yarbrough, Robert W. (2018), *The Letters to Timothy and Titus*, PNTC (Grand Rapids: Eerdmans).

Other commentaries, monographs and articles

Aageson, James W. (2007), *Paul, the Pastoral Epistles, and the Early Church*, Library of Pauline Studies (Grand Rapids: Baker Academic).

Adams, Edward (2013), *The Earliest Christian Meeting Places: Almost Exclusively Houses?* LNTS 450 (London: T&T Clark).

Alexander, Loveday (1993), 'Acts and Ancient Intellectual Biography', in Bruce W. Winter and Andrew D. Clarke (eds.), *The Book of Acts in Its Ancient Literary Setting*, Vol. 1, *The Book of Acts in Its First Century Setting* (Grand Rapids: Eerdmans), pp. 31–63.

(1994), 'Paul and the Hellenistic Schools: The Evidence of

Galen', in Troels Engberg-Pedersen (ed.), *Paul in His Hellenistic Context*, SNTW (Edinburgh: T&T Clark), pp. 60–83.

Arnold, Clinton (1995), *The Colossian Syncretism: The Interface between Christianity and Folk Belief at Colossae*, WUNT 2/77 (Tübingen: Paul Siebeck).

Badcock, F. J. (1937), *The Pauline Epistles and the Epistle to the Hebrews in Their Historical Setting* (London: SPCK).

Baldwin, Henry (2005), 'An Important Word: αὐθεντέω in 1 Timothy 2:12', in Andreas Köstenberger and Thomas Schreiner (eds.), *Women in the Church: An Analysis and Application of 1 Timothy 2:9–15*, 2nd edn (Grand Rapids: Baker Academic).

Barclay, John M. G. (2007) '"There Is Neither Old Nor Young?" Early Christianity and Ancient Ideologies of Age', *NTS* 53, pp. 225–241.

——(2015), *Paul and the Gift* (Grand Rapids: Eerdmans).

Barrett, Matthew (2021), *Simply Trinity: The Unmanipulated Father, Son, and Spirit* (Grand Rapids: Baker).

Bassler, Jouette M. (1984), 'The Widow's Tale: A Fresh Look at 1 Tim 5:3–16', *JBL* 103, pp. 23–41.

Bauckham, Richard (2008), *Jesus and the God of Israel: God Crucified and Other Studies on the New Testament's Christology of Divine Identity* (Grand Rapids: Eerdmans).

Baum, Armin (2001), *Pseudepigraphie und literarische Fälschung im frühen Christentum: mit ausgewählten Quellentexten samt deutscher Übersetzung*, WUNT 2/138 (Tübingen: Mohr Siebeck).

Baur, F. C. (2016), *Lectures on New Testament Theology*, ed. Peter C. Hodgson, trans. Robert F. Brown (Oxford: Oxford University Press).

Bavinck, Herman (2002–2008): *Reformed Dogmatics*, 4 Vols. Trans. John Bolt (Grand Rapids: Baker Academic).

Beiser, Frederick C. (1996), *The Sovereignty of Reason: The Defense of Rationality in the Early English Enlightenment* (Princeton: Princeton University Press).

Billings, J. Todd (2011), *Union with Christ: Reframing Theology and Ministry for the Church* (Grand Rapids: Baker).

Bosman, Philip (2003), *Conscience in Philo and Paul: A Conceptual History of the* synoida *Word Group*, WUNT 2/166 (Tübingen: Mohr Siebeck).

Brandt, Hartwin (2002), *Wird auch silbern mein Haar: Eine Geschichte des Alters in der Antike* (Munich: C. H. Beck).

Bruce, F. F. (1985), *The Pauline Circle* (Grand Rapids: Eerdmans).

Campbell, Constantine (2012), *Paul and Union with Christ: An Exegetical and Theological Study* (Grand Rapids: Zondervan).

Campbell, R. Alastair (1994), *The Elders: Seniority within Earliest Christianity*, SNTW (Edinburgh: T&T Clark).

Clarke, Andrew D. (1996), "'Refresh the Hearts of the Saints'': A Unique Pauline Context?' *TynBul* 46, pp. 277–300.

—— (1999), *Serve the Community of the Church: Christians as Leaders and Ministers* (Grand Rapids: Eerdmans).

—— (2008), *A Pauline Theology of Church Leadership*, LNTS 362 (London: T&T Clark).

Doering, Lutz (2012), *Ancient Jewish Letters and the Beginnings of Christian Epistolography*, WUNT 298 (Tübingen: Mohr Siebeck).

van Driel, Edwin C. (2021), *Rethinking Paul: Protestant Theology and Pauline Exegesis*, Current Issues in Theology (Cambridge: Cambridge University Press).

Duff, J. (1998), 'P[46] and the Pastorals: A Misleading Consensus?' *NTS* 44, pp. 578–590.

Dunn, James D. G. (1997), *The Theology of Paul the Apostle* (Grand Rapids: Eerdmans).

Eckstein, Hans-Joachim (1983), *Der Begriff* Syneidesis *bei Paulus: eine neutestamentlich-exegetische Untersuchung zum Gewissensbegriff*, WUNT 2/10 (Tübingen: Mohr Siebeck).

Evanson, Edward (1792), *The Dissonance of the Four Generally Received Evangelists and the Evidence of Their Respective Authenticity Examined* (Ipswich: Jermyn).

Feyel, Christophe (2009), Dokimasia: *La Place et le Rôle de l'Examen Préliminaire dans les Institutions des Cités Grecques*, Études Anciennes 36 (Nancy: Association pour la diffusion de la recherche sur l'antiquité).

Fiorenza, Elisabeth Schüssler (1994), *In Memory of Her: A Feminist Theological Reconstruction of Christian Origins*, 10th edn (New York: Crossroad).

Fitzgerald, John T. (1988), *Cracks in an Earthen Vessel: An Examination of the Catalogues of Hardships in the Corinthian Correspondence*, SBLDS 99 (Atlanta: Scholars Press).

────'Virtue/Vice Lists', *ABD* VI, pp. 857–859.

────(2007), 'Early Christian Missionary Practice and Pagan Reaction: 1 Peter and Domestic Violence against Slaves and Wives', in M. W. Hamilton, T. H. Olbricht and J. Peterson (eds.), *Renewing Tradition: Studies in Texts and Contexts in Honor of James W. Thompson* (Eugene: Pickwick Publications), pp. 24–44.

────(2010), 'The Stoics and the Early Christians on the Treatment of Slaves', in Tuomas Rasimus, Troels Engberg-Pedersen and Ismo Dundeberg (eds.), *Stoicism in Early Christianity* (Grand Rapids: Baker Academic), pp. 141–175.

Frei, Hans (1974), *The Eclipse of Biblical Narrative: A Study in Eighteenth and Nineteenth Century Hermeneutics* (New Haven: Yale University Press).

Frey, Jörg (2018), *The Glory of the Crucified One: Christology and Theology in the Gospel of John*, trans. Wayne Coppins and Christoph Heilig, BMSEC (Waco: Baylor University Press/ Mohr Siebeck).

Fuhrmann, Christopher J. (2012), *Policing the Roman Empire: Soldiers, Administration, Public Order* (Oxford: Oxford University Press).

Gathercole, Simon J. (2002), *Where Is Boasting? Early Jewish Soteriology and Paul's Response in Romans 1–5* (Grand Rapids: Eerdmans).

────(2006), *The Preexistent Son: Recovering the Christologies of Matthew, Mark, and Luke* (Grand Rapids: Eerdmans).

Gehring, Roger (2004), *House Church and Mission: The Importance of Household Structures in Early Christianity* (Peabody: Hendrickson Publishers).

Harrison, P. N. (1921), *The Problem of the Pastoral Epistles* (Oxford: Oxford University Press).

Hengel, Martin (1974), *Judaism and Hellenism: Studies in Their Encounter in Palestine during the Early Hellenistic Period*, trans. John Bowden (Philadelphia: Fortress Press).

Herzer, Jens (2017), 'Zwischen Mythos und Wahrheit: Neue Perspektiven auf die sogenannten Pastoralbriefe', *NTS* 63, pp. 428–450.

Hoklotubbe, T. Christopher (2017), *Civilized Piety: The Rhetoric of*

Pietas *in the Pastoral Epistles and the Roman Empire* (Waco: Baylor University Press).

Hölkeskamp, Karl J. (2004), 'Under Roman Roofs: Family, House, and Household', in Harriet I. Flower (ed.), *The Cambridge Companion to the Roman Republic* (Cambridge: Cambridge University Press), pp. 113–138.

Horrell, David G. (2005), *Solidarity and Difference: A Contemporary Reading of Paul's Ethics* (London: T&T Clark).

Hübner, Jamin (2015), 'Revisiting αὐθεντέω in 1 Timothy 2:12: What Do the Extant Data Really Show', *Journal for the Study of Paul and His Letters* 5, pp. 41–70.

Huizenga, Annette (2013), *Moral Education for Women in the Pastoral and Pythagorean Letters*, NovTSup 147 (Leiden: Brill).

Jenson, Robert W. (1997), *Systematic Theology. Vol. 1: The Triune God* (Oxford: Oxford University Press).

Jipp, Joshua W. (2015), *Christ Is King: Paul's Royal Ideology* (Minneapolis: Fortress Press).

Joshel, Sandra R. (2010), *Slavery in the Roman World*. Cambridge Introductions to Roman Civilization (Cambridge: Cambridge University Press).

Keener, Craig (2012–2015), *Acts: An Exegetical Commentary* (Grand Rapids: Baker).

—— (2021), *1 Peter* (Grand Rapids: Baker).

Kidson, Lyn M. (2020), *Persuading Shipwrecked Men: The Rhetorical Strategies of 1 Timothy 1*, WUNT 2/526 (Tübingen: Mohr Siebeck).

Kloppenborg, John S. (2019), *Christ's Associations: Connecting and Belonging in the Ancient City* (New Haven: Yale University Press).

Kloppenborg, John S., Richard Ascough and Philip Harland (2013), *Associations in the Greco-Roman World: A Sourcebook* (Baylor: Baylor University Press).

Knight, George (1984), 'ΑΥΘΕΝΤΕΩ in Reference to Women in 1 Timothy 2:12', *NTS* 30, pp. 143–157.

Lau, Andrew (1996), *Manifest in the Flesh: The Epiphany Christology of the Pastoral Epistles*, WUNT 2/86 (Tübingen: Mohr Siebeck).

Lightman, Marjorie and William Zeisel (1977), '*Univira*: An Example of Continuity and Change in Roman Society', *CH* 46, pp. 19–32.

von Lips, Hermann (2008), *Timotheus und Titus: Unterwegs für Paulus*, Biblische Gestalten 19 (Leipzig: Evangelische Verlagsanstalt).

López Salvá, Mercedes (2018), 'Introducción al Libro Cuarto de los Macabeos', in Natalio Fernández Marcos and María Victoria Spottorno Díaz-Caro (eds.), *La Biblia Griega. Septuaginta II. Libros Históricos* (Salamanca: Ediciones Sígueme), pp. 931–942.

Macaskill, Grant (2019), *Living in Union with Christ: Paul's Gospel and Christian Moral Identity* (Grand Rapids: Baker Academic).

McLean, B. H. (1996), 'The Place of Cult in Voluntary Associations and Christian Churches in Delos', in J. Kloppenborg and S. Wilson (eds.), *Voluntary Associations in the Graeco-Roman World* (London: Routledge), pp. 186–225.

Malherbe, Abraham (1986), *Moral Exhortation: A Greco-Roman Sourcebook* (Philadelphia: Westminster Press).

—— (1989), *Paul and the Popular Philosophers* (Minneapolis: Fortress Press).

—— (2014), *Light from the Gentiles: Hellenistic Philosophy and Early Christianity. Collected Essays, 1959–2012 by Abraham Malherbe*, 2 Vols. Carl Holladay, John T. Fitzgerald, Gregory E. Sterling and James W. Thompson (eds.), NovTSup 150 (Leiden: Brill).

Martin, S. C. (1997), Pauli testamentum: *2 Timothy and the Last Words of Moses*, TGST 18 (Roma: Pontifica Università Gregoriana).

Meade, David (1986), *Pseudonymity and Canon: An Investigation into the Relationship of Authorship and Authority in Jewish and Earliest Christian Tradition*, WUNT 39 (Tübingen: Mohr Siebeck).

Merz, Annette (2004), *Die Fiktive Selbstauslegung des Paulus: Intertextuelle Studien zur Intention und Rezeption der Pastoralbriefe*, NTOA/SUNT 52 (Göttingen: Vandenhoeck & Ruprecht).

Milgrom, Jacob (1990), *Numbers*, JPS Torah Commentary (Philadelphia: Jewish Publication Society).

Mitchell, Margaret (2003), *Journal of Religion* 83, pp. 116–119.

Moltmann, Jürgen (1974), *The Crucified God: The Cross of Christ as the Foundation and Criticism of Christian Theology*, trans. R. J. Wilson and John Bowden (New York: Harper & Row).

Morgan, Teresa (2015), *Roman Faith and Christian Faith: Pistis and Fides in the Early Roman Empire and Early Churches* (Oxford: Oxford University Press).

Mutschler, Bernhard (2010), *Glaube in den Pastoralbriefen: Pistis als Mitte Christlicher Existenz*, WUNT 256 (Tübingen: Mohr Siebeck).

van Nes, Jermo (2018), *Pauline Language and the Pastoral Epistles: A Study of Linguistic Variation in the* Corpus Paulinum, Linguistic Biblical Studies 16 (Leiden: Brill).

North, Helen (1966), Sophrosyne: *Self-Knowledge and Self-Restraint in Greek Literature*, Cornell Studies in Classical Philology 35 (Ithaca: Cornell University Press).

Oakes, Peter (2009), *Reading Romans in Pompeii: Paul's Letter at Ground Level* (Minneapolis: Fortress Press).

Padilla, Osvaldo (2016), *The Acts of the Apostles: Interpretation, History and Theology* (Downers Grove: IVP Academic).

—— (forthcoming), *The Vicarious Incarnation of Christ*, Studies in Christian Doctrine and Scripture (Downers Grove: IVP Academic).

Pao, David (2003), *Thanksgiving: An Investigation of a Pauline Theme*, NSBT 13 (Downers Grove: InterVarsity Press).

Parkin, Tim (2003), *Old Age in the Roman World: A Cultural and Social History* (Baltimore: Johns Hopkins University Press).

Pfitzner, V. C. (1967), *Paul and the Agon Motif: Traditional Athletic Imagery in the Pauline Literature*, NovTSup 16 (Leiden: Brill).

Porter, S. and G. P. Fewster (2013), *Paul and Pseudepigraphy*, Pauline Studies 8 (Leiden: Brill).

Provan, Iain (2017), *The Reformation and the Right Reading of Scripture* (Waco: Baylor University Press).

Rapske, Brian (1994), *Paul in Roman Custody. The Book of Acts in Its First Century Setting*, Vol. 3 (Grand Rapids: Eerdmans).

Reicke, B. (1976), 'Chronologie der Pastoralbriefe', *TLZ* 101, pp. 81–94.

Richards, E. Randolph (1991), *The Secretary in the Letters of Paul*, WUNT 2/42 (Tübingen: Paul Siebeck).

Ridderbos, Herman N. (1975): *Paul: An Outline of His Theology*, trans. John Richard de Witt (Grand Rapids: Eerdmans).

Saller, Richard (1994), *Patriarchy, Property, and Death in the Roman*

Family, Cambridge Studies in Population, Economy, and Society in Past Time 25 (Cambridge: Cambridge University Press).

Sanders, E. P. (2001), *Paul: A Very Short Introduction* (Oxford: Oxford University Press).

Schleiermacher, F. E. D. (1807), 'Ueber den sogenannten ersten Brief des Paulos an den Timotheos', *Friedrich Schleiermacher. Sämtliche Werke. Abteilung 1: Zur Theologie. Band 2.* Ed. Jacob Frerichs (Berlin: De Gruyter), pp. 221–320.

Schnabel, Eckhard J. (2004), *Early Christian Mission*, 2 Vols. (Downers Grove: InterVarsity).

—— (2008), *Paul the Missionary: Realities, Strategies and Methods* (Downers Grove: IVP Academic).

Schnelle, Udo (2009), *Theology of the New Testament*, trans. M. Eugene Boring (Grand Rapids: Baker Academic).

Schrage, Wolfgang (1988), *The Ethics of the New Testament*, trans. David E. Green (Philadelphia: Fortress Press).

Schreiner, Thomas (2005), 'A Response to Linda Beleville', in James R. Beck (ed.), *Two Views on Women in Ministry*, 2nd edn (Grand Rapids: Zondervan), pp. 105–109.

von Siebenthal, Heinrich (2019), *Ancient Greek Grammar for the Study of the New Testament* (Berlin: Peter Lang).

Smith, Julien C. H. (2020), *Paul and the Good Life: Transformation and Citizenship in the Commonwealth of God* (Waco: Baylor University Press).

Sterling, Greg (2001), '*Mors Philosophi*: The Death of Jesus in Luke', *HTR* 94, pp. 383–402.

Stettler, Hanna (1998), *Die Christologie der Pastoralbriefe*, WUNT 2/105 (Tübingen: Mohr Siebeck).

Stirewalt, M. Luther (2003), *Paul, the Letter Writer* (Grand Rapids: Eerdmans).

Stowers, Stanley Kent (1986), *Letter Writing in Greco-Roman Antiquity*, LEC 5 (Philadelphia: Westminster Press).

Stuhlmacher, Peter (2018), *Biblical Theology of the New Testament*, trans. Daniel P. Bayley (Grand Rapids: Eerdmans).

Torrance, T. F. (2008) *Incarnation: The Person and Life of Christ* (Downers Grove: IVP Academic).

Verner, David C. (1983), *The Household of God: The Social World of the Pastoral Epistles*, SBLDS 71 (Chico, CA: Scholars Press).

von Wagener, Ulrike (1994), *Die Ordnung des "Hauses Gottes": der Ort von Frauen in der Ekklesiologie und Ethik der Pastoralbriefe*, WUNT 2/65 (Tübingen: J. C. B. Mohr).

Wallace, Daniel (2000), *The Basics of New Testament Syntax: An Intermediate Greek Grammar* (Grand Rapids: Zondervan).

Wilckens, Ulrich (2002–2016), *Theologie des Neuen Testaments*, 7 Vols. (Neukirchen-Vluyn: Neukirchener).

Winter, Bruce W. (2003), *Roman Wives, Roman Widows: The Appearance of New Women and the Pauline Communities* (Grand Rapids: Eerdmans).

Witt, William G. (2020), *Icons of Christ: A Biblical and Systematic Theology for Women's Ordination* (Waco: Baylor University Press).

Wolter, Michael (1988), *Die Pastoralbriefe als Paulustradition*, FRLANT 146 (Göttingen: Vandenhoeck & Ruprecht).

—— (2014), *Der Brief an die Römer. Teilband 1: Röm 1–8*, EKK (Neukirchen-Vluyn: Neukirchener Theologie/Patmos Verlag).

—— (2015), *Paul: An Outline of His Theology*, trans. Robert L. Brawley (Waco: Baylor University Press).

Wolters, Al (2009), 'αυθεντης and Its Cognates in Biblical Greek', *JETS* 52, pp. 719–729.

Wright, N. T. (2013), *Paul and the Faithfulness of God*, 2 Vols. Christian Origins and the Question of God, Vol. 4 (Minneapolis: Fortress Press).

Yeago, David (1994), 'The New Testament and the Nicene Dogma: A Contribution to the Recovery of Theological Exegesis', *ProEccl* 3, pp. 152–164.

INTRODUCTION

1. Authorship

a. Early church to the eighteenth century

Each of the Pastoral Epistles claims to have been written by Paul the apostle, who introduces himself as the author in the salutation of each letter. Christians, from very early, accepted these letters as written by Paul. As far as we know, only very few rejected Pauline authorship at the early stage of the church (e.g., Marcion). Beginning in the eighteenth century and up to the present time, however, many scholars, especially from mainline Protestantism, hold that the Pastoral Epistles are pseudonymous: not written by Paul but by someone else as if he (or they) was the apostle. In the pages that follow I will state my view of the matter, attempting at the same time to bring the reader up to date on how things stand in the academy on the subject of the Pastoral Epistles' authorship. Given the nature of this commentary series, we can only offer a sketch of the subject. Those who desire a longer account should turn to the longer commentaries. In English, the treatments of Johnson, Marshall and Towner are particularly helpful.

The view taken in this commentary is that the author of the Pastoral Epistles is Paul the apostle. This view is taken because this is what we find in the text of Scripture, which I believe to be a trustworthy, written account of the Word of God. In saying this I am aware that some objections may be presented that could make my statement seem naïve, or perhaps even the result of some hidden fundamentalism. For example, it may be easy to point out that my statement about 'the text of Scripture' is anachronistic. Since neither our modern language Bibles nor the Greek New Testament (the NA[28] is employed throughout this commentary) fell pristinely from heaven, what do we mean by 'the text of Scripture'? *What* Scripture? From what period? This provides an opportunity to briefly comment on the manuscripts on which our Greek New Testaments and modern Bibles depend, particularly as it relates to the Pastoral Epistles.

Our modern Bibles are based on a Greek text reconstructed from the earliest and best manuscripts of the New Testament texts, including early papyri, which are often fragmentary. The most important manuscripts are the two dominant majuscules Codex Sinaiticus (א) and Codex Vaticanus (B), both dating to the fourth century AD. Codex Sinaiticus includes the Pastoral Epistles in the order we have in our modern Bibles. Just as in our Bibles, each Pastoral letter begins with 'Paul, apostle' (1 and 2 Timothy), or 'Paul, a servant of God' (Titus). Codex Vaticanus contains all the letters Paul wrote to churches, but lacks those written to individuals (i.e., the Pastoral Epistles and Philemon), which tend to come at the end of the Pauline Corpus in manuscripts and canon lists. Since there are a number of pages missing from Codex Vaticanus after Hebrews 9:14 (note that many in the ancient church thought Paul wrote Hebrews), it is probable that Philemon and the Pastoral Epistles *were* once part of the manuscript but have been lost. There is no significant debate on this point. Two other early major manuscripts – Codex Alexandrinus and Codex Ephraemi Rescriptus (both fifth century) – also include the Pastoral Epistles as part of the Pauline Corpus, with Paul's name in the salutations.

Of the numerous yet often fragmentary papyri, the letter to Titus is found in P[32] (c. AD 200). Unfortunately, only fragments of Titus chapters one and two survive (Tit. 1:11–15; 2:3–8). This is the oldest manuscript of any of the Pastoral Epistles in existence today. This tells us that at least Titus was being read and copied very early. Perhaps the most important papyrus for the Pauline letters is P⁴⁶, which dates near AD 200 and was a collection of Paul's letters. Because the Pastoral Epistles are missing from this papyrus, and because it dates so early, some scholars have suggested that perhaps here we have textual evidence that at least in some regions of the early church the Pastoral Epistles were not viewed as Pauline. This would be significant. On the other hand, since there are missing pages at the back end of the manuscript (the last surviving part of the papyrus is 1 Thess. 5:28, the last verse of that letter), it is possible that the Pastoral Epistles were once present in the circulation of this corpus. Jeremy Duff has argued that the scribe of P⁴⁶ increased the number of words per page (by compressing) from the middle of the document onward. He did this because he would have realized that he would run out of space to include the Pastoral Epistles. With more words per page than was the case in the first half of the quire, the scribe would have been able to include up to 2 Timothy.[1] Duff considers it a viable hypothesis that the scribe of the papyrus would then have added extra pages to the quire, or a new quire altogether, in order to include Titus.[2]

Another hypothesis was put forth by Joachim Jeremias who argued that P⁴⁶ was probably a collection of Paul's letters to *churches*, not individuals.[3] Thus, the last missing seven pages would have included 2 Thessalonians, which is also currently absent in the papyrus. Jeremias' hypothesis receives support from the Muratorian Canon (mid-second century), where the author clearly differentiates between Paul's letters to churches and letters to individuals.

Whatever the solution with respect to P⁴⁶, it is fair to say that some scholars have placed an undue amount of weight on this single papyrus to reach the conclusion that Paul was not the author of the Pastoral Epistles. Much more evidence is needed to reach

---

1 Duff, 'P⁴⁶ and the Pastorals', pp. 578–587.
2 Ibid., pp. 587–589.
3 Jeremias, p. 4.

such a conclusion, particularly in light of the testimony of the early church, where Pauline authorship of the Pastoral Epistles was held unanimously.

To conclude this section, we can say that the Pastoral Epistles are found in the most important codices of the NT, just as the other letters of Paul. That the letters are missing from Codex Vaticanus is recognized as an accidental loss (Vaticanus is also missing Philemon and Revelation). This also may be the explanation for the omission of the letters in P^{46}. We do find fragments of Titus in P^{32}, which dates to approximately AD 200. As a whole, then, the Pastoral Epistles are stable in the manuscript tradition as both Pauline letters and canonical documents.

I now turn to the evidence of the Apostolic Fathers. The Fathers provide an important window into early Christianity, from AD 70 to around 150.[4] In their treatment of Scripture, the Fathers normally do not cite the names of the biblical authors when quoting Scripture. Nevertheless, they do quote or echo material that they clearly viewed as apostolic and therefore authoritative. There are many statements in the Fathers that are also found in the Pastoral Epistles, thus opening the possibility that they were quoting these letters as authoritative Scripture. However, these possible quotations or echoes are often so traditional in their content that one cannot say with confidence that the Fathers are referring to the Pastoral Epistles exclusively. Consider the following example: in *1 Clement* 61:2 the author speaks of God as 'the King of the ages'. This exact phrase is found in 1 Timothy 1:17. Should we conclude that Clement is quoting from 1 Timothy? This is a possible conclusion. However, the phrase 'King of the ages' is also found in sufficient Jewish writings (e.g., Tob. 13:6, 10 and the Hebrew text of Jer. 10:10) to lead us to conclude that Clement may have picked it up from other sources, not necessarily from Timothy. This type of example with respect to the Pastoral Epistles can be shown in numerous places in the Fathers.

There are, however, at least two examples where the author's statement does appear to be a reference to the Pastoral Epistles.

---

4 Holmes, *Apostolic Fathers*, p. 3.

One such example is found in Polycarp's letter to the Philippians (c. AD 117). At 4:1 he states: 'But the love of money is the beginning of all troubles. *Knowing, therefore, that we brought nothing into the world and cannot take anything out*, let us arm ourselves with the weapons of righteousness.' The highlighted portion, although expressing a sentiment that can also be found in the Old Testament and Greek philosophers (see commentary), is so similar and even identical in language to 1 Timothy 6:7, 10, that we probably do have here a quotation from 1 Timothy.[5] A second example comes from 1 Clement (c. AD 95–97). At 2:7 Clement tells the Corinthians: 'You never once regretted doing good, *but were ready for every good work*.' Again, the highlighted portion is probably a quotation from Titus 3:1 in light of identical language. In addition, the phrase is not common in Jewish or Greco-Roman literature.[6]

Thus, it is probable that the Pastoral Epistles (at least 1 Timothy and Titus) were known and used authoritatively by Clement and Polycarp. This is significant, since these authors wrote at the end of the first and beginning of the second century AD.

I conclude this sketch by looking at documents from the early church outside the Apostolic Fathers. It is helpful to begin with the statements on the Pastoral Epistles found in the Muratorian Canon, which probably dates to approximately AD 200. This document is the oldest list of the New Testament books that we possess. The pertinent section reads:

> [Paul also wrote] out of affection and love one to Philemon, one to Titus, and two to Timothy; and these are held sacred in the esteem of the Church catholic for the regulation of ecclesiastical discipline. There is current also [an epistle] to the Laodiceans, [and] another to the Alexandrians, [both] forged in Paul's name to [further] the heresy of

---

5 Another potential allusion is found in 2:1–3 of Polycarp's letter to the Philippians, alluding to 2 Tim. 4:8.

6 A TLG search of 'ready' (*hetoimos*) plus 'work' (*ergon*) yielded an insignificant amount of texts. The closest may be Dio Chrysostom, *Or.* 64.5.

Marcion, and several others which cannot be received into the catholic
Church—for it is not fitting that gall be mixed with honey.
(Trans. Metzger)

This is an important statement for at least four reasons. First, and
most obvious, is the declaration that Paul wrote what we call the
Pastoral Epistles. Second, as indicated previously, there is evidence
here for grouping the Pastorals with Paul's letter to individuals.
Third, it should be noted that the author reinforces the view that
these letters were received into the universal church and so can be
employed in church life. It is likely that the author added this statement because these epistles were written to individuals. One could
then ask: do they have the same authority as the other letters of Paul,
which were written to *churches*? Are they *applicable* to the government
of the church even though they were not written to congregations?
The author answers this in the affirmative. Lastly, we may note that
the author mentions letters forged in Paul's name. They are not to
be accepted because they are forgeries and because they forward
Marcion's heresy. This helps us see that pseudepigraphic letters in
Paul's name existed in the early church (cf. 2 Thess. 2:2) yet were
not accepted (see further comments below).

Other authors from the second to fourth centuries who cite the
Pastoral Epistles, almost always mentioning Paul as their author,
include Theophilus, *ad Autolycus* 3.14; Irenaeus, *A.H.* Preface; 1.18.3;
2.14.7; 3.3.3; 3.14.1; Clement of Alexandria, *Strom.* 1.350; Tertullian,
Adv. Marc. 5.21; Athanasius, *Ep. fest.* 39.

To conclude this section on the authorship tradition of the Pastoral Epistles, it can be noted that there is strong evidence, dating
to the second century, that these were letters authored by Paul. That
the letters were used authoritatively is suggested by the quotation
from *1 Clement*. It is fair to say, therefore, that the early, orthodox
church held the view that the Pastoral Epistles were canonical documents whose author was Paul, not pseudonymous writings. To hold
the view of Pauline authorship today is to be in continuity with the
earliest witnesses of the formation of the New Testament canon.
And, in fact, Christians throughout the centuries have held this
view on the basis that their Bibles have 'Paul the apostle' as the
author of the letters.

b. Eighteenth century to the present

It is not surprising that negation of the Pauline origin of the Pastoral Epistles began in the eighteenth century, for a century earlier the period that we call the Enlightenment had taken its first steps. There is much that could be said about the effects of the Enlightenment on biblical studies.[7] I mention two aspects that may help us understand (partly) why the Pastoral Epistles began to be rejected as Pauline. First, during the Enlightenment there was a loud call on the part of many philosophers and theologians for emancipation from the traditional doctrines of the church: the Trinity, revelation, the incarnation and miracles, for example. According to these academics the time had come to stop basing our most essential beliefs on the Bible and the creeds of the church. All doctrines should be subjected to reason before they could be accepted.[8] Second, biblical studies began to be dominated by historical, not theological questions. Something had to take the place of theology if it would no longer serve as the framework for the study of the Bible. This was filled with the newly developed 'scientific' discipline of history. For those biblical scholars who placed philosophy before revelation, study of the Bible became one of 'purely historical' interest.[9] That is, biblical studies were to be, not foundationally a theological discipline, but mostly a rational quest of what the men who wrote the Bible intended to communicate to their original audiences. What the church had said about the origins of biblical texts should be laid aside in exegesis, for its statements were dominated by a theological framework that was not sufficiently scientific. This was the prevalent intellectual atmosphere, especially in England and Germany, when we begin to hear doubts of the Pauline provenance of the Pastoral Epistles.

---

7 See Frei, *The Eclipse of Biblical Narrative*; Provan, *The Reformation and the Right Reading of Scripture*, chapters 14–16. See also, forthcoming, Padilla, *The Vicarious Incarnation of Christ*.

8 See helpfully Beiser, *The Sovereignty of Reason*, pp. 3–19.

9 The phrase 'purely historical' to refer to the goal of biblical studies in modernity I owe to Wilckens, *Theologie des Neuen Testaments*, 1:1, pp. 15–18: 'rein historisch'.

Jermo van Nes has recently shown that the campaign to question the originality of the Pastoral Epistles began in England, not Germany, as is usually believed.[10] In 1792 the English clergyman Edward Evanson wrote a work that argued for the pseudonymity of most of Paul's letters, Romans included! He also viewed the Pastorals as pseudonymous, based partly on their language but primarily on their theology. Evanson viewed the theology of the letters as 'most malicious, illiberal'.[11] It should be noted that Evanson had strong Socinian and Unitarian affinities, even arguing for the removal of the Nicene Creed from the Book of Common Prayer.[12]

In Germany Friedrich Schleiermacher questioned the authenticity of 1 Timothy in an open letter in 1807.[13] He argued that the letter was pseudonymous, actually drawn from 2 Timothy and Titus (van Nes, p. 10). Since many of Schleiermacher's arguments are still basically the arguments used today, it may be helpful to list them here. As van Nes summarizes, according to Schleiermacher, 1 Timothy was not authentic because: (1) There was a high number of *hapax legomena* (words only found in 1 Timothy) in the letter. (2) The language of 1 Timothy at times follows that of 2 Timothy and at other times that of Titus, thereby showing dependence. (3) It is difficult to locate when Paul would have written 1 Timothy if we use Acts as a biographic template. (4) There seemed to be no genre parallels between 1 Timothy and the other letters of Paul. (5) 1 Timothy is less theologically coherent, and is even inferior, to Paul's other letters (van Nes, pp. 10–13).[14] Although the arguments of both Evanson and Schleiermacher were initially received with considerable criticism, their views did not die out; in fact, they began to receive support from other scholars.

In his massively influential introduction to the New Testament (3 Vols., 1810–14), J. G. Eichhorn extended Schleiermacher's arguments to all three Pastoral Epistles (van Nes, pp. 15–17). In a

---

10   Van Nes, *Pauline Language and the Pastoral Epistles*, pp. 8–10.
11   Evanson, *The Dissonance*, pp. 267–269.
12   ODCC3d, p. 585.
13   'Über den sogenannten ersten Brief des Paulos an den Timotheos'.
14   See also the helpful summary in Roloff, pp. 23–24.

number of publications between 1835 and 1860, F. C. Baur argued carefully for the relationship between the Pastorals and second-century gnostic polemic, thereby making it impossible for Paul to have written these letters, since he was executed in the mid-60s.[15] In 1880 H. J. Holtzmann published an important commentary on the Pastoral Epistles, which both assumed the pseudonymity of the letters and also argued in the most rigorous way to date for the non-Pauline provenance of the letters. Holtzmann argued in such a way so as 'to destroy objections, and convincingly establish the impossibility of the Pauline authorship of the epistles' (Roloff, p. 24). This commentary had a profound effect on the future negation of the authenticity of the letters.[16]

In the English-speaking world the most persuasive and momentous work against Pauline authorship of the Pastoral Epistles was that of P. N. Harrison.[17] His goal was to demonstrate that the letters were written by a Paulinist during the late reign of Trajan and the early reign of Hadrian (c. AD 101–120). His three major arguments were as follows: (1) the language of the Pastoral Epistles is very different from the accepted Pauline letters in vocabulary, grammar, and style. (2) The language is more like that of second-century Hellenistic authors. (3) The unknown author of the Pastoral Epistles weaved in material from Paul's other letters into the Pastorals in order to show his admiration for Paul and thereby his faithfulness to the apostle (van Nes, pp. 26–35).

As the years passed, the supposed pseudonymity of the Pastoral Epistles gained the upper hand in both liberal Protestant and liberal Roman Catholic educational institutions and churches. However, evangelical and conservative Roman Catholics continue to hold to the traditional view of Paul as author.

---

15 Ibid., p. 24. See also the recently translated Baur lectures: *Lectures on New Testament Theology*, pp. 325–31.

16 See van Nes, *Pauline Language and the Pastoral Epistles*, pp. 18–26, for a categorization of Holtzmann's arguments.

17 Harrison, *The Problem of the Pastoral Epistles*.

c. Conclusion

The view taken in this commentary is that belief in Paul's author-ship of the Pastoral Epistles is not something that can be proved by engaging in argument and counter-argument with those schol-ars who deny Pauline authorship. As Protestant evangelicals who submit to the authority of the Scriptures, we look to those same Scriptures for belief in Paul as the author of these letters. In other words, we should believe the biblical texts that state 'Paul, apostle of Christ Jesus' (1 Tim. 1:1; 2 Tim. 1:1) and 'Paul, a servant of God and apostle of Jesus Christ' (Tit. 1:1). The testimony of Scripture is the strongest of proofs (Calvin, *Inst.* 1.7). Nevertheless, since many of the arguments proffered by those who deny Pauline authorship are faulty in many respects, it is necessary to engage with those arguments with the best evidence and method. In addition, it is often in cordial disagreement that we come to understand our own positions best. Below are three broad statements and arguments that contest the pseudonymous view of the Pastoral Epistles.

First, one of the arguments that originated with Schleiermacher, and which continues to be employed in the present, is the apparent lack of connection between Paul's missionary movements and the composition of the Pastoral Epistles. That is, the situations reflected in the Pastorals do not seem to fit with the information about Paul found in the Acts of the Apostles.

This argument, however, is problematic, for it assumes that Acts is a comprehensive history of the early church, and of Paul in particular. While Acts is a historical work that provides a true account of the contents narrated therein, it is not an exhaustive account. That is, the Acts of the Apostles is a selective history that includes and omits in accordance with the historical and theologic-al goals of the author.[18] This selectivity in the historical genre has also been recognized by historians of antiquity and modernity.[19] Therefore, not being able to locate in Acts when Paul would have

---

18 See Padilla, *The Acts of the Apostles*, pp. 75–107; Keener, *Acts*,
    1:90–220.

19 For the literature, see Padilla, *The Acts of the Apostles*, pp. 108–122;
    Marguerat, *Les Actes des Apôtres*, 1:24–30.

written the Pastoral Epistles is not a strong argument against the letters' authorship. Having said this, it is worth pointing out that a number of able scholars have presented plausible scenarios within the known history of Paul in Acts where the Pastoral Epistles could have been composed.[20] On the other hand, even while raising this possibility, scholars who deny Pauline authorship quickly speak of it disparagingly as no more than a possibility.[21] And yet, 2 Timothy in particular, if one holds that Paul was executed in Rome after a period of imprisonment there, would not at all be implausible (see below in the section on the Occasion of the Letters for the church tradition). Whether it is possible or not to find in Acts episodes where Paul could have written 1 Timothy and Titus, there may be a lack of historiographical sophistication in expecting that Acts (or most historical works) provide comprehensive coverage of the events of a person's life.

The second argument often used against Pauline authorship is linguistic. The argument has at least three layers. First, there are numerous words that are found in Paul's so-called authentic letters which are lacking in the Pastorals. Second, the Pastorals contain a high number of *hapax legomena*. Third, there are some apparent syntactical idiosyncrasies in the Pastoral Epistles that differ significantly from Paul's other letters.

While the present author is not a professional linguist, a few comments can be offered against the linguistic argument, particularly at the methodological level. First, Schleiermacher, who again was the first to raise vocabulary as a problem, only conducted an 'impressionistic' analysis of the data.[22] Second, it is likely that the Pauline Corpus (even including the Pastoral Epistles), does not provide a sufficiently large sample to carry out a methodologically satisfactory analysis of the data. Third, those who deny Pauline

---

20 Reicke, 'Chronologie der Pastoralbriefe', pp. 81–94; Johnson, pp. 65–68.

21 Merkel, p. 8, raises the possibility of Paul's journey to Jerusalem (from Acts 20:2) as a time when the letters could have been written but quickly states that this is no more than a far-off possibility.

22 So, Johnson, p. 68.

authorship tend to minimize how much the specific situation that
an author is addressing can affect the choice of vocabulary. Many
more arguments can be offered that weaken the supposedly solid
evidence of linguistic disparity leading to difference of authorship.
As we note below, the recent work of van Nes is to date the most
sophisticated rebuttal of the linguistic argument against Pauline
authorship of the Pastorals.

Employing modern linguistic criticism, which for some time
has already been used in classical studies, van Nes mounts an
impressive argument from the linguistic perspective. In particular, van Nes shows the advantage of employing quantitative and
qualitative methods that include regression analysis (a basic stat-
istical analysis to explain the relationship of data, in this case the
vocabulary of Paul in the Pastorals in relationship to his other
letters), as well as explanatory models used by modern linguists
of the Indo-European languages (pp. 113–139). Concentrating on
vocabulary and syntax, van Nes concludes that the differences
between the Pastoral Epistles and the other Pauline letters should
not lead to the necessity of positing for author variation (i.e., the
respective letters *must* have been written by different persons).
In his view the data simply do not allow for the type of overly
confident statements against Pauline authorship that are regularly
found in New Testament scholarship. The variations found in the
data can lead to other conclusions, including the view that Paul
could have been the author of the Pastoral Epistles. Van Nes
suggests that the argument to disqualify these letters as Pauline
from the point of view of the language they use should be off the
table.[23] Those who question Pauline authorship – should they
continue to do so – may have a better argument in the direction
of the apparent shadowy circumstances behind the composition
of the letters. We should note that van Nes does not argue for
Pauline authorship as such. His task is rather to question the anti-
quated linguistic methods that are still found in commentaries
and New Testament introductions. This modest conclusion is in

---

23   See ibid., pp. 221–224 and the helpful appendices summarizing the
     data.

sharp contrast to those who state with great confidence that Paul did not write the Pastorals.[24]

The third observation that plays a part in the debate of Pauline authorship falls more into the 'social' side of the argument. It is the following: a number of leading, non-evangelical voices in the academy are themselves questioning the status quo on the pseudonymity of the Pastoral Epistles. I give two examples. First, in his 2001 Anchor Bible commentary on 1 and 2 Timothy, Luke Timothy Johnson, Professor Emeritus at Emory University, raised eyebrows in the academy when he argued vigorously that the letters were authored by Paul. This was not received very well by other scholars.[25] Nevertheless, Johnson's careful research both of the textual evidence as well as the history of interpretation led him to conclude that in reality there were 'extra-evidential factors' (p. 55) for the consensus against Pauline authorship. Some of these 'extra-evidential factors' included the following: (1) the power of construal: 'The more one construal is handed on to the generations that have not examined its premises and arguments as settled "fact," the more natural and self-evident it becomes' (p. 56). (2) The desire to use Paul for particular social or theological cause may lead to discharging him when some of his writings go *against* the cause we may wish to use him for (pp. 56–57; see e.g., 1 Timothy 2:9–11 and the ordination of women). (3) The quality of the criteria, which is to say the criteria used to deny Pauline authorship, is not particularly scientific: 'In light of recent scholarship, the various criteria that were developed willy-nilly … increasingly appear to be simplistic and possibly even misleading' (p. 58). (4) Lastly, Johnson speaks of the consequences of grouping 1 Timothy, 2 Timothy and Titus (pp. 63–64). That is, there seems to be an 'all or nothing' approach in the verdict of authenticity: either all are authentic or all are pseudonymous.

---

24 For example, Meade, *Pseudonymity and Canon*, p. 118, who speaks of the pseudonymous view of Ephesians and the Pastoral Epistles as a 'foregone conclusion'!

25 See the scathing review by Margaret Mitchell in *JR* 83 (2003), pp. 116–119.

While Johnson perceives *some* potential evidence to question the authenticity of the Pastoral Epistles, at the end it seems to him that what gives pulse to the rejection of the letters is a social consensus. He concludes: 'But I remind the reader that this consensus resulted as much from social dynamics as from the independent assessment of the evidence by each individual scholar' (p. 55).

The second example of recent mainline scholars who are questioning the pseudonymous view of the Pastoral Epistles is Jens Herzer, who is the chair of New Testament Exegesis and Theology at the University of Leipzig in Germany. From a number of publications questioning the consensus, I call attention to his recent essay, published in the journal of the Society of New Testament Studies, the most prestigious academic society in New Testament studies.[26] First, Herzer argues that we should move away from viewing these letters as one corpus, namely 'the Pastoral Epistles'. Only when we proceed in this manner can we appreciate the uniqueness of each letter and their potential Pauline origin. Second, when this is done, he concludes that 1 Timothy should still not be viewed as Pauline;[27] third, however, Herzer argues that 2 Timothy and Titus may perhaps be authentic, even though they sound a bit different from Paul's other genuine letters. The reason why they ring different from the accepted letters is that they were composed during a special situation in Paul's life. Titus, for example, constitutes a 'snapshot' during Paul's journey to Rome, fresh from Jewish rejection of the Gentile offering (p. 449).

It is time to summarize. From the earliest period that we know of the development of the New Testament canon, the Pastoral Epistles were received as letters from Paul the apostle. The few who denied their authenticity (along with other NT writings) did so for heretical reasons, Marcion being the best-known example (see Tertullian, *Adv. Marc.* 5.21). Otherwise, the church held the letters as Pauline, with a stream of the tradition classifying them as letters that Paul

---

26 Herzer, 'Zwischen Mythos und Wahrheit.'

27 For Herzer, the main argument against authenticity is the lack of *concrete* local and personal statements in the letter, as opposed to 2 Timothy and Titus (pp. 438–441 and *passim*).

wrote to individuals. Pauline authorship was never questioned until the Enlightenment period, when most of the New Testament and Christian doctrine was subjected to the erosive doubt of rationalism, particularly in the academy. First Timothy was the first to be denied by Schleiermacher, who on the basis of linguistic variation concluded that it was a compilation of 2 Timothy and Titus. As time continued all three letters would eventually be considered pseudonymous. This view dominates secular and mainline Protestant and Roman Catholic institutions and churches today. However, for the last twenty years there have been strong arguments by a few mainline Protestant authors themselves against the Enlightenment-based rejection of the Pastoral Epistles as Pauline. To be sure, this is a minority voice; but they are those of experts on the field. These scholars call attention to the pressure in the academy to follow the status quo as a significant reason for why the letters are held as non-Pauline. In addition, the argument has been made that grouping the letters as one corpus has had the result of each letter being painted with the same brush. Thus, Jens Herzer has contended that if we do away with 'the Pastoral Epistles', it would be possible to argue that both 2 Timothy and Titus stem from Paul. From evangelical circles, the recent work of Jermo van Nes has thoroughly called into question the linguistic basis for the pseudonymity theory. In this view the argument from language that goes all the way back to Schleiermacher simply cannot stand in light of sophisticated methodology from modern linguistics.

The position taken in this commentary is that Paul is the author of the Pastoral Epistles. The reasons can now be summarized as follows: (1) The biblical texts read, 'Paul, an apostle ... Paul a servant.' (2) Pseudepigraphy was not acceptable in the early church. [28] (3) With the exception of false teachers, the early church did not question the Pauline provenance of these letters. (4) The arguments against Pauline authorship from language, geography and theology are flawed (as argued above). (5) It is probable that the 'majority position' has been deeply influenced by academic/social pressures,

---

28   See Baum, *Pseudepigraphie und literarische Fälschung*; Porter, *Paul and Pseudepigraphy*.

which lead to the rejection of Pauline authorship without sufficiently nuanced analysis of the data.

2. Genre

The Pastoral Epistles are clearly letters: but what kind of letters? During the Greco-Roman period there were many types of letters.[29] Understanding the genre of the Pastoral Epistles provides significant aid in their interpretation.

For many years the conclusions of Dibelius and Conzelmann dominated the mainline academic opinion of the genre of the Pastorals. In their opinion, 1 Timothy and Titus are examples of *church orders*, similar to the *Didache* and Polycarp's letters.[30] Second Timothy was considered an example of *paraenesis* (exhortation), similar to Isocrates and Ps. Isocrates (pp. 7–8). These choices of genre, particularly on 2 Timothy, assumed pseudonymity, although they need not have done so.[31] However, especially with the papyri discovery of Adolf Deissmann at the beginning of the twentieth century, more attention has been given to the relationship between Greco-Roman letters and the New Testament letters. Comparisons have been made not only with the papyrus letters that survived in Egypt but also with ancient handbooks on letter writing (e.g., Libanius and Demetrius). Drawing on the evidence provided by this literature, this commentary takes the view that the Pastoral Epistles provide an example where both the official/administrative and individual/friendship letters meet.[32]

Official/administrative letters were written to give orders and advice from a superior to a person governing in a province (e.g.,

29 See Stirewalt, *Paul, the Letter Writer*; Stowers, *Letter Writing in Greco-Roman Antiquity*.

30 Dibelius and Conzelmann, pp. 5–7.

31 See Collins, pp. 6–9, who accepts the above classifications along with the pseudonymous character of the Pastoral Epistles.

32 For the primary sources, see particularly Stirewalt, *Paul, the Letter Writer*; Richards, *The Secretary in the Letters of Paul*; Doering, *Ancient Jewish Letters*.

the Emperor Trajan to Pliny the Younger, governor in Bithynia). Individual letters/letters of friendship, although at times containing mandates from a superior, had a different tone, more often urging and exhorting on the basis of love. The official/administrative aspect of the Pastoral Epistles is seen in the fact that Paul gives commands to his co-workers Timothy and Titus, and that often the rationale for these commands is Paul's authority as an apostle. As to the individual/friendship letter aspect, we can point to Paul's emotive expressions of love for his co-workers (e.g., 2 Tim. 1:3–5). We should note, of course, that the official/administrative *tone* of a letter does not preclude friendship/love and vice versa.

Some scholars have attempted a more precise classification under the canopy of official letters. They categorize the Pastoral Epistles (esp. 1 Timothy and Titus, although Johnson includes 2 Timothy) as examples of *mandata principis* ('orders from a ruler'), the best example being the correspondence between Trajan and Pliny cited above.[33] The primary problem with this classification is that it seems to be too narrow to account for all the phenomena present in the Pastoral Epistles.

In order to make proper decisions about the genre of the Pastoral Epistles it is crucial to have a clear concept of the category of genre itself.[34] In particular, it must be remembered that genres are not pure. Under the same genre (say, poetry) we can find exemplars that may differ considerably from one another, like siblings in a large family. We also know that Paul was very creative in his handling of Jewish and Greco-Roman generic features. In fact, Paul *needed* to be creative in his communications given the depth and dialectical nature of the Christian message (e.g., a crucified Lord; already/ not yet; justified yet facing eschatological judgment, etc.). And so it should not be surprising if in his composition of the Pastoral Epistles he drew on different types of letters. Above we noted the similarities between the Pastoral Epistles and the official letter. But it is also clear that Paul's letters as a whole and the Pastoral Epistles

---

33 See esp. Wolter, *Pastoralbriefe*, pp. 164–170; Johnson, pp. 96–97.

34 I have attempted to provide some clarity on this in another work: Padilla, *The Acts of the Apostles*, pp. 39–74.

specifically share in the ancient 'letter of exhortation'.[35] This blending does not mean that the Pastoral Epistles are *sui generis*; it simply means that genre is flexible. And so I view the Pastoral Epistles as examples of the letter of exhortation, which contains both elements of official and friendship letters.

These letters of exhortation were rich in *paraenesis*, that is, exhortations on what to believe, what type of life to lead and what to avoid. These letters could also be called *protreptic* in that they encourage the recipients to adopt a particular type of lifestyle. A very clear example of the paraenetic/protreptic genre is Clement of Alexandria's *Protrepticus*. Understanding the Pastoral Epistles as letters of exhortation sheds light on a number of important features. Consider the following:[36] (1) *Paraenesis* often uses personal examples (*exempla*) as persuasion to follow in a way of life. Paul often presents himself in the Pastoral Epistles as an example to follow (e.g., 1 Tim. 1:12–16; 2 Tim. 3:10–14) and asks Timothy and Titus to be examples to others (1 Tim. 4:12; 2 Tim. 2:1–2; Tit. 2:7). He mentions both positive (Lois and Eunice, 2 Tim. 1:5) and negative examples (Hymenaeus and Alexander, 1 Tim. 1:18–20; Hymenaeus and Philetus, 2 Tim. 2:17–18; Alexander, 2 Tim. 4:14; Cretans, Tit. 2:12–13). (2) It is common in *paraenesis* to use the language of *disease* and *health* to speak of the spiritual state of individuals. This is very common in the Pastoral Epistles (see e.g., 1 Tim. 1:10; 2 Tim. 2:17; Tit. 1:15). (3) *Paraenesis* employs short precepts, often with the assumption that the readers *already* know them; they just need reminders. (4) *Paraenesis* is well known for using *lists of virtues and vices*. Many modern scholars complain of the constant use of such lists in the Pastoral Epistles, arguing that they are foreign to the authentic Paul. But this is simplistic: when authors choose, consciously or subconsciously, to compose in a particular genre, they commit themselves to integrate most of its features. (5) *Paraenetic* letters give commands and make significant truth-claims, but often do not provide extended *reasons* for following those orders or believing the truth-claims – it

---

35   See Stowers, *Letter Writing*, pp. 91–152.
36   For what follows I build on the helpful work of Malherbe, *Light from the Gentiles*, 1:407–430.

is ultimately a matter of the authority of the author. This explains why Paul's theological anchoring of some of his deepest doctrinal statements tends to be short, often made up of traditional, liturgical material of the church (e.g., Tit. 2:11–15; 3:3–8). Again, many scholars find here a drastic difference from, say, Romans and Galatians. This is then supposed to be proof that Paul did not write the Pastoral Epistles. But such conclusions ignore the extent to which genre determines how one argues and presents evidence.

To sum up, when authoring letters to individual co-workers whom he had placed over certain regions or churches, Paul availed himself of a letter genre that would help him accomplish his task best. There existed official letters, employed to give orders to a junior official who was stationed in a foreign region. But there were also letters of exhortation, a sub-genre of which were called *paraenetic* or *protreptic*. These letter types worked with the ethos of the authority of the writer in order to provide precepts and exhortations (*paraenesis*), but they were not as such official or administrative letters. As a whole, the Pastoral Epistles are examples of paraenetic letters: 1 Timothy and Titus provide numerous precepts; 2 Timothy, while providing many precepts, also includes features of the farewell genre. Moral philosophers like Seneca used the paraenetic letter. Paul adopts this genre, although he ultimately grounds his *paraenesis* on the gospel of the Lord. Philosophers (mostly Stoic), on the other hand, grounded their *paraenesis* on more immanent realities.

3. Reading the Pastoral Epistles

The two letters to Timothy and the letter to Titus began to be called the 'Pastoral Epistles' in the eighteenth century with a commentary by P. Anton (1753).[37] The reason for this label was not a discovery of ancient sources that used this title for the letters. Rather, the reason for the label stemmed from the observation that in these letters there were many instructions to ministers of the church. These were 'pastoral letters', evidently written to help Timothy

---

37   Thus, Oberlinner (1994), p. xxii.

and Titus shepherd churches entrusted to them. The phrase stuck. However, as noted under Authorship, in the last two decades there have been calls to do away with the designation Pastoral Epistles.[38] The argument is being made that there is more to be gained by separating the letters than by holding them together as a distinct corpus.[39]

There are certainly gains in separating the letters, particularly in providing a more straightforward reading of linguistic data when comparing, say, Titus, to another letter in the Pauline Corpus. In addition, dialogue could increase between scholars of different persuasions on the matter of authorship. Perhaps we could study together 2 Timothy without necessarily also including, say, 1 Timothy. On the whole, however, I would suggest that we preserve the label 'Pastoral Epistles' and carefully consider the positive results that may emerge from such classification. In particular, it is important to clarify just what it means to read these letters as one corpus. One of the reasons why there has been a call to read the epistles individually is a misunderstanding of what it means to read the letters as a unit. For some scholars, exegeting these letters as the corpus 'Pastoral Epistles' is a historicist operation. That is to say, they believe that to interpret them as a discrete body is a tacit admission that the letters *share in the same historical origin*: same author, same period, same reasons to write, same false teaching to oppose, etc. To use the technical language of biblical studies, the *Sitz im Leben* (that is, what was happening on the ground that demanded the writing of the Pastoral Epistles) of the letters must be identical or very similar. Otherwise, how can they be one body? No wonder there is the suggestion to abandon the label Pastoral Epistles, for these letters are notoriously difficult to place in Paul's missionary movements – their historical origin is particularly obscure. But unity is not just a matter of historical origination. This attitude betrays the historicist mindset which is the heritage of biblical studies from the eighteenth century and which afflicts

---

38   In addition to Herzer and van Nes above, see also Towner, pp. 88–89.

39   Cf. Aageson, *Paul.*

the discipline to this day. Again, unity is not just about historical uniformity; it is also a *theological matter.*

This would mean that, while certainly respecting the uniqueness of each of the letters, we can still read them as one corpus, because the letters are bound together theologically. And although there is theological overlap in a number of areas, what makes them stand out as one body is their *ecclesiological concerns to preserve the sound apostolic teaching.* To wit, the Pastoral Epistles are those letters whose primary canon contribution is *their instruction to church leaders.* In this sense, too, we can speak of a historical unity, for Paul wrote the letters to address problems in local congregations. Throughout the centuries the church has discerned in these letters injunctions for how church leaders 'ought to behave in the household of God' (1 Tim. 3:15); what it means to be a 'servant of God' (2 Tim. 2:24); how to 'put in order' the churches (Tit. 1:5). Again, this does not mean that the rest of the Bible is useless in the instruction of church leaders and church life. Yet, we do not wish to lose the singularity that the Pastoral Epistles offer on the subject.[40]

To conclude, it seems preferable to suggest we keep the label 'Pastoral Epistles', understanding their theological emphasis on the subject of church life, particularly the instructions for those who seek to lead the church in different capacities. There is also helpful material in these letters on the missional relation of the church to the different members of society. Admittedly, these *are* three separate letters, and we must respect their individual uniqueness lest we flatten what we can learn from the gains that can be attained by paying attention to the occasion of each. Methodologically, I will call attention to the effects of approaching the letters as a discrete body in the different sections of the commentary proper.

4. The occasion of the Pastoral Epistles

As indicated above, it is particularly challenging with the information we have to place the composition of the Pastoral Epistles

---

40 See in particular Yarbrough, pp. 43–51, on the connection between pastoral leadership and the Pastoral Epistles.

to a distinct stage in Paul's career. Only 2 Timothy can be placed with some assurance to the end of Paul's life. The reason for this is the language of 2 Timothy 4:6–8 and 18, where Paul speaks with certainty about his imminent death. If Paul was executed during Nero's late reign, as is acknowledged nearly unanimously from the early church, it is likely that 2 Timothy was written between AD 64–67 in Rome.

First Timothy and Titus are more difficult to place. The tradition from Eusebius (*E.H.* 2.22) is the following: Paul was released from the Roman imprisonment briefly described in Acts 28:30–33, then left Rome to continue his missionary work, probably in Spain, and finally returned to Rome, where he was imprisoned a second time under Nero and shortly thereafter martyred under the same emperor. This is a very strong tradition (see also *1 Clement* 5:6–7; Muratorian Canon), later confirmed by Athanasius and Jerome. It would be possible, then, to think of the composition of 1 Timothy and Titus as somewhere between Paul's first and second imprisonment.

Another option for the composition of the letters was put forth by Badcock.[41] His reading of the evidence is that Titus was written first while Paul was at Ephesus (see Acts 19:1–11). First Timothy was written second, during Paul's journey to Jerusalem (see Acts 20). Second Timothy was last, written while Paul was imprisoned at Caesarea (see Acts 24–26). I. H. Marshall acknowledges the difficulty in establishing with precision the location and date of the letters' composition. He suggests that Titus be read first, followed by 1 Timothy, and that 2 Timothy is meant to be read last, as Paul's final letter.[42]

Since we do not possess an exhaustive itinerary of Paul's movements, it may be that we are not able to gain as much precision as we would like in discovering when and where Paul wrote the Pastorals, especially with respect to 1 Timothy and Titus.

We must now ask the more specific question of what prompted

---

41   Badcock, *The Pauline Epistles*, pp. 73–158.

42   Marshall, p. 2. Note that for Marshall this reading order does not necessarily mirror their order of composition.

Paul to compose these three letters. Again, since these are three different letters lacking in an *identical* historical genesis, we must think of the occasion in very general terms: more or less, we can reflect on whether or not there are overlapping reasons for which Paul wrote the letters. The path I take in this commentary is to state some *general* reasons for their composition, which seem applicable to all letters. These reasons serve as a framework for the interpretation of the Pastoral Epistles, always with the willingness to revise the framework in light of fresh reading of the evidence.

It may be helpful to recall the statements on 1 Timothy 3:14–16 made by C. Spicq in his classic commentary. In light of the language and themes of this text, Spicq argued that the section is 'not only the climactic point of the epistle, but itself the key to the Pastorals' (p. 103). This is a defensible thesis since the themes raised by Paul here *in nuce* are also found in 2 Timothy and Titus. I will therefore use 1 Timothy 3:14–16 to point to three likely reasons for the composition of the Pastoral Epistles.

First, Paul wrote these letters to stress the importance of godly leadership if the church is to thrive. Verse 15 accentuates the importance of the leaders' *conduct* (see *anastrephō* in v. 15). And, in fact, all the Pastorals come back to this theme. At 1 Timothy 3:1, Paul acknowledges that it is a 'noble task' (*kalos ergon*) to desire the office of 'overseer'. But that is not enough. There must also be present (*dei*, 'it is necessary', 3:2) a particular type of *conduct* which is commensurate with leadership in the household of God. There follows a list of virtues and vices to help guide in the discernment of church leadership (3:2–13). In many other places in the letters Paul emphasizes the necessity of godly conduct in the leaders (e.g., 1 Tim. 4:6–8, 12; 6:11–14; 2 Tim. 1:6–8, 13–14; 2:1–7; 15–24; 3:10–12, 14–17; Tit. 1:5–9; 2:7).

It will not do, nevertheless, simply to be a virtuous person. So, in the second place, Paul wrote to remind the believers that conduct must be grounded on 'sound doctrine', also called 'truth', 'faith', and 'gospel'. This is the second discernible reason for Paul writing the letters. Sound doctrine is a *sine qua non*, not only for thriving but for the very existence of the church. Notice how Paul, immediately after touching on the leaders' necessary godly conduct in 3:14, speaks of the church of the living God in connection with

the 'truth'. While a life of virtue ('good works') is one of the goals
of Christian existence, such virtues are only possible for those
who have experienced salvation, regeneration, justification and
are being 'trained' (*paideuō*) to live godly lives (Tit. 2:12; 3:5–7). In
the Pastoral Epistles – as well as in Paul's other letters – there is
no such thing as a church or church leadership without adherence
to the sound, apostolic doctrine, the 'deposit' that Timothy must
guard by the power of the Holy Spirit (1 Tim. 6:20; 2 Tim. 1:14),
pass along to others (2 Tim. 2:1–2) and be willing to suffer for
(2 Tim. 2:9–10).

   Third, while all of the sound doctrine is essential, the emphasis
in the Pastoral Epistles falls on Christology and soteriology. Verse
16 of 3:14–16 moves to a great and climactic confession, probably
the result of church tradition with Paul's own final touch. The
great confession is stated poetically, and it is probably a liturgical
statement that moves from incarnation to exaltation. And there
are many other important Christological texts in the Pastoral Epistles (e.g., 1 Tim. 2:5–6; 6:13; 2 Tim. 2:8; 4:1; Tit. 2:13; see below
on the Theological Emphases of the Pastoral Epistles). Soteriology also figures greatly in these letters, with powerful statements
found in 1 Timothy 2:3–7; 2 Timothy 1:9–10; Titus 2:11–14 and
3:3–7. These too reflect the language of church tradition, including
Paul's.

   Is it possible to be more specific regarding the occasion of the
letters? Within the framework suggested above, it is natural that
we encounter in the Pastoral Epistles much polemic against false
teachers. For these opponents were attacking the church with
destructive false doctrine. Yet, what specific false teaching they were
disseminating is much more difficult to know with exactness. We
hear of Hymenaeus and Alexander (1 Tim. 1:18–20), of Hymenaeus
and Philetus (2 Tim. 2:17–18), and of Alexander the coppersmith
(2 Tim. 4:14). However, what they and the 'certain people' (*tines*,
1 Tim. 1:4) were teaching specifically is unclear. Paul mentions
'myths and endless genealogies' (1 Tim. 1:4; Tit. 1:10–16; 3:9) in the
context of some 'of the circumcision' who apparently were teaching
the Mosaic law. However, they did not really know the law, because
they did not understand the goal of the law or its relationship to the
'glorious gospel' (1 Tim. 1:6–11). They were also forbidding some

material blessings, such as eating certain foods and marriage, that were created by God for sharing and enjoyment with thanksgiving (1 Tim. 4:1–4). They claimed to possess 'knowledge' (*gnōsis*, 1 Tim. 6:20), and made the claim that the (likely) final resurrection had already taken place (2 Tim. 2:18). Furthermore, the false teachers are presented as those who sneak 'into households and captivate silly women' (2 Tim. 3:6–8). They are compared to the paradigmatic Jewish magicians Jannes and Jambres. We thus have a combination of elements that include law, food regulations, celibacy, (proto) gnosticism and itinerant teachers who may have practised magic. This combination is difficult to find in just one group. Therefore, there are numerous debates as to who the opponents are in the Pastoral Epistles.

The hypothesis suggested in this commentary is that the opponents, whose false teaching was broadly similar in the situations presented in all three letters, were Jewish Christians. As to their Jewish identity, there existed Jewish itinerant teachers, such as those found among the Essenes, who combined the aspects of law, food regulations, celibacy and even magical practice mentioned above. Speaking of the Essenes (second century BC–first century AD), M. Hengel makes the following statement: 'When the Essenes were occupied with astrology and iatromantics [magical alchemy] they believed this to be something fundamentally different from what was happening outside the community in the same area … One could speak of a Hasidic-Essene "gnosticism".'[43] There is now enough evidence that in the first century AD there were Jews who had added to their devotion to the law the type of thought-forms that we would call proto-Gnostic. It would not be surprising if the Jewish opponents of the Pastoral Epistles held to similar beliefs as the opponents Paul resisted in Colossians.[44]

As to the Christian identity of the opponents, it is quite probable

---

43 Hengel, *Judaism and Hellenism*, 1:243. On marriage restrictions, see 2:119.

44 Kelly, pp. 10–12, reached a very similar conclusion to the one sketched above. On the false teachers at Colossae, see esp. Arnold, *The Colossian Syncretism*.

that they were part of the churches, yet were beginning to separate at the time of writing (cf. 1 Tim. 1:18–20; 2 Tim. 2:14–26; Tit. 3:10–11). We have enough evidence from 1 Corinthians to state that Christians who were once part of the congregations had misunderstood/perverted Paul's teaching on marriage and the resurrection and they were causing great problems to the rest of the believers. The situation may be similar in the churches Paul addresses in the Pastorals.

To conclude on the possible identity of the opponents addressed in the Pastoral Epistles, we find Marshall's description attractive (p. 51):

> A combination of the Jewish, Christian and ascetic elements suffices to explain the nature of the opposition in the Pastoral Epistles. We have to do with a group of Jewish Christians, perhaps travelling teachers with an ascetic streak, who were active within the Pauline mission area. They attached importance to the law … and from it they derived a radical set of ascetic restrictions regarding purity.

While the identity of the opponents envisaged in the Pastorals is cloudy, the effects they were having on the different congregations come to the surface in particular in Paul's descriptions and exhortations to the women (see, e.g., 1 Tim. 2:9–11; 2 Tim. 3:5–9; Tit. 2:2–5). These problems can be discerned in each letter. It appears that the opponents were targeting some of the women in the churches, probably wealthy wives and widows (1 Tim. 2:9–15; 5:3–16). The women may have hired some of those who later turned out to be false teachers to instruct them, in the same way some wealthy women of the Greco-Roman period hired moral philosophers as private tutors.[45] But these teachers were deceiving them (2 Tim. 3:6–7). Some of the women, for their part, appeared to be growing bold on the basis of their learning. It is probably for this reason that Paul censures some of them so severely, even prohibiting them from teaching.

---

45   See, e.g., Lucian, *Merc. cond.* 6–7, 8–9; *Fug.* 5, 18, 19–20, 22.

5. Theological emphases in the Pastoral Epistles

a. The God of the Pastoral Epistles[46]

Paul begins each of these epistles with the common opening elements of letters from the Greco-Roman period (see comments under 1 Tim. 1:1–2). Nevertheless, he expands the common template by enlarging on each aspect, particularly theological statements about God. This aspect signals to the reader how the letters are to be read – they are to be read 'under' God. But who is this God? I offer four theological statements about the God of the Pastoral Epistles.

i. God is the God of Israel

The language Paul uses to speak about God is without question OT language. In the salutations God is referred to in the singular, thereby contrasting him with the many gods of the nations. In addition, the blessings he pours on his people ('grace', 'mercy' and 'peace') are the blessings we read about in the OT, when it speaks of God blessing his people Israel. We should note in this respect that the last blessing in each letter's salutation is 'peace'. This is probably an echo of the priestly prayer of Numbers 6:26: 'The Lord lift up his countenance upon you and give you *peace*.' In the salutation to Titus, Paul speaks of God as the God 'who never lies' (1:2), an attribute of God with OT roots (Numb. 23:19; 1 Sam. 15:29).

The doxology of 1 Timothy 1:17 uses vocabulary present in Hellenistic Judaism: 'king eternal' (Tob. 3:16); 'immortal' (*Wis.* 12:1; 18:4; Philo, *Sacr.* 95; *Mos.* 2.171). Most striking of all is the phrase 'the only God' (1:17), which singles out the God of Israel over the gods of the nations. This is strengthened in 1 Timothy 2:5 with the phrase: 'For there is one God.' These last two statements look back to the Shema of Deuteronomy 6:4.

Another important indicator to think of God as the God of Israel is found in the language and concept of election found in 2 Timothy 1:9. Paul speaks of God as the one 'who saved us and called us with

---

46 I recommend Köstenberger's detailed discussion on the God of the Pastoral Epistles (pp. 413–431).

a holy calling ... according to his own purpose and grace.' This
resonates with OT language of Israel's election and salvation. For
God makes it clear that Israel is the people of God not because of
any merit of its own (be it religious or social) but because Yahweh
freely loved Israel and chose it in covenant love (see Deut. 7:7–8).
This call sets Israel apart from all the nations. This is the same God
who Timothy (along with his mother and grandmother) and the
Christians now serve in Jesus Christ.

ii. God is the Father of the Lord Jesus Christ

From the salutations through to the rest of each letter, God is
rarely mentioned in the abstract. Instead, in each salutation he is
God 'the Father' and is placed in apposition to 'Christ Jesus' (or
'Messiah Jesus'). I note in the commentary that God is not often
called Father in the OT. However, in the Gospels Jesus often calls
God his Father, then invites the disciples also to call God Father,
particularly in the context of prayer (e.g., Matt. 6:9; cf. also John
14 – 17). We should therefore think of God as Father firstly in the
Christological context: Jesus is the Son of God, and because we are
'in' Christ, we also may call God our Father.

Clearly the relationship between God the Father and Jesus
is a spiritual relationship, since God does not produce children
through biological means (contrast the Greek gods, who often
impregnated women, even against their [the women's] will). What
does it mean, then, to speak of God as the unique Father of Jesus
and Jesus as the unique Son of the Father? The phrase 'Son of
God' is used in the OT and Second Temple Judaism in a messianic
sense to speak of the unique relationship between God and his
anointed (see Ps. 2:7; 2 Sam. 7:14; Isa. 42:1). At the same time, it
is clear from a number of texts (see John 5:18; 10:33, 36) that to
be the Son of God is to be equal to God. Combining these two
ideas, we can say that God being the Father of Jesus speaks to the
latter's messianic, human identity as well as his divine identity,
for he shares in God's nature as his Son. We should add to this
discussion 2 Timothy 2:8, where Jesus Messiah is said to be 'a
descendant of David'. Jesus is therefore the Messiah, who is, to be
sure, human, but also divine (cf. Rom. 1:3–4). To use the helpful
language of Richard Bauckham, which is applicable to the Pastoral

Epistles, the NT 'includes Jesus in the unique divine identity as Jewish monotheism understood it'.[47]

There are two more observations to make in the context of the salutations. First, we should note that the blessings invoked by Paul – grace, mercy and peace – are blessings that in the OT God alone can grant in a lasting manner. And yet, the blessings in the salutations come from God the Father *and* 'the Messiah Jesus our Lord'. The second observation is lexical. The title 'Lord' is used of Jesus Christ. While the word can simply mean 'sir' or 'master', the context suggests the connotation of Lord, as in reference to the God of Israel. We recall that, with a few exceptions, the Greek *kyrios* is the Septuagint translation of the Hebrew tetragrammaton YHWH, the name (*shem*) of the God of Israel. To call Jesus LORD is to say that he *is* the God of Israel (see Isa. 45:24; 1 Cor. 8:6; Phil. 2:5–11).

The climax of Christology in the Pastoral Epistles is found in Titus 2:13. In referring to the return of Christ, Paul speaks of *our great God and Saviour, Jesus Christ*. As I note in the commentary on this verse, there is a single article governing 'God and Saviour', with 'Jesus Christ' standing in apposition, thus further marking out who is the great God and Saviour. This is a remarkable statement, for Paul is identifying not just the eternal, pre-incarnate Logos as God but Jesus Messiah, the man who was born of Mary in Bethlehem. The Pastoral Epistles thus make a powerful contribution to our understanding of God, a contribution that is later picked up by Nicene theologians in their 'definition' of the person and nature of Christ.

---

47 Bauckham, *Jesus and the God of Israel*, p. 19. Van Driel, *Rethinking Paul*, p. 19, has helpfully added to Bauckham's identity Christology by using the phrase 'identity characteristic' as opposed to 'functional characteristic'. He explains: '"Being president of the United States" is a functional characteristic—it does not express an intrinsic quality of the person who fulfills this role, but it is a function one is endowed with at some point and that passes to someone else at a later point.' Jesus' 'identity characteristic' as God is *intrinsic* to his existence.

iii. The God of the Pastoral Epistles is Triune

We have seen above that both the Father and the Son are viewed as God, without the positing of two gods and without the thought that in reality the Father is the Son or the Son is the Father. We can rather speak of two persons constituting one God.[48] Our suggestion with the above subheading is that the Holy Spirit is also presented as God in the Pastoral Epistles, although with less elaboration than we saw with respect to the Son. In fact, the Pastoral Epistles are comparatively brief in their references to the Holy Spirit. We primarily see the Spirit as the source of *gifting* and *empowerment* for ministry (see 1 Tim. 4:14; 2 Tim. 1:6–7). However, in the well-known passage of Titus 3:3–8, we find the Spirit linked with God and Jesus Christ in the activity of salvation. In verses 5–6 in particular Paul speaks of the God who saved us 'through the water of rebirth and renewal by the Holy Spirit … [whom] he poured out on us richly through Jesus Christ our Saviour'.

Two points need to be made at this stage with respect to Titus 3:5–6 (see further Commentary section). First, we should note the relationship between the Father, Son ('Jesus Christ our Saviour') and the Holy Spirit. Paul uses a number of prepositional phrases to interlink the work of each in salvation. Whatever the precise meaning drawn out from the prepositions, it is fair to say that Paul views all three united in the *ad extra* operation of salvation.[49] Anticipating our conclusion, this is *one* God at work. Second, we note that the Holy Spirit is the author, the one who effects salvation 'through the water of rebirth and renewal'. We recall that Titus 3:3–8 speaks of salvation from different perspectives ('to save', 'to justify'). The Holy Spirit is the one who performs that aspect of salvation that the Bible calls

---

48 See helpfully Lau, *The Epiphany Christology*, pp. 260–270, with the insightful comment that the divine (he calls it 'pre-existent') Christology of the Pastorals particularly shines in the exaltation of Jesus.

49 The phrase *ad extra* is a theological way of speaking of the work of the Father, Son and Holy Spirit on entities outside the Trinity. For example, working on creation (not an inherent part of God) would be God working *ad extra*.

'regeneration' or 'renewal' or 'new birth' (see Commentary for the different scriptural texts). Since God alone can effect our salvation, and since the Holy Spirit can be interpreted as the one who saves us by washing and regeneration, we can conclude that the Holy Spirit is also constitutive of the being of God in the Pastoral Epistles.

But can this be called 'the doctrine of the Trinity'? All depends on what we mean by 'the doctrine'. For many scholars, the doctrine of the Trinity must include definitions, lengthy explanations, negations and affirmations, the closing of logical circles, and so on. With these criteria, by definition the Bible would not contain many doctrines, since there is not much systematization in the Bible itself in comparison to a later period. But systematization and doctrine are not coterminous. After all, the word 'doctrine' simply means teaching or instruction. And so I conclude that it would not be disingenuous to say that the God of the Pastoral Epistles (and the NT) is trinitarian in that in both terminology and activity the work of God is the work of the Father, the Son and the Holy Spirit; and yet these are not three different gods. I expand on this a little more under the Theology section of Titus 3:3–8. For now, if we agree that the God of the Pastorals can correctly be called trinitarian, we must be willing to follow this affirmation in such a way that it forms a framework for the exegesis of these letters.

iv. The God of the Pastoral Epistles is the Saviour
To the extent that titles for God are used in the Pastoral Epistles, the dominant one is 'Saviour' (Greek, *sōtēr*). It is used a total of ten times in the Pastoral Epistles. Without question the theological background for this title is the OT and the use of the early church.[50] The OT is replete with both the noun and verbal formulations such as 'Yahweh saves' (Deut. 32:15; 1 Sam. 10:18–19; Pss 23:5; 24:5 [LXX];

---

50 On the background of *sōtēr* in the Pastoral Epistles, see Marshall, pp. 291–292; Stettler, *Christologie*, pp. 28–33. The Hellenistic concept of gods or emperors as 'deliverers' or 'saviours' may be present in the language of *sōtēr*. However, in light of what constitutes salvation in the Pastoral Epistles, the OT/Second Temple material is the more fitting background.

Isa. 12:2; 45:21; 62:11). The title is also used in Second Temple Jewish literature (e.g., 1 Macc. 4:30; *Pss. Sol.* 8:33; 17:3). The verb 'to save', which refers to God delivering and rescuing from dangers and crises, is equally abundant in the OT, with Yahweh as the subject. In addition to the many usages in the Psalms and Jeremiah, we call attention to the following texts: Deuteronomy 33:29; Isaiah 43:3; 45:17, 22; 60:16; 63:9. What marks out the God of Israel is the fact that he is the Saviour of his people, the one who delivered them once from Egypt, [51] delivers them when they pray, and will deliver them again at the end (Isa. 43:5–7; Rom. 8:17; 1 Thess. 1:10;). In this final salvation, which includes acquittal and ultimate deliverance from God's wrath, God will include all the nations of the earth who call upon his name, not only Israel.

The use of 'Saviour' also has Christological ramifications for the Pastoral Epistles. The reason is that the title is used equally of God (1 Tim. 1:1; 2:3; 4:10; Tit. 1:3; 2:10; 3:4) and of Jesus Christ (2 Tim. 1:10; Tit. 1:4; 2:13; 3:6). Stettler concludes: 'That at the same time God … and Jesus … are called σωτήρ ('Saviour') in the Pastorals signifies for Christology that the Pastorals see a unity between God and Jesus Christ in the salvific act.'[52] This unity of action not only presupposes unity of being but *is* the unity of being as one God.

b. Salvation

There are two primary themes that are present in the Pastoral Epistles with respect to salvation: it is a gracious work of God and it cannot be gained by human effort. Although there is some nuancing of these themes that are particular to the Pastoral Epistles, the themes are essentially those found in Paul's so-called 'undisputed' letters. It is fascinating that F. C. Baur, who has had such a profound effect on NT studies to this day, can agree on the two themes above as the foundation of soteriology in the Pastoral Epistles.[53] Nevertheless, he finds the following to be the clue that the

---

51 As Jenson puts it: 'Asked about who God is, Israel's answer is, "Whoever rescued us from Egypt"' (*Systematic Theology*, 1:44).

52 Stettler, *Christologie*, p. 28.

53 Baur, *Lectures*, pp. 321–322.

letters' theology is ultimately not from Paul himself: 'He does not set faith over against works in such a way that the teaching about justifying faith stands out *as the central point of the entire teaching about salvation*' (p. 322, italics added). Evidently, only a type (or caricature) of Lutheran understanding of salvation could qualify as a genuine Pauline soteriology for Baur! However, studies of Pauline theology during the last fifty years have shown that although justification by grace through faith is crucial to Paul's understanding of salvation, it is not necessarily the *central* point of the apostle's doctrine of salvation. Below I mention two areas of emphasis in the Pastorals' concept of salvation.

First, God, as Father, Son and Holy Spirit, is the subject of salvation. The soteriology of the Pastoral Epistles is God-centred. Attention is called to each person of the Trinity as the actor of salvation: the Father (1 Tim. 4:10; 2 Tim. 1:9), the Son (1 Tim. 2:5–6; 3:16), the Holy Spirit (Tit. 3:5–6). There is a coalescing of the trinitarian work in the climactic soteriological text of the Pastoral Epistles, namely Titus 3:4–8.

Second, salvation is God acting to bring us back to himself that we might enjoy fellowship with him. Although it can be artificial because there is overlap, we can think of salvation in the three tenses: past, present and future. As to the *past* aspect, we notice Paul juxtaposing 'not according to our works' with 'according to his own purpose and grace ... given to us in Christ Jesus before the ages began' (2 Tim. 1:9). The language of 'election' and 'grace' together makes one think of Romans 11:5: 'chosen by grace' (NIV). The thought is also similar to Romans 9:11. In short, Paul speaks of salvation as something that is determined by God in eternity past, before the creation of the universe (see Rom. 8:28–30; Eph. 1:4–5). At that 'time', God, in his freedom and love, determined to be for us – to love us – in Jesus Christ. Salvation in Christ was not 'Plan B' for God; he always determined to make a people for himself with Jesus Christ as the head of the new creation (Col. 1:15–18; see further under Commentary on 2 Tim. 1:9). If this is true, then there is nothing human beings can do to gain God's favour or salvation. The law itself was not given in order that we in the present might be justified by the keeping of it. The ultimate goal of the law was to lead us to Christ (Gal. 3:19–25); it was put in place to convict 'the lawless and disobedient ... the godless and sinful ... the unholy and profane', and so on (1 Tim. 1:8–10). This teaching is in accord with some of the best-known passages from Paul (e.g., Rom. 2:13; 3:20; Gal. 2:16).

The present reality of salvation highlights the work of Christ as the incarnate Lord in relationship to the reception of his work in our lives. In one sense, the entire life of Jesus, including his resurrection, was for our salvation: from his incarnation to his glorification (see particularly 1 Tim. 3:16). At the same time, Paul, with preformed liturgical tradition that may have been in use by Christians, speaks of the death of Jesus as a sacrifice for our sins: 'who gave himself as a ransom for all' (1 Tim. 2:6); 'he it is who gave himself for us that he might redeem us from all iniquity' (Tit. 2:14). This work of Christ must be received in the present for salvation to become effective in those who believe. Those who do not believe will be judged at the second coming of Christ (2 Tim. 4:1). This is stressed by Paul in 1 Timothy 4:10. The Holy Spirit is also present in the 'now' of salvation in that he is the one who causes us to experience rebirth and renewal (Tit. 3:5).

The future of salvation is primarily expressed in the Pastoral Epistles with language of eternal life and the parousia or return of Christ. First, in the Pastoral Epistles, eternal life often refers to the future (and also to the experiencing of salvation in the present). For example, Paul encourages Timothy to 'take hold of ... eternal life' (1 Tim. 6:12), which implies that sharing in salvation is possible in the here and now. Most uses of the phrase, however, point to the future (e.g., 1 Tim. 1:16; Tit. 1:2). A good example is found in Titus 3:7: 'So that, having been justified by his grace, *we might become heirs according to the hope of eternal life*' [italics added]. The qualification of 'life' with 'eternal', while referring to unending time, is not primarily about raw chronology: as if the hope was plain and simple to live for ever! This thought might actually be frightful if our experience of life in the present is marked by depression and sadness. The qualifier 'eternal' has primarily to do with a share in the life of God. Thus, Paul speaks of the future of believers as sharing in 'the life that really is life' (1 Tim. 6:19). And at 2 Timothy 2:10, again primarily speaking of the future deliverance of believers, he links salvation in Christ Jesus with the phrase 'eternal glory'. Eternal life, the beginning of which is in the present, is ultimately about an experience in *God's* life, where the sheer joy of his blessed being is so overwhelming that the experience of the succession of time is no longer conscious: it is an eternal present of joy.

The second main theme about the future of salvation in the Pastoral Epistles is the second coming of Christ. In Titus 2:13 the coming of Christ is called 'the blessed hope'. Paul the prisoner is encouraged by knowing that the Lord will one day return, will judge justly and will grant him 'the crown of righteousness' (2 Tim. 4:8). At that time the Lord will rescue Paul and introduce his 'heavenly kingdom' (4:18). Although Paul has been faithful to the end in his God-given missionary task, there is always the possibility of failure. But Paul does not lose hope in the face of human failure, for persevering in the kingdom of God is ultimately tied to God's nature as a faithful God: 'If we are faithless, he remains faithful – for he cannot deny himself' (2:13).

c. The Christian life

In the Pastoral Epistles salvation is ineluctably followed by a new type of life. Paul expresses this new conduct of the believer primarily in two ways. First, there is the phrase translated into English as 'good works'. The phrase translates the somewhat uncommon Greek phrase *ergon agathos* as well as the much more common *ergon kalos* (or *kalos ergon*, which is the dominant word order). What are these 'good works'? To help shed light on Paul, it is important to refer to a number of authors from the Hellenistic period onwards. They linked the phrase 'good works' with the common Greek virtues (*aretē*).[54] The four cardinal virtues for the majority of philosophers were *phronēsis* ('prudence'), *sōphrosynē* ('moderation'), *dikaiosynē* ('justice') and *andreia* ('courage').[55] In some ways, then, we can think of 'good works' as those works the expressions of which

---

54 See Posidonius, *Frag.* 416 l. 9; Musonius Rufus, *Diatr.* 3.1; Plutarch, *Comp. Per. Fab.* 2.2.3; *Mar.* 9.4.1; *Alex.* 34.4.2; Dio Chrysostom, *Or.* 3.52.7; Galen, *PHP* 5.5.7.

55 See Plato, *Resp.* 4.427E, 435B; Dio Chrysostom, *Or.* 13.31–32; cf. Malherbe, *Light from the Gentiles*, 1:467–468.

are commensurate with the virtues. Of course, early Christians held
to other virtues as well, the main one being love (1 Cor. 13:8–13).
We can see how Paul concretized these 'good works' when we pay
attention to the specific contexts where the phrase appears in the
Pastoral Epistles. Thus, 'good works' would include church ministry
(1 Tim. 3:1; 2 Tim. 3:17), helping the poor (1 Tim. 6:18), caring for
the saints in need (1 Tim. 5:10; Tit. 3:14) and potentially benefaction
of the city (1 Tim. 6:17–19).

The fact that Paul has used a phrase such as 'good works' to
explain the nature of new Christian existence is itself telling. For
this language was at home in the Greek vocabulary of virtuous
living in the context of the city-state, where to live virtuously was
viewed as a benefit to the city-state.[56] Paul is thus contextualizing
for these believers what it means to live like a Christian in a situation where unbelievers may be suspicious of this new 'sect' from
the east. He is probably using this language to remind believers
that the best apologetic for Christian mission is often good works.
Two conclusions emerge from this. First, what Paul is asking of
the believers is not some unattainable goal. As we comment in the
section on overseers and deacons as well as the household code of
Titus 2, Paul simply wants the believers to display solid, grounded
morality: sobriety, courtesy, faithfulness, raising children well, being
respectful of spouses, and so on. These were the kinds of virtues
to which much lip service was given in the Greco-Roman world,
especially by moral philosophers, but which few in the populace
actually practised. Second, 'good works' were not an end in themselves but had a *missional* function. Particularly telling is the phrase
in Titus 2:10, where godly conduct is there to 'adorn the teaching
of God our Saviour'. Good works have a purpose: to win for the
faith the unbelievers who are carefully observing the Christians.

The second way in which Paul expresses the new conduct of the
believer is by his constant use of the word *eusebeia*, variously translated as 'godliness', 'piety', 'reverence'. To measure the importance

---

56 See Smith, *Paul and the Good Life*, pp. 5–113, for the relationship
    between Paul, the virtuous life advocated by classical philosophers,
    and the Christian life of flourishing.

of this term in the Pastoral Epistles it is worth noting that while it
never shows up in the other letters of Paul, it appears ten times in
the Pastoral Epistles (1 Tim. 2:2; 3:16; 4:7–8; 6:3, 5–6, 11; 2 Tim. 3:5;
Tit. 1:1). We must ask why Paul has chosen to give such prominence
to *eusebeia*. To answer this it is necessary to briefly explore how the
term was used in the Greco-Roman world.

We could say that the Greek term *eusebeia*, along with its Latin
counterpart *pietas*, refers to religious conduct, as long as we
remember that religion in the ancient world encapsulated not only
behaviour towards the gods but also conduct in the family and
political arena. To be *pious* meant to live properly in the religious,
civic and familial spaces. A common phrase in Greek literature is
the following: to have '*eusebeia* towards/with the gods'.[57] *Eusebeia*
was adopted by some Hellenistic Jewish authors, particularly the
author of *The Letter of Aristeas* and, above all, 4 Maccabees. These
Jewish authors were attempting to incorporate and contextualize
Greek terms and concepts with the Jewish law in order to help their
audiences navigate life in the diaspora, especially in the defence
of Judaism before Gentile audiences. For the author of 4 Maccabees, *eusebeia* (and its connotations) is the key term. Mercedes López
Salvá explains the meaning of the adjective of *eusebeia* in 4 Maccabees in the following way: 'This adjective, which he includes in the
announcing of his thesis, is the distinctive seal of our author, since
"pious" in the Jewish world means "he who adheres to the Law."
With terms from Greek philosophy, the author encourages the ful-
fillment of the commands of the Torah.'[58] We quote this statement
because this is also what Paul the Jewish Christian is doing with his
use of the term. The difference is that Paul encourages his readers to
live according to the 'sound doctrine' of the gospel of Jesus Christ,
not the law as such (see 1 Tim. 1:3–11).

A second observation with respect to this term is that just as the
phrase 'good works' was linked with the Greek virtues, so it was

---

57 E.g., Isocrates, *Hel. enc.* 31.4; *Bus.* 15.11; Plato, *Euthyd.* 13B4; *Symp.*
193D4; Demosthenes, *Cor.* 7.14; Polybius, 5.10; Posidonius, *Frag.* 102A,
l. 13.

58 López Salvá, *Introducción*, p. 935.

also the case with *eusebeia/pietas*.[59] The author of 4 Maccabees even comments: '[Our philosophy] teaches us moderation [*sōphrosynē*] … teaches us courage [*andreia*] so that we might bear up under all kinds of pain with ease … It educates us in justice [*dikaiosynē*] … and it teaches us godliness [*eusebeia*], so that we might reverence the only God who exists' (5.23–24, my trans.). The author cites the Greek cardinal virtues, but replaces *phronēsis* ('prudence') with *eusebeia*. The point to be made here is that this term used by Paul was not only in the same domain as the virtues but could also be presented as one of the four virtues. Lastly, we note that *eusebeia* can also be linked with 'beauty' and 'love'. In fact, in *Letter of Aristeas* 229.2 we hear that 'the power of *eusebeia* is love'. This is in line with the use of *pietas* in some Roman authors, where it becomes clear that to define *pietas* these authors tell stories that actually describe what we would call mercy, compassion and even love.[60]

To sum up, as Paul instructs the believers in the new Christian life in the Pastoral Epistles, he uses the terminology of 'good works' and 'godliness' (*eusebeia*), which he does not use in his other letters. In attempting to clarify with some concreteness what type of conduct is envisioned by these words, I have noted that they were often employed in relation with the cardinal virtues of the Greco-Roman world. *Eusebeia* also expresses love and compassion, virtues that are found in the Scriptures. And so, we can say that the Christian life in the Pastoral Epistles is portrayed as a life of virtue. Mention of these virtues is scattered throughout the different sections of the Pastoral Epistles. I have also suggested that the good works and piety of the Christians are not ends in themselves. By using the specific terminology noted above, it is likely that Paul is teaching the believers who resided in different cities of the Empire how to relate to non-Christians. By leading virtuous lives they could potentially silence unbelievers who may have viewed the Christians

---

59 E.g., Isocrates, *De pace* 33.1; 34.5; 63.2; Demosthenes, *Mid.* 12.3; Posidonius, *Frag.* 309A, l. 83; *Letter of Aristeas* 131.2.

60 On the Roman authors, I depend on Saller, *Patriarchy, Property and Death*, pp. 106–114. The authors he uses as examples are the elder Seneca, Pliny the Elder and Valerius Maximus.

as a dangerous sect. Their mode of life was itself a type of context-ualization in order ultimately to win their neighbours to the faith.[61]

d. The church

The ecclesiology of the Pastoral Epistles is similar to that found in the other letters of Paul. Lexically speaking, however, whereas the term *ekklēsia* ('assembly') dominates in the other letters, in the Pas-toral Epistles it is found only three times (1 Tim. 3:5, 15; 5:16). More common is the language of 'household' (*oikos/oikia*) to speak of the church (e.g., 1 Tim. 3:15; 2 Tim. 3:6; Tit. 1:11). In addition, Paul uses filial language (1 Tim. 5:1–16) and the household code (Tit. 2:1–10), thereby suggesting that the church is similar to an *oikos*.[62] This is not foreign to Paul's other letters, where the phrase *tēn kat'oikon ... ekklēsian* ('the church/assembly in the household of ...') shows the connection between the household and the assembly (see Rom. 16:5; 1 Cor. 16:19; Col. 4:15; Phlm. 2). The household in the Greco-Roman world could refer both to the material house as well as to the members of the house. Furthermore, whereas the North American and Western European household usually only includes parents and children, the ancient household included extended family members, and, often, slaves. Paul refers to the church as a household for at least two reasons: churches often met in homes and the Lord Jesus used family language to refer to his followers.[63]

The fact that Paul uses the metaphor of the household implies that the church structure in the Pastoral Epistles was to some extent hierarchical. Thus, just as fathers were the leaders of the house-holds, so also adult males were the leaders of the churches. To be sure, there is evidence that there was flexibility in this respect, with couples like Aquilla and Priscilla probably leading the church that met at their home (Rom. 16:5). In addition, as I will argue (1 Tim. 3:8–13), there were female deacons, which implies a measure of lead-ership, including the activity of teaching. Furthermore, although

---

61 See Towner, pp. 55–56. The commentary by Saarinen, pp. 23–28, provides a sophisticated yet clear explanation of this theme.

62 See further Verner, *Household*; Gehring, *House Church and Mission*.

63 On both, see Gehring, *House Church and Mission*, pp. 260–268.

the Pastoral Epistles emphasize the importance of overseers, elders and deacons for the congregation to thrive (cf. Tit. 1:5) – and therefore an overt church organization – it is an exaggeration to claim that this is evidence that the letters were composed in the second century, where church organization was more detailed. A reading of the Ignatian letters, for example, suggests that in comparison to the church of the Apostolic Fathers, the hierarchy in the Pastoral Epistles was still relatively simple.

One last observation to make about Paul's view of the church in the Pastoral Epistles is its importance in the keeping and guarding of the gospel. One of the key texts in this respect is 1 Timothy 3:14–16. Paul expressly tells Timothy why he is writing him this letter: it is so that Timothy and the Christians may know 'how one ought to behave in the household (*oikō*) of God'. He then more closely defines the *oikos* as 'the church of the living God', an expression redolent of OT language to speak of Yahweh and his people (e.g., Deut. 23:2, 3, 4, 9; Judg. 20:2; 1 Chr. 28:8; Mic. 2:5). Paul goes on to further define the church by using temple imagery: it is 'the pillar and bulwark of the truth'. As I will note throughout the commentary, Paul often uses the word 'truth' as synonymous to sound doctrine and the gospel. Therefore, the duty of the church as presented in the Pastoral Epistles is to remain faithful to apostolic doctrine found in Scripture, to 'guard the deposit' (1 Tim. 6:20, ESV), 'the good treasure … with the help of the Holy Spirit living in us' (2 Tim. 1:14).

ANALYSIS

FIRST TIMOTHY

1. SALUTATION (1:1–2)

2. TEACH ONLY WHAT IS IN KEEPING WITH THE GOSPEL (1:3–20)
   A. A correct understanding of the law in light of the gospel (1:3–11)
   B. Paul the former blasphemer saved by grace and made a minister of the gospel (1:12–17)
   C. Encouragement to Timothy to fight the good fight (1:18–20)

3. INSTRUCTIONS FOR BEHAVIOUR IN CHURCH MEETINGS – A MISSIONAL GROUNDING (2:1 – 3:16)
   A. Corporate prayer and the mission of the church (2:1–7)
   B. The behaviour of men and women in community worship and the mission of the church (2:8–15)
   C. The qualifications of overseers and deacons (3:1–13)
   D. The church as the household of God (3:14–16)

4. INSTRUCTIONS FOR TIMOTHY AND THE CHURCH (4:1 – 6:2a)

A. How Timothy can be a good minister of Jesus Christ (4:1–16)
B. How to care for the household of God (5:1–6:2a)
    i. Instructions for the old and young (5:1–2)
    ii. Instructions for widows (5:3–16)
       a. Honour the true widow (5:3–6, 9–10)
       b. Refuse the younger widows (5:11–15)
       c. Younger widows should marry (5:14–16)
    iii. Instructions on the treatment of elders (5:17–25)
    iv. Instructions for slaves (6:1–2a)

5. FINAL SET OF INSTRUCTIONS (6:2b–21)

A. False teachers and the love of money (6:2b–10)
B. Exhortation for Timothy to remain faithful (6:11–16)
C. Final exhortations and closing (6:17–21)

SECOND TIMOTHY

1. SALUTATION (1:1–2)

2. INITIAL INSTRUCTIONS: A CALL FOR TIMOTHY TO PERSEVERE IN GUARDING THE GOSPEL (1:3 – 2:13)

A. Timothy's pedigree of faith (1:3–5)
B. The call to guard the gospel: duty, grounding and empowerment (1:6–14)
C. Onesiphorus as an example for Timothy (1:15–18)
D. Renewed call for perseverance: wisdom from life and the example of Jesus Christ (2:1–13)

3. FURTHER INSTRUCTIONS – A CALL FOR PERSEVERANCE IN DOCTRINE AND LIFE IN LIGHT OF FALSE TEACHERS AND PAUL'S DEATH (2:14 – 4:8)

A. How Timothy can be an approved worker (2:14–26)
B. The last days that are already present (3:1–9)

C. Timothy's hope for distressing times (3:10–17)
D. Proclaim the word in season and out of season (4:1–8)

4. FINAL INSTRUCTIONS AND GREETINGS (4:9–22)
A. Personal requests, news of the judicial hearing and letter closure (4:9–22)

TITUS

1. SALUTATION (1:1–4)
A. Opening (1:1–4)

2. INSTRUCTIONS FOR THE LIFE OF THE CHURCH ON THE BASIS OF GOD'S MERCIFUL SALVATION (1:5 – 3:11)
A. Instructions concerning leaders in the churches of Crete (1:5–9)
B. The reason for the appointment of leaders (1:10–16)
C. Instructions for the household (2:1–10)
D. Soteriology as the basis for Christian behaviour (2:11–15)
E. The behaviour of the church towards society and the theological reason (3:1–11)
 i. Commands towards authorities and outsiders (3:1–2)
 ii. The theological basis for obeying the commands (3:3–7)
 iii. Closing, bookend exhortations (3:8–11)

3. FINAL INSTRUCTIONS AND CLOSURE (3:12–15)

FIRST TIMOTHY
COMMENTARY

This letter is structured in three parts. First, there is a salutation, similar to the salutations of secular letters (1:1–2). Second, there is the extensive body of the letter (1:3 – 6:21a). In this body we find commands, exhortations and explanations, all related to the 'sound doctrine' of the church. Third, the letter closes with a very brief greeting, the shortest in all of Paul's letters (6:21b).

1. SALUTATION (1:1–2)

Context

A salutation was standard in ancient letter writing in the Greco-Roman world.[1] The names of the author and recipient(s) as well as an invocation of the gods for the well-being of the recipients were included. Paul takes up this custom in his letters but enlarges the commonly brief salutation by adding theological statements about God and the recipients. In this way he provides a theological framework for the entirety of the letter. As such, we often find theological themes expressed in the greetings, themes that will often be taken up in the body of the letter. The articulation of these themes in the body of the letter is in large part meant to form the character of the reader, which in Paul's letters is always accomplished on the basis of the gospel. It was a common view of ancient moral philosophy that character formation would partly be done by means of communications such as letters (Stowers, pp. 36–47).

---

[1] For a helpful introduction, see Stowers, *Letter Writing.*

Comment

1. *Paul, an apostle of Christ Jesus.* Paul begins by identifying himself as the author. As he does in almost all his letters (exceptions being Philippians, 1 – 2 Thessalonians and Philemon), he explains his identity by stating that he is an *apostle*. The verbal form of the term *apostle* (i.e., *apostellō*) means 'to send', with the emphasis falling on the identity of the individual as 'one who is sent'. Although the term *apostle* in the New Testament can be used of others like Barnabas (Acts 14:14) and Junia (Rom. 16:7), it is clear that, beginning with Jesus' commission (Matt. 10:1–4// Mark 3:13–19//Luke 6:12–16), a distinctive role fell on the Twelve as the authoritative tradents and interpreters of the life, death and resurrection of Jesus. Paul, as 'one untimely born' (1 Cor. 15:8), was called to be an apostle by the risen Lord and received the same authority as the original Twelve. As such, we should view him as one who has been sent by Jesus Christ to communicate the authoritative word of God to the people of God, in this case to Timothy and the churches at Ephesus. Paul understands himself as an apostle, and as such an envoy of God who proclaims the gospel of God (Rom. 1:1; 15:16; 2 Cor. 11:7; 1 Thess. 2:8, 9) and thus writes to congregations, and individuals such as Timothy, with the authority of God's envoy. This means that the words of Paul in this letter are the written word of God and must be taken as possessing the authority of God himself. To read this letter otherwise is to read against the grain of the document, thereby compromising the reader's potential understanding of it.

Paul expands on the nature of his apostleship by adding the prepositional phrase *by the command of God our Saviour and of Christ Jesus our hope.* With this modifying phrase Paul gives us to understand that his apostleship is not a self-willed vocation but one which is a response to God's command (see Acts 9:1–18; 22:6–16; 26:12–18; Gal. 1:1, 15–16). Also to be noted is that when speaking of God, Paul does not do so here in the abstract. The true and only God is the God who is the *Saviour.* This predicate of God, as we explained in the Introduction, is essential in the Pastoral Epistles, appearing ten times (2:3; 4:10; 2 Tim. 1:10; Tit. 1:3, 4; 2:10, 13; 3:4, 6). Crucially, it is a predicate that is also used of Jesus Christ, thereby linking the activity of God with that of Jesus.

When Paul uses *Saviour* he is employing OT language about the nature of God. In the OT, God is the one and only Saviour of his people (Exod. 15:2; Deut. 32:15; 1 Sam. 10:19; Ps. 24:5; Isa. 17:10; 45:15, 21; 60:16; 62:11). The paradigmatic event of salvation in the OT is God's mighty deliverance of his people in the exodus from Egypt; but in Isaiah 40 – 66 we learn of a new exodus, where God would deliver his people once and for all from their sins and their enemies. This new exodus dawned in the life, death and resurrection of Jesus, and will be completed in his future parousia or second coming.

The designation of Jesus as *our hope* is important, for just as *Saviour* was a predicate of God in the OT, so also was *hope* (e.g., Pss 22:9 [LXX] 21:10; 40:4 [LXX] 39:5; 91:9 [LXX] 90:9). Particularly pertinent to our text is Psalm 65:5 (LXX 64:5), where God is both Saviour and hope: 'By awesome deeds you answer us with deliverance, O God of our *salvation*; you are the *hope* of all the ends of the earth and of the farthest seas.'

2. *To Timothy, my loyal child in the faith.* Timothy is a *loyal* or faithful (*gnēsios*) *child* of Paul in the Christian faith.[2] This statement is probably meant to reassure Timothy that, in contrast to the many false teachers that Paul will unmask in this letter, Timothy is for his part a true believer and bearer of the faith (cf. 1:18–20; 6:11–12; 2 Tim. 1:3–5). Paul calls him *my … child* because Timothy's faith was shaped by the apostle (in addition to Timothy's mother and grandmother: 2 Tim. 1:1–5; cf. Acts 16:1–5).

To close the salutation Paul invokes a blessing on Timothy, expressed by the terms *grace, mercy, and peace.* We will return to explain the first two terms in more depth later (see under 1:14; 2 Tim. 1:9; Tit. 3:5). The following may briefly be said now. *Grace* (*charis*) is similar to the Greek *chairein* ('Greetings!'), often found in the opening of Greek letters (see Johnson, p. 158). It is also found in the LXX of finding God's 'favour' (e.g., Gen. 6:8 of Noah). *Mercy* (*eleos*) often translates the Hebrew *hesed*, which refers to God's faithful love for his people and which is both the motivation

---

2   For a 'biography' of Timothy, see Bruce, *The Pauline Circle*, pp. 29–34. In German, Lips, *Timotheus und Titus*, pp. 33–34, is helpful.

and ground of his free covenant with them (see Exod. 34:6; Ps. 103:8; Mic. 7:18). It is because of this faithful love that he forgives his people when they deserve punishment, and why he does not abandon them when they disobey him. Lastly, Paul invokes God's *peace* on Timothy. Again, the concept expressed by the term has OT roots, referring to *shalom,* a multivalent term that refers to peace with God, neighbours and enemies. The language of *peace* may be echoing the priestly prayer of Numbers 6:26: 'The Lord lift up his countenance upon you, and give you *peace.*'

Theology

Paul introduces theological themes that will be foundational in the Pastoral Epistles. The first theme is soteriological (and therefore also necessarily *theo*logical). God is designated as our Saviour, our deliverer. The blessings that Paul invokes on Timothy are blessings of salvation that have already reached the believers but will be fully realized at the second coming of Jesus Christ. God alone has the capacity to save us from sin and death. And this leads to the second theme found in the salutation, namely, the identity of God the Saviour.

It is clear from Paul's language that this God is the God of Israel. Yet, the identity of this God of Israel is clarified so that it *fundamentally* includes Jesus Christ. This is so because the designations and the acts of God are equally attributed to Jesus Christ. God alone is the hope of Israel – *Christ Jesus our hope* (1:1). Grace, mercy and peace come from God the Father *and Christ Jesus our Lord* (1:2). Who God is and what he is capable of doing, Jesus Christ also is and is able to do. Indeed, he is the *Lord* (*kyrios*) (1:2), a title that in the Septuagint mostly refers to God. This does not mean that there are two gods! Rather, it means that God is Father, Son – and as we see from other letters of Paul and Titus (e.g., 2 Cor. 3:17; 13:4; Tit. 3:5) – Holy Spirit. Thus, Paul opens his letter with an indication as to who this God is who saved Timothy and whom Timothy must serve and obey.

We must now recall the statement made under Context about letters in the Greco-Roman world, namely, that they were vehicles to instruct pupils in the teacher-student relationship. It is thus crucial to observe that Paul's letters begin by speaking of God. The implication is that character formation in the Christian disciple must begin, not with internal possibilities for change ('I can do this if I give it my best!'), but rather with experiential knowledge of God. This is our only hope for transformation.

2. TEACH ONLY WHAT IS IN KEEPING WITH THE GOSPEL (1:3–20)

We can divide this section into four parts. First, Paul urges Timothy to instruct 'certain people' (1:3) not to become attached to 'different doctrine', which, instead of being concerned with 'God's work' (NIV), is interested in 'myths and endless genealogies' (1:4). This people think that they are experts in the law. But they really are not (1:3–7). This leads to the second part of the section. The law, Paul argues, was not put in place for the righteous. Instead, the law was given 'for the lawless and disobedient, for the godless and sinful', and so on. This is likely to mean that the law was given by God to demonstrate human sinfulness (1:8–11; see further explanation below). In the third part of the section Paul recalls for Timothy how he himself (Paul) behaved before encountering Messiah Jesus. He was a 'blasphemer, a persecutor, and a man of violence' (1:13). Despite this conduct, God was gracious to Paul, even placing him in the ministry. Paul is then moved to a brief doxology (1:12–17). The section ends with Paul reminding Timothy of his ministry. Timothy was empowered to fight the good fight of the ministry 'having faith and a good conscience'. This is in contrast to Hymenaeus and Alexander, who have shipwrecked their faith (1:18–20).

A. A correct understanding of the law in light of the gospel (1:3–11)

Context
One of the most important aspects of this section is Paul's use of a catalogue of vices to describe those for whom the law was written. In the Pastoral Epistles there are catalogues of virtues and vices at 1 Timothy 1:8–10; 4:1–3; 6:3–5; 2 Timothy 2:22–23; 3:1–9; and Titus 3:3. Catalogues of virtues and vices were common in the writings of moral philosophers of the period, often employed as a response to criticism.[1] These catalogues were highly stylized. For example, many of the terms for vices began with the Greek letter alpha which negates the virtue (e.g., English *un*righteous, *un*loving). Because the catalogues were so conventional, we must remember they are *general* descriptions that do not apply to every single individual. Their effect is meant to be cumulative rather than individual.

Paul uses these catalogues for at least two reasons. First, the catalogues were a common feature of the type of protreptic writings of which the Pastorals are an example (i.e., writings made up primarily of exhortation; see Introduction). Second, the vice catalogues were a rhetorical manoeuvre in polemic situations, giving a negative portrayal of opponents. Modern readers may find these catalogues offensive, especially when the vices of the enemies are highlighted. We must bear in mind, however, that they were part of contemporary culture. Paul's aim in using the catalogues of vices is not to insult opponents but to warn the believers of false teachers who were destructive to the faith.

Comment
3–4. *I urge you, as I did when I was on my way to Macedonia.* On the potential historical background of this statement, see Introduction.

---

1 See Malherbe, *Moral Exhortation*, pp. 138–141; Fitzgerald, 'Virtue/Vice Lists', *ABD* 6:857–859.

To the extent that this reference can be pinpointed, it may refer to Paul's travels and delegations as found in Acts 20:1–38. Paul had left Ephesus, travelled through the churches in Macedonia, and, having sent for the elders of the Ephesian churches, warned them of future false teachers who would infiltrate the churches. That this is the period being referred to in vv. 3–4 is only a possibility, however.

Paul's charge to Timothy at a previous time is related to the present charge. So in a sense this is a reminder, which is common in the paraenetic genre. The charge given Timothy is described as follows: *instruct certain people not to teach any different doctrine.* The verb *instruct* (*parangellō*) is often used by Paul with the weight of his apostolic authority behind it (e.g., 1 Cor. 7:10; 11:17; 1 Thess. 4:11; 2 Thess. 3:6, 12). Therefore, what Timothy was commanded to instruct in the past, and is also now to instruct, has as its source apostolic authority. To reject it would be to reject the commands of Jesus Christ.

The phrase *teach any different doctrine* (NRSV) translates the Greek verb *hetererodidaskalein*, which occurs in the NT only here and in 6:3 and is not attested prior to the NT. It is common in early Christian literature (e.g., Ignatius, *Polycarp* 3.1; Origen, *Fragmenta in Psalms 1–150* 3.4; Eusebius, *E.H.* 2.10.2), often either echoing or quoting 1 Timothy. As will be clear in the rest of the letter, this *different* teaching is such because it does not correspond to the sound apostolic doctrine (see further under 1:10).

One aspect of the false instruction is mentioned in verse 4 with the statement concerning *myths and endless genealogies.* The term *myth* (Greek *mythos*) can simply mean 'speech', 'statement', or a 'story, tale' (Homer, *Od.* 3.94; 4.324), without distinguishing between its truthfulness or falsity. Plato uses *mythos* (e.g., *Resp.* 359D [*mythologousin*]; *Tim.* 22C; 23B *Leg.* 636C) of primeval stories beyond the possibility of falsification or verification, stories that help explain origins and the reasons for current states of affairs in a culture. But *mythos* can also mean fiction as opposed to the truth (e.g., Herodotus, *Hist.* 2.23; 2.452; Plato, *Phaed.* 61B; *Prot.* 320C; *Resp.* 330D). This is likely the sense in 1:4 as well as 2 Timothy 4:4 and Titus 1:14 (where 'myth' is contrasted with 'truth'). Equally important is the use of *mythos* in Greek moral philosophy. The term could be employed to polemicize against those who, instead of careful use of reason to reach the truth, preferred to be led by old, fabulous

tales that could not be proved one way or the other.[2] Thus, *myths*
were viewed as unworthy pieces of corroboration for serious philosophers.[3] By using this language to label the teaching of the
opponents, Paul is portraying them as dangerous men who offer
exotic, fabulous teaching that is not in accord with the truthful
apostolic doctrine or even with good use of reason.

With *endless genealogies* Paul clarifies the content of the myths.
More than likely, this refers to OT genealogical trees that filled gaps
in biblical history and served as starting points for the construction
of stories (Jewish haggadah: e.g., *Jubilees* 8.1–30; Ps. Philo 1–2). As
Roloff suggests, the study of false myths and genealogies must have
exerted 'considerable fascination' given their esoteric and secretive
nature (Roloff, p. 64).

Paul now provides one of the reasons why devotion to *myths and
endless genealogies* is prohibited: they *promote speculations*. This last term
(*ekzētēsis*) is only used once in the NT with the meaning 'useless
speculation' (BDAG, p. 303). The term is related to *zētesis*, which
some manuscripts read.[4] This last term is found in Acts (15:2, 7;
25:20) and the Pastoral Epistles (6:4; 2 Tim. 2:23; Tit. 3:9, used with
'genealogies'). These *speculations* were Jewish in nature; they had to
do with an improper use of the law, for they led to useless quarrels
and baseless conjectures. Paul will return later (v. 8) to explain the
proper use of the law.

By contrast, teaching in the church should be concerned with
divine training which is known by faith. The Greek *oikonomia*, translated
by the NIV as 'God's work', usually conveys the sense of 'management' or 'plan' (BDAG, pp. 697–698). An alternative reading accepts
the term *oikodomēn* ('edification', so KJV), based on the original
hand of Codex Bezae, Latin traditions and Irenaeus. The reading
oikonomia is to be preferred due to superior manuscript support and
to being the more difficult reading. The meaning *training* (NRSV)

---

2 See, e.g., Clement of Alexandria, *Protr.*1.

3 See, e.g., the pejorative use of the word in Marcus Aurelius, *Med.* 8.25
   (twice); 12.27 (twice).

4 E.g., D F G. The reading adopted in the NA[28] is preferred, being
   supported by Alexandrian witnesses: ℵ 33 81.

is listed in BDAG, but seems unlikely given that a term like *paideuō* ('to train, discipline'; cf. Tit. 2:12) or *paideia* would have been a better fit if Paul were attempting to communicate 'training' in godliness (cf. 2 Tim. 3:16 and Tit. 2:12).

Perhaps a comparison with other Pauline texts may lead to clarification. In Ephesians 3:2 and Colossians 1:25 Paul uses a similar phrase (*oikonomia theou*). In those texts the emphasis falls on a gracious commendation given to Paul to unveil the mystery of the gospel. I suggest we understand Paul as communicating in 1:4 that the proper focus of church instruction should be on apostolic doctrine that concentrates on the gospel, not mythic speculations.[5] That is to say, there is nothing wrong in careful, deep inquiry into mystery – as long as it is the mystery of the gospel.

Paul concludes by saying that this *oikonomia* is by *faith*. That is, from beginning to end (cf. Rom. 1:17), both the content and appropriation of the gospel has to do with God's work in Jesus Christ (objective faith or *fides quae*) that must be accepted in full trust (subjective faith or *fides qua*).

5. Paul shifts to an explanation of his instruction by concentrating on its *aim* (*telos*). The aim or goal of Paul's orders to Timothy as found in the entirety of 1 Timothy is *love*. The noun *agapē* occurs numerous times in the Pastoral Epistles (e.g., 1 Tim. 1:14; 2:15; 4:12; 6:11; 2 Tim. 1:7, 13; 2:22; 3:10; Tit. 2:2). Love is linked with God's grace and faithfulness as underlying his marvellous rescue of the former blasphemer Paul (1:13–14). The love of God has been poured out on the believers by the Holy Spirit (2 Tim. 1:7), with the result that they can love God and neighbour, the two pillar commands of the Law and the Prophets (cf. Matt. 22:36–40). In fact, therefore, it is the teaching of the gospel – or rather the gospel itself – that Paul passes down to Timothy and which has the power to move believers to the fulfilment of the law (cf. Rom. 5:5; 13:8–10). Ironically, Paul's teaching actually leads to the *true* fulfilment of the law, in contrast to those who claim to be teachers of the law (1:7)! Paul's point is that the teaching of sound doctrine leads to love of God and love of neighbour. One is reminded of

---

5 For other suggestions, see Marshall, pp. 367–368.

Augustine's famous statement, where the theologian indicates that the understanding of Scripture is nothing if it does not lead to love: 'Whoever, then, thinks that he understands the Holy Scriptures, or any part of them, but puts such an interpretation upon them as does not tend to build up this twofold love of God and our neighbour, does not yet understand them as he ought' (*Doctr. chr.* 1.36).

Paul expands on the concept of *love* by means of a prepositional phrase: this love stems *from a pure heart, a good conscience, and sincere faith*. The cluster of words that appear here is very common in the Pastoral Epistles. The adjective *pure* (*katharos*) occurs with 'conscience' at 3:9; with 'heart' at 2 Timothy 2:22; and at other times by itself. The phrase *pure heart* appears in the Septuagint (e.g., Pss 24:4; 51:12) with reference to ritual purification and integrity at the seat of the person's being. Johnson explains the pure heart as a 'symbol for being rightly related to God' (p. 165).

The use of *conscience* in the Pastoral Epistles is disproportionate to the rest of Paul's letters, where, apart from Romans and the Corinthian correspondence, it does not appear at all. By contrast, in the relatively brief Pastoral Epistles, *conscience* appears six times. Two important monographs on the use of conscience in Paul[6] unfortunately restrict themselves to the so-called 'undisputed letters' of Paul, thereby commenting only very briefly (Bosman, not at all) and parenthetically on the use of conscience in the Pastoral Epistles. Eckstein concludes that conscience in Paul (including the Pastoral Epistles) is an anthropological category, that is, it is something shared by all humans irrespective of their spiritual state. Conscience is an authority in people that can judge their acts as positive or negative in accordance with previously given norms (pp. 311–320). To Eckstein's analysis the following may be added: in the Pastoral Epistles conscience is not a neutral apparatus capable as such of receiving and judging God's revelation. Rather, the term is always qualified (e.g., 'good' or 'pure' on the one hand, and 'seared' or 'corrupt' on the other). This pushes the reader to

---

6 Eckstein, *Der Begriff* Syneidesis *bei Paulus*; Bosman, *Conscience in Philo and Paul*.

ask the question: on what basis is the person's conscience 'good' or 'corrupt'? Judging from the context of each usage, the state of the conscience is directly related to the person's response to the apostolic teaching, the sound *didaskalia* of the Pastoral Epistles. Rejection of the apostolic gospel leads to a 'seared' (4:2) or 'corrupt' (Tit. 1:15) conscience. On the other hand, acceptance of the apostolic gospel leads to a 'good' conscience because the individual has been saved and washed by God the Saviour (Tit. 3:4–6). And so, the *good conscience* of 1:5 is similar to *pure heart* in that both are the result of God's cleansing of the person.

The third phrase qualifying *love* is *sincere faith*. The phrase is also found in 2 Timothy 1:5 to speak of the genuine faith found in Timothy but firstly in his grandmother and mother. In the other Pauline letters there are examples of *sincere (anhypokritos)* qualifying 'love' (e.g., Rom. 12:9; 2 Cor. 6:6). To understand this phrase better one must inquire into the nature of *faith (pistis)* in this verse as well as others in the Pastoral Epistles.

Pistis in the Pastoral Epistles is found in 1 Timothy 1:2, 4, 14, 19 (twice); 2:7, 15; 3:9, 13; 4:1, 6, 12; 5:8, 12; 6:10, 11, 12, 21; 2 Timothy 1:5, 13; 2:18, 22; 3:8, 10, 15; 4:7; Titus 1:1, 4, 13; 2:2, 10; 3:15. Two observations can be made about Paul's frequent use the word. First, its meaning is irreducible to just one or two significations. In other words, it is a polyvalent term that can have more than one meaning. Second, the use of *pistis* has been somewhat conventionalized as part of a Christian pattern of speech. As a consequence, in those cases where *pistis* is used in a formula in the Pastorals, it is difficult to pin down the precise meaning. With these comments in place, we add that there are concrete patterns of meaning in the Pastoral Epistles. (1) Faith can refer to an objective body of belief (*fides quae*), namely the apostolic teaching. Those who reject the apostolic teaching end up in perdition (e.g., 1 Tim. 1:19; 2 Tim. 3:8; Tit. 1:13; 2:2). (2) Faith can refer to the act of believing in the God of the apostolic gospel (*fides qua*; e.g., 1 Tim. 1:4; 2:7; 2 Tim. 3:15; Tit. 1:1). This act of trust is not a result of human willpower but of God's grace working in the sinner (1 Tim. 1:14). (3) Faith can refer to a virtue of the Christian, which is accompanied by love, holiness, purity and other virtues (e.g., 1 Tim. 2:15; 4:12; 6:11; 2 Tim. 1:13; 2:22; 3:10; Tit. 2:2). As such, the translation *faithfulness* may at times be appropriate.[7] These uses of *pistis* are not hermetically sealed from one another. In view of 1:3–20, the meaning of *pistis* in verse 5 denotes all three senses: faith is belief and trust in the apostolic doctrine, which leads to faithfulness to the gospel in Christian existence.

To sum up, verse 5 serves as a contrast to verses 3–4, which briefly mention the content of the false teaching that Timothy must order to stop. In contrast to this false teaching, which only produces endless speculations, apostolic instructions from Paul, which concentrate on 'God's work', aim to lead to the true fulfilment of the law, namely love of God and love of neighbour. Such love is no self-produced achievement; rather, it stems from the work of God that purifies and which enables sincere trust in God and faithfulness to the apostolic teaching in conduct.

6–7. Verse 6 basically reiterates verse 4, albeit in more polemical language. Having *deviated* (*astocheō* is the language of apostasy in the Pastoral Epistles: 1 Tim. 6:21; 2 Tim. 2:18) from the virtues listed at the end of verse 5, the false teachers *turned to meaningless talk* (*mataiologia*). This term and its cognates are often used in debate in moral philosophy in order to knock down an opponent's argument by speaking of it as no better than a 'false tale' or a mere 'rambling' with no true content.[8] The term is also found in Titus 1:10, where it is used of 'rebellious people' who speak meaningless things. Thus, abandonment of apostolic teaching leads to the adoption of fabulous tales and useless chatter that do not produce love. Paul is about to specify in verse 7 what the empty chatter is about.

The false teachers whom Timothy is to silence desire to be *teachers of the law* (*nomodidaskaloi*). This may suggest that the opponents are Jewish; but it is also possible that the false teachers are Gentile believers who have added aspects of Judaism to their philosophical system (see Introduction). In the NT the term *nomodidaskalos* is

---

7 On this use of *pistis* in the Pastoral Epistles, see also Mutschler, *Glaube in den Pastoralbriefen*; Köstenberger, pp. 492–498. On faith in Paul, see Morgan, *Roman Faith and Christian Faith*.

8 See, e.g., Plutarch, *Lib. ed.* 9; Porphyry, *Abst.* 4.16.52, used with 'superstitious tales' (*deisidaimonia*); Athenaeus, *Deipn.* 14.7.27.

found in Luke 5:17 and Acts 5:34; it is not employed in a disparaging manner, as the teaching of the law as such is not the problem (see verse 8 below). Rather, it is the fact that they 'teach' the law *without understanding either what they are saying or the things about which they make assertions* that constitutes the problem. The *mēte ... mēte (either ... or)* construction intensifies the depth of ignorance of the opponents: 'They do not even know the meaning of what they are saying, let alone teaching, as doctrine' (Marshall, p. 373). Such a statement by Paul may appear arrogant if the false teachers were Jewish – and thereby also potentially experts on Scripture. This leads us to ask the question: how can Paul make such strong claims? The answer from the New Testament in general and the Pastoral Epistles specifically is that the false teachers cannot understand the law because they do not read it with Jesus Christ as its centre and culmination (see 1 Tim. 1:10–11; 6:3; Tit. 1:10–13; also Matt. 5:17; Rom. 10:4; Gal. 3:15–22). As long as the law is read as the climax of God's revelation, it cannot be properly grasped. Only in light of the advent of Jesus Christ can the law be understood as God wishes it to be understood. The problem with the false teachers is therefore not a matter of intelligence or erudition: it is ultimately a Christological problem. Namely, it is about their failure to understand the relationship between the Messiah and the law. Paul and the early Christians read the law in light of their experience of the risen Jesus.[9] Paul in particular possessed a keen understanding of the place of the law in salvation history – it was given to him through a revelation from the risen Lord Jesus (e.g., Gal. 1:1, 11–12).

8. The statement about the activity of the opponents *vis-à-vis* the law may be twisted to implicate Paul as anti-law as such. He therefore clarifies his stance on the law: *Now we know that the law is good*. Paul had to make similar qualifications in Romans (7:7, 12, 16; cf. 3:31). In this verse his declaration is akin to the many statements of the goodness of the law found in the Psalter (19:7–11; 119; etc.). Paul adds a qualifier by means of a conditional clause: *if one uses it*

---

9 It is necessary to add that, on the other hand, the identity of the risen Jesus could not be recognized without knowledge of the law – we have a dialectic, that is, a back-and-forth between one horizon and the other.

legitimately ('if one uses it *lawfully*' [*nomimōs*]). Clearly Paul is using a play on words with *nomos* ('law') and *nomimōs*. But what does he mean by 'lawfully?'

9–11. *This means understanding that the law is laid down not for the innocent but for the lawless and disobedient.* The participle *eidōs* (*understanding*) that begins verse 9 explains the previous verse by clarification: the law, in fact, is not instituted for *the innocent* (the NIV translation of *dikaios* as 'righteous' is superior to the NRSV's 'innocent'. In what follows I will use the NIV's rendering). Thus, the goodness of the law is tied up with God's intention for it.[10] The statement that the law was not intended by God for the righteous would have been rejected by a large strand of Judaism. For in the mind of many Jews the reason why God gave the law to Israel as opposed to other nations was because Israel was *worthy* of it. Election, which was made concrete in the giving of the law, was a matter of merit in the minds of many Jews. There existed a broad tradition that had the *individual* Abraham as the righteous man whose obedience won the merit necessary for Israel to receive the written law in due course (e.g., *2 Esdras* 19:6; Philo, *Abr.* 50; 83; 89–90; 167; 204; 261; *Genesis Rabah* 44.3, 5). Paul's statement about the law not being instituted for the righteous is therefore a contradiction of a large swath of Judaism. In addition, it implies that Israel was not righteous just because it had received the law.

What follows in verse 9 is a vice list (cf. Rom. 1:29–31; Gal. 5:19–21), which describes the activities of those for whom the law was instituted. The head term is *lawless (anomos)*, which is expanded by the remaining words in verses 9–10. The idea conveyed is that of individuals who live as if there is no law. Although the accent here falls on the Mosaic law (Torah), it may also include 'natural revelation' given by God apart from Israel's Torah (cf. Rom. 1:18–32). *Disobedient (anypotaktos)* refers to rebels who refuse to be subject to any type of authority (see 1:10 and Tit. 1:6, of disobedient children).

The second pair speaks of those who are *godless and sinful*. The first term (*asebēs*) conveys the sense of impiety. It is the opposite of *eusebeia*, which as we saw in the Introduction is the key term for ethics

---

10 See Köstenberger, p. 74.

in the Pastoral Epistles. In Titus 2:12 *godlessness* is a condition from which God saves us. The second word (*hamartolos*) is often found paired with *asebēs* and is used 'to refer to people who flout God's authority, deny his existence, and thus are sinful' (Marshall, p. 379).

The third pair of vices speaks of the *unholy and profane*. Prior to the NT this pair appears together in Jewish texts (e.g., 3 Macc. 2:2 and Philo, *Mos.* 2.199.) *Profane* (*bebēlos*), which is often employed in contrast to that which is holy, can also be found in a catalogue of vices in Philo, *Sacr.* 32.6 (see further under 4:7 and 2 Tim. 2:16). In 2 Timothy 3:2 *unholy* (*anosios*) appears in another catalogue of vices, where Paul lists the characteristics of evil men who will rise on the last days.

For those who kill their father or mother. Both in the Jewish (Exod. 20:12; Deut. 6:16) and Greco-Roman contexts (Marcus Aurelius, *Med.* 6.34; Plato, *Leg.* 881A), the honouring of parents was viewed as a sacred duty, an act of *pietas*. To kill father or mother was therefore one of the vilest offences a human being could commit. Paul adds *for murderers* (*androphonos*), who by their action are breaking the sixth commandment (Exod. 20:13).

For *fornicators, sodomites.* These two examples of lawlessness refer to sexual acts. The NIV translation of *pornos* as 'adulterers' is too restrictive, since *pornos* could also refer to fornication and even homosexuality and incest. Of course, *pornos* also does refer to adultery. Thus, a *pornos* was always a fornicator but not always an adulterer. More than likely, *pornos* is here harking back to the seventh commandment (Exod. 20:14), which prohibits sexual intimacy between a married man and the wife or fiancée of another man (see also Lev. 18:20; 20:10; Deut. 22:22, 23–27). It was so serious an offence that it was punishable by death. The composite word *arsenokoitēs* ('male' + 'bed'), translated by the NRSV as *sodomites* refers to 'a male who engages in sexual activity with a person of his own sex' (BDAG, p. 135). The word can refer to both the active and passive party in the homosexual act. When Greek writers wanted to refer specifically to the passive party, they used the term *malakos* (which Paul uses in addition to *arsenokoitēs* in 1 Cor. 6:9). The OT clearly prohibits homosexual acts, for which the death penalty was stipulated (e.g., Lev. 18:22; 20:13). Greek culture was open to homosexual behaviour, including acceptance of an agreed sexual relationship between an adult male and a pre-pubescent boy. The Romans viewed this as perverse.[11] The suggestion that the NT does not condemn same-sex relations as long as the partners are in a committed relationship does not have any exegetical or historical merit.[12]

The vice list continues with *slave traders, liars, perjurers*. Slavery was pervasive in the ancient world, although it should be noted that in the Greco-Roman world slavery did not have to do with race, skin colour or education. People became slaves as a result of military conquest, or because they were born from slaves. The term used here (*andrapodistēs*) could refer to a slave dealer or a kidnapper. In the case of the latter, Johnson incisively comments: 'It is a dramatic example of breaking the commandment of the Decalogue against stealing, since it is the very freedom of a person that is taken away' (p. 171). The last two vices, *liars, perjurers* (*pseustēs, epiorkos*), are covered by the ninth commandment: 'You shall not bear false witness against your neighbor' (Exod. 20:16).

And whatever else is contrary to the sound teaching. Paul cuts short the vice list in order to move to the centre of gravity of 1:3–11. Note that Paul does not say: 'and whatever else is contrary to the *law*'. The law is no longer the ultimate measure or judge of conduct. Rather, *sound teaching* is the measure of the conduct of God's people, which includes the law as interpreted in the light of the life, death and resurrection of Jesus Messiah. *Sound teaching* (*hygiainō didaskalia*, which can also be translated as *sound doctrine*) is one of the most important phrases in the Pastoral Epistles, appearing four times (2 Tim. 4:3; Tit. 1:9, 2:1). The almost identical phrase, *logos hyiēs* ('sound word'), is found in Titus 2:8. Paul links *sound teaching* with 'the word' and 'the truth' when he exhorts Timothy to preach the word, 'for the time is coming when people will not put up with *sound doctrine*, but having itching ears, they will accumulate for themselves teachers to suit their own desires, and will turn away from listening to the truth and wander away to

---

11 See Halperin, *OCD*, pp. 700–703.

12 For a biblical and thoughtful response to the view that committed homosexual relationships are not in view in Scripture, Hays, *The Moral Vision of the New Testament*, pp. 379–405, is very helpful.

myths' (2 Tim. 4:3–4). Titus is urged to teach that which is 'proper to' or 'fitting' (*prepo*) with sound teaching (Tit. 2:1).

We should also note that the opposite of *sound* or *healthy* was the concept of a 'sick soul' or 'sick mind'. This was very common in the language of moral philosophers, particularly the Cynics. Furthermore, moral philosophers often portrayed themselves as 'healers of the soul'. They believed that they could bring health or soundness to the soul by their *rational* teaching, delivered with frankness of speech. Paul is using the language of moral philosophers when he speaks of *sound* or *healthy* teaching. Most of Paul's hearers would have recognized this. For Paul and the early Christians, the gospel was that which made the sick soul well.

It is notable that *sound teaching* is teaching that *conforms to the glorious gospel*. *Sound teaching* is therefore a phrase that refers to the *standard* of the church, the norm that divides truth from error. It is thus another way of referring to the gospel. Marshall explains that the phrase stands for 'the approved apostolic doctrine. The dominant use of the singular διδασκαλία in the Pastoral Epistles (14 times) reflects an emphasis on the concept of a fixed body of Christian doctrine' (p. 381). The teaching is *sound* (*hygiainō*) because, having God as its source, it leads to the healing (salvation) of the individual who adheres to it.

Paul concludes this section by indicating the source of the gospel: it is *the blessed God*. God is here designated as *blessed* (*makarios*; see 6:15; cf. Tit. 2:13), an epithet that is not used of God in the Septuagint. The term is often found in the Imperial Cult; perhaps its use here indicates a soft polemic. Paul was *entrusted* with this gospel (see Gal. 2:7; 1 Thess. 2:4; Tit. 1:3), a theme he will develop in the following section.

Theology

Before drawing some theological lessons from the section above, some thoughts on preaching and liturgy from this text may be helpful, particularly in relation to the catalogue of vices. When preaching from these texts it is probably unhelpful to spend many minutes explaining *each* virtue or vice, for these catalogues were meant to strike the hearers *as a whole*, in cumulative fashion. It is probably more in keeping with the goals of the text to select one or two virtues or vices that the church needs to hear about at that moment and expound them carefully, instead of the entire material. In a liturgical setting, texts like these that include a catalogue of vices may be *read* entirely for their cumulative effect, followed by the congregation responding: 'Lord, have mercy upon us.'

Let us now summarize the content of 1:3–11. On a previous occasion Paul had urged Timothy to remain at Ephesus so that he would command certain people not to teach against apostolic doctrine. Now, through this letter, he reminds Timothy of this command. These opponents seem to have been teaching from the law of Moses. They were apparently using the law to engage in the tantalizing practice of filling gaps in OT history – perhaps the type of midrashic haggadah (stories) that one finds in later rabbinic writings. Whatever the specific content of their teaching, Paul views it as profoundly harmful because it did not conform to the gospel of Jesus Christ. This lack of conformity was evident in at least two ways.

First, it was not Christological (i.e., centred on Jesus Christ) in the way it went about interpreting God's revelation. Had it been so, the teachers would have been using the law in the right or 'lawful' way, that is, as an instrument whereby God demonstrated the deep sinfulness of *all* humanity; it was to show humanity that it was not righteous. As we learn from Paul in Romans 3:20 and Galatians 2:16, 19, 21; 3:19–22, the law was not the climax – and therefore not the centre – of salvation history in the way that most Jews typically believed. Rather, the law was given to lead humanity to Christ, the real climax – and therefore the centre – of salvation history. Any interpretation that displaced Jesus Messiah from the centre and replaced him with the law had to be resisted, for ultimately such interpretation was theologically malignant.

Second, the teaching of the opponents was not Christological (and therefore harmful) because in *content* it did not conform to the good news of the life, death and resurrection of Jesus for our salvation.

In his Jewish context, Paul's statements about the law would have been found astonishing. How could he – as a Jew – ever give the law a subordinate place? This would seem unthinkable. In the verses that follow Paul will explain.

B. Paul the former blasphemer saved by grace and made a minister of the gospel (1:12–17)

Context

One of the most important questions facing the interpreter of these verses is how they function in the flow of the argument. Why would Paul seemingly interrupt the flow of thought by introducing an autobiographical statement? How does this autobiographical sketch move his argument forward?

For some of the scholars who reject Pauline authorship, verses 12–17 are viewed as employed by the pseudonymous author in a rhetorically clever way to establish his authority. That is, he uses Paul's conversion narrative to authenticate the gospel communicated in his instructions to Timothy.[13] This is an example of the pseudonymous approach to the Pastoral Epistles affecting its exegesis. If, on the other hand, one holds Pauline authorship, there is no need to understand verses 12–17 as authentication of the gospel preached by Paul. For Timothy, the long-time co-worker and disciple of Paul, well knew that the apostle's gospel came from the risen Lord.

It is better to understand this autobiographical section as a word of encouragement and hope to Timothy. If God through his gospel was capable of saving someone like Paul – a persecutor of the church – then he certainly could save those to whom Timothy was ministering. Paul's conversion is a *regulative* example of the power of God to save. Timothy is therefore to continue teaching the gospel, for God can save through it – even the opponents who loom large in this letter.

Rhetorically speaking, the above conclusion regarding the function of these verses fits very well with the view that 1 Timothy is an example of a paraenetic letter (see Genre in Introduction). For one of the ways to make an argument in this type of letter was by the use of *examples* (*exempla*). Thus, the author used examples in order

---

13 Roloff, pp. 84–88, 99, who is certain that the real Paul could not have written these words, states: 'It is evident that this retrospective narrative [of Paul's conversion] cannot be formulated by Paul himself'! (p. 85).

to make concrete an idea that may have seemed too abstract or theoretical; or in order better to persuade a pupil.[14] It is likely that this is what Paul is doing in this section, where he offers his own life as an example of the power of the gospel that Timothy must protect.

Comment

12. *I am grateful to Christ Jesus our Lord.* Paul opens this subsection with a report that gives us a window into his prayer life. What he urges other believers to do ('give thanks in all circumstances', 1 Thess. 5:18) he himself practices. The object of Paul's thanksgiving is Jesus Christ, whom he designates as the *Lord*. As we noted in the Introduction and in 1:2, the title *kyrios* is often used in the Septuagint to render the Hebrew Tetragrammaton. To say that Jesus is the *kyrios* is to affirm that the identity of the God of the OT is not understood if it does not also include Jesus Christ.

With the phrase, *who has strengthened me*, Paul provides another designation of Jesus. In 2 Timothy 4:17 Paul also speaks of the Lord who gave him strength during his trial. The Lord gives Paul strength to endure all circumstances (Phil. 4:13). But why would Paul use this designation of the Lord in this verse, instead of, say, 'who loved me,' or 'who saved me?' After all, he is speaking of his salvation-call. It is possible that the portrait of Paul in Acts at the time of his salvation-call may shed light on this question.

The image of Paul in Acts during the days of his salvation-call is one of a man who had been utterly broken (Acts 9:8–9). He needed the Lord's power to embark on the ministry to which he was called. Interestingly, the Acts text says that after being baptized and eating, Paul 'regained strength' (*enischyō,* 9:18). And during his initial preaching in Damascus we are told that he 'became increasingly more powerful' (*enedynamouto,* 9:22). Paul is thus probably using the description *who has strengthened me* in 1:12 because he recalls the empowering of the Holy Spirit that he had received during his call. This historical memory is simultaneously a reminder to Timothy, encouraging him to press on with his work at Ephesus, for the Lord will strengthen him as he had strengthened Paul.

---

14   See Malherbe, *Moral Exhortation*, pp. 135–138.

Because he judged me faithful and appointed me to his service. Another reason why Paul gives thanks to Christ is expressed in this subordinate causal clause (*because*, Greek *hoti*). Christ's appointing him to his *service* (*diakonia*, cf. 3:8–13) is related to Paul's faithfulness. This is a puzzling idea, for it sounds as if Christ's call was based on Paul's faithfulness! This mentality does not fit with Paul's thought elsewhere, however (1 Cor. 15:10!). In order to interpret this verse correctly most commentators have rightly called attention to 1 Corinthians 7:25: 'But I give my opinion as one who by the Lord's mercy is trustworthy [*pistos*]'. Towner's conclusion is sound: 'Paul is not arguing that Christ foresaw that in spite of his sin Paul would prove himself faithful; rather, the sense here is of the potency of divine calling to achieve certain results in human lives. As Paul reflects on this process, his argument is that his ministry to this point has demonstrated the effectiveness of Christ's choice in appointing him apostle to the Gentiles' (p. 138).

13. *Even though I was formerly a blasphemer, a persecutor, and a man of violence.* Here Paul introduces a concessive statement that links back to the previous verse and forward to the following clause. God gave Paul strength and called him to his service *despite* his disturbing pre-conversion behaviour. With two consecutives 'ands' in the Greek that raise the intensity of the language, Paul reminds Timothy of what he used to be *vis-à-vis* the church. There is great pathos in this sentence, highlighting the enormity of Paul's former *hubris*. First, as a *blasphemer* Paul behaved irreverently towards God. Paul probably indicates that he spoke of Jesus as a false prophet and seducer of Israel rather than what he truly was, the Messiah of Israel.[15] Paul's irreverence was accompanied (or perhaps deepened, if we view the second two descriptions as variations of the first) by being a *persecutor* of the Christian community (*diōktēs*; see 1 Cor. 15:9; Gal. 1:13, 23; Phil. 3:6). The NRSV translation *man of violence* for the last statement is too restrictive as a translation of the Greek *hybristēs*. While violence is characteristic of the *hybristēs*, it is better to think of his fundamental condition as one of insolence and defiance of the gods (so especially in Greek tragedy), an attitude that often resulted

---

15 This was the view of Jesus in rabbinic Judaism: e.g., *b. Sanh.* 43a; 107b.

in unhinged violence against other humans. Marshall rightly states that in using the three terms Paul is portrayed as a *theomachos*, a 'god-fighter'.

But I received mercy because I had acted ignorantly in unbelief. With a strong adversative conjunction (*alla,* 'but'), Paul comments on the incongruous result of his blasphemous behaviour: instead of being severely punished as he deserved, he instead *received mercy.* The passive voice of the verb shows that Paul was acted upon by God; his conversion was God's free initiative. *Mercy* in the Septuagint often renders the Hebrew *hesed*, a term used to articulate God's faithful love which initiates and maintains his covenant with those he chooses (cf. 1:2). Karl Barth has captured the biblical sense of mercy when he states: 'The mercy of God lies in his readiness to share in sympathy the distress of another, a readiness which springs from His inmost nature and stamps all his being and doing' (*CD* II.1 p. 369). The giving of mercy is therefore based on the character of God, not on human achievement or potential. This is why the dependent causal clause that is found at the end of this verse is jarring: *because I had acted ignorantly in unbelief.* Is Paul saying that the *reason* he was shown mercy was his acting in ignorance? Does this mean that, had he acted knowingly, God would *not* have been merciful to him? Clearly Paul believes that the ultimate ground for salvation lies in God's free love; and in fact 1:14 makes this abundantly clear. We probably must therefore understand the present clause as working *within* this framework. But what shall we say about the second question? Did Paul believe that God would have withheld his mercy had the former acted in full consciousness of what he was doing in persecuting the church?[16]

To understand Paul's meaning it is prudent, as most commentators suggest, to view the statement through the OT concept of 'high-handed' sins versus sins of ignorance (see Lev. 4:22–35; 22:14; Num. 15:22–31). The latter category refers to sins committed 'inadvertently'.[17] The person does not realize at the moment that he/she is breaking a commandment. This does not absolve the person, who

---

16   Cf. Collins, p. 38.

17   The term is found in Milgrom, *Numbers*, pp. 402–405.

must still offer a sacrifice to atone for sin. It is clear from Galatians 1:13–16 and Philippians 3:4–6 that Saul of Tarsus' activities were more the result of blind, ignorant zeal than careful consideration of the faith. M. Wolter suggests that we should understand Paul's persecution of the church not as a campaign against another religion but as an *intra-Jewish* operation to preserve the purity of Israel, in line with Pharisaic ideals. Like Phinehas and Elijah in the OT and their zealous attempt to keep Israel pure, so Paul attempted to cleanse from Israel what seemed to him at the time a polluting sect.[18] Yet, this was all done in *ignorance*. But could the same be said of the opponents Timothy was facing? It appears that they were not acting in ignorance but that they consciously rejected the apostolic faith. Thus, it may be that this last clause of verse 13 is also an indirect way of warning the opponents: perhaps God will not much longer be patient with them if they continue consciously to reject the truth of the gospel.

14. Despite Paul's action as an enemy of God, *the grace of our Lord overflowed for me*. The word *grace*, used previously in the salutation, appears again. It is a fundamental term in Paul's theology and appears thirteen times in the Pastoral Epistles. J. M. G. Barclay has shown that the concept of grace was abundant in the Judaism of the Second Temple period, and that the basic concept of grace was that of a *gift*. Barclay argues that what was unique about Paul's use of the word was his *perfection* of the concept of grace so that it communicated the *incongruous* nature of the gift that was grace, that is, the gift of grace was given on account of Jesus' atoning death and resurrection to those *who did not deserve it*.[19] This undeserved gift *overflowed* (*hyperpleonazō*) over Paul. The thought is identical to Romans 5:20: 'The law was brought in so that the trespass might increase. But where sin increased [*pleonazō*], grace increased all the more [*hyperperisseuō*]' (NIV).

15. *The saying is sure and worthy of full acceptance*. This is one of the most important formula statements in the Pastoral Epistles, appearing five times (1 Tim. 1:15; 3:1; 4:9; 2 Tim. 2:11; Tit. 3:8). Marshall

---

18 Wolter, *Paul*, pp. 15–23.

19 Barclay, *Paul and the Gift*, pp. 565–566.

investigates the phrase from three angles: origin, reference and significance (Marshall, Excursus 9, pp. 326–330). As to the origin of the phrase, despite many hypotheses, there is no certainty. As to reference, the formula can refer both to material quoted prior to and after the formula. As to significance, it lies in its function to confirm traditional, authoritative statements, even though it is probable that the author has played a part in the shaping of these authoritative statements. In sum, when Paul uses the formula he is laying stress on the fact that what has just been said, or is about to be said, has the full weight of apostolic authority. It is for this reason that the content of the formula deserves *full acceptance*.

The authoritative statement that is of particular significance to the situation with Timothy, and which deserves full acceptance is the following: *Christ Jesus came into the world to save sinners.* There is little doubt that this statement originated with the 'I have come...' sayings of Jesus (e.g., Mark 2:17; Luke 19:10), which were fundamental for the early church's understanding of the advent of Jesus (see Rom. 5:8; Heb. 9:11–28; 1 Pet. 2:21–25; 1 John 4:7–16).[20] The 'faithful saying' that Paul announces here is thus a fundamental statement, a creedal-like sentence that was accepted and confessed by the apostolic church. In view is the mission of the Messiah Jesus, who became incarnate and died an atoning death on the cross for our sins. *Of whom I am the foremost* [*prōtos*]. Given his violent persecution of the people of the Messiah Jesus, Paul understood himself as the ultimate sinner, the one who could least expect God's mercy. On this sentiment of Paul, see 1 Corinthians 15:9 and Ephesians 3:8.

16. *But for that very reason I received mercy.* The prepositional phrase *dia touto* ('for this reason') expresses purpose, which is stated in the following clause. Paul explains the aim of God showing mercy to him, the worst of sinners. *So that in me, as the foremost, Jesus Christ might display the utmost patience, making me an example to those who would come to believe in him for eternal life.* Paul once again uses *prōtos* in the sense of 'foremost' or 'prominent' (BDAG, pp. 892–894). In light of the context of this verse, NIV's translation of 'worst' is appropriate:

---

20 See helpfully Gathercole, *The Preexistent Son*, pp. 83–111, on this formula in Matthew, Mark and Luke.

Paul was the 'worst' offender, who as such provides a pattern of God's mercy to similar offenders.

It should further be noted that the subject of this purpose clause is *Christ Jesus*. It is he who *display[s] the utmost patience* to sinners. Paul uses the same verb, *display (endeiknymi)*, in Romans 9:17 (Septuagint quotation of Exod. 9:16) and 9:22 with God as subject, in a context of public demonstration of God's attributes. Here, it is Jesus Messiah who publicly displays an attribute (*utmost patience*, Greek: *tēn hapasan makrothymian*), which is commonly ascribed to God. As we argued in the Introduction and 1:1–2, Jesus performs the same activities that God performs, thereby showing equality with God. Paul knows no God whose identity does not also include Jesus Messiah.

Paul, then, understands that one of the purposes for Jesus Christ's display of great mercy towards him, the worst of sinners, is that it might serve as an example of hope to those who will believe. His life, particularly his conversion, is a 'pattern' or 'prototype' (*hypotypōsis*) of God's dealing with sinners. For God is such 'who desires everyone to be saved and to come to the knowledge of the truth' (1 Tim. 2:4). This entire verse should encourage Timothy. It is a reminder of God's longsuffering mercy even towards those who oppose his word. It is God's patience *vis-à-vis* the opponents that should encourage Timothy to hope that his correction of them would lead to repentance (see 2 Tim. 2:24–26).

17. *To the King of the ages, immortal, invisible, the only God, be honor and glory forever and ever. Amen.* Reflecting on the unfathomable mercy that God showed him, and which serves as a pattern of God's mercy for sinners in the present and the future, leads Paul to a doxology. In view of what we said above about Jesus Christ being constitutive of the identity of God, it is likely that the object of praise in this verse is the Father *and* the Son. The predicates of God used here echo OT and Hellenistic Jewish language. God is the *King eternal* (NIV; see Jer. 10:10; Tob. 13:6), the one whose rule over things visible and invisible is from everlasting to everlasting. The language is analogical, using the human experience of the succession of time to describe eternity.[21] God is also *immortal* or 'imperishable'

---

21   See Bavinck, *Reformed Dogmatics*, 2:159–164.

(*Wis.* 12:1; 18:4; Philo, *Sacr.* 95; *Mos.* 2.171). This means that God does not possess the possibility of perishing, something that is constitutive of creation. This is implicitly therefore a statement about God's transcendence (see Rom. 1:23, where the imperishable God is juxtaposed with perishable humanity). *Invisible* is related to God being Spirit (John 4:24) and therefore to the human incapacity to see him or represent him in an image. Statements in the OT about God being seen (e.g., Exod. 34; Isa. 6) refer to a mediate, not immediate perception of God.[22] Yet, Paul says that the Son is the image of the invisible God (Col. 1:15). *The only* [*monos*] *God* recalls the OT and Jewish tradition, where *only* is always used in contrast to other gods (see Deut. 32:12; 1 Sam. 7:3; 2 Kgs 5:17; 19:15, 19; Isa. 37:18; *2 Esd.* 19:6; 2 Macc. 7:37; 4 Macc. 5:24). That is, the God of Israel alone is deliverer, or Lord. This therefore means that Yahweh alone is God. In Second Temple literature this leads to a clearer metaphysical statement of monotheism in the sense that there exists only one God. As we have noted throughout chapter one, this God includes Jesus Messiah as constitutive of his identity.

To this God alone belong *honor and glory*. These two terms can occur together in both the OT and the NT (e.g., Exod. 28:2; Rev. 4:9). According to Marshall (pp. 405–406), the terms as used in the NT are synonymous. *Honor* and *glory* are properties that fittingly belong to God alone. To give God *honor* and *glory* is thus to acknowledge that he alone is God.

Theology

Commentators often call 1 Timothy 1:12–17 a 'digression'. If what is meant by a digression is a move away from the main topic of discourse, then 1:12–17 cannot be labelled a digression. For, just as at 1:3–11 the centre of gravity was the gospel, so it is here. In 1:3–11 the theme was the gospel in its relationship to the unlawful use of the law: it was the gospel that actually determined that the place of the law was as a pointer to our unrighteousness, and therefore to the Christ who forgives our trespasses. In 1:12–17 the theme is the gospel in its relationship to Paul in his pre-conversion life. Paul

---

22 Again, see ibid., 2:187–188.

makes it clear that in God's work of salvation there is a fundamental incongruity: the sinner who deserves nothing but God's wrath is instead, in Jesus Christ, shown mercy. In the clash between sin and grace, grace abounded all the more: *The grace of our Lord overflowed for me* (1:14). The reason this occurs is because God is a God whose essence is grace (Exod. 34:6–7). He deeply desires not the death of the sinner but life and a relationship with him (which *is* life). This is our God. 'Any other idea of God, in which He is not yet gracious, or not yet essentially, decisively and comprehensively known as gracious, is really … a theology of the gods and idols of this world, not of the living and true God' (Barth, *CD* II.1 p. 357).

It is in light of who God is that Paul, despite being a blasphemer, persecutor and hubrist, was saved and called to be a servant of Christ. This is of a piece with the 'trustworthy sayings' of the Pastoral Epistles, that is, the apostolic – and therefore authoritative – teaching that *Christ Jesus came into the world to save sinners* (1:15). Timothy, therefore, must not lose heart but continue to uphold this gospel: for God's mercy to Paul is a pattern of God's merciful posture to sinners, even the worst of sinners. But is this a possibility even with the opponents of 1 Timothy? Yes – but there must be repentance on the part of the false teachers, as Paul puts it in 2 Timothy 2:24–25: 'correcting opponents with gentleness. God may perhaps grant that they will repent and come to know the truth, and that they may escape from the snare of the devil, having been held captive by him to do his will.' Nevertheless, Paul sounds a warning in the next section: prideful, conscious rejection of the apostolic gospel may lead to terminal reprobation.

C. Encouragement to Timothy to fight the good fight (1:18–20)

Context

Paul returns to encourage Timothy *directly*. This is evident in the correlation between 1:3 and 1:18, shown to be a correlation by grammatical and lexical equivalence. First, we note that Paul addresses Timothy with the second-person singular pronoun, which was not used in verses 4–17. 1:3: 'I urged *you* [*sē*]'; 1:18: 'I am giving *you* [*soi*] these instructions.' Second, we note that Paul returns to the use of *parangellō* and cognates, thereby picking up from 1:3: 'that you may *instruct* [*parangeilēs*] certain people'; 1:18: 'I am giving you these *instructions* [*parangelian*].'

Paul is thus returning to the beginning theme of exhorting Timothy directly; but in 1:18–20 he will add a new motif in order to encourage Timothy, namely, the prophecies previously made about him.

Comment

18. *I am giving you these instructions, Timothy, my child.* On a previous occasion Paul charged Timothy to command 'certain people' (1:3) not to teach false doctrine, which is anything that does not correspond to the glorious gospel (1:11). Paul again puts this charge before his 'child' Timothy. Paul develops the current thought by means of two prepositional phrases: *in accordance with* [*kata*] *the prophecies made earlier about* [*epi*] *you.* What is the relationship between the current charge to stop the opponents and the previous prophecies made over Timothy? It is probably a reminder that Timothy was set apart to face opponents of the truth. For these prophecies probably refer to a word from the Holy Spirit, through prophets, setting Timothy aside for this very task (cf. 4:14 and Acts 13:1–3). This would mean that Timothy has been called and empowered for the work before him at Ephesus.

You may fight the good fight. Paul uses a military metaphor (cf. 2 Tim. 2:4; 4:7) to suggest how Timothy should defend the gospel. The choice of this metaphor to explain Timothy's task shows that it is a demanding, arduous and painful task that will require total dedication on his part.

19. *Having faith and a good conscience.* In order to fight the good fight successfully, Timothy must continually keep hold of faith and a good conscience. As we saw earlier (1:5), so also here *faith* and *good conscience* are linked. Mutschler (p. 272) suggests that we view the conjunction *and* between *faith* and *good conscience* as epexegetical, that is, as further defining the meaning of the first item by the second. With this in view, he suggests that we understand *faith* here as *habitus*, an orientation to life with the emphasis on character (p. 273). On the one hand, then, Timothy has been set apart by God through prophecies for his current ministry. On the other, he must continue to strive and persevere in faithfulness, all the while knowing that it is Christ Jesus himself who strengthens him (1:12).

By rejecting conscience, certain persons have suffered shipwreck in the faith. Timothy certainly does not want to end like this. Some of the opponents have 'repudiated' (*apōtheomai*) good conscience.[23] This rejection led to shipwreck. This metaphor was vivid and well known in a world that was constantly aware of the Mediterranean Sea and the numerous shipwrecks that occurred there. The metaphor was also used by philosophers (e.g., Philodemus, *Vit.* p. 33J; Diogenes Laertius, 5.5).

20. *Among them are Hymenaeus and Alexander.* The former is mentioned in 2 Timothy 2:17–18 as one who left the truth by saying that 'the resurrection has already taken place'. *Alexander* 'the metalworker' is mentioned in 2 Timothy 4:14 as one who harmed Paul and 'strongly opposed our message'. It is difficult to be certain if this is the same Alexander, the name being widely used.

Whom I have turned over to Satan. The verb for *turned over* (*paradidōmi*) was used by Paul in 1 Corinthians 5:5, where he ordered the Corinthians to 'hand over such a one to Satan'; that is, a man involved in an incestuous relationship. It is likely that the handing over was for rehabilitation, even though the language is certainly strong. It is not at all clear what this process looked like in Pauline communities. We may gain some clarity, however, from Matthew 18:15–17, where the final step of discipline is the treatment of the unrepentant as an unbeliever, with the ultimate goal of restoration.

That the ultimate goal of the discipline of Hymenaeus and Alexander was restorative is clear from the terminology used in the purpose clause at the end of the verse: *so that they may learn not to blaspheme.* The verb *learn* translates the Greek *paideuō,* which has a *corrective* sense, not at all the destruction of the person being disciplined.[24]

The discipline they are to receive is one controlled by God but through the instrumentality of Satan (cf. Job 1–2; Luke 22:31–32;

---

23 Marshall, p. 411, indicates that the verb *apōtheomai* 'conveys a picture of deliberate rejection'.

24 The monograph by Kidson, *Persuading Shipwrecked Men*, argues cogently for the view that the ultimate goal in view was restorative.

2 Tim. 2:25–26). As grim as this sounds, the hope is that repentance will result. For Paul himself had been a blasphemer, yet the Lord showed him mercy (1:13).

Theology

In this final section of chapter one Paul comes full circle. His *direct* exhortation to Timothy *vis-à-vis* the opponents is formally taken up again, so that we have symmetry between 1:3 and 1:18. However, Paul adds a new layer to his instruction: Timothy's battle with the opponents is not to be done through his own strength. To be sure, Paul hinted at this in 1:12, when he spoke of Jesus Messiah who strengthened him and put him in the ministry. In 1:18 he is more direct: Timothy's capacity to fulfil his charge is based on God's call on his life, which was communicated through prophecies. This means that Timothy's task is not self-imposed or human-imposed. It is the Lord God himself who has set Timothy apart for his current task. And this means that God will continue to empower Timothy in the same manner in which he empowered Paul.

If the statement in 1:18 is positive in the encouragement of Timothy, the statement in 1:19–20 is negative. Paul reminds Timothy of two examples of men who did not persevere in the apostolic doctrine. The result was the shipwreck of their faith, which led Paul – in an act of compassion and preservation of the church's purity – to hand them over to Satan so that they might repent. Paul is thus simultaneously warning and reminding Timothy of the scope and object of the latter's task. His task is to fight the good fight, which includes the disciplining of those who oppose the apostolic gospel. The goal is that the opponents might be saved. For, after all, 'the goal of our instruction is love from a pure heart and a good conscience and a sincere faith' (1:5, NIV).

3. INSTRUCTIONS FOR BEHAVIOUR IN CHURCH MEETINGS – A MISSIONAL GROUNDING (2:1 – 3:16)

A. Corporate prayer and the mission of the church (2:1–7)

Context

In 3:14–15 Paul tells Timothy that he is hoping to come to him soon. If he is delayed, however, he is writing this letter to instruct Timothy on how to behave in the household of God. Although these words apply to the entirety of the letter, they do so in an even more specific way to 2:1–3:13. For in this section Paul gives orders to the church as the *household* of God. Thus, in 2:1–7 Paul gives instructions concerning *prayer as a community*. In 2:8–15 Paul gives instructions concerning *the behavior of men and women in community*. And in 3:1–13 Paul gives instructions for those *who take care of God's community*. As will be seen in the comments that follow, these instructions are held together by the church's mission to outsiders, a mission that has a Christological basis.

Comment

1. *I urge (parakalō)* connects this verse with 1:13, thus presenting the instructions that follow as a continuation of apostolic orders. The verb is common in paraenetic letters.

First of all. In this context, *first (prōtos)* can refer to the first injunction in a series, without implying priority of importance; or it can refer to something that deserves priority (BDAG, pp. 892–894). Both senses were present in 1:15–16. It is probable that in 2:1 the word refers to the first in a series of acts of worship carried out by the community. For although the command to pray appears in other letters of Paul (e.g., Rom. 12:12; 15:30; 1 Cor. 14:13–16; 1 Thess. 4:17), there is never the sense that this was the most important act of worship in church meetings. We must also keep in mind the occasional nature of Paul's letters when seeking to glean church order for the present.

Supplications, prayers, intercessions, and thanksgivings. Paul lists the different types of prayers to be made by the community. Marshall, p. 419, helpfully notes: 'The four terms which describe prayer characterise it *in its totality*' (emphasis added). In vv. 1–2 intercession is highlighted.

For everyone. Two terms are used here that will continually appear in verses 1–7: *pas* ('all, every, everyone') and *anthrōpos* ('person, human, man'). A combination of the two, or each term in isolation, appears in verses 1, 2, 4, 5 and 6. Prayers are for *every person*, for God desires *every person* to be saved through Jesus Christ the *human person* ('man'). As we indicated under Context, this universal, missional point of view provides the framework for understanding 2:1–7; indeed, for understanding the entire section that runs through 3:16.

2. *For kings and all who are in high positions.* Included in 'everyone' are those in positions of rule. *Basileus* ('king') was used of regional rulers and client kings in the east (e.g., the ruling members of the Herodian dynasty), as well as the Roman emperor (BDAG, pp. 169–170; Johnson, p. 189). There existed a long tradition in Judaism where the priests, while certainly not sacrificing *to* the foreign king, would offer sacrifices on his behalf and commit to pray *for* the king.[1] This tradi-

---

[1] See, e.g., Ezra 6:8–10. The tradition of praying for kings and rulers is also found in the synagogue: Josephus, *J.W.* 2.197, 409; Philo, *Flacc.* 49;

tion was authorized by Jesus for his disciples (Matt. 22:15–22//Mark 12:13–17//Luke 20:26) and followed in the early church (Rom. 13:1–7; Tit. 3:1; 1 Pet. 2:13–17). Paul continues it in the present command. The phrase *and all who are in high positions* (*en hyperochē*) refers to those who worked *with* but *under* kings, such as officials and representatives. For further details, see on Titus 3:1.

Paul now provides the purpose for these prayers: *that we may lead a quiet and peaceable life in all godliness and dignity*. The words *quiet and peaceable life* are emphasized both by their position in the clause and the use of alliteration (*ēremon kai ēsychion*). They convey the sense of a life free of tumult, allowing the person to go about his or her business without the fear of civic violence or uproars, which was a constant possibility in the cities of the eastern regions of the Roman empire. This does not mean that Christians should aspire to lead a life of reclusion (so, rightly, Oberlinner, 1994, p. 68). As the context demonstrates, the goal is to enjoy lives free of civic turmoil with a view to the proclamation of the gospel. It should also be noted that peaceful existence is what God wishes for his creation.

3. *This is right and is acceptable in the sight of God our Saviour.*[2] The demonstrative pronoun *this* harks back to the community's prayer for all people and includes verses 1–2. The phrase *is acceptable* (*apodekton*) probably reflects OT sacrificial language, where worthy sacrifices were deemed pleasing and *acceptable* before the Lord. But 'in the NT community of God prayer in the church replaces sacrifices' (Marshall, p. 425). The designation of God as *Saviour* links back to 1:1 (see comments there and Introduction under Theological Emphases) and continues a theological theme (Saviour), that is constitutive of God in the Pastoral Epistles.

4. *Who desires everyone to be saved and to come to the knowledge of the truth.* The relative pronoun *who* may have a causal sense here (Marshall, p. 425). The logic may be arrived at by asking a question: why is prayer for everyone pleasing to God? Because he is the kind of

---

Legat. 157, 317. For other examples in the Hellenistic Jewish literature, see Johnson, p. 189.

2 Some Greek manuscripts include *gar* ('for') at the beginning of this verse: ℵ D, etc. A slightly better textual tradition omits it.

God who wants *everyone* to be saved (cf. Oberlinner, 1994, p. 72). The ABA'B' pattern of this verse suggests that *to be saved and to come to the knowledge of the truth* are related in the manner of hendiadys. That is, the second phrase further defines the first. Thus, *to be saved* means *to come to the knowledge of the truth*. A number of comments are necessary to elucidate this phrase. First, the phrase highlights the initial aspect of salvation, or 'conversion' (Marshall, p. 428). Several texts confirm this (1 Tim. 4:3; 2 Tim. 2:25; 3:7; Titus 1:1). Second, we should note that the *truth* in the Pastoral Epistles is often used by Paul to refer to the *gospel* that has been received and passed down by the apostles (e.g., 1 Tim. 2:7; 3:15; 2 Tim. 2:18; cf. also Gal. 2:5, 14; 5:7; Eph. 1:13; Col. 1:5, 6). The reason *truth* is chosen is probably polemical: in contrast to the heterodoxy (1:3) of the opponents, the apostolic gospel is true in that it conforms to the life, death and resurrection of Jesus Christ as proclaimed by the prophets and apostles. That is, he uses *truth* in order to throw into relief the error or falsity of corrupt teachers. In this respect *truth* has an intellectual nuance, suggesting that the false teachers are mentally broken, which is demonstrated in their rejection of the gospel. This was a common polemic of moral philosophers against their opponents.[3] This does not mean that salvation is restricted to the intellectual domain. The concepts of knowledge and truth (*alētheia*) in the Pastoral Epistles are inclusive, referring to the volitional, existential and noetic (i.e., what/how one wills, lives and thinks).

The statement that God wants *everyone* to be saved has a seemingly universalistic ring to it. Many scholars have thus sought to bring further precision to the meaning of the statement. On the one hand, some point to the situation at Ephesus, claiming that Paul was battling a form of salvation by special knowledge (gnosis). Paul, they suggest, is insisting that there are no boundaries to God's salvation; it is not the possession of only a few 'enlightened' (see 6:20).[4] Although possible, there is not sufficient evidence of a fully flowered gnosticism behind the Pastoral Epistles (see further Introduction and on 6:20). Marshall (p. 426) and Towner (pp. 177–178) point to Gentile inclusion

---

3   See Malherbe, *Light from the Gentiles*, 1:124, n. 16.

4   See esp. Roloff, p. 119; Oberlinner (1994), p. 72.

as the reason why Paul speaks in such a universal manner. On the other hand, some scholars suggest that the phrase should be translated as 'all *kinds* of people'.[5] Although this is grammatically possible, it is unlikely in light of the Bible's clear representation of God as one who desires all his creation to be redeemed (e.g., Ezek. 18:23; John 3:16; 1 John 2:2). More than likely Paul is speaking of Gentile inclusion. It may have been the case that the Jewish opponents, although not judaizing in the way we see in Galatians, for example, have boasted of Jewish superiority on the basis of the biblical statements on the election of Israel.

5. *For there is one God; there is also one mediator between God and humankind.* It is probable that in verses 5–6 Paul is drawing on an early Christian liturgical tradition (some of which may have been written by Paul himself: cf. 1 Cor. 8:6).[6] The statements thus function similarly to the 'trustworthy sayings' in other parts of the Pastorals. That is, they serve to confirm a theological declaration by referring to authoritative apostolic tradition (see comments on 1:15). In this case, verses 5–6 support verse 4 in part by further explaining it.

This forces us to examine the relationship between God's desire that everyone be saved (v. 4) and the confessional statement of verses 5–6, more specifically, the relationship of the fact that God is *one* and that there is *one* mediator. More than likely, the logic is that since there is one God (e.g., Deut. 6:4) and one mediator, there is only *one way* of salvation for all, Jews and Gentiles alike. Perhaps we can call this divine symmetry, reflecting the beauty of God.

Christ Jesus, himself human. Paul now names the one and only mediator between God and humanity: the Messiah Jesus. Paul emphasizes the humanity of Jesus as the mediator (cf. Heb. 9:15). It would of course be a mistake to think that Paul is hereby negating the divinity of Jesus. As we have seen (1:1–2) and will see again (Tit. 2:11–14), Jesus is clearly presented in the Pastorals as God. This theological affirmation should serve as a framework for our

---

5 For example, Knight, p. 119.

6 This is rejected by Johnson, p. 191, but accepted by Roloff, p. 120 and Oberlinner (1994), pp. 73–74. See also Dunn, *Theology of Paul the Apostle*, pp. 174–177.

Christological and soteriological comments in these letters. And it is precisely through this framework that we can make the best theological sense of 2:5. For the statement about the *human* Messiah Jesus may assume his divine yet enfleshed existence as God. To this divine existence he has added humanity (cf. Phil. 2:5–11). In this way he could be a mediator both from the side of God and from the side of human beings. Calvin understood this well: 'Who could have done this [restoration] had not the self-same Son of God become the Son of man, and had not so taken what was ours as to impart what was his to us, and to make what was his by nature ours by grace?'[7]

6–7. *Who gave himself a ransom for all.* This verse stands in remarkable parallelism to the words of Jesus in Mark 10:45: 'For the Son of Man [*ho hyios tou anthrōpou*] came not to be served but to serve, and to give [*didounai*] his life a ransom [*lutron*] for many.' Paul echoes these words of Jesus, which, along with his explanation of the bread and the wine at the last supper (Matt. 26:26–29; Mark 14:22–26; Luke 22:15–20), became the normative explanation of Jesus' death in the early church (see, e.g., Gal. 1:4; Eph. 5:2; see also Towner, pp. 183–185).

The compound *antilytron* ('ransom') appears only here in the NT but is basically a synonym to the simple *lytron*. Cognates of this term are found elsewhere in the NT (Luke 1:68; 2:38; 24:21; Acts 7:35; 28:19; Tit. 2:14; Heb. 9:12; 1 Pet. 1:18). In the LXX *lytron* is a 'sum payable as ransom' (GELS, p. 436; cf. Jeremias, p. 15), including payment given to free a slave (see Exod. 21:30; 30:12; Lev. 19:20). Jesus' death is presented as payment, as the rescue-ransom to deliver from 'wickedness', as we will learn in Titus 2:14. This payment was, in keeping with the universal thrust of the text, *for all*. The preposition *hyper* ('for'), in addition to the context, explains this ransom as substitution. Jesus died *in the place* of others, indeed *all*.

The testimony (*this was attested at the right time*) of this stunningly gracious act was given at the time set by God, and includes Paul's own preaching. In a way that continues the accent on God's grace, we are told that none other than the former blasphemer Paul was

---

7 Calvin, *Inst.* 2.12.1–2. See also Torrance, *Incarnation*, esp. p. 82; Ridderbos, *Paul*, p. 196.

himself made *a herald and an apostle ... a teacher of the Gentiles in faith and truth*. The thought here reflects what Paul states in other places (e.g., Rom. 1:1–5; 15:14–16; Gal. 2:7), namely, God's gracious call on his life as an apostle to the Gentiles.

Theology

Worship and mission are linked in this text in two ways. First, worship of God, which is presented here as prayer (v. 1), has a soteriological horizon. On this side of the eschaton, prior to final judgment, worship is incomplete without proclamation of the good news to all people. Second, mission is based on worship. It is only because God in the first place 'desires everyone to be saved' (v. 4) and has thus sent Jesus Christ to become 'the man Christ Jesus' in order to serve as ransom, that mission is at all possible. Otherwise, the mission of the church would be an entirely immanent affair. That is, without the transcendent reality that God in Christ has taken on flesh and taken a cross for our sins, the church could ultimately only offer a self-help message, dependent only on anthropological possibilities. Therefore, we can say that church mission without God's act of love in giving Jesus Christ for our sins cannot exist. And worship – again, this side of the eschaton – includes the *missio Dei* as its necessary outcome. In this way the reality of the church stands in imitation to the reality of God. For God, although completely blessed in the fellowship of Father, Son and Holy Spirit, and therefore not in any need of creating, nevertheless, in an overflow of his love, has in the person of the Son become the man Christ Jesus to include others in the Triune fellowship. So also the church, though blessed in its contemplation of God in worship, nevertheless, precisely because of that worship, proclaims the good news of Jesus Christ. Without this proclamation flowing out of worship, the church does not have an identity.

B. The behaviour of men and women in community worship and the mission of the church (2:8–15)

Context

The section at hand contains instructions to the men and women of the congregations at Ephesus when they meet to worship. It is notable that the injunctions to the women are in disproportion to the injunctions to the men. That is, while the injunctions to the men only take up one verse in our modern Bibles (2:8), the injunctions to the women take up seven verses (2:9–15). This probably implies that there were significant problems with the women in the congregations at Ephesus when Paul wrote to Timothy (see Introduction under Occasion for the Pastoral Epistles). To be clear, this does not mean that the women were the only ones creating problems; or that all the women were reflecting poor Christian conduct. As we saw on 1 Tim. 1:18–20, Paul also spoke of men who were shipwrecking their faith.

It is possible to deduce from Paul's statements in 2:9–15 that there were at least two significant issues with some of the women. The first is relatively easy to recognize; the second less so. The first problem is evident by the type of language Paul employs in both the prescriptions and proscriptions of verses 9–15. One of the key terms is *sōphrosynē*, which appears at both verse 9 and verse 15, thus forming an *inclusio*, a bookend that frames the understanding of 2:9–15. The term *sōphrosynē*, or the adjective *sōphrōn*, was one of the four cardinal virtues of Greek philosophy.[8] As the virtues were applied to women, *sōphrosynē* was viewed as the most important virtue that a woman should display. *Sōphrosynē* can be translated with different words. The standard lexicon for the period of the NT gives the following translations: 'good judgment, moderation, self-control'. When the term is applied to women, the translation can be nuanced to mean 'decency, chastity' (BDAG, p. 987). 'Modesty' can also be a good translation (cf. NIV translation of the term in v. 9). In light of the broad semantic domain of the word, the transliterated form *sōphrosynē* will be used in the following paragraphs.[9] Following are some examples of the contexts in which *sōphrosynē* had to be displayed by women.

---

8 See Plato, *Resp.* 4.427E, 435B; Dio Chrysostom, *Or.* 13.31–32; cf. Malherbe, *Light from the Gentiles*, 1:467–468.

9 Thus also North in her magisterial work, *Sophrosyne*, xi.

1   Language. A woman who is careful with her speech
    possesses *sōphrosynē*. In Sophocles' play, *Ajax* (fifth century
    BC), Ajax the ancient Greek hero tells a woman the
    following: 'Do not ask me, do not question me! It is best to
    show some sense (*sōphronein*).' That is, the statement of Ajax
    conveys the common sentiment that women show
    sōphrosynē when they are quiet (Sophocles, *Aj.* 586). Another
    example is found in Euripides (fifth century BC). One of
    the daughters of Heracles, another (perhaps *the*) Greek
    hero, interrupts a conversation and says: 'Strangers, please
    do not consider my coming out to be overbold: this is the
    first indulgence I shall ask. I know that for a woman silence
    is best, and modest behavior (*sōphronein*), and staying quietly
    within doors' (Euripides, *Heracl.* 475–476). Here we can see
    how *sōphrosynē* includes silence, modest behaviour and the
    woman caring for the home. The Platonist philosopher
    Plutarch (c. AD 50–120) tells a story that once again
    illustrates the importance of silence as a display of
    sōphrosynē: 'The Roman senate was once for many days
    debating … and since the matter gave rise to much
    uncertainty and suspicion, a woman, prudent (*sōphrōn*) in
    other respects, but yet a woman, kept pestering her
    husband and persistently begging to learn the secret'
    (*Garr.* 507B). Two things should be noted here. First,
    Plutarch expresses one of the stereotypes against women in
    antiquity ('but yet a woman'!), namely that they spoke more
    than necessary. Second, we can glean from the statement
    that for women *sōphrosynē* was demonstrated with silence,
    not in 'pestering' the husband in public. It is to be noted
    that in verse 11 of this section of 1 Timothy, Paul will call
    on the women to 'learn in silence'. This is one way they
    could work out *sōphrosynē*.

2   Sexuality. For the Stoic female philosopher Phintys
    (approximately 3 BC), a woman is *sōphrōn* when she
    understands that the marriage bed is only for procreation
    with her husband (Stobaeus, *Anthology* 61). The Jewish
    philosopher/exegete Philo describes Potiphar's wife, who
    attempted to seduce Joseph, as a woman lacking in

sōphrosynē. After trying to seduce Joseph, 'She put on the air of a chaste [*sōphrona*] and modest woman' (*Ios.* 50.5). This is the opposite of what she truly was, a sexually immoral woman. In another place Plutarch speaks of *sōphrosynē* as 'a mutual self-restraint which is a principal requirement for marriage' (*Amat.* 767E).

3   Modesty. *Sōphrosynē* is the opposite of the immodest wearing of expensive clothes and jewellery often critiqued by Greco-Roman authors. Musonius Rufus can speak of a *sōphrōn* woman as one who 'avoid[s] unlawful loves … hate[s] strife, *extravagance, and ornamentation*' (North, p. 230, emphasis added). The Christian Clement of Alexandria (second century AD) understood *sōphrosynē* for women as, among other things, not wearing jewellery and expensive clothing (*Paed.* 2.12.121; 3.2.13).

To sum up, the similarity of language between 1 Timothy 2:9–11 and Greco-Roman literature suggests that one of the major problems Paul was attempting to solve was the presence of women who lacked *sōphrosynē*, the primary feminine virtue, one exemplified in the household by a woman who was virtuous as a wife, mother and manager of the home.[10]

The second problem addressed in this section appears to be false teaching. Although not much is said about the topic directly, we do find the language of deception used twice in vv. 13–14: 'And Adam was not *deceived*, but the woman was *deceived* and became a transgressor.' Since deception is something generally accomplished by false teachers, it may be that false teaching was also one of the problems with some of the women.

Comment

8. *I desire, then, that in every place the men should pray, lifting up holy hands without anger or argument.* Paul returns to the subject of prayer, which he began in verses 1–3 and paused in verses 4–7. With the term *men* (*andras*), Paul gives instructions specifically to males.

---

10   Huizenga, *Moral Education for Women*, pp. 11–12.

This does not mean that women cannot or do not pray. Paul is simply arranging the commands in a way that reflects the different members and genders in the household of God; furthermore, it may be that the men in the church were struggling in this area and therefore needed to be corrected. The command here is to *pray*, which is then modified with two qualifications. First, prayer is to be done *in every place*. Second, the men are to pray by *lifting up holy hands*. The concept of lifting holy hands in prayer is found both in pagan literature (e.g., Aesop, *Fab.* 49) and in Jewish tradition, particularly the Septuagint (e.g., Ps. 134:2/LXX 133:1). The emphasis in verse 8 is on the hands being *holy* (*hosious*), suggesting cultic or ritual purity. What precisely this means is specified with the negative phrase *without anger or argument* (*dialogismos*). That is, purity is related to the treatment of other brothers, probably going back to the teaching of Jesus (see Matt. 5:21–26). Philippians 2:14 also helps us understand Paul's qualification: 'Do all things without arguing [*dialogismos*] or murmuring' (cf. also Rom. 14:1). The necessary attitude during prayer must be one of accord and unity, foregoing quarrelling.

9–10. These verses speak of the deportment of women in a positive–negative–positive structure (ABA'). A–Dress modestly (positive command); B–Do not dress with expensive hairdos, jewellery and clothing (negative command); A'–Dress (metaphorically speaking) with good works (positive command). Verse 9 reads: *Also that the women should dress themselves modestly and decently in suitable clothing, not with their hair braided, or with gold, pearls, or expensive clothes.* The main verb of this verse is *kosmeō* which means 'dress or 'adorn' (BDAG, p. 560) and is often found with the term *sōphrosynē* (Plato, *Gorg.* 507E–508A; Aristotle, *Eth. nic.* 1109A16). Injunctions on the deportment of women in public were a common theme in the Greco-Roman literature of Paul's period, especially but not exclusively from the pen of moral philosophers.[11] In addition, there existed in Greece and Asia Minor the office of the *gynaikonomos*. This office, of which evidence exists from the fourth century BC to the second

---

11 Wagener, *Die Ordnung*, p. 79, calls attention to the term *kosmeō* as often referring to women in inscriptions.

century AD, was tasked with regulating luxury laws for women
during religious processions. The duty of the office was to ensure
that excessive jewellery or non-decorous dressing by women would
be minimized in public.[12] Paul's orders for women to dress dec-
orously, therefore, would not have been strange to the readers of
this letter.

Paul continues in verse 9 by instructing the women how *not*
to adorn themselves. The extravagant attire that Paul criticizes
here was also the target of many writers in the Greco-Roman
world. Indeed, an examination of the terms used by Paul reveals
that in the contemporary literature the words were often used
together to describe (and castigate) materialism, luxury and vanity.
Not with their hair braided (or 'plaited') refers to an elaborate hairdo
that reflected excessive vanity and which was prohibited by the
office of the *gynaikonomos* (e.g., *IG* v.1 1390, *ll.* 16–26: prohibited for
the woman was 'gold jewellery, or rouge, or white lead, or a hair-
band, nor *plaited hair* nor shoes, unless of felt or sacred leather').[13]
The ostentatious wearing of *gold* (*chrysion*) or *pearls* (*margaritēs*) in
public was also regularly condemned by authors of the period.
With respect to gold, the neo-Pythagorean letter from Melissa to
Clearete is illuminating, not least because of its striking similarity
to 1 Timothy 2:9–11: 'A wife's adornment [should be] ... with quietness, white and clean in her dress, plain but not costly, simple but
not elaborate or excessive. For she must reject garments shot with
purple or gold ... For it is not in expenditure on clothing and
looks that the modest woman should express her love of the good
but in the management and maintenance of her household.'[14] The
Roman satirist Juvenal raged against the flashy wearing of *pearls*:
'There is nothing that a woman will not permit herself to do,
nothing that she deems shameful, when she encircles her neck

12   See Winter, *Roman Wives*, pp. 85–91; Schnabel, *Der erste Brief des Paulus
     an die Korinther*, pp. 589–590. I am grateful to the series editor for
     pointing out to me the office of the *gynaikonomos*.

13   On excessive hairstyles, especially by wealthy women, see Winter,
     Roman Wives, p. 104.

14   *P. Haun.* 13, *ll.* 6–29 (Winter, *Roman Wives,* p. 107).

with green emeralds, and fastens huge pearls to her elongated ears' (*Sat.* 6.458–459). The final phrase of v. 9, *expensive clothes* (*polytelēs*), is also found numerous times in literature criticizing sensuality and materialism. The following statement by Plutarch is helpful in understanding Paul's prohibition. Plutarch joins the word *polytelēs* with 'homes' to speak of those things that one desires to obtain in order to gain tranquillity of soul: 'And so it is that no costly house [*oikia polytelēs*] nor abundance of gold [*chrysiou plēthos*] nor pride of race nor pomp of office ... impart so much calm and serenity to the life as does a soul free from evil acts' (*Tranq. an.* 19). In other places Plutarch speaks of *expensive clothes* to criticize avarice (e.g., *Cat. Min.* 11.3.6). In one essay he states that it is not *expensive clothes* that make a woman decorous: 'It is not gold [*chrysos*] or precious stones or scarlet that make her such, but whatever invests her with that something which betokens dignity, good behavior and modesty [*aidous*]' (*Conj. praec.* 26).

With an adversative conjunction (*alla*, 'but, rather') Paul returns to the positive side of the command on the deportment of women. They should adorn themselves *with good works, as is proper for women who profess reverence for God.* The emphasis is placed on the correspondence between profession of faith and conduct. The verb 'to profess' (*epangellomai*) has a strong declarative sense (BDAG, p. 356). These are women who publicly confess their Christian faith. As such, they must 'back up' their profession; and the fitting way (*prepei*) to do this is by *good works* (*ergōn agathōn*). The good works that Paul has in mind may be clarified by permitting the use of the phrase in 5:10 to shed light on this text. They are: 'One who has brought up children, shown hospitality, washed the saints' feet, helped the afflicted.' Although this is not an exhaustive list, it helps to clarify the thought of verse 10.

Thus, in order to describe what the deportment of women should be, Paul uses both literal and metaphorical language – the women are to dress modestly and they are to 'put on' good works. In contrast to the life of immodesty, sensuality and materialism often exhibited (and prohibited) by certain women in the Greco-Roman world, the Christian women should make it their business to lead lives of modesty, chastity and humility. The basis for this life is the woman's profession of belief in the gospel.

The modern reader should not miss the fact that Paul employs the language of the period to exhort the women, probably to ensure that the exhortations were clearly understood. By quoting the texts from the primary sources my goal has been to show how the type of behaviour displayed by the immodest use of clothing, hairdo and jewellery would have been scandalous in Paul's culture. If our missional reading of this text is correct (see esp. on 2:4–6), part of the reason why this behaviour is forbidden is that it would have acted as a deterrent for those unbelievers who were interested in exploring the gospel.

11. *Let a woman learn in silence with full submission.* As we saw above, one of the aspects of *sōphrosynē* was the capacity to control one's speech. It is not surprising, therefore, that this verse begins with a command to 'quietness' (NIV). The context continues to be Christians meeting for worship, of which teaching and learning sound doctrine was an important part. That women should learn sound doctrine is not in question. It is clear that this was the norm in the early church (see e.g., Luke 10:38–42; Acts 21:7–9; 1 Cor. 14:33–35). The emphasis here is on the proper attitude while learning: they are to learn *in silence*. The term *ēsychia* has shades of meaning: 'quietness, rest, silence' (BDAG, p. 440). As suggested above, the NIV's 'in quietness' is probably the most appropriate translation. This does not mean that in a worship gathering women are to be mute: 1 Corinthians 11:3–10 envisages women prophesying and praying in the public worship of the local congregation. In addition, as we indicated previously, it is implied in 1 Timothy 2:1–15 that both men and women prayed publicly. The limitation here is to 'speaking out of turn and thereby interrupting the lesson' (Marshall, p. 453).

With the second prepositional phrase, *with full submission*, Paul clarifies the meaning of *ēsychia*. The issue turns out to be a matter of respect or *submission*. The verbal form of the noun *submission* in Greek is *hypotassō*, and is also used of the submission of wives to husbands (e.g., 1 Cor. 14:34; Eph. 5:21–22 [possibly mutual submission]; Col. 3:18; 1 Pet. 3:1). Some nuance on the meaning of the term may be found in a comparative text from Plutarch, although the Greek philosopher uses language that goes beyond Paul's in severity. It does provide us, however, with a view of how some in the culture understood the place of married women: 'So it is with women also; if they subordinate themselves (*hypotattousia*) to their husbands, they are commended, but if they want to have control, they cut a sorrier figure than the subjects of their control' (*Conj. praec.* 33). The picture is that of a wife who, in the company of her husband and others, attempts to seize control of the discussion. Such action would have been distasteful in Greco-Roman culture, in large part because it would shame the husband. Consider Plutarch once again: 'For a woman ought to do her talking either to her husband or through her husband, and she should not feel aggrieved if, like the flute-player, she makes a more impressive sound through a tongue not her own' (Ibid., 32). Although Paul does not go to this extreme, the statement from Plutarch may help us understand the cultural view of women and speech, at least from the perspective of the elite, of which Plutarch was a part. We should thus probably view Paul's statements in verse 11 as a way of protecting the good witness of the Christian congregations: for a woman (married or single) in the congregation to disrespect the teachers or their husbands by constantly taking over or interrupting the teaching would have been as much of an obstacle to the Christian mission as unsubmissive children in the household of an overseer (3:4); it would have turned away outsiders who were initially attracted by the Christian message (see further comments on Tit. 2:5).

12. *I permit no woman to teach.* With verse 12 more light is shed on the commands to quietness and submission of the previous verse. The context, as indicated above, is that of instruction in the congregation. *To teach* (*didaskein*) is the first word of the clause, indicating the main emphasis. The activity of teaching is of utmost importance in the Pastoral Epistles. Timothy is himself instructed about his own teaching; the ability to teach is one the qualifications in the list of the overseer; the noun 'teaching' (*didaskalia*) occurs numerous times (1 Tim. 1:10; 4:6, 13, 16; 2 Tim. 3:10, 16; Tit. 1:9). With respect to women, Paul says in this verse: *I permit no woman to teach.* What this means cannot be understood properly until the next sentence is engaged.

Or to have authority over a man. With the use of the conjunction 'or' (Greek, *oude*) in relation to the previous clause, further light can be shed on the nature of Paul's prohibition. We begin by asking how we should understand the little word *or.* Is Paul thinking of *two separate* activities? If this were the case, we would have to think of teaching *and* another undefined activity, namely, *to have authority*;

we would thus have two separate prohibitions for the women. The other option is to view *oude* ('or') as conjoining two similar concepts. In this case we would have an example of hendiadys, where the second term explains the first. This is the view of most commentators, regardless of how they interpret the rest of the verses in 1 Timothy 2:9–15. We could thus paraphrase verse 12 as follows: 'I do not permit a woman to teach, that is to say.' And this leads to the debated question of how to understand the Greek verb that follows, *authenteō* ('to have authority'). Does this term mean 'to have authority' without any nuance as to *how* that authority is exercised? Or does the term contain a negative sense, namely, to exercise authority *in a manner that is overbearing*, for example? These options are not arbitrary intrusions into the argument: they stem from the conclusions of scholars regarding the sense of *authenteō* and its cognates in the primary sources.

Prior to weighing the options, it is important to note the work of Köstenberger on the relation between *to teach* and *to have authority*. Köstenberger has put forth the argument that since 'to teach' and 'have authority' are related in this verse, and since teaching is a positive activity in the Pastoral Epistles, it follows that 'to have authority' *also* possesses a positive nuance in this verse (pp. 81–103). The conclusion is then reached that Paul is not prohibiting the 'domineering' or 'overly independent' exercise of authority, but that he actually prohibits women from teaching men. In other words, the problem is not the teaching but the *gender* of the one doing the teaching.

Köstenberger's argument, however, is problematic, for the verb *didaskō* ('to teach') and the noun *didaskalia* ('teaching, doctrine') are not positive or negative. It depends on the context whether the teaching activity is positive or negative. This is why Paul often qualifies *didaskalia* with another word that clarifies whether the teaching in view is sound or unsound. For example, in 1 Timothy 1:10 he speaks of 'sound' *didaskalia*. But at 4:1 he speaks of the *didaskalia* 'of demons'! One cannot, therefore, effectively turn the vocabulary of teaching in the Pastoral Epistles into a technical term that means, as such, 'to teach sound doctrine'. Marshall is correct when, speaking of *didaskalia*, he says the following: 'In itself the term says nothing as to the acceptability or otherwise of the teaching as such' (p. 455).

The observations above require us to return to the meaning of the verb *authenteō* ('to have authority'). In light of the importance of the term in understanding Paul's prohibition, it is not surprising that the word has been rigorously studied and debated.[15] At the risk of oversimplifying, it seems that three general options have emerged as to the connotation of *authenteō*. We can call one of these options the *neutral* one, the second *positive*, and the third *pejorative*.[16] For some scholars *authenteō* simply means 'to have authority', without any indication as to how this authority is exercised.[17] T. Schreiner has suggested on the basis of his examination of the evidence that *authenteō* actually conveys a *positive* connotation.[18] Another group of scholars concludes from the evidence that *authenteō* carries with it a *negative* connotation, adding the nuance of 'domineering' or 'independent'.[19] Marshall (p. 460), uses the phrase 'heavy-handed' as a way to explain what Paul is prohibiting in the exercising of authority.

The view taken in this commentary is that *authenteō* and its cognates carries with it a *pejorative* sense. That is, the word portrays the exercising of authority as carried out in a way that is *negative*. The following are the two main reasons for adopting this interpretation. First, the evidence from the primary sources, especially as it has been explained by Hübner, appears to be strong in demonstrating the negative connotation of *authenteō* and cognates. Second, it should be noted that Paul had at his disposal a number of terms to express the concept of exercising of authority. Examples are *exousia* ('authority') and cognates, *kyrieuō* ('to rule over, have power'), and *proistēmi* ('to lead, manage, have authority'). Paul uses these terms in his writings. And yet in 1 Timothy 2:12 he has chosen to employ a relatively rare word (used only once in the NT). The suggestion here is that Paul chose this particular word precisely because it could

---

15 In addition to the commentaries, see Baldwin, 'An Important Word'; Wolters, 'αυθεντης and Its Cognates'; Hübner, 'Revisiting αὐθεντέω'.

16 See Hübner, 'Revisiting αὐθεντέω', pp. 62–65.

17 E.g., Knight, 'ΑΥΘΕΝΤΕΩ', pp. 143–157.

18 E.g., Schreiner, 'A Response to Linda Belleville', p. 108, and Köstenberger as discussed above.

19 E.g., Hübner, 'Revisiting αὐθεντέω', pp. 65–70.

carry the nuance that he wanted to communicate. And the nuance is without question a pejorative one. I would thus paraphrase 2:12 as follows: 'I do not permit a woman to instruct men *in a domineering fashion, by teaching on their own authority.*' The Message Bible renders the phrase as follows: 'I don't let women take over and tell the men what to do.'

When we combine Paul's concern with the *sōphrosynē* of the women in the congregations (which called for modesty and quietness on their part) with this verse, it becomes probable that Paul is forbidding a particular type of woman from teaching men: immodest women who desired to instruct the men in a 'heavy-handed', domineering and disrespectful fashion. We should note that Paul also forbids *men* who behave in such a way from overseeing and teaching the congregations (see 1 Tim. 3:1–7; 2 Tim. 2:24–25).

13. *For Adam was formed first, then Eve.* With a causal conjunction ('for', *gar*) Paul signals his move to provide another basis for the injunctions of verses 11–12. Paul goes to Scripture, particularly Genesis 2:4–22, to demonstrate that the attempt of women in the congregations in Ephesus to dominate during instruction is not biblical. For in the creation account the woman is clearly presented as Adam's helper and therefore she is not to act in a manner that is domineering and disrespectful to him. The argument here is almost identical to 1 Corinthians 11:2–16. It is possible that Paul is using a rabbinic hermeneutical key, where 'the first is best' argument was widely applied.[20] However, Paul partly relativizes this hermeneutic in 1 Corinthians 11:11: 'Nevertheless, in the Lord woman is not independent of man *or man independent of woman.*'

14. *And Adam was not deceived, but the woman was deceived and became a transgressor.* Paul marshals a second biblical basis for his argument. He moves forward in the Genesis account to the fall (Gen. 3:1–24). The emphasis is on the verb 'to deceive', which is used twice in this verse (*apateuō* and the cognate *exapataō*). We are told that while *Adam was not deceived*, by contrast the woman, having been deceived, *became a transgressor.* By focusing on the deception of Eve, Paul is harking back to her own words in Genesis 3:13: 'The serpent tricked

---

20 For the Jewish texts, see Towner, pp. 226–227.

me, and I ate.' While both Adam and Eve sinned, the emphasis in Paul's exposition is on the fact that Eve's transgression came about by deception.[21]

Granted that Paul bases the arguments of verses 11–12 on the Genesis text, just *how* is he using them as his basis? That is, is the Genesis account being used as a 'timeless truth', a universal proof-text that demonstrates that women are somehow fundamentally more prone to being deceived and therefore should not be allowed to instruct men? Some commentators have taken this view. The Roman Catholic priest C. Spicq (p. 71), for example, says the following: 'A woman will always be easier to deceive than a man, and that is why the apostle cannot allow women … not only to have authority over their husbands, but above all to teach the truth in the church.' A more recent commentator, while denying that Paul suggests that the woman is as such more gullible than the man, nevertheless views verses 13–14 as providing a rationale that is 'permanently applicable' for the exclusion of women from public teaching.[22] The reason is that 'Paul is rooting his directive in the order of creation rather than providing a cultural rationale' (ibid.). The problem with this view is that it fails to ask just *how* Paul is using Scripture as the basis of his injunctions. It is likely that what Paul is doing is *illustrating* what can happen (and has happened) when women take a dominating attitude *vis-à-vis* the men who are put in place as their teachers. This is exactly what happened with Eve when she, independently of Adam, engaged the serpent. She was deceived and monumental consequences followed.

We conclude this section of 1 Timothy 2:9–15 by suggesting that Paul's prohibition of women teaching men in the congregations at Ephesus was based on a problem of *character* not gender. Some of the women lacked the basic modesty that was the hallmark of women who confessed the faith. This lack of modesty may have been manifested in the women attempting to co-opt instruction in the church and instruct men in a manner that was 'heavy-handed'

---

21 For the Jewish background on the supposed greater weakness of the woman to sin by being deceived, see Ecc. 25:24; Philo, *QG* 1.33.46.

22 Köstenberger, pp. 116–118.

and domineering. This would have shamed the husbands and men in the congregations. This shaming behaviour had the potential of destroying the missional work of the church with outsiders. It is also possible that the women who lacked godly modesty were being deceived by false teachers. Paul's emphasis on deception in his interpretation of Genesis 3:1–24 may indicate that the women were being deceived – and it is generally the case that false teachers are the ones doing the deceiving.

15. *Yet she will be saved through childbearing.* Paul concludes on a positive note on the fate of the women at the churches of Ephesus. The *she* of this verse no longer refers to Eve but to the women in the churches. The main verb is the passive form of *sōzō*, which appears numerous times in the Pastoral Epistles (1 Tim. 1:15; 2:4; 4:16; 2 Tim. 1:9; 4:18; Tit. 3:5). Without exception, the verb is used of God's deliverance of humans from their sins and into knowledge of the living God. What is perplexing is the prepositional phrase modifying the verb: *through childbearing.* This has given rise to a number of interpretations that attempt to unravel the meaning of 'save' here, and has led to two main interpretations of the meaning 'to save'; here, namely that it refers to spiritual salvation or to physical preservation.

When we keep the context of vv. 9–15, that is, women lacking *sōphrosynē,* at the forefront, a satisfying interpretation of verse 15 may emerge. For as we saw on vv. 9–11, one of the most important aspects of *sōphrosynē* was *caring for the home.* We should thus understand Paul as saying that if the women at Ephesus are to be saved, they need to reject the pattern of women who rejected the feminine cardinal virtue *sōphrosynē.* B. Winter suggests that rebellion against *sōphrosynē* may have also included avoidance of pregnancy and/or termination of pregnancy by abortion (Winter, pp. 110–113). Thus, Paul speaks in a blunt and dramatic manner (just as he did in vv. 11–12): either follow the pattern of immodest women (probably nourished by false teaching) or follow the pattern that is 'proper for women who profess reverence for God' (v. 10), which includes a virtuous home life, with the bearing of children. This latter pattern leads to salvation. This is the meaning of the final clause of the verse, a conditional clause that modifies the verb 'to save': *Provided they continue in faith and love and holiness, with modesty.* These are qualities that *all* believers are to display, and which stem from adherence to sound doctrine (see 1:5). Paul closes the section with the mention of *modesty* (*sōphrosynē*), the same term used in verse 9 to begin the section. Cognates of this term will also be used of overseers (3:1; Tit. 1:8), older men (Tit. 2:1) and younger women (Tit. 2:5). In short, Paul's statement in verse 15 regarding the salvation of women is not that much different from his statements about the salvation and Christian life of *every* believer. Childbearing is singled out for cultural reasons and possibly the influence of the so-called New Wives movement (see Winter for this movement; Towner, p. 235).

Theology

In the context of the church's mission to unbelievers (2:1–7) and worship (2:8–15), Paul wants to make sure that the behaviour of the women of the church is commensurate with the faith they profess. Many women (perhaps particularly wealthy wives and widows – see Occasion for the Pastoral Epistles in the Introduction) were behaving in a manner contrary to the faith. This behaviour consisted in immodest, materialistic and sensual deportment, more than likely in the context of the local congregations meeting in family homes. In addition, the behaviour consisted in domineering and overly independent attitudes in the context of teaching, and perhaps false teaching. This behaviour was unacceptable for women of faith in any period – but perhaps especially in the Greco-Roman world, where modesty was a highly prized virtue for women. Consequently, Timothy is to order the women to adorn themselves with utter modesty and to cease from attempting to dominate the instruction in the church. This also includes concentrating on the care of their homes.

By way of application, it does seem unlikely that we should take this passage to mean that women are forbidden from teaching men. This reading fails to grapple consistently with the occasional nature of Paul's letters and the culture in which they were written. In addition, this text should not be the basis for denial of women's ordination. In some ways this is a very strange text. For there are many examples in the Bible of women instructing the whole assembly and/or men (e.g., Deborah and Huldah). First Timothy

2:9–15 may even be viewed as an exception to the rest of Scripture, and certainly Paul, who counted on women as his co-labourers in the gospel. The uniqueness of the passage is all the more reason to believe that in 1 Timothy 2:9–15 we are dealing with a unique problem. Therefore, to use this text as the final word on women's ordination is precisely what we should not do.[23] The most concrete application from this text should be a reminder that women (as well as men!) must lead lives of modesty that would attract outsiders to the gospel (see further on Tit. 2:1–10).

C. The qualifications of overseers and deacons (3:1–13)

Context
One of Paul's goals in writing to Timothy is that the latter would understand how to conduct himself in God's household (3:15; see Introduction under Occasion and comments on 1:3–8). Timothy also has the duty of shepherding the congregations at Ephesus so that, negatively, they would not fall into false doctrine but, positively, would pursue godliness. One of the ways that this goal would be accomplished was through the appointing of good leaders.[24] Therefore, in this section Paul introduces two offices of church leadership, namely 'overseer' and 'deacon'. The logic, well represented in the entire Bible, is that without godly leadership the people of God easily deviate. Therefore, it is necessary that churches have godly leadership.

To help the reader navigate this section it is important to understand the language of leadership in its sociohistorical background. First, there is the word *episkopos* ('overseer'), which is found in the Septuagint (Num. 4:16; 31:14; Judg. 9:28; 2 Kgs 11:15, 18; 2 Chr. 34:12; Neh. 11:9; 14:22; Job 20:29; Isa. 60:17 [used with *archontes*]; 1 Macc. 1:51; *Wis.* 1:6). It almost always translates the Hebrew root *pqd*. The term refers to those who lead or are in charge. The context can be cultic, military or tribal. In the Greco-Roman context *episkopos* is

---

23 On this history of the use of this text, as well as the question of women's ordination (i.e., denial of it), see the recent work of Witt, *Icons of Christ*.

24 See also Titus 1:5–16 and our comments there.

also used for officials of Greek cities: for example, for the super-
visor of the mint in Ephesus, local officials in towns and officers of
associations, clubs or religious cults. In the voluntary associations in
particular, *episkopos* could be used to designate an administrator of
the association.[25] There was a broad range of voluntary associations:
fishermen, physicians, silversmiths, dyers, and so on. It should be
noted that these associations often used of their members family
terminology such as: fathers, mothers, brothers and sisters.[26] Some
scholars have thus suggested that the family and household language used in the Pastoral Epistles as a whole and in 1 Timothy 3 in
particular is taken from the context of the associations, given their
apparent similarities to church language (thus, ibid.). Furthermore,
it is suggested that the leadership structure found in the Pastoral
Epistles is borrowed from voluntary associations.

The data in this respect can be interpreted in at least two ways.
One way is to say that the church borrowed family language *directly*
from voluntary associations. The other is to say that since the
nucleus of society was the *familia*, both the associations and the
church found it natural to use the language of family to speak of
inter-relations and structure.[27] This does not mean that the church
was *not at all* influenced by the common voluntary associations: it
means that it is a reductionist and overly simplistic explanation of
the data to conclude that family language in the church stemmed
exclusively from associations. As we indicated in the Introduction
(see under Church), the concept of the family is often evoked in the

---

25 See McLean, 'The Place of Cult in Voluntary Associations', pp. 186–225.
    By way of definition of voluntary associations, consider the following:
    'A broad cross section of people in the ancient Mediterranean world was
    affiliated with some type of unofficial association. These associations
    provided members with a sense of belonging, along with some practical
    benefits such as opportunities for networking, regular banquets, and a
    decent burial' (Kloppenborg et al., *Associations in the Greco-Roman World*,
    p. 1).
26 See Kloppenborg et al., *Associations in the Greco-Roman World*, nos. 88, 91,
    215, 319.
27 See Clarke, *Serve the Community of the Church*, pp. 79–101.

Pastoral Epistles as akin to the identity of the church. It is thus not surprising that the family structure is the one used as an analogy in the context of church leadership.[28] Like the head of the family (*paterfamilias*), for example, the overseer must manage his household well and have a good reputation (*pietas*) with outsiders.

To conclude on the overseer, it is essential to note that in its use in the verbal form (*episkeptomai* or *episkopeō*) the dominant nuance is that of 'to manage', 'to look after' or 'to care for' (TDNT II, pp. 600–605). This is precisely what the verb conveys in 1 Peter 2:25 and 5:2. It is also likely that we should view this office in the Pastoral Epistles as often, but not always, held by heads of family who could accommodate a meeting of believers in their homes. Lastly, from texts like Philippians 1:1 we should think of more than one overseer in the cities where churches existed. This is in contrast to the second century, where often there was a single overseer over an entire group of churches in a city (e.g., Ignatius, *Eph.* 1:3; 2:1–2; 4:1; 5:3; 6:1; *Magn.* 2:1; 3:1; 6–7; 12–13; *Trall.* 2:1–3; 7:1–2). For the NT period an overseer was someone who had the means *and* desire (3:1) to serve as a caring leader over Christian meetings at his home (and possibly the homes of others). But that was not enough. He also had to display the virtues mentioned in 3:2–7. Just *how* the overseer went about fulfilling the responsibilities of this office is not entirely clear. Teaching was involved (3:2); and from the virtues mentioned in the text, as well as primary sources outside the Bible, it appears that the type of person who Paul was searching for in an overseer was someone who cared deeply for the believers under his responsibility. Therefore, the overseer also had to possess pastoral gifts, which could be exercised in hospitality, visiting the sick and vulnerable, helping in reconciliation between believers who had quarrelled, and so on (see Matthew 25:36, 43; Acts 7:3, with the verbal form *episkeptomai*).

The second office mentioned is that of deacon (*diakonos*). The term and its cognates are not very much used in the Septuagint (the noun is found in Esth. 1:10; 2:2; 6:3, 5; Prov. 10:4; 4 Macc. 9.17). It

---

28   See ibid., pp. 160–166; Gehring, *House Church and Mission*, pp. 260–268; Campbell, *The Elders*, pp. 182–193.

is more common in Greco-Roman literature, where it referred to a helper (sometimes servile – whether as a servant, messenger or attendant; see LSJ, s.v.). The noun (in both the masculine and feminine) is found in inscriptions of voluntary associations to refer to an office in the respective guilds and is often translated as 'assistant'.[29] Given that the qualification of being a competent administrator of his household is also required of the deacon (3:12), it is likely that as was the case with the overseer, so also the contexts of the deacons' duties were the household churches. This would imply a less formalized structure than what we find in second-century ecclesial contexts; and this should deter us from reading our contemporary denominational ideas of the office of deacon into the text of the Pastoral Epistles.

Comment

1. *The saying is true.* The syntax of verse 1 suggests that this phrase should go with what follows. As indicated earlier (1:15), this phrase is used in the Pastoral Epistles to underline the traditional and authoritative nature of that which the phrase is referring to, and therefore the obligation of the readers to accept it. By beginning the section in this manner, Paul communicates his desire for the churches at Ephesus to accept the leadership of the overseers and deacons.

Whoever aspires to be an overseer (episkopē) desires a noble task (NIV). The term *episkopē* refers to the office of overseer, although the term 'office' is not present in the Greek. Yet, we can think of the duty as an 'office' of overseer in the sense that this is a position that exists irrespective of the person holding it. What matters, then, is the carrying out of the tasks delineated in the obligations of the overseer, not holding a title. To desire *to be an overseer* is to desire *a noble task* (*kalos ergon*). This phrase is often used in the Pastoral Epistles (see Introduction; 1 Tim. 3:1; 5:10, 25; 6:18; Tit. 2:14. See also 1 Tim. 3:13, where *kalos* is used with *bathmos* ['standing, status']).

2. *Now the overseer [episkopos].* On the term *episkopos*, refer to the Context section. *Above reproach.* Rather than viewing this quality

---

29 See Kloppenborg et al., *Associations in the Greco-Roman World*, nos. 1, 4,
     19, 29, 36, 38. Cf. also Spicq, p. xlvi.

in the abstract and therefore as unrelated to other qualities, it is better to understand *anepilēmptos* (BDAG: 'irreproachable', p. 77) as the heading for the qualifications that follow. In other words, what it means to be *above reproach* is filled in by the qualities that follow.

Married only once. Such is the NRSV translation of the Greek phrase *mias gynaikos andra.* The ESV's 'the husband of one wife' is an improvement on the NRSV. Marshall (pp. 155–157) helpfully presents five possible views on the meaning of the phrase: (1) one who has not committed polygamy. However, since polygamy was not known to have been practised in Greco-Roman culture, it is unlikely that Paul would be addressing it here. (2) One who is married, not a celibate. It is probable that Paul mentions marriage because it is likely that the overseer was the head of a household (*paterfamilias*) and therefore normally married. Thus, the office of overseer is not denied to a person who is single. (3) One who has not remarried after experiencing widowhood. This interpretation is also unlikely, since remarriage after a spouse's death was not considered sinful (see 1 Cor. 7:8, 39). (4) One who has not remarried after divorce. In Matthew 5:32 and Mark 10:11 Jesus prohibited remarriage after a divorce. However, in Matthew 19:9 and 1 Corinthians 7:15 this prohibition is relaxed. Furthermore, the language used in this verse does not seem to be pointing to the situation of divorce. (5) One who is faithful to his wife. Since the statement in the verse is put by Paul in a positive sense, it is quite likely that Paul's emphasis is on the overseer being faithful to his wife.[30] This is the NIV translation: *Faithful to his wife.* This could have been difficult in a Greco-Roman culture in which married men often visited brothels or engaged in sex with prostitutes during banquets. Most Gentile men grew up with a conception of sexuality that included this type of sexual behaviour. While this behaviour was condemned by the moral philosophers (but only to some extent: see Plutarch, *Conj. praec.* 16!), other ancient sources suggest that it was normal for married men to give free rein to their sexual desires with prostitutes. The overseer, by contrast,

---

30 See esp. Knight, pp. 157–159.

must be faithful to his wife. Marshall's conclusion (p. 157) is sound: 'It can undoubtedly be assumed that the marriage would have to conform to the standards of acceptability within the church (i.e. monogamous and if a remarriage, then a legitimate one).'

The next quality is *temperate* (*nēphalios*), a virtue that is also to be displayed by female deacons (3:11) and older men (Tit. 2:2). Outside the NT, the term was used of being moderate in the drinking of wine (BDAG, p. 672; Spicq, p. 79). In the NT, the term is used figuratively to express a life not given to excess or flippancy. 'Moderation', 'temperance', 'seriousness', all get at the meaning of the word. BDAG, p. 672, offers the meanings: 'sober … restrained in conduct, self-controlled.' Just as the head of the family (*paterfamilias*) had to be a serious man, so also the overseer of the family of God had to be serious, that is, *temperate*.

Sensible (*sōphrōn*). We have commented on this term and the cognate *sōphrosynē* on 1 Timothy 2:9–15. This was one of the four cardinal virtues in most circles of Greek philosophy and the principal virtue that a woman was to display. *Sōphrōn* is also used in Titus 1:8 of the overseer, in 2:2 of older men and in 2:5 of young wives. In this context, words like 'self-control' and 'temperance' are good English terms to get a sense of the meaning of the Greek (Spicq, p. 80; BDAG, p. 987).

Respectable (*kosmion*). As was the case with the previous two terms, so also this one is used of the qualities of the godly woman (2:9). As we have indicated, *sōphrōn* and *kosmion* were often used together, with the second term highlighting temperance and 'decorum' (Hutson, p. 93).

Hospitable. This should be a quality of *all* Christians (Rom. 12:13; Heb. 13:2; 1 Pet. 4:9; 3 John 5), but perhaps especially so of Christians who owned larger homes, as we have argued may have been the case with overseers in the early church. If we keep in mind the often appalling and dangerous conditions of inns in antiquity, we can see how important hospitality was, especially among people like the Christians who understood themselves as being family members and who often travelled as missionaries.

An apt teacher. The word *didaktikos* is used elsewhere in the Pastoral Epistles of a quality that the 'servant of the Lord' must possess (2 Tim. 2:24). The sense is not that the overseer must be an uncommonly eloquent teacher. Rather, the overseer must have the capacity to instruct in sound, apostolic doctrine (cf. Spicq, p. 81). His knowledge of the gospel must be such that he can refute false teachers (2 Tim. 2:24).

3. *Not a drunkard.* See also Titus 1:7, where someone who drinks alcohol excessively is denied the office of overseer. *Not violent but gentle.* The first of these prohibitions was often linked with drunkenness. The drunk person would often engage in violent behaviour or bullying (Marshall, p. 162). Malherbe suggests that Paul may also be alluding to the potential of domestic abuse. If overseers were also heads of their homes, they had to be careful in not engaging in the type of violent behaviour that a *paterfamilias* could. Thus, *not violent but gentle* could be a warning against domestic violence.[31] Instead of being *violent*, the overseer must be *gentle* (*epieikēs*). This is a quality that all Christians must exhibit (Tit. 3:5; see also Phil. 4:5). BDAG (p. 371) provides the following meanings: 'yielding, gentle, kind, courteous, tolerant'.

Not quarrelsome (*amachos*). This is a quality required of all believers in Titus 3:2. LSJ, s.v. 2, is helpful in explaining the meaning as 'disinclined to fight, not contentious'. The definition provided by BDAG is 'peaceable' (p.52). *Not a lover of money* (*aphilarguros*). This is another virtue that all believers should have, given that 'the love of money is a root of all kinds of evil' (6:10; on love of money, see further on 6:6–10, 17–19). The exhortation against the love of money may have been of particular importance with respect to the overseer, who as such probably handled money for church distribution. In addition, generosity, the opposite of love of money, was publicly highly valued in leaders of communities and cities in the Greco-Roman world (i.e., civic benefaction; see Johnson, p. 215).

4–5. *He must manage his own household well.* The household would have included the overseer's wife, children and slaves (if he had any). The management of the household included maintaining order, administration and caring for those in the household (cf. Rom. 12:8; 1 Thess. 5:12; BDAG, *proistēmi*, p. 870). In fact, it was a common *topos* in Greco-Roman moral philosophy that only a

---

31 Malherbe, *Light from the Gentiles*, 1:565.

virtuous man could manage his household well, which would mean that he could also manage the city-state well.

The NIV translates the next qualification as *and see that his children obey him*. The children in view here were not just necessarily the 'minors' in the home but also may have included adult children living in the house, the *domus*.[32] In general, during the Greco-Roman period it was expected that children would show absolute respect to their father. Not to do so was a scandal, a profound violation of *pietas*.[33]

For if someone does not know how to manage his own household, how can he take care of God's church? The logic of the argument is from the lesser to the greater. The inability to manage in private affairs demonstrates that in a corresponding but larger public duty he will also fail. This was a common *topos* in Greco-Roman ethics. For a list of texts, see under Context in Titus 1:5–9. For the term *church* (*ekklēsia*), see 3:15.

6–7. *He must not be a recent convert.* The term *neophytos* appears only here in the NT and means 'newly planted'. The overseer must not be a new believer. Paul explains the reason in the next statement: *or he may be puffed up with conceit and fall into the condemnation of the devil.* Holding the office of overseer without sufficient spiritual maturity may lead to being *puffed up*. The same verb (*typhoō*) is used in 6:4 of false teachers who, no longer holding to sound doctrine, have become conceited.

Becoming conceited or arrogant can lead 'to the judgment of the devil'. The genitive is probably an objective genitive, suggesting that the overseer may fall *under the same judgment as the devil* (NIV). A similar idea is expressed in verse 7. The overseer must have a good reputation with outsiders, lest he fall *into disgrace and the snare of the devil. Snare (pagis)* means a 'trap' (BDAG, p. 747; see on 6:9 and 2 Timothy 2:26). The devil is presented here as active in seeking the disgrace of the overseer. The logic here is that a damaged reputation with unbelievers would lead to speaking evil of the gospel (see Marshall, p. 484).

---

32 See Hölkeskamp, 'Under Roman Roofs', pp. 134–136.
33 See Clarke, *Christians as Leaders*, pp. 89–92. For more in-depth exploration of this subject, see Saller, *Patriarchy*, pp. 102–153.

8–9. *Deacons likewise.* As indicated above (Context), the deacons served as assistants to the overseer(s). Other uses of *deacons* in the Pauline epistles (Rom. 16:1; Phil. 1:1) do not suggest that the assistantship of the deacons was limited solely to administration, as the language in 3:9 appears to suggest (this is also pointed out by Towner, pp. 261–262).

Serious (*semnos*) was also used in the overseer qualifications to speak of the respect that his children had to show him. The deacons are to carry themselves with seriousness and dignity worthy of the office. *Not double-tongued*, that is, not insincere (BDAG, p. 250). *Not indulging in much wine.* The prohibition is the same as in 3:3. *Not greedy for money.* The NIV translation, 'not pursuing dishonest gain', better renders the meaning of the Greek *aischrokerdēs*. The same term is used to prohibit dishonest gain from the overseer in Titus 1:7. This prohibition parallels 3:3.

They must hold fast to the mystery of the faith with a clear conscience. The term *mystery* (*mystērion*) anticipates 3:16. Paul uses the word *mystery* (Eph. 1:9; 3:4; Col. 1:26; 2:2; 4:3) to refer to God's plan of salvation that was previously veiled but which now has been graciously unveiled to the apostles. The content of the mystery is centred on Christ, yet with linkages to the church (Eph. 1:9) and salvation (Col. 1:26–27). The latter is the case here, with the genitive *of the faith* being in apposition: the mystery, which is the faith (cf. Johnson, p. 228; on faith in the Pastoral Epistles, see 1 Tim. 1:5). The manner in which the deacons are to hold on to the faith is *with a clear conscience.* The phrase is similar to 1:5 ('good conscience'). As we have seen, the emphasis on 'conscience' in the Pastoral Epistles is on the fact that it has been cleansed by God and therefore the individual is free to serve God. With this *clear conscience*, the deacons must persevere in the apostolic faith in the knowledge that they have been saved on the basis of God's grace in Jesus Christ and therefore lead lives of sincere faith (see Marshall, p. 491).

10. *First be tested … if they prove themselves blameless.* Deacons must first model the qualities in the list of the previous verses. Paul uses the verb *dokimazō*, which the NRSV translates as *tested.* The verb and noun were used in ancient voluntary associations to speak of 'vetting' an individual to judge if he or she had the required virtues to belong to that community. This vetting was called a *dokimasia*.[34] In a similar way, deacons (and one would assume overseers) first had to be vetted in light of the standards set by Paul. Success in this (probably carried out by observation of the candidate's life) would demonstrate that they were *blameless*, thereby ready to take on the office of deacon.

11. *Women likewise.* Paul may be referring to wives of deacons or to female deacons (i.e., deaconesses). The view taken in this commentary is that the meaning of 'women' should be *deaconesses* for at least the following reasons. First, it would be odd in a passage dealing with church offices for there to be a sudden parenthetical shift to give orders to women or wives as such, especially after the injunctions of 2:9–15. Second, there are no explicit directions to the wives of overseers; why should there be for those of deacons? Third, we have a clear case of a deaconess in Phoebe (Rom. 16:1). More than likely, then, Paul is referring to female deacons. For the implications of this conclusion for the ministries of women in the church today, see below (under Theology).

Serious. This is the same qualification used for male deacons in verse 8. *Not slanderers* (*me diabolous*), which correlates to 'double-tongued' of verse 8, adds an element of insidiousness that may accompany the act of slandering. *Temperate*, on which see comment on verse two. *Faithful in all things*: with the use of *pistos* Paul parallels the requirement of deaconesses with that of deacons in verse 9 (*echontas … tēs pisteōs*). Therefore, although faithfulness applies to all spheres, the emphasis would be on faithfulness to the apostolic doctrine (see also 1:12; 2 Tim. 2:2).

12–13. *Let the deacons be married only once.* Paul returns to the qualifications of male deacons. The qualities are the same that the overseer is to model (3:2, 4). On this qualification, see the comments in 3:2.

For those who serve well as deacons. With the causal *gar* ('for') Paul introduces motivation for deacons who do their work well. Furthermore, with the use of *kalos* a parallel is made with 3:1: 'Whoever aspires to be an overseer desires a noble [*kalos*] task.' *Gain a good standing … and great boldness in the faith that is in Christ*

---

34 See Feyel, *Dokimasia*.

Jesus. The word *standing* means a 'step', as in movement upwards (BDAG, p. 162). It was used metaphorically of a promotion, for example, in the army. In the context of 1 Timothy 3 it probably refers to advancement in the sense of further trust and respect from the community (cf. Dibelius and Conzelmann, p. 59; Roloff, p. 167; Marshall, p. 496). Such good standing is related to *boldness* (*parrēsia*). Here the sense of the term is that of confidence and assurance (cf. Eph. 3:12; Heb. 10:35) at both an existential and eschatological level. That is, the noble service of the deacons will provide them with the assurance of eternal life (cf. 1 John 3:21) and that in the final judgment they will not be condemned.[35] Of course, this confidence is not ultimately based on human achievement. The final phrase of the verse reminds the readers that this happens in the sphere of *faith that is in Christ Jesus*, both the objective, sound, apostolic doctrine (*fides quae*), as well as appropriation of that body of doctrine by means of trust (*fides qua*).

Theology

The terms used to describe the leaders in the congregations – overseers and deacons – have a long history of church usage. It is easy to read contemporary meanings back into the biblical text. Although contemporary uses may be legitimate theological extensions of the biblical text, we cannot assume that they always are. Thus, it was necessary to examine the sociohistorical context of the Greco-Roman period where these terms were employed.

One of the striking features of this passage is the similarity between the overseers and deacons. The similarities are both in qualifications and functions. As for the former, it can be shown that the same character traits are expected of both. Nevertheless, it would appear that 'an apt teacher' (v. 2) and 'not be a recent convert' (v. 6) are unique to the overseer. On the other hand, it could be argued that the qualification 'they must hold to the mystery of faith' (v. 9), said of the deacons, is parallel to 'an apt teacher' of the overseer. In fact, 3:9 is virtually identical to Titus 1:9: 'He must

---

35 See, e.g., *Wis.* 5:1, where *pollē parrēsia* ('great boldness') is used in an eschatological context.

have a firm grasp of the word that is trustworthy in accordance with the teaching' (*antechomenon … tou pistou logou*). This is said in Titus of the *overseer*. This parallels well with 1 Timothy 3:9 (*echontas … tou pistou logou*), of the *deacon*. Furthermore, the qualification of the overseer, 'not be a recent convert', parallels with 'and let them first be tested', required of the deacons in verse 10. In addition to equality of character traits, the adjective/adverb *kalos/kalōs* is linked to both functions of overseeing and serving as deacons, operating as bookends to the entire section (vv. 1 and 13). Lastly, Timothy, who probably served as an overseer of the churches at Ephesus, is encouraged to be 'a good servant of Christ Jesus' (*kalos … diakonos*, 4:6), language which is similar to 3:13 (of deacons).

As for function, we have seen that in 3:1–13 there is little indication of the respective concrete work of overseers and deacons. Apart from the functions inherent in their titles, there is not much clarity with respect to the differences of their actual duties. We may say that the *episkopoi* had the responsibility of a more general oversight over their congregation, while the *diakonoi* assisted the *episkopoi* in their oversight. But what did this oversight of the *episkopoi* mean *concretely*? And are we to say that deacons did not serve the believers *directly* but only indirectly through the overseers? This is not convincing. The usual approach has been to say that the difference in function is one of teaching and instructing (e.g., Köstenberger, pp. 125–126). This has some support in light of 1 Timothy 5:17. However, in view of the parallelism just suggested between 3:2 and 9, and the example of Timothy in 4:6, it would be hard to maintain a rigid difference such as: the overseers taught; the deacons did not teach. The difference (apart from titles) seems to have been one of *degree*, not kind. Thus, the overseers *tended* to concentrate on teaching and pastoral care, while the deacons *tended* to concentrate more on assistance to the overseers and congregation. But their respective functions were not as sealed off from one another as is often thought.

A final word of application may be offered on the relationship between the modern pastor and the overseer. In many modern denominations and non-denominational churches the overseer tends to be conflated with the pastor. There is some warrant for this in the text of 1 Timothy. But a warning is necessary. What many churches look for in a pastor is a set of skills and personality traits. These often include a charismatic personality, powerful and eloquent preaching, a visionary, great administrative skills, and so on. By contrast, the biblical model of the pastor (to the extent that it can be distilled from 1 Tim. 3:1–13) focuses on *character and pastoral attitudes*. The leaders in the churches must be godly men and women who have been gifted by the Holy Spirit to teach the Scriptures competently and care pastorally for the congregation, similarly to the way parents care for their children.

D. The church as the household of God (3:14–16)

Context
This section constitutes the hinge of 1 Timothy. In many ways the injunctions of chapters 4–6 parallel those of 1–3.[36] Thus, 3:14–16 looks backwards and forwards; it is the hinge of the letter. As such, the entire letter hangs together on 3:14–16. For what we shall discover in these verses is that the church is nothing less than the dwelling of the living God. This demands beliefs and behaviour that are commensurate with the character of the living God, who is identified with the incarnate and risen Lord Jesus Christ.

Comment
14. *I am writing these instructions to you so that.* The pronoun *these* looks backwards and forward. Although Paul expects to come to Timothy soon, he found it necessary to write this letter, just in case he was delayed. The purpose (*hina*, 'so that') for writing the letter follows.

15. *You may know how one ought to behave in the household of God.* The complementary infinitive *to behave* refers to the believer's conduct. The emphasis is on conduct which is visible to others and stems from a committed relationship to God. This behaviour is related to godliness (*eusebeia*), a clean (because cleansed) conscience and sincere faith (1:5). It encompasses both belief and practice.

Careful attention to conduct is particularly urgent because of the sphere of the believer's life. That is, the fellowship of the Christians at Ephesus happens in *the household of God* (*oikō theou*). The biblical

---

36 For example, see the following parallels: 1:3, 18/4:11; 1:12/4:6; 1:19/4:1.

background here is that of the temple in the OT, which is often called the house of God or the house of the Lord (1 Kgs 3:1; 8:1, 14–66; 12:27; 2 Kgs 21:4). God would dwell there, answering prayer, forgiving sins and receiving sacrifices and thanksgiving. In other texts, Paul writes of the church as God's temple: 'Do you not know that you are God's temple and that God's Spirit dwells in you?' (1 Cor. 3:16). And in Ephesians 2:19–22 he combines household and temple imagery to speak of the Christians as the dwelling place of God. More than likely, Paul speaks of the church here as the house of God because of the ecclesiastical metaphor of the household, which he has been using throughout 1 Timothy.

Paul further identifies the house of God as *the church of the living God. Ekklēsia* ('assembly') was the term for the democratic assembly of Greek city-states, made up of the elected council (*boulē*) and the well-to-do male citizens (*dēmos*). This term would have evoked for the readers associations of the powerful and elite citizens of a city. In the Septuagint, however, *ekklēsia* was often used of the people of God, Israel, gathered before the Lord (e.g., Deut. 4:10; 9:10; 18:16; 31:30; Josh. 9:2; Judg. 20:2). The phrase 'assembly of God' is found in Nehemiah 13:1, while 'assembly of the Lord' is found in Deuteronomy 23:2–4. The phrase *living God*, which is here linked to the church, is very common in the OT and Septuagint. It appears in contexts where the God of Israel is contrasted with the dead gods of the nations (e.g., Deut. 5:26; 1 Sam. 17:36; 2 Kgs 19:4, 16; 3 Macc. 6:28), or in liturgical language (e.g., Pss 42:2; 84:2; Hos. 1:10; Tob. 13:2). Both senses come together in 1 Timothy 3:15.

The pillar and bulwark of the truth. The metaphor now moves with more precision to temple imagery, used by Paul in other places also to speak of the church (1 Cor. 3:11; Eph. 2:20). The key question is how to understand the relationship between the church (*pillar and bulwark*) and the *truth*, the latter understood as a reference to the gospel (see explanation in 2:4).[37] The church is a bulwark of the gospel in that it defends it and is also the place where the gospel is found in preaching and the sacraments. Fear that this verse places the church over the

---

37 Among many examples of *alētheia* referring to the gospel in the Pastoral Epistles, see: 4:2; 2 Tim. 2:25; 3:7; Tit. 1:1.

gospel[38] stems from excessive Western individualism and from the history of the church, where sometimes the office (papacy) and creeds have trumped the gospel. The gospel is indeed found in the church because the Holy Spirit, who points to Jesus, dwells in the church, not in culture. It is in this sense that we must understand Augustine's statement: 'For my part, I should not believe the gospel except as moved by the authority of the catholic church' (*Fund.* IV.131).

16. *And without any doubt, the mystery of our religion is great.* With a simple 'and' Paul moves to the climax of the passage, which is probably a reworked piece of liturgy from the early church to which Paul himself may have contributed. Prior to the statement itself, however, he makes the powerful declaration above. The term translated *religion* is *eusebeia*, which, as we have seen (Introduction, under Christian Life), is central in the Pastoral Epistles. In this verse the objective aspect of *eusebeia* is highlighted, namely the apostolic doctrine, which is the gospel. It is probable that the connection between *mystery* and *religion* in this verse is epexegetical, that is, the mystery *is* the *eusebeia*, the gospel. With the use of *mystery* Paul underlines the fact that the gospel has been unveiled by God, not discovered by human religiosity or ingenuity (see further on 3:9 for 'mystery').

Most commentators agree that the following lines stem from a confession, probably in the form of a hymn. We follow Towner (pp. 278–285) in examining the 'hymn' in six lines.

1. *He was revealed in the flesh.* The verb *phaneroō* ('to reveal') appears three times in the Pastoral Epistles (1 Tim. 3:16; 2 Tim. 1:10; Tit. 1:3). God is always the one doing the revealing. What is revealed is God's grace and eternal life. In Romans 16:25–26 what is revealed is the 'mystery', which the context makes clear is Jesus Christ, who can only be revealed by God through his prophets, not 'discovered' by humanity.[39] Combining these verses with the use of *flesh* here, it is

---

38 See discussion in Hutson, pp. 105–106.
39 To be sure, humans can learn about the historical figure of Jesus by doing research. However, the perception that this same Jesus is the Son of God whose crucifixion and resurrection from the dead did away with our sins – this perception can only be graciously revealed by God through the Spirit.

clear that the reference is to the climactic salvation-historical event of Jesus Christ coming for our salvation. Although the crucifixion is not mentioned in this hymn, it is probably implied. Redemption begins already in the incarnation and climaxes in the crucifixion, resurrection and ascension of Jesus.[40]

2. *Was vindicated by the Spirit* (NIV). Jesus was crucified, a manner of death reserved in the Roman world for the worst of criminals; and in the OT, the one who hung upon a tree was cursed by God (Deut. 27:26; cf. Gal. 3:13). Jesus' resurrection from the dead demonstrated that he was no criminal or imposter when claiming to be the Son of God. Rather, *by* his resurrection 'he was declared to be the Son of God in power according to the Spirit of holiness' (Rom. 1:4). By his resurrection Jesus was vindicated as the obedient Son of God who won our justification (Rom. 4:25).

3. *Seen by angels.* There is debate on what event this phrase is speaking of here. Given the fact that the same verb in the passive form (*ōphthē*, 'seen') is used in Acts 13:31 and 1 Corinthians 15:5–8, where it refers to the post-resurrection appearances, it is likely that the phrase is referring to the angelic witness of the resurrection on Easter morning, which is the beginning of the post-resurrection appearances in the gospel tradition (see also Knight, p. 185).

4. *Proclaimed among the gentiles.* What was confessed in lines 1–3 was nothing less than the gospel, the good news of the Lord's advent and resurrection. In lines 4–5 Paul follows the trail of the missionary proclamation of the gospel and then returns to Christ in line 6. *Proclaimed* is the translation of the verb *kēryssō*, used in the NT for the missionary proclamation of the gospel (e.g., Rom. 10:8, 14, 15; 1 Cor. 1:23; 15:11, 12; 2 Cor. 1:19; Gal. 2:2; 1 Thess. 2:9; also Acts 8:5; 9:20; 10:37; 15:21; 20:25; 28:31; cf. the noun *kerygma*, Rom. 16:25; 1 Cor. 1:21; 2:4; 15:14; Tit. 1:3; see further on 2 Tim. 4:2). The preaching of the gospel of which Paul speaks is extensively described in the Acts of the Apostles.

5. *Believed in the world.* Jesus Christ was not only proclaimed among the Gentiles (the parallel to *world* in this line) but he was actually believed in by faith, thereby demonstrating the effectiveness and

---

40 See Torrance, *Incarnation*, pp. 37, 195.

power of the gospel (see Towner, p. 283). The thought is very similar to Colossians 1:6.

6. *Taken up in glory.* Paul now returns to the glorification of Christ. The verb *analambanō* ('to take up', 'lift up') is used in Acts to speak of the ascension (Acts 1:2, 11, 22; cf. Mark 16:19). This line thus probably refers to Christ's ascension to the right hand of the Father (see also Phil. 2:9).

Theology

It now becomes clear why Paul insists on Timothy correcting the false teachers and installing leaders (overseers and deacons). Their duty is to guard and protect nothing less than the gospel, which is *without any doubt ... great* (3:16). It is great because the gospel is God himself taking on our human flesh to participate in our misery as human beings and redeem us from sin, then being vindicated in his resurrection and returning to his previous glory at the right hand of the Father. Thus, *the mystery of our religion* is the incarnate, crucified, risen and exalted Jesus Messiah. We may boldly say that *God* is the gospel. The gospel is not a formula that one believes in the same way one 'believes' a mathematical equation or formula. For formulae cannot save humans; only the living Lord, who 'for us and for our salvation ... came down from heaven ... For our sake was crucified ... On the third day he rose again ... He ascended into heaven and is seated at the right hand of the Father' (Nicene Creed).

4. INSTRUCTIONS FOR TIMOTHY AND THE CHURCH (4:1 – 6:2a)

A. How Timothy can be a good minister of Jesus Christ (4:1–16)

Context

One of the salient features of 4:1–16 is the use of words and themes that Paul already employed in chapters 1–2. Consider the following: 'later times' (*husterois kairois*) 4:1/'right time' (*kairois idiois*) 2:6; 'renounce the faith' (*apostēsontai ... tēs pisteōs*) 4:1/'some have rejected ... with regard to the faith' (*apōsamenoi peri tēn pistin*) 1:19; 'consciences' 4:2/'conscience' 1:19 (twice); 'a good servant [*diakonos*] of Christ Jesus' 4:6/'appointed me to his service [*diakonia*]' 1:12; 'the sound teaching [*didaskalia*] 4:6/'sound teaching [*didaskalia*]'1:10; 'myths' 4:7/'myths' 1:4.

It would thus appear that in 4:1–16 Paul repeats the themes of chapters 1–2. I suggest that while this is true, he also includes two layers to the discussion. First, he brings an eschatological framework to the forefront that previously was not as pronounced. Second, he gives more direct commands to Timothy *himself*, that is, how he is to lead a life that does not contradict his teaching.

From a rhetorical perspective, the observations above should not be surprising. First, with respect to the matter of repetition with variation, we should remember that this is precisely how paraenesis worked. By repetition the teacher continually reminded his students of proper conduct. Second, it was crucial for a person of virtue that there would not be a gap between his speech and his actions. The famous Stoic philosopher Seneca said: 'Let this be the kernel of my idea: let us say what we feel, and feel what we say; let speech harmonize with life. That man has fulfilled his promise who is the same person both when you see him and when you hear him' (*Ep.* 75.4; cf. also 108.35). This was a common sentiment in moral philosophers. Paul may be alluding to this well-known concept to encourage Timothy in a life of integrity.

Comment

1. *The Spirit expressly says.* Paul may refer to the speech of the Spirit as found in *Holy Scripture* or to Spirit-inspired prophetic speech in the early church, or perhaps to private revelation from the Holy Spirit. In light of 4:14, the second option may be in view (cf. Marshall, pp. 536–537).

In later times. The theme of the last days as a period ripe with false teaching and apostasy is common in the Pastoral Epistles (e.g., 2 Tim. 3:1–9; 4:3) and in the NT as a whole. More than likely, it stems from Jesus' teaching (e.g., Matt. 24:4–14 and Synoptic parallels), which itself is the heritage of biblical and Second Temple eschatology. Paul often speaks of the last days as *already* having dawned with the advent of Jesus; indeed, this is common NT teaching (see 1 Cor. 10:11; 1 Pet. 1:10–12; 4:17; 1 John 2:18–25; 4:1–6).

Renounce the faith. This is the first 'vice' that Paul lists in his description of behaviour during the later times. As indicated earlier (cf. 1:7–11), catalogues of vices were often employed by Greco-Roman moral philosophers (including Jewish philosophers) of Paul's period in polemical contexts (see further 2 Tim. 3:1–9). The idea in this verse is very similar to 1:19, where the object of the verb is also 'faith'. The reality of the later times (which are already here) is that there will be apostasy from the apostolic doctrine.

By paying attention to deceitful spirits and teaching of demons. The instrument through which the false teachers are persuaded to abandon the faith is demonic in nature; it is the work of *deceitful spirits* (cf. 2 John 7), which is further described as the *teaching of demons*. In contrast to the sound doctrine, which has its source in the Spirit-inspired Scriptures (2 Tim. 3:16), the doctrine disseminated by the false teachers has its source in demons. The thought is similar to Colossians 2:8, 22, which itself goes back to the teaching of Jesus (see Mark 7:7 = Isa. 29:13). The idea is that in their distortion of the law (by reading it without Jesus Messiah as the centre and goal) and their prohibitions of marriage and certain foods (see below), the false teachers are being inspired by demons.

2. *Through the hypocrisy of liars whose consciences are seared with a hot iron.* The *liars* are the demonic-inspired false teachers, who are further accused of hypocrisy. This is in sharp contrast to the genuine (*anhypokritos*) faith that accompanies the love produced by the gospel (1:6). Paul concludes the false teachers' description with a visceral metaphor. Their state, viewed from the point of view of their consciences, is like that of cauterized skin, such as was found in branded animals (see Marshall, pp. 540–541). The result is callousness – total lack of sensitivity to the gospel. The following verses explain, by means of participles, both *why* they are in such state and the *result* of being in such state.

3. *They forbid marriage.* The union between a man and a woman in marriage was instituted by God and declared to be good (Gen. 2:18–25). This union is so sacred that man cannot dissolve it (Matt. 19:1–9). Marriage is never prohibited in the NT, although Paul explains that in certain situations it might be better to remain single (see 1 Cor. 7:6–9, 25–38). By contrast, the false teachers appear to be forbidding the very institution of marriage. It is also possible that what the false teachers are encouraging is sexual abstinence (cf. the problems addressed by Paul in 1 Cor. 7).

Demand abstinence from foods. Another example that shows the cauterization of the teachers' consciences is their command to refrain from consuming (certain) foods (cf. Rom. 14:15, 20; Col. 2:16, 21–22). But this should not be so, for Jesus declared all foods clean (Mark 7:19; Acts 10).

Which God created to be received with thanksgiving by those who believe and know the truth. With the verb *created* (*ektisen*) Paul echoes the creation narrative (cf. v. 4), where all God created was good, precisely because *he* created it. Therefore, all foods are to be received with the appropriate thanksgiving due the creator. It should be noted that the term translated as *to be received* (*metalēmpsis*) also connotes 'sharing'. Thus, God created foods to be enjoyed not only for oneself but to share with others in thanksgiving (see Rom. 14:6 and comments on 1 Tim. 6:17–19).

Since the law prohibited certain foods, Paul concludes the verse with the phrase *by those who believe* and thus *know the truth*. This does not mean that only Christians can enjoy God's provision of food. What it means is that, in contrast to Jews (and some Jewish Christians: e.g., Rom. 14; Gal. 2:11–14), believers could eat all foods with confidence because they know that Jesus had declared all foods clean. Paul reads the OT creation account through the lens of Christology, not Torah. This hermeneutic (i.e., approach to understanding the Scriptures) has already been seen in 1 Timothy 1:8–11.

4. *For everything created by God is good.* Paul now gives the reason (*hoti*, 'for') why all foods should be received with thanksgiving. Quite simply, it is because everything God has created is good, a clear echo of Genesis 1:31.

And nothing is to be rejected, provided it is received with thanksgiving. Because everything created by God is good, therefore *nothing is to be rejected*. We should note the contrast between 'everything' and 'nothing' in verse 4. The participle *lambanomenon* ('receive') is conditional, providing a stipulation. No food is to be rejected as long as there is recognition that it is the good gift of the Creator.

5. *For it is sanctified by God's word and prayer.* Paul adds another reason why no food is to be rejected: it is *sanctified*, that is, set aside, made holy, by God's word (*logos theou*). This phrase in the anarthrous form (without an article) is used by Paul in 1 Thessalonians 2:13. In 2 Timothy 2:9 and Titus 2:5 the phrase is used with the article. In all these examples the context suggests that the word of God refers to the good news of Jesus Christ. The thought, then, is that on the basis of the words and work of Christ, all food could now be consumed.

The second agency for the sanctification of food is *prayer*. The context may have to do with the eating of meat sacrificed to idols, which the hosts may inadvertently, without knowing the meat's origins, have offered to others. The words of John Chrysostom may help us understand: 'Grace before meat disinfects even what has been offered to idols' (cited in Marshall, p. 547).

6. *If you put these instructions before the brothers and sisters, you will be a good servant of Christ Jesus.* Having described and rebutted some of the commands of the demonic-inspired teachers, Paul now once again exhorts Timothy directly. The term *hypotithemenos* ('put before') carries the sense of careful reasoning while teaching (see Roloff, p. 241). In other words, Timothy's pastoral work in teaching is not just the hurling of orders but rather careful explanation and reasoning with the flock.

In contrast to the false teachers, Timothy will be a good *servant* (*diakonos*) of Jesus Christ if he instructs the church with the teaching handed down by Paul; in fact, he would be a servant just like Paul (see 1:12). We can thus say that the goodness of a Christian servant is directly related to his or her passing down the apostolic teaching.

Nourished on the words of the faith and of the sound teaching. With the term *entrephomenos* (*nourished*) Paul further describes what a good servant of Jesus Christ looks like.[1] The verb *entrephō* with the dative is found in the discourse of moral philosophy in a metaphorical sense of that on which someone is 'weaned' in order to grow and develop in virtue (see LSJ, s.v.). Paul switches from what Timothy was to give to what he receives. To continue to be a good servant of Jesus Christ, Timothy's spiritual diet must be from the same source as that which he passes down: apostolic teaching. Here the teaching is described as *the words of the faith* and *the sound teaching*. The first phrase refers to the objective aspect of faith, namely the gospel. The second phrase is an expansion of the first, with the language of *sound* or 'healthy' teaching being employed due to the polemical context of the section. That is, the *sound teaching* is being contrasted with the demonic instruction of the false teachers (4:1).

That you have followed. Paul encourages Timothy by saying that in fact he *has* followed, and continues to follow (the verb is formulated

---

1   See Marshall, p. 549; Towner, p. 303: 'Paul … pauses to deepen the definition of the "good servant of Jesus Christ".'

with the perfect tense) the sound doctrine. Paul will develop this motif in 2 Timothy 1:4–5 and 3:10–16.

7. *Have nothing to do with profane myths and old wives' tales.* Paul now gives two commands to Timothy. First, there is a negative command. Both the Greek sentence structure as well as the verb (*paraiteomai*) show this to be a strong prohibition, well communicated by the NRSV with the phrase *have nothing to do.* The first description of the myths Timothy is to reject is *profane* (*bebēlos*). Among Hellenistic Jewish authors the word is found mostly in Philo. It is usually employed in juxtaposition to something that is sacred or holy.[2] The second description of the myths is *old wives' tales* (*graōdēs*), which denotes legendary and false stories. These myths stand in comparison to the sound teaching of verse 6. Thus, rather than giving himself to *profane* myths (as the false teachers do in the name of teaching the law), Timothy is to give himself to the 'sacred [*hiera*] Scriptures' (2 Tim. 3:15).

Train yourself in godliness. The positive command is announced here. The metaphorical use of exercise language for training in morality was popular, and found in moral discourse of the Greco-Roman period. We will develop this in comments on 2 Timothy 2:3. On *godliness*, see 2:2.

8–9. *For, while physical training is of some value, godliness is valuable in every way.* In order to bring out the importance of spiritual training, Paul draws a comparison with physical training. His readers would have easily understood the comparison, given the Greco-Roman world's obsession with athletics (cf. S. Instone, *OCD*, pp. 198–199). The comparison is communicated by the contrast between *some* (*oligos*) and *every* (*pās*), captured in the NRSV translation. To be sure, Paul says, physical training has some value; but godliness is of value in *every* way. In his next comment he provides the reason.

Holding promise for both the present life and the life to come. The promise of godliness moves *beyond* this life to the life to come. The point is not that the future life is spiritual (and therefore better as such) while the present is physical. This kind of thought would have more in common with Plato than with the Bible. As Marshall (pp. 553–554)

---

2 See Philo, *Leg.* 1.62; *Migr.* 69.3; *Fug.* 114; *Abr.* 20.

shrewdly observes, it is the *kind* of life that is in view. The life to come is glorified existence in the fully realized kingdom of God (see Phil. 3:20–21). This kind of life has already dawned with the presence of the Holy Spirit in the existence of the believers (Col. 3:1–4; see further under 6:12, 19). On the 'faithful sayings' in the Pastoral Epistles see comment on 1 Timothy 1:5.

10. *For this end we toil and struggle.* Syntactically, there is debate on how this verse relates to the previous ones (cf. Marshall, p. 555). The connection may be that since godliness has an eternal promise, Paul is willing to *toil and struggle (agōnizomai)*. The struggle refers to the challenges and sufferings of the ministry.

Because we have our hope set on the living God. More than likely, the clause adds a new layer: not only do we toil and struggle in the ministry because our gospel has hope for the life beyond this one, but we also toil and struggle because the *living* God is our *hope* (cf. 1:1). And so, the adjective *living* is not accidental: since he is the living God, the one 'who alone has immortality' (6:16), he is able to give new life to those who perish in the toiling and preaching of the gospel (cf. Johnson, p. 251). The thought is similar to 2 Corinthians 1:3–11.

Who is the saviour of all people, especially of those who believe. Paul rounds off his thought with a statement that has a liturgical ring. As we have noted, the predication of God as *Saviour* is central in the Pastoral Epistles (see Introduction under Theological Emphases and comments on 1 Tim. 1:1 and 2:4). The universality of God's salvation in this verse is similar to 2:4. Scholars rightly point out that Paul is not here affirming universal reconciliation, that is, that all people are ultimately saved (cf. Knight, p. 203). Just in what sense, however, is God *the saviour of all people*? The idea is probably that for anyone to be saved, it must be through God the Saviour Jesus Christ, who died for all (2:6; Tit. 3:4; see also Rom. 5:18; 2 Cor. 5:15).

The final clause issues in a paradox: although God is the Saviour of all people, only those who believe are saved. Towner (p. 312), has helpfully added the polemical context of the letter to help explain this verse. His words are worth quoting:

> There is no ... need to posit two shades of meaning for the term 'Saviour.' Rather, in this primary missiological and polemical conclusion, Paul brings his own ministry again to the fore, linking

salvation and godly living to it. In so doing, he denounces both the extreme exclusivist claims and ascetic rigors of the heresy.

11. Paul returns to giving Timothy direct commands. On the verb *parangellō* ('insist'), see comments on 1:3. On 'teach' (*didaskō*), see 2:12.

12. *Let no one despise your youth.* With Timothy serving as Paul's apostolic extension in the congregations in Ephesus and therefore having authority over them, the question may be raised: might his youth not be an obstacle in being taken seriously when he commands the churches? Some might 'look down' or *despise* (*kataphroneō*) Timothy's relative youth. In fact, a long tradition in Greco-Roman literature looked down on youth as a time of rashness, impulsivity, lack of wisdom, etc.[3] Paul goes against cultural norms in not automatically linking authority with seniority. As we shall see below and in verse 14, it is the fact that Timothy has been called, gifted by the Holy Spirit and leads a godly life that matters.

But set the believers an example in speech and conduct, in love, in faith, in purity. Rather than letting others' view of his youth be a ministerial detriment, Timothy is to concentrate on giving them an example. To be recalled here is the widespread motif in ancient moral philosophy that in order to command others, the individual must first demonstrate virtue in his own life (Seneca, *Ep.* 108.35). This will potentially do away with any criticism of his youth. The areas where Timothy is to be exemplary are many. *Speech* refers to his use of language, probably implying self-control of the tongue (cf. Col. 3:8). *Conduct* (*anastrophē*) appears in its verbal form in 3:15 and is related to behaviour that is commensurate with the believers' reality as the dwelling of God. On *love* and *faith*, see on 1:5. *Purity* is also used in 5:2 with reference to Timothy's sexual purity towards women.

13. *Until I arrive, give attention to the public reading of Scripture, to exhorting, to teaching.* As he already mentioned in 3:14, Paul hopes to come to Ephesus soon. Until then, his representative Timothy is to devote himself *to the public reading of Scripture.* Although *public* and *Scripture* are not part of the Greek text, the context implies both

---

3 Cf. Malherbe, *Light from the Gentiles*, 1:483–6, with primary sources.

specifications. On the public reading of Scripture, see Nehemiah 8:1–8; Luke 4:16; Acts 13:15. Paul follows synagogue practice in this (cf. Johnson, p. 252). The *Scripture* Paul refers to is the OT. It is probably not coincidental that next to Scriptural reading Paul mentions exhorting and teaching. What is envisioned is a group of believers (probably some unbelievers too) meeting at a home, an overseer or elder reading Scripture, then exhorting and teaching from it (cf. Acts 13:15; Heb. 13:22). Timothy is one of the leaders doing this, and he is to continue in it.

14. *Do not neglect the gift that is in you.* If Timothy is going to accomplish the task set before him, it will not be on his own strength. Therefore, he cannot neglect the *gift* (*charisma*) in him. Spiritual gifts are given by the Holy Spirit (1 Cor. 12:4, 7–9) for the purpose of accomplishing tasks that build up the church. Romans 12:6–8 speaks of gifts of the Spirit that were mentioned above in 4:13: exhortation and teaching (see also on 2 Tim. 1:6).

Given to you through prophecy with the laying on of hands by the council of elders. With two prepositional phrases that link to the verb *given*, Paul describes the circumstances of God's ministerial gift to Timothy. The gift was accompanied by prophecy, probably meaning that the Holy Spirit spoke to either Paul (2 Tim. 1:6) or a group of church leaders, or both. Acts 13:1–2 gives us a picture of what this might have looked like: 'Now in the church at Antioch there were prophets and teachers … While they were worshipping the Lord and fasting, the Holy Spirit said, "Set apart for me Barnabas and Saul for the work which I have called them".'

The *laying on of hands* was common in the OT and NT for the conferring of an office, the invoking of God's blessing, for healing and for the giving of the Holy Spirit (see Exod. 29:10; Deut. 34:9; Acts 8:17). Here the laying on of hands by the council of elders and Paul was a recognition of God's antecedent calling and gifting of Timothy (cf. Marshall, pp. 567–569).

15–16. *Put these things into practice, devote yourself to them, so that all may see your progress. … Continue in these things, for in doing this you will save both yourself and your hearers.* There is a contrast between verses 14 and 15. Timothy is not to 'neglect' (*ameleō*) the gift of the Spirit; instead, he is to 'take pains with' (*meletaō*, BDAG, p. 627) these things, namely the injunctions of verses 6–13, which is only possible by the power of the Holy Spirit in and through him. One of the purposes for which Timothy is to be devoted to godliness is that other believers would see his *progress* (*prokopē*), language also used in moral philosophy (but not exclusive to it) to speak of progress in philosophy from being a beginner to a proficient philosopher in the life of morality.[4] His progress will win the respect of other Christians and help him lead them with less hesitation on their part.

The reason (*gar*) why Timothy is to pay close attention to his life and doctrine is that ultimate, eschatological deliverance depends on it. Paul is of course not suggesting salvation by works (note Tit. 3:4–7). He is simply reminding Timothy of the danger of preaching to others while he, Timothy, perishes (see Roloff, p. 261). The thought is similar to 1 Corinthians 9:27: 'I punish my body and enslave it, so that after proclaiming to others I myself should not be disqualified.' The false teachers, by contrast, have forsaken sound teaching and are therefore in danger of being eternally lost along with their hearers.

Theology

Direct exhortations to Timothy abound in chapter 4. The main line of thought is how Timothy is to be a 'good servant of Christ Jesus' (4:6). This is crucial not just for Timothy's sake but also for his hearers. For Timothy, being a good servant of Christ Jesus directly impinges on the well-being of his hearers. If he fails to pay close attention to his life and doctrine, both his hearers and he will perish. What a tall task for Timothy! In fact, it is quite impossible for him, and us, to accomplish it left to our own devices. And this is why Paul reminds him of the gift he has received from God. Only by relying totally on the Holy Spirit can Timothy (and we) be good servants of Jesus Christ.

---

4 See Epictetus, *Enc.* 12–13, 48, 51; Plutarch, *De prof. virt.* See also Sir. 51:17 and 2 Macc. 8:8.

B. How to care for the household of God (5:1–6:2a)

Context

Paul continues to instruct Timothy on how to care for the church. In this section he counsels him on how to relate and care for the different ages and categories of people in the church. The text resembles the household codes (*Haustafeln*) found in Ephesians 5:21–6:9 and Colossians 3:18–4:1 (cf. also 1 Pet. 3:1–7). Nevertheless, this section is not strictly speaking a code (see comments on Titus 2:1–10, which more closely resembles a household code). Rather, the probable background is the exhortations found in moral philosophers (see Dibelius and Conzelmann, p. 72). Common in the Greco-Roman world, these exhortations encouraged groups to treat one another as family members. Since Paul viewed the church as a household (see 3:4–5, 15 and Introduction), it is natural that he would avail himself of contemporary communication structures that employed family language in order to package his counsel.

One area that receives seemingly disproportionate treatment in 5:1–6:2 is the situation of widows (14 verses in total). Two main proposals as to why Paul dedicated so much space to widows are the following. First, some suggest that there existed at Ephesus a formal 'order' of widows who dedicated themselves to work in the church. For their labour they were in return cared for by the church (see Dibelius and Conzelmann, pp. 74–76). It is suggested that this order of widows was emancipating itself from the hierarchy of the church.[5] What the author (who, according to Dibelius and Conzelmann, is assumed not to be Paul, but an author writing at a later time) was attempting in this passage was to suppress the overly independent and egalitarian attitudes and activities of this order of widows.[6] His strategy was to order younger widows to be taken off the 'list' (and thereby no longer receive funds) in order that they might marry and dedicate themselves, in good patriarchal order, to their homes.

---

5 E.g., Bassler, 'The Widow's Tale', pp. 23–41.
6 See also Wagener, *Die Ordnung des 'Hauses Gottes'*, pp. 115–233; Schüssler-Fiorenza, *Memory*, pp. 284–342.

The second reading of the situation sees the basic problem as one of limited funds. L. T. Johnson puts it this way: 'the most obvious and central concern in the passage [was] the effort to balance the needs of the poor and the resources of the intentional community' (p. 271). Thus, Paul's principal aim was to help Timothy *discern* which widows had a real need. This concern to discern which widows had a real need may be seen at the beginning and end of the section, thereby forming an *inclusio* or bookend: 'Honor [i.e., assist financially] widows who are really widows ... Let the church not be burdened, so that it can assist those who are real widows' (5:3/16).

To be sure, a subsidiary aim of the passage is to correct younger widows who were acting in a harmfully independent manner (5:6, 11–16; cf. 2:9–15). But to order these to marry was not to re-establish a patriarchal ethos (as the first option suggests); rather, younger widows who were able to work or marry (and thereby procure necessary funds) should have done so in order to leave sufficient funds for older widows (60 plus) who had no one to help them. Thus, the aim of the command was love for those in direst need (cf. 1:5).

Comment
i. Instructions for the old and young (5:1–2)
1–2. Clearly the expression *an older man* does not have as its primary reference the church leaders called 'elders' (see 5:17–19) but an older man in age. When it is necessary to address an older man, it should not be done *harshly* (*epiplēssō*, which denotes lack of tact in exhorting). The command not to be harsh towards an older man is also found in Leviticus 19:32, and, indeed, in much Greco-Roman literature (Malherbe, 1:486–490). Rather than being harsh, Timothy is to exhort him *as to a father*, that is, with love and respect.

Timothy should exhort (the verb *parakaleō* is implied in the rest of vv. 1–2) younger men *as brothers*, that is, as family members. With the category of *younger women* Paul adds the prepositional phrase *with absolute purity*. The term *hagneia* has here the sense of sexual purity (see Philo, *Abr.* 98; BDAG, p. 12).

ii. Instructions for widows (5:3–16)

a. Honor the true widow (5:3–6, 9–10)

In these verses Paul explains who the real widows are who should receive material help. The main verb in verse 3 is the imperative *honor* (*timaō*). The term denotes not just 'respect' and 'regard' but also material compensation (BDAG, pp. 1004–1005; see also on 5:17). Which widows in the churches should be honoured, that is, financially compensated this way?

Widows who have living children or grandchildren should *not* receive material compensation from the church. Rather, their children and grandchildren should provide for them. This provision is presented by Paul as a religious duty: it is a form of *eusebeia (godliness)*. By providing for their widows, the children and grandchildren can *make some repayment to their parents*. This was a common attitude and mindset in the ancient world; and it still is in many parts of the majority world where pensions, social security payments, and the like either do not exist or are too small. The idea is that as parents made innumerable sacrifices in caring for their children, so it is in turn the duty of children to care for them in old age. Paul closes verse 4 by providing a theological reason for his command: such care of parents *is pleasing in God's sight*. This is probably a reference to the fifth commandment (Exod. 20:12/Deut. 5:16; cf. Eph. 6:1–3). The sentiment was also common in Greco-Roman authors (e.g., Xenophon, *Oec.* 7.19).

Paul's second guideline on what is a true widow and therefore worthy of honour (compensation) is given in verse 5. Beginning with an adversative conjunction (*de*, 'but', not included in NRSV), Paul sets up a contrast. The real widow, on the one hand, is one who has been *left alone* (*memonōmenē*). Because she has no earthly source of support, she therefore has put all her hope in God. The concrete expression of her having put all hope in God is the fact that she continuously remains in prayer. In fact, she is given to prayer *night and day*. She is much like the widow Anna in Luke 2:37. On the other hand, a widow *who lives for pleasure* (*spatalaō*) should not receive material help. The Greek verb carries negative connotations of indulgent living. It is used, for example, in Ezekiel 16:49 (LXX): 'This was the guilt of your sister Sodom: she and her daughter had pride, excess of food, and prosperous ease, but did not aid the poor and needy.' This type of widow, Paul says, *is dead even while she lives.*

In verses 9–10 Paul sets out further conditions for the recognition of a true widow. First, she must not be under sixty years of age. Although this might not seem like an advanced age to us, it was so in the ancient world (see R. Garland, *OCD*, p. 37). Second, she must have been *married only once.* Literally, the phrase is 'a one-man woman'. It is quite likely that Paul is referring to the *univira*, that is, a widow who, having been widowed, took a vow never to remarry so as to honour the memory of her deceased husband. The *univira* was praised in the Roman world for what seemed to many to be a virtuous mindset.[7] It should be noted that in many countries of Latin America this is also viewed as virtuous. One of the reasons is that remarrying is considered a dishonour to the dead husband. This attitude is common in patriarchal societies that value the honour of the dead male over the possibility of the widow having funds to survive! Is Paul capitulating to the Roman patriarchal culture in which he lived when he makes it a condition that in order to receive funds the widow should be a *univira*? This is unlikely. It is more probable that Paul is thinking in practical terms. For a widow who was already sixty *and* had married only once was less likely to have many children who could care for her. Given the limited funds of the church, Paul had to think of those widows who were most vulnerable: the *univira* would have been such. Thus, the qualification here is not a matter of virtue but of the harsh realities of poverty and being an older woman in the ancient world.

Third, *she must be well attested in good works (ergois kalois,* cf. 2:10; 5:25; 6:18; Tit. 2:7, 14; 3:8, 14). A general list of what these good works are follows: she raised children (perhaps including orphans, thus Marshall, p. 595); she has shown hospitality (also expected of the overseer at 3:2 and Tit. 1:8); she has *washed the saints' feet* (a demonstration of hospitality and humility, cf. Luke 7:36–50); she has given aid to those afflicted, probably including the giving of alms (a quintessential Jewish demonstration of piety); in short, she

---

7   See G. Clark, *OCD*, p. 1573; Lightman and Zeisel, *'Univira'*, pp. 19–32; Malherbe, *Light from the Gentiles*, 1:491–492.

has devoted herself to every kind of good work (thus bringing the 'list' to a close in parallel with the good works of verse 9).

b. Refuse the younger widows (5:11–15)

Under *Context* we indicated that the fundamental problem with regard to widows was, on the one hand, the obligation of the church to aid widows, and, on the other hand, the reality of limited funds. Paul's solution had been to instruct Timothy to give aid to 'real' widows, a category that he defined for Timothy. The ones who were not real widows should not be helped, lest funds run out to help those widows who truly needed help. Paul defines this former group of widows as 'younger', and tells Timothy why they should not receive aid.

In this text Paul presents a number of criticisms against younger widows. But it should be noted that Paul is not criticizing young widows *as such*, as if it were more virtuous in itself to be an older rather than a younger widow. Clearly, many younger widows in the congregations in Ephesus were behaving in ways that were not in accord with godliness – and this is one of the reasons why Paul tells Timothy to refuse to put younger widows on the help list. But another reason is that the younger widows could work and still had a chance to be married and raise a family.

The command to *refuse* younger widows is given a reason in the clause that follows: *For when their sensual desires alienate them from Christ, they want to marry, and so they incur condemnation for having violated their first pledge* (11–12). This phrase is confusing, for in 5:14 Paul counsels the younger widows to marry. Yet here it is viewed as incurring condemnation (the participle *echousai* probably being causal). How can we explain this apparent contradiction? The two most viable options are the following: (1) When powerful sexual desires (*katastrēniaō*, see BDAG, p. 528) awake, the younger widow breaks an initial vow or agreement (*tēn prōtēn pistin*, 'their first pledge' v. 12) in which she promised to serve Christ wholeheartedly as a widow. (2) Moved by sexual desires, the younger widow is even willing to marry an *unbeliever*, or possibly cohabit with him before marriage. In the case of remarriage, the wife will probably also have to adopt the gods of her new husband (assuming the husband was not a Christian). Remarrying into *this* situation essentially means abandoning the

Christian faith. This second option seems the better one because: (1) Paul does encourage marriage (v. 14) as long as it is 'in the Lord' (1 Cor. 7:39); (2) One can read *pistis* in verse 12 with the common Pastoral Epistles understanding of belief/trust for salvation. Here it is likely that the initial act of conversion is in mind.

Next, Timothy is to refuse the younger widows because they become *busybodies* (v. 13). Another disqualification is provided on the basis of the fact that, in addition to the behaviour described in verses 11–12, they simultaneously (*hama ... kai*, 'besides that') cause harm with their tongues. The terms used to describe their activities, namely *idle ... gossips ... busybodies* (*argē, phlyaros, periergos*) paint a picture of a woman who has nothing better to do than to make the rounds around homes in order to meddle and engage in tantalizing gossip. In doing this they are *saying what they should not say*. The language is strikingly similar to Titus 1:11, where it is said of the false teachers that they 'are upsetting whole families (*holous oikous*)' and teach 'what is not right to teach' (*didaskontes ha mē dei*). We may thus imagine that these widows, in the context of their useless chatter, may be passing down false teaching (Marshall, p. 603; Towner, pp. 354–355).

c. Younger widows should marry (5:14–16)

With the inferential conjunction *oun* (*so*) Paul brings his instructions about widows to a close. With three consecutive complementary infinitives he expresses what the younger widows should do: *marry, bear children, and manage their households*. Why the younger widows should dedicate themselves to their homes is answered in terms of a goal: *so as to give* (*didonai*) *the adversary no occasion to revile us*. The phrase *no occasion* is frontloaded in the Greek text for emphasis: Paul's concern is that *the adversary*, that is, Satan, would use the behaviour of the women (exhibited by the younger widows of the church) to possibly goad unbelievers to speak against the believers and the gospel (see Introduction under Occasion).

That Satan could hijack the widows' behaviour to attempt to derail the mission is not some far-off possibility. By beginning verse 15 with *already* (*ēdē* is frontloaded in the Greek) Paul provides the logic for the statement in verse 14. The fact is that *some* (*tines*) have already *turned away to follow Satan*. The verb *ektrepō* ('to turn, turn

away', BDAG, p. 311) is used two other times in the Pastoral Epistles in a negative way: to turn to 'meaningless talk' (1:6); to turn to
'myths' (2 Tim. 4:4). The current verse is more intense in expression,
as the turning is to the actual source of false teaching, Satan. The
thought here is similar to 1:19–20.

iii. Instructions on the treatment of elders (5:17–25)

Paul continues providing Timothy instructions on how to shepherd
the different groups in the churches. In these verses he shifts to
the treatment of leaders in the church, namely elders. This is not a
reference strictly to older men, which Paul has already mentioned in
5:1. Rather, the instruction refers to that group of men who bore the
honorific title of 'elder' (on which see comments under Tit. 1:5–9).

17–18. *Let the elders who rule well be considered worthy of double honor.*
Paul introduces here a group of leaders of the early church. In his
letters the title is also found in 1 Timothy 5:19 and Titus 1:5. In
1 Timothy 4:14 Paul spoke of the *presbytery*, probably the council
of elders. The title is found in the Septuagint to refer to rulers of
Israel (e.g., Exod. 3:16, 18; Lev. 4:15; Num. 11:16; Josh. 7:6; 8:10). The
title is also found in Jewish inscriptions (e.g., *CIJ* 1:294, §378; 1:432,
§595) and in Philo to speak of leaders of the synagogue (e.g., Philo,
Flacc. 74, 76, 80). In the Greco-Roman contexts elders could refer to
leaders in a number of contexts (e.g., city leaders: Diodorus Siculus,
Hist. 21.18.1; Aristotle, *Pol.* 1272A).[8] As the title suggests, the *presby-
teroi* in view were senior members of the congregation. We should
think of the elders as a collective term for a group of leaders, not
necessarily an office.[9] Other scholars, however, think of the elders
as synonymous with the overseers, and thereby holding an office
(see esp. Marshall, p. 177). On the relationship between elders and
overseers, see the comments in Titus 1:5–9.

Paul speaks here of *the elders who rule well.* The verb 'rule' (*proistēmi*),
which was used in 3:4 of the work of the overseer, is used here with the

---

8 I am indebted to Keener, *1 Peter*, pp. 355–359 for many of these sources.
9 Clarke, *A Pauline Theology*, p. 56: 'Accordingly, "eldership" is not an
   individual office, but an honoured status, bringing with it membership
   of an influential and respected body.'

adverb *well*. The use of *honor* (*timē*) has the same sense as in 5:3, namely monetary compensation. The term *double* could refer to *acknowledging* worth in addition to monetary payment, or to the ruling elders receiving double *monetary* reward (e.g., Roloff, p. 308; Johnson, pp. 277–278).

Especially those who labor in preaching and teaching. Paul singles out those who work 'in the word' and teaching. This statement assumes that not all elders were teachers, suggesting that a large part of the labour of the elder was simply leading. As regards the connection between 'in the word' and *teaching*, we probably have an example of hendiadys, although Towner (p. 363) sees a potential distinction from the perspective of the audience: the first activity refers to evangelizing unbelievers (cf. 2 Tim. 4:2) while the second refers to church instruction.

For the Scripture says. Paul grounds his command on *graphē*, Scripture (see 2 Tim. 3:16). The first Scripture is Deuteronomy 25:4, which Paul quotes word for word from the Septuagint but puts the imperative at the end, while the Septuagint has it at the beginning (following the Hebrew text). Paul uses the same Scripture with the same purpose in 1 Corinthians 9:9, where he states that God gave the command not solely for the sake of the ox but for ministers of the gospel. The second Scripture is a word for word quotation from Luke 10:7. It is likely that Paul's source is either a proto-form of Luke or a written source such as Q (see Marshall, pp. 616–617, for the different possibilities). It should not be missed, whatever the nature of the source, that the words of Jesus are viewed as *graphē*, Scripture inspired by God (2 Tim. 3:16).

19. *Never accept any accusation against an elder except on the evidence of two or three witnesses*. Given the type of work of the elder as well as their dignity as elders, accusations against them should be examined carefully. Paul therefore commands Timothy to use the biblical procedure of Deuteronomy 17:6; 19:15, where a legal case could not be settled with fewer than two witnesses.

20. *But those elders who are sinning* (NIV). The use of the present tense in this phrase probably suggests continuous action. These would be *elders*, therefore, who perhaps have been warned before yet continue in sinful behaviour.

Rebuke them in the presence of all. The verb *elengchō* is used five times in the Pastoral Epistles (1 Tim. 5:20; 2 Tim. 4:2; Tit. 1:9, 13; 2:15).

As the context makes clear, the goal is to rehabilitate: *so that the rest may also stand in fear.* The public nature of the rebuking as well as the goal link this passage with others in the NT that have to do with church discipline (e.g., Matt. 18:15–20). The public rebuking of an elder will instil fear of God in the other elders.

21. Given the difficulty of being willing to rebuke an elder (probably because of his respected status), Paul concludes this section with a solemn warning. He needs to impress upon Timothy the gravity of impartial judgment. *I warn you* (*diamarturomai*) is also used in 2 Timothy 2:14 and 4:1 and can be rendered as 'solemnly urge' (BDAG, p. 233). The seriousness of the charge is highlighted by invoking *God and … Christ Jesus and … the elect angels.* Paul wants Timothy to envision the heavenly court (or throne room) as the witnesses of the command he is receiving. The content of the command is given with a *hina* clause, with *these instructions* looking backwards. What Timothy must do is to *keep* the instructions, with the emphasis falling on *how* he is to keep them: *without prejudice, doing nothing on the basis of partiality.* The two phrases give a sense of completion to the command: 'The first phrase says that one is not to come with pre-formed opinions, the second one that one is not to be ruled by partiality to one party or the other' (Marshall, p. 620).

22. *Do not be hasty in the laying on of hands, and do not share in the sins of others.* Without more specific context, it is difficult to offer a precise explanation of this verse. Two clues, however, may help. First, there is the phrase on *the laying on of hands*, which was also employed at 4:14. Second, the use of cognates *mēdeni* ('no one') and *mēde* ('and not, but not, nor' [BDAG, pp. 644–647]) shows a connection between the two prohibitions. Thus, in context, the command is probably that Timothy should not commission or 'ordain' a person to a ministry without previous, careful consideration of their life and doctrine (cf. 3:10).[10] The result of hasty ordination (to use a later term) will be that Timothy will end up being part of any corruption in the church (cf. Johnson, p. 281). Rather than doing this, Timothy is to keep himself *pure* (*hagnos*, see on 5:2, 11).

---

10 Thus the majority of commentators, going back to the Greek fathers; cf. Marshall, pp. 620–622.

23–25. Like a wisdom teacher who is like a father (1:2), Paul adds statements that will be helpful for the younger Timothy: both for his own health struggles and wisdom as a minister of the gospel.

Timothy is to avoid drinking only water and instead drink a little wine. The reason for this is Timothy's apparent delicate health and the often bad quality of water in the ancient world. The advice to drink wine for digestive problems was common (cf. Johnson, p. 282, for primary sources).

Verses 24–25 are wisdom statements that, in context, continue instructing Timothy in the evaluation of elders for the church. The contrast in these verses is between *sins* in verse 24 and *good works (erga kala)*. Timothy must understand that in some cases the sins of some people (in view are probably elders) will be *conspicuous* or evident (*prodēlos;* see also Heb. 7:14) even prior to final *judgment.* While for other people, their sins will be uncovered only in final eschatological judgment. This proverbial statement is probably meant to ease the pressure on Timothy as he does his best to discern those qualified for leadership in the church.

Likewise for good works, sometimes they are apparent in the present life and sometimes not. Yet Paul adds that good works will nevertheless shine through, possibly echoing Jesus' statement as found in Matthew 5:14.

iv. Instructions for slaves (6:1–2a)

1–2. Paul wraps up the 'household' orders that began in 5:1 with instructions for slaves. The use of *yoke* to speak of the burden of slavery was common in antiquity.[11] The fact that Paul speaks of the *yoke* of slavery rather than simply saying 'Those who are slaves', implies that for Paul this was not an ideal condition in which to exist. Although slaves could be found labouring in different spheres of society (e.g., public office, fields and, worst of all, the mines), it is likely, given the context of 5:1–6:2a, that Paul is referring to household slaves. Most slaves had become enslaved as prisoners of war, although many also came to this state as a result of piracy

---

11   Used in Sophocles, Herodotus and Plato (BDAG, p. 429). For the
     Roman period, see 1 Macc. 8:17.

and brigandage; and children of slaves were also slaves (K. Bradley, *OCD*, pp. 1375–1376). It should be noted that, in contrast to American slavery, ancient slavery was not based on skin colour. Furthermore, especially in the case of Roman households, many of the Greek slaves were educated and taught the children of elite Romans to speak and read Greek (with its highly regarded classical literature among Romans).

In contrast to Ephesians 6:5–9 and Colossians 3:22–4:1, where the emphasis lies on the eschatological rewards of the slaves when they serve 'as to the Lord', here the framework is more *missional*. The slaves need to honour their masters (verse 1 envisions unbelieving masters while verse 2 believing masters; cf. Oberlinner, 1994, pp. 263–264): *so that the name of God and the teaching may not be blasphemed*. The first part of this negative purpose clause (*hina mē*) alludes to Isaiah 52:5 (LXX): 'This is what the Lord says: "Because of you my name is continually blasphemed among the nations".' The actions of the slaves who bear the name of Jesus Christ, if not respectful of their masters, could lead to slandering God's holy name, a name whose character is explained in *the teaching*.[12]

Verse 2 shifts to those slaves who belonged to believing masters. The temptation for the Christian slaves in this scenario was to show less honour, in fact to be *disrespectful*. The verb here is *kataphroneō*, which was also used in 4:12 of the potential of believers 'looking down' on Timothy because of his youth. Why would this be a temptation for slaves with believing masters? *Because they are brothers*, and thereby of equal worth in the *ekklesia* of the Lord (Phil. 16). The refrain, 'familiarity breeds contempt', may be the potential attitude that develops from the perspective of the slave. Rather (*alla*) than letting the slave's spiritual kinship be a cause for disrespect, it should actually lead to *serving them all the more*. With another causal clause (*hoti*), Paul gives the reason why slaves should behave this way: *Since those who benefit by their service are believers and beloved*. The logic is that their work is an act of Christian service to their beloved brothers. The thought is

---

12 *Didaskalia*. See on 1:3, 10. For the connection of 'the teaching' with God's action as 'Saviour', see Tit. 2:10.

similar to Galatians 6:10: 'So then ... let us work for the good of all, *and especially for those of the family of faith.*'

The phrase *by their service* (*tēs euergesias*) translates a noun that was often used to refer to wealthy citizens who made civic contributions to the *polis* or city-states (cf. Johnson, p. 284). What is surprising is that Paul uses this language to refer to the acts of service of Christian slaves! It was the wealthy master who was the patron and benefactor of those inferior to him. Here Paul subverts traditional mores by placing the slaves as ones who by their service actually become benefactors of their masters![13]

On the other hand, there are those who, based on the syntax of the sentence, understand the thought to be the following: slaves need to be even more keen to serve believing masters because these believing masters actually practise kindness to the slaves. In this case Paul would be making the more common comment that slaves benefit from the kindness of their masters, especially when those masters are believers.[14]

Theology

This section, probably inspired by the household code, shows us Paul's practical outworking of the reality of the church as a *familia*, a household. One of the crucial aspects that Paul highlights is the missiological grounding of the ethic that governs the logic of the relationships in the church. That is, the precepts are given with one eye towards unbelievers: improper behaviour on the part of believers can jeopardize the winning of unbelievers to the Christian faith.

What defines behaviour as improper is often taken from the moral codes of Paul's contemporary culture. This is most jarring in the commands to slaves. For those of us living in Western liberal

---

13 Cf. Seneca, *Ben.* 3.18–20, who speaks of slaves providing a *beneficium* to their masters by means of their service. It seems that Seneca bases this possibility on anthropology, i.e., the equality of humans, while Paul bases it on ecclesiology, i.e., on the fact that masters and slaves are brothers.

14 For this interpretation see Fitzgerald, 'The Stoics and the Early Christians', pp. 145–146, citing Xenophon, *Oec.* 12.5–7.

democracies, we might have expected Paul, in the name of Christ, to exhort slaves to strive for and attempt their liberation. Should not a Christian society be intolerant of slavery? Yet here Paul does not exhort slaves to free themselves but actually to be the best slaves possible! On this basis some scholars view the ethos of 1 Timothy as a return to patriarchal structures, a devolution from the egalitarianism of Galatians 3:28 (e.g., Fiorenza, p. 279). Was Paul championing structures that kept slavery in place? And what would this mean for us as we seek to apply this part of Scripture?

It would be a simplistic answer to say that Paul had capitulated to the structures of his contemporary period. As modern readers, we must do our best to understand that slaves in the Roman empire could not attempt a *social revolution* without suffering devastating consequences; or, thinking, equally anachronistic, that slaves could 'peacefully' march against slavery in the Roman forum. This is by no means an attempt to justify or soften the brutal slavery of that or any other period. On the one hand, then, it is clear that Paul envisions a life where the kingdom of God is gaining ground and the result is that there is no slavery, beginning with the Christian assembly (Gal. 3:28). This is clearly his desire and what he is instituting in the sphere of the local congregations of believers. On the other hand, he could not simply command slaves to free themselves given the socio-economic realities of the Roman world. This strategy could have hurt slaves severely,[15] for (for example) those slaves who worked in the household or estates received food, clothing, housing and medical care, among other benefits. If a slave was suddenly freed, he/she might not have the means to stay alive. The Greco-Roman world did not have the infrastructure to free slaves and give them work and housing the next day.

Paul's strategy, in fact, is much more subtle, but in no way less effective for that. By inculcating on his readers the transcended reality of the kingdom of God – a reality where Christian slaves were the brothers of their believing masters and where the former

---

15 Not to mention the possibility that this strategy could have caused an immediate and violent clampdown on the congregations Paul established and its leaders. I owe this insight to the editor of the series.

could be called benefactors of the latter – Paul quietly subverts the values of his society from inside the structure itself; it is a transformation from below. For the only true Christian way for the transformation of the structure is if the gospel penetrated deeply into the lives of people. Then there may be hope for the Christian world view to affect government institutions. The paradox is that this is the reason why Paul wants slaves to be respectful, lest the progress of the gospel be abated. For to stop the progress of the gospel is to stop the only possibility of lasting change in culture.

5. FINAL SET OF INSTRUCTIONS (6:2b–21)

A. False teachers and the love of money (6:2b–10)

Context

Two broad statements need to be made about the literary context of this section. First, several terms and concepts have already appeared in two previous sections of 1 Timothy: *didaskō* ('to teach'), *parakaleō* ('to urge, encourage'), *heterodidaskaleō* ('to teach otherwise') and *didaskalia* ('teaching'). Most of these terms also appeared at the heading of the two previous major sections, namely 1:3–11 and 4:11–16 (cf. Roloff, pp. 326–329). We thus have, beginning at 6:2b, a *third set* of similar instructions. In this final round Paul returns to previous themes; but he also adds a new layer: *the relationship between false teaching and money.*

The second broad contextual theme has to do with the *coherence* of 6:2b–21. In their influential commentary, Dibelius and Conzelmann (pp. 83–91) suggested that the material consists of miscellaneous and *ad hoc* instructions without a dominant theme. However, the majority of commentators have now rejected this. While different

themes have been suggested as holding together the coherence of
6:2b–21, Marshall's suggestion that the thread that goes through
this section is the connection between wealth and false teachers
appears sound (Marshall, pp. 633–636).

Comment

2b. *Teach and urge these duties* looks both backwards and forwards.
On the one hand, Timothy is to continue addressing the *duties* he
is to engage in as a servant of Jesus Christ, which may refer either
to the entire epistle to this point, or, more probably, the material
from 5:3 – 6:2. On the other hand, the pronoun *these* may also be
referring to the final exhortations in the letter, namely the warning
against false teachers and love of money.

3–5. In verse 3 Paul repeats the thought of 1:3–4. Notable here is
the linkage between *the sound words of our Lord Jesus Christ and the teaching that is in accordance with godliness.* In 1:10 we saw the adjective *sound*
(*hygiainō*) modifying *teaching* (*didaskalia*); here we see *hygiainō* linked
with *Jesus Christ.* More than likely, the idea is that the 'sound words'
stem from Jesus Christ and are *about* Jesus Christ.[1] These words
from and about Jesus are the content of the teaching, expressed
with the noun *didaskalia.*

In verse 4 Paul makes a declaration that serves as the apodosis
(the 'then' part in an 'if … then' clause) to verse 3: the state of the
person who does not hold to the apostolic teaching is one of blindness and foolishness (perfect tense of *typhoō*; cf. BDAG, p. 1021).
Because the person is in such a state, Paul can add the following:
understanding nothing ('nothing' is emphatic). Rather than (*alla*) *understanding,* what such a person has is *a morbid craving for controversy and
for disputes about words.* The verb *noseō* ('to be sick, ailing', BDAG,
p. 678) is often used figuratively to express an overwhelming desire
for something.[2] The false teacher, rather than being consumed with

---

1   Thus we have a combination of a genitive of source with an objective
    genitive.
2   See, e.g., Plato, *Phaedr.* 228B, where it is used with 'words' or 'speech' (*tō
    nosounti peri logōn*); Plutarch, *De laude* 546F, of someone who is obsessed
    with his own reputation: *tois peri doxan nosousin.*

the gospel, is consumed with *controversy* (*zētēseis*, cf. 1:4) and *disputes about words*. This last phrase translates a single Greek word, *logomachia*, which means 'word-fight'. It is also used at Titus 3:9 and 2 Timothy 2:14 (cognate).

The result that comes from this obsession with words and arguments rather than the sound *didaskalia* is expressed with a list of vices: *envy, dissension, slander, base suspicions*. The first vice translates *phthonos*, which often appears in Paul's catalogue of vices (e.g., Rom. 1:29; Gal. 5:21; Tit. 3:3). The word is used to describe people who are far from God. *Eris* ('dissension, strife') is used in Titus 3:9 in the context of false teaching: 'But avoid stupid controversies, genealogies, dissensions (*ereis*), and quarrels about the law, for they are unprofitable and worthless.' On *slander* (*blasphēmia*), see on 1:13. The last vice is *hyponia* ('suspicion, conjecture', BDAG, p. 1040; on the verbal form, see Acts 13:25; 27:27). Sirach 3:23–24 provides a parallel: 'With matters greater than your affairs do not meddle, for things beyond human understanding have been shown to you. For their presumption has led many astray, and their evil fancy [*hyponia ponēra*] has diminished their understanding.' Thus, *base suspicions* may have to do with doctrinal 'conjectures', which often lead to unfounded suspicions between fellow believers. The vice expressed with *wrangling* (*diaparatribē*; used only here in the NT) is often used elsewhere figuratively in the discourse of moral philosophers. The term suggests a sickly, diseased state that is brought about by constant arguing.[3]

Paul expands on the character of false teachers with three participles. Their teachings produce unhealthy attitudes and activities among believers because the false teachers are spiritually sick. They are described as *depraved in mind* (*diaphtheirō*), again suggesting disease (the noun can describe something that is 'rotting or decaying', BDAG, p. 239). The term *mind* (*nous*) refers to the individual's 'way of thinking' (BDAG, p. 680) or mentality (see 2 Tim. 3:8; Tit. 1:15, referring to false teachers). Paul asserts that the false teachers are *bereft of the truth* (NIV 'who have been robbed of the truth'), that is, have lost the gospel and sound teaching (on 'truth', see on 2:4). Lastly, Paul says of the false teachers that they view *godliness* (*eusebeia*,

---

3 See Malherbe, *Paul and the Popular Philosophers*, p. 126.

see Introduction and on 2:2 and 3:16) as *a means of gain*. For the first time in the Pastoral Epistles the concept of using doctrine in a corrupt way, namely for self-enrichment, is employed. The specific context for understanding precisely how the false teachers could use godliness as a means of financial gain is not made clear. There are some clues in 2 Timothy 3:6–7. In any case, the problem was not that of making a living from the gospel (see 5:18). The problem was their corrupt motivation, greed, and the fact that they were teaching a *false* gospel, characterized by the telling of myths and the stirring of controversies.

To sum up verses 3–5, then, it is clear that Paul returns for the third time to speak of the false teachers. The theme of the teachers as simultaneously corrupt and corrupting is repeated with new terminology. We thus have variations of a theme in verses 3–5. The new motif is the use of godliness as a source of wealth. This motif is expanded in what follows.

6–8. These verses pick up the theme of material gain and compare the proper attitude to that of the false teachers (v. 5). The section unfolds with a proverb-like declarative statement followed by a corroboration.

Of course, there is great gain in godliness combined with contentment. Paul makes a play on words with *porismos* (*gain*) and *peirasmos* (*temptation*, v. 9): *godliness* does actually lead to *gain*, but not when the thought is only of economic profit. One of the key terms in this verse is *contentment* (*autarkeia*; cf. 2 Cor. 9:8; Phil. 4:11). The word is very common in the moral philosophers to speak of the good (or virtuous) life (cf. Johnson, p. 294). Paul probably uses the language of popular philosophy, even if his theological foundations are from the OT. The sense is that a life of godliness, which is content with God's provision, is a life of plenty. The thought is similar to Proverbs 30:8–9: 'Give me neither poverty nor riches; feed me with the food that I need' (LXX: *syntaxon … moi ta deonta kai ta auterkē*). It is clear from Philippians 4:10–13 that this contentment is only possible through the power of Jesus Christ.

Paul now corroborates the sapiential statement: *For we brought nothing into the world and we can take nothing out of it* (NIV). This statement has affinities with both Jewish wisdom (e.g., Job 1:21; Ecc. 5:14; *Wis.* 7:6) and Greco-Roman philosophy (e.g., Seneca; cf. Roloff,

p. 355). There is a syntactical difficulty at the beginning of the second line, for the best textual tradition reads *hoti* (translated with 'and'), which means 'because, for, that' (see the discussion in Marshall, pp. 646–648). I have chosen the NIV's translation as it seems to best carry the logic of the text.[4] Whatever the precise sense of the syntax, the general meaning is clear, namely the futility of accumulating wealth in light of death (Oberlinner, 1994, p. 280). Rather than engaging in wealth-seeking futility, we shall be content[5] *if we have food and clothing.* The second direct object (*skepasma*, 'covering', BDAG, p. 927) can refer to both clothing and shelter.

9–10. With the use of the phrase *those who want to be rich* (*hoi boulomenoi*), Paul returns to speak of the dangers of seeking wealth. In these verses it is more than likely that he has in mind not just the false teachers but all Christians.

What is the result of those whose chief goal is to become wealthy? They *fall into temptation and are trapped by many senseless and harmful desires.* This sentence is full of pathos in Greek, linking three nouns rapidly with the conjunction *kai* ('and'). Furthermore, each of the three words has the letter *p*, thereby showing partial alliteration: *peirasmos, pagis, epithymia.* The first term, not very common in Greek literature, carries the sense of being goaded into doing something wrong. That is, those who want to get rich will find themselves in situations full of potential for evil.[6] The second term was used in 3:7 to speak of the overseer falling into 'the snare (*pagis*) of the devil'. It is also used in 2 Timothy 2:26. The third word is *epithymia* ('desire', neutral), which is modified by *senseless* and *harmful.* The language is

---

4 Some manuscripts (ℵ[2] D[1] and Majority Text), include 'it is clear that' (*dēlon hoti*). Although not original, this reading understands the logic of the passage. I paraphrase the verse as follows: 'We brought nothing into the world, [and it is clear] that we can take nothing out of it.'

5 The future of *arkeō*, 'to be content, satisfied', probably has an imperative sense to it: 'We *must* be content.'

6 As indicated above, there may be a play on words here: the Greek *peirasmos* sounds very much like *porismos* ('gain'), used in vv. 5–6. The point is that a life consumed with the accumulation of wealth actually does not lead to gain but to potential entrapments.

similar to the critique of moral philosophers against avarice, which leads to destruction.

Just as he did in verses 7–8, Paul corroborates his statement with a proverb that was (in different forms) found in many Greco-Roman authors (Seneca, *Ep.* 87.31–34; Philodemus, *Oec.* 14.5–6). *For the love of money is a root of all kinds of evil.* Two comments must be made about this statement. First, the word *root* is the very first in the sentence, thereby showing how foundational for evil love of money can be. Second, there is the question of how we should translate the Greek *pas* ('all, every'). Many translators add 'kinds' in order to make clear that love of money is not the *absolute* source of evil. However, we must remember that this is a proverbial statement, and it is in the nature of proverbs to absolutize or hyperbolize. This in part is what makes proverbs function so well: they strike the reader, thereby causing careful reflection. Thus, I prefer the KJV translation: *For the love of money is the root of all evil.*

The topic of love of money (*philargyria*) is expanded with the following dependent clause: *and in their eagerness to be rich some have wandered away from the faith and pierced themselves with many pains.* The main verb of the first clause is the compound *apoplanaō* ('to mislead, go astray'), accompanied by the prepositional phrase *from the faith* (*apo tēs pisteōs*). An identical use of this prepositional phrase is found in Acts 13:8: 'But the magician Elymas ... tried to turn the proconsul *away from the faith.*' The second clause should be read as expressing result: *and* [as a result, they] *pierced themselves with many pains.* Apostatizing from the faith because of love for money has painful outcomes. The verb *peripeirō* can mean 'to impale' (BDAG, p. 803). The pain of apostasy is so profound that Paul uses gruesome language to express it. The thought is similar to what he said before about false teachers in 1:19, although there he used the metaphor of shipwreck.

B. Exhortation for Timothy to remain faithful (6:11–16)

11–12. Paul returns to exhorting Timothy directly. In order to encourage him, he uses the epithet *man of God.* This appellation has a distinguished history in the OT, being used of Moses (Deut. 33:1; Josh. 14:6; 1 Chr. 23:14), Samuel (1 Sam. 9:16), Elijah (1 Kgs 17:24), David (2 Chr. 8:14), as well as other prophets

(1 Sam. 2:27; 1 Kgs 12:22; 13:1). It was an honour for Timothy to be called a *man of God*. Precisely because this is who he is, Timothy must *shun* love of money. Instead, he should *pursue righteousness, godliness, faith, endurance, gentleness* (*praypathia*, see comments on 2 Tim. 2:25 and Tit. 3:2). This list of 'virtues' is similar to the fruit of the Spirit of Galatians 5:22.

The third command uses an athletic and military metaphor to make the same point, namely the need for perseverance in the Christian life. Timothy is to *fight the good fight of the faith*. The language used (*agōnizou ton kalon agōna tēs pisteōs*) indicates that Christian faithfulness is a struggle that demands discipline and determination, not unlike that of an athlete or soldier (see further under 4:10; 2 Tim. 2:3–5; 4:7).

The fourth command reads: *take hold of the eternal life*. The verb *epilambanomai* ('to take hold') is almost always used of taking hold of something material.[7] Here the idea is of *seizing*, which implies alertness and focus. As we will see (cf. 6:19), the practice of being generous with money is given as a way of keeping this command. What Timothy is to seize, then, is *eternal life* (cf. 1:16; see also Rom. 2:7; 5:21; 6:22, 23; Gal. 6:8). Paul uses eschatological language, which is based on the Jewish concept of the two ages: the present evil age and the one to come, which will begin at the end. For Paul and the early Christians the age to come is *already* here, inaugurated in the resurrection of Jesus and the giving of the Spirit.[8] Eternal life can begin now with the renewal of the Holy Spirit at conversion: 'If you sow to your own flesh, you will reap corruption from the flesh, but if you sow to the Spirit, you will reap eternal life from the Spirit' (Gal. 6:8; cf. Tit. 3:5). This command should not be understood in some Pelagian way, that is, as if God will grant salvation as a response to human action. The thought is more subtle and dialectic, calling Timothy to persevere in the sound doctrine that includes the concrete actions of faith. *Eternal life*, then, is not something that was initiated by any human work of Timothy, as if he could grasp it by

---

7   Thus the majority of uses in the literature. We find a figurative use in Prov. 4:13 ('Take hold of instruction') and Polybius, *Hist.* 15.8, of taking hold of hope.

8   See Ridderbos, *Paul*, pp. 205–206; Dunn, *Theology of Paul*, pp. 317–319.

sheer self-will. Rather, he was *called* (the passive form of the verb indicates that the initiative lies with God), a term that is used soteriologically in the Pastoral Epistles: 'God, who saved us and called us with a holy calling, not according to our works but according to his own purpose and grace' (2 Tim. 1:9).

For which you made the good confession in the presence of many witnesses. Most scholars agree that the nature of the confession alluded to is Christological, probably: 'Jesus is the Messiah' or 'Jesus is Lord' (cf. Towner, pp. 411–412; cf. Rom. 10:9). The *occasion* for this confession is more difficult to determine. It could refer to (1) ministry ordination (Knight, pp. 264–265); (2) confession at baptism (Johnson, p. 307); or (3) a trial (Holtz, p. 141). The connection with 2 Timothy 2:2 probably tips the scale in favour of the first option.

13–16. As Paul continues to exhort Timothy, he raises the seriousness of the latter's vocation by calling on God himself as witness (see also 5:21). *In the presence of God, who gives life to all things.* The predicate of God as the life giver (*zōogonōn*) appears only once in the Septuagint referring to God (1 Sam. 2:6).[9] Why would Paul use this uncommon appellation of God? More than likely, it is a more solemn way of speaking of God as creator (so Marshall, p. 662), particularly in view of the direct object *ta panta* ('all things'), which looks back to creation.

The second witness is Jesus Christ, the one *who in his testimony before Pontius Pilate made the good confession.* Paul employs the faithfulness of Jesus as an example for Timothy. In particular, Paul harks back to Jesus' trial, where he confessed that he was the Messiah instead of denying it to avoid execution (Matt. 27:11// Mark 15:2//Luke 23:3). Paul, who himself will bear witness to Christ until the end (2 Tim. 1:8; 4:6–8), wants Timothy to do the same. This entire phrase has a liturgical ring to it, perhaps pointing to an early confession.

Having called God and Christ Jesus as witnesses, Paul now specifies, with a complementary infinitive, what Timothy's task is: *to*

---

9 א and the Majority Text read the more common *zōopoieō* (e.g., Rom. 4:17; 8:11, etc.). The reading accepted here (the more difficult reading) is found in D A as well as the Alexandrian minuscules 33 and 81, among others.

keep the commandment without spot or blame. The commandment is probably a reference to 6:2 and what follows. However, it may also include the entire letter (cf. 1:5). Using alliteration (both adjectives begin with alpha and have the letter *p*), Paul clarifies *how* the commandment is to be kept: it is to be kept *without spot or blame* (on the second adjective, *anepilēmptos*, see on 3:2 and 5:7).

Timothy is to remain faithful, keeping the commandment until *the manifestation of our Lord Jesus Christ.* This clearly refers to the return of Christ. However, instead of using the more common *parousia* (1 Thess. 4:15) or *phaneroō* ('to make manifest', Col. 3:4), Paul uses *epiphaneia.* The term is found abundantly in the Christological language of the Pastoral Epistles (2 Tim. 1:10; 4:1, 8; Tit. 2:12; 3:4–7). *Epiphaneia* has a rich history of use in the Hellenistic period, where it refers, besides other uses, to the intervention of kings in battle to procure the victory for a city. These kings were viewed as representations of the gods. In the OT and Hellenistic Jewish literature the word is used to speak of the Lord's appearance to save his people (e.g., Ps. 117:27; Zeph. 2:11; 2 Macc. 2:21; 3:24; 5:4; 3 Macc. 2:9; 5:8, 51; see also our discussion of Tit. 2:11). Towner (p. 416) summarizes the meaning of the data: 'From the Jewish (canonical and extracanonical/Judaistic writings), it is evident that the language … was quite compatible for discussing God's divine appearances and interventions to save his people.' It is thus Christologically significant that the word is used of the appearance of Jesus Christ, for it supports his deity by using language of Christ that is also used of God.[10]

The salvific manifestation of Jesus Christ will occur *at the right time.* The thought is similar to 2:6, where we saw that the timing of God's salvific revelation belongs to God's prerogative.

He who is the blessed and only sovereign, the King of kings and Lord of lords. Talk of God, particularly of his future manifestation in Jesus Christ to rescue his people, moves Paul to a doxology. On *blessed* (*makarios*), see on 1:11. *Sovereign* (*dynastē*) can be used of human rulers,

---

10 On *epiphaneia* as Paul's appropriation of Hellenistic Jewish language and conceptuality to highlight the transcendent yet immanent breaking-in of Christ, see the work of Lau, *Manifest in the Flesh.*

but is often found in doxological contexts praising the Lord (e.g., Gen. 49:24; Job 13:15 [LXX]; 2 Macc. 3:24 [with *epiphaneia*]; 12:15, 28; 3 Macc. 2:3; 5:51; 6:39; Sir. 46:5, 7, 16). Here Paul tells us that God is the *only* ruler.

In 1:17 Paul spoke of God as 'the King of the ages'. The expression *King of kings* (the phrase is also found in 3 Macc. 5:35; Dan. 4:37), is similar, but the language is more glorious. A variation of this phrase is used of Christ in Revelation 17:14 and 19:16, showing the early Christian fluidity of language between God and Jesus. The same occurs with the second expression, *Lord of lords*. With the use of these two phrases, it is difficult to imagine the readers *not* making a connection with imperial Rome. In the Roman propaganda in the east, the emperor was hailed as king and lord. By making this statement Paul is unmasking the imperial claims without calling on his readers to revolt.[11]

Paul continues the doxology, switching to the use of apophatic language. That is, in order to speak of God, he must say what God is *not*, for human language is incapable of speaking directly of the transcendent God unless analogy or negation is used. The first predicate is *immortality (athanasia)*, which God alone possesses. The word is not found in Hellenistic Judaism but stems from the Greco-Roman language of gods and emperors (Marshall, p. 667). The emphasis falls on the fact that life, although shared with creation as a gift, properly belongs to God alone. The thought is akin to Psalm 90:2: 'Before the mountains were brought forth, or ever you had formed the earth and the world, from everlasting to everlasting you are God.' In the NT, John's prologue also comes to mind: 'In him was life, and the life was the light of all the people' (John 1:4).

With another alpha privative (*aprositos*, 'unapproachable') Paul continues the doxology with beautiful symmetry. God is the one who *dwells in unapproachable light*. The OT texts to which Paul alludes are at least Exodus 33:17–23 and Psalm 104:1–2. The statement

---

11   See Wright, *Paul and the Faithfulness of God*, pp. 1305–1319, who uses the language of 'implicit confrontation' to speak of this type of Christian language *vis-à-vis* the Roman empire.

speaks of God's transcendence and holiness (see also 2 Tim. 6:18). As such, God cannot be known by creation in the same unmediated way that he knows himself in the immediacy of Father, Son and Holy Spirit. Because this is who God is, it follows that no human *has ever seen or can see* him. Calvin provides a helpful clarification: 'We cannot see God in this nature, as it is said elsewhere, "Flesh and blood shall not possess the kingdom of God." … We must be renewed that we may be like God, before it be granted to us to see him' (*The First Epistle to Timothy*, p. 169).

Given this reality of God, Paul concludes the doxology in the following way: *To him be honor and eternal dominion. Amen.* God already and always has all honour and dominion. Ascribing these perfections to him in worship is therefore simply *acknowledging* who he already is.

C. Final exhortations and closing (6:17–21)

17. The dominant theme of this section is the subject of wealth, which was first seen in the polemics of 6:5–10. The term for 'rich' (*plousios*) and its cognates appears four times in this section. *As for those who are rich in the present age.* In the Greek, the transition from verse 16 to 17 is much brusquer than the NRSV would lead us to believe. There are no conjunctions or particles between the 'Amen' of verse 16 and the beginning of 17. Paul simply launches: 'Command those who are rich' (NIV). Two comments may be helpful. First, warnings to the wealthy were a common *topos* in the popular morality of the period.[12] Paul is thus availing himself of a well-known practice in order to exhort rich believers to behave in a way that is commensurate with their Christian profession. Second, the warning is couched in eschatological language: they are the rich *in the present age.* The effect of this way of phrasing things is to begin deflating any potential pride: they may be rich now, but this 'now' will pass quickly!

There are two prohibitions that Timothy is to command the rich (which implies that there were wealthy believers in the congregations

12 For this section I build on Malherbe, *Light from the Gentiles*, 1:507–557.

of the province of Asia): *not to be haughty or to set their hopes* on wealth. The verb *hypsēlophroneō* ('to be proud, haughty') is a *hapax* in the NT. As Malherbe demonstrates (see previous footnote), the use of the term in philosophical and popular literature emphasizes the self-centredness to which wealth can lead. The second prohibition, also common in popular literature, is equally important in OT wisdom (see esp. Pss 49; 52:7; 62:11; Prov. 23:4–5). One should not put hope on wealth. With a dative that serves as the object of the infinitive (Knight, pp. 272–273), Paul speaks of the *uncertainty* (*adēlotēs*) of wealth. The thought is similar to Proverbs 23:5: 'When your eyes light upon it [wealth], it is gone; for suddenly it takes wings to itself, flying like an eagle toward heaven' (see also Luke 12:16–21).

Instead of putting their hope in fleeting wealth, the rich must rather (*alla*) put their hope *on God who richly provides us with everything for our enjoyment*. The emphasis falls on the phrase *panta plousiōs*, which can be translated as 'all things richly.' Thus, God not only provides for his children, but he does so richly or splendidly. The point is not that being a Christian will inexorably lead to wealth. Rather, God is not only the proper object of our hope but also the one who is dependable to provide for our every need. We note also the play on the word for 'wealth' or 'rich', namely *plousios*. Whereas Paul has been using the term exclusively to refer to money, and, further, with a negative connotation, now the adverb *plousiōs* does not refer to money but to the manner in which God provides.

Interestingly, Paul closes the thought with a prepositional phrase that has the function of purpose or goal. God provides richly *for our enjoyment*. Malherbe suggests that this goal of wealth stands in contrast to the popular moral philosophy of the period (e.g., Cynics, Stoics, Epicureans). The popular Cynic view was that money was worthless and thus good for nothing. The Epicurean view was more complex, at times suggesting that wealth was to help others in order that in the future the gift would be reciprocated. By contrast, Paul views wealth as a good gift of the creator and thus to be enjoyed. What this enjoyment looks like is unpacked in what follows.

18–19. *They are to do good, to be rich in good works, generous, and ready to share.* The verbal forms in this list are all in the infinitive, thereby going back to the imperative (*command*) of verse 17 (Knight, p. 273; Towner, pp. 426–427). The infinitives of the verse may be a *concretization* of the command. On the other hand, Malherbe argues that the infinitives of verse 18 should be viewed as *epexegetical* to the phrase *for our enjoyment* at the end of verse 17. We could thus paraphrase as follows: 'God provides for our enjoyment, *namely*, doing good, being rich in good works, and so on.' This reading explains enjoyment as an experience that is related to that which is done for the other. 'The reason for enjoyment is that this is what God intends in providing richly. What is required is not reflection but action' (Malherbe, p. 92). This interpretation means that the possibility of enjoying God's good gifts is irreducibly linked to our sharing those gifts with others. Material goods are ultimately of no enjoyment if they are selfishly hoarded: 'For it is in giving that we receive', said St Francis.

With the participle *apothēsaurizontas* ('to store up, lay-up', BDAG, p. 110; the verb is a *hapax*), Paul explains the *result* of obeying the commands of verses 17–18.[13] It is *a good foundation (themelios) for the future*. The thought is similar to 3:13, which speaks of the reward of deacons who serve well: '[They] gain a good standing for themselves and great boldness.' The framework is eschatological, more specifically referring to final judgment. Paul clarifies the thought with a purpose clause: *So that they make take hold of the life that really is life*. On the verb 'to take hold', used with 'life' as referring to eternal life, see comments on 6:12. This verse does not teach some form of Pelagianism (meaning that our present deeds win eternal life for us); this would be an unequivocal contradiction of what we find elsewhere in the Pastoral Epistles (e.g., 2 Tim. 1:9; Tit. 3:4–5) and Paul's other letters. Marshall thus explains the clause as follows: 'We have the normal NT teaching that lack of the expression of faith in good works is an indication of the lack of faith itself, and conversely' (pp. 673–674). Another way of grasping Paul's thought is more straightforward: eschatological judgment will indeed be based on the storing up of good deeds, but these deeds are only possible by the enabling of the Holy Spirit, thus excluding any possible pride on the part of the person.

---

13   Thus most commentators. The NRSV brings out this function of the participle by adding *thus* to the beginning of the verse.

20. After the exhortation to the wealthy, Paul returns for one final time to exhort Timothy directly: *Guard what has been entrusted to you.* The Greek sentence reads: 'Guard the deposit.' The phrase is found in Greco-Roman literature to speak of the process 'of entrusting some commodity with a person who is to ensure its safe-keeping … and eventually return it to its owner' (Towner, p. 430). The deposit that Timothy is to guard is the gospel, more specifically, the gospel as Paul has passed it down to Timothy. This is a theme that is developed further in 2 Timothy (see comments on 2 Tim. 1:11–18). Paul elsewhere speaks of the gospel tradition he had received and passed down (see, e.g., 1 Cor. 11:2; 15:1–7; 2 Thess. 2:15). In these other letters he uses the vocabulary of *paradosis* ('tradition'), or *paralambanō* ('to receive') or *paradidōmi* ('to transmit'). In the Pastoral Epistles, by contrast, he prefers *parathēkē* ('deposit'). It is probable that this shift is due to the particular circumstances apparent in the Pastoral Epistles. That is, since Paul is writing to one of his delegates in a situation where false teaching is threatening sound doctrine, he must emphasize the keeping and protection of the gospel (cf. Marshall, p. 675; Towner, p. 431).

One of the ways in which Timothy will be able to guard the deposit is by avoiding *the profane chatter and contradiction of what is falsely called knowledge.* The adjective *profane* (*bebēlos*) was used in 4:7 with the old wives' tales that Timothy must have nothing to do with. *Chatter* (*kenōphonia*) is also used with *bebēlos* in 2 Timothy 2:16. The term was also used in popular philosophy to refer to speech devoid of any meaning (Roloff, p. 374, n. 223). *Contradiction* was a word used in rhetoric and logic for the presentation of an opposite proposition (Johnson, p. 311). Thus, Timothy is to stay away from rhetorically charged argumentations that really have no substance (i.e., scriptural content) and are thus profane.

Although it is probable that the false teachers called this type of empty chatter 'knowledge', Paul unmasks it by labelling it *falsely called.* Because the gospel is not the content of the speech of the opponents, it necessarily is false. In their holding and profession of false knowledge, *some have missed the mark as regards the faith.* The thought is identical to 1:6, thus forming an *inclusio* for the letter.

21. *Grace be with you.* This repeats the wish of 1:2. On *grace*, see comments on 1:2 and 1:14. With this ending, Paul reminds Timothy of the need to depend on the grace of God daily as he ministers the gospel.

Theology

As ministers of Jesus Christ, it is our obligation to protect the gospel. Paul has presented two significant dangers. First, there is the danger of false teaching. Both the numerous exhortations to stop false teaching, as well as the brief descriptions of the false teaching, make it clear that this is an aspect of ecclesial life that needs constant attention. The way to combat false doctrine is to remain committed to the gospel in the context of congregations that honour the Scriptures as their ultimate authority. In this framework, commitment to the ancient creeds and their recitation in worship (e.g., the Apostles Creed, the Nicene Creed) is extremely helpful. The second danger presented in this text is the love of money. Wisdom is necessary to avoid this evil: (1) we need to remember that the greatest wealth is 'godliness with contentment'; (2) we need to remember that material wealth is only temporary; (3) we need to remember that God is the good provider of all our needs, but that this provision is inherently for sharing; (4) we need to remember that true life is only complete in eschatological fulfilment by union with the God of verses 15–17.

SECOND TIMOTHY
COMMENTARY

1. SALUTATION (1:1–2)

Context

On the background of the salutation in Paul's letters, see comments on 1 Timothy 1:1–2.

Comment

1–2. While in 1 Timothy Paul's apostleship was based on God's command (*epitagē*), here it is based on (or 'accords with', Greek *kata*) *the promise of life that is in Christ Jesus*. The text is thus similar to 1 Timothy 4:8 where *promise* and *life* are joined. As 2 Timothy 1:10 will go on to make clear, it is only on the basis of the gospel that the individual can have a share in this eschatological and blessed life. Paul thereby connects his apostleship to the gospel, the guarding of which is the main thrust of 2 Timothy. This is another way of saying that he is a servant of the gospel, which defines his apostolicity (see 1:10–11; 1 Tim. 2:7; Tit. 1:3). On Timothy, see 1 Timothy 1:2. The blessing that Paul invokes on him is the same as in 1 Timothy 1:2. See commentary there.

2. INITIAL INSTRUCTIONS: A CALL FOR TIMOTHY TO PERSEVERE IN GUARDING THE GOSPEL (1:3 – 2:13)

Second Timothy is divided into two large sections, both of which are exhortations to Timothy to persevere in protecting the gospel. The first section (1:3 – 2:13) begins with Paul reminding Timothy of the fact that both his (Paul's) and Timothy's ancestors served the true God, who is the God and Father of Jesus Christ. Therefore, Timothy must continue to persevere; and Paul is certain that he will because the same faith of his mother and grandmother is also alive in Timothy (1:3–5). Paul then moves on to remind Timothy that faithfulness to the gospel can only happen if Timothy depends on the power of the Holy Spirit to rekindle the gift. For the Holy Spirit, which has been given to Timothy, is a Spirit of 'of power and of love and of self-discipline'. Timothy must therefore press on by suffering with Paul for the purpose of gospel proclamation and preservation. For Paul himself is a prisoner, being treated as a common criminal even though he is actually a messenger of the good news (1:6–14). In fact, Timothy must follow the example of Onesiphorus, who was not ashamed of the gospel, or of Paul, a prisoner on account of his adherence to Christ and his promulgation of the gospel. Onesiphorus ministered to Paul while the latter was in jail (1:15–18).

The first main section concludes with Paul exhorting Timothy to be strong 'in the grace that is in Christ Jesus' and to communicate the sound doctrine to others who could teach it. Paul gives Timothy three illustrations that highlight the dedication needed to accomplish the task: soldier, athlete and farmer. The most important example is Jesus Christ himself, who suffered and yet was vindicated by God by being raised from the dead. Timothy must be faithful to the Messiah Jesus even unto death. But Paul reassures Timothy that even when his faithfulness lacks, God's does not: he will not turn his back on Timothy (2:1–13).

A. Timothy's pedigree of faith (1:3–5)

Context

Of the Pastoral Epistles, 2 Timothy begins with the formal section most like the other letters of Paul, that is, with Paul's thanksgiving for his addressees. The giving of thanks is normally based on the gifts and spiritual fruit of his addressees. For example, 1 Corinthians begins with the following words: 'I give thanks to my God always for you … for in every way you have been enriched in him, in speech and knowledge of every kind' (1:4–5). This way of starting a letter or speech was known in the Greco-Roman period as an *exordium*. Two things characterize an *exordium*. First, the speaker mentions the virtues of his listeners, which, in the case of Christians, have been granted by the Holy Spirit. This serves to build rapport with the audience and gain its good will. Second, the subject matter of the speech is briefly announced (see, e.g., *Rhetoric to Alexander* 3.14). Paul, who was certainly aware of the conventions of ancient rhetoric and used them to communicate persuasively to the communities he pastored, begins 2 Timothy with an *exordium*. However, instead of thanking 'the gods', as was the case in pagan letters, he thanks 'God the Father and Jesus Christ our Lord'. Second, Paul's thanksgivings are much longer than those found in pagan letters. He uses the thanksgiving section in order to accent God's gracious work in the lives of his readers. Thus, he mentions Timothy's *sincere faith*, which simultaneously shows both a virtue of the addressee as well as the main theme of the letter,

namely the guarding of the faith. In addition, Paul mentions another
virtue of Timothy: the excellent pedigree of faith that belongs to him
through his grandmother and mother. Paul will use this last theme
to encourage Timothy to guard the faith.

Comment

3. One of the key questions for understanding these verses is why
Paul includes the following phrase in his mention of thanksgiving to
God: *whom I worship with a clear conscience, as my ancestors did*. He probably mentions his ancestors to create symmetry between Timothy
and himself: just as Paul and his ancestors served God with a clean
conscience, so do Timothy and his grandmother and mother (i.e.,
his ancestors), who have a *sincere faith* (*anypokritou pisteōs*, as also found
in 1 Tim. 1:5 along with *clean conscience*). This is to say that Timothy's
faith 'pedigree' is as strong as that of Paul, the persevering apostle.

Paul qualifies his service (*latreuō*, on which see Rom. 1:9) in two
ways. First, he links his ancestors and himself with respect to the
God they served. Second, he affirms that this service has been
carried out with a *clear conscience*. As we explained in 1 Timothy 1:5,
one of the emphases on conscience in the Pastoral Epistles is the fact
that God has cleansed it in salvation, thereby helping the believers
discern what is according to the gospel and what is not.

The last clause – *when I remember you constantly in my prayers night
and day* – is temporal, indicating Paul's constant prayer for Timothy
when he (Paul) gives thanks to God.[1]

4. *Recalling … I long to see you.* These two verbal forms are participles of attendant circumstance in Greek, revealing to Timothy
Paul's inner state as he prays for him. The Greek *epipotheō* ('I long')
expresses a sentiment that is 'both tender and fervent' (Spicq,
p. 703). Paul's desire to see his son in the faith is kindled when, as he
prays, he recalls the latter's *tears*. Most commentators agree that this
refers to their sad parting, the last occasion Paul had seen Timothy.

The purpose ('so that', Greek *hina*) for which Paul longs to see
Timothy is so that the former *may be filled with joy*. Here we have a

---

1   For the similar construction in Paul's letters, see Rom. 1:8–10; 1 Cor.
    1:4; Eph. 1:15–16; Phil. 1:3–4; Col. 1:3; 1 Thess. 1:2; 2 Thess. 1:3.

very vulnerable portrait of Paul: he may be lonely in prison, and the presence of Timothy would fill him with joy. The thought that church leaders must mask their sadness for fear of not appearing like strong leaders has no biblical support but probably stems more from the (false) image of the modern 'superhuman' CEO.

5. *I am reminded of your sincere faith.* Paul attaches a third participial phrase (*labōn*) that goes back to verse 3, that is, his declaration of constant prayer on behalf of Timothy.[2] As he prays, he remembers Timothy's genuine faith. This is in contrast to the hypocrisy of the false teachers, who use the faith as a means of gain (3:2; 1 Tim. 6:5–10).

First in your grandmother Lois and your mother Eunice. In fact, the same type of faith that dwells in Timothy first dwelled in his ancestors (just like Paul's!), namely his grandmother and mother.[3] The name *Lois* has not been attested. *Eunice* is more common, going as far back as Hesiod's *Theogony* 246 (BDAG, p. 409; LPGN has thirteen references). From Acts 16:1 we know that Timothy's mother was a Jewish Christian. She taught him the faith from the Scriptures since the time Timothy was an infant (2 Tim. 3:14–15). Paul is persuaded (perfect tense of *peithō*, 'I am sure') that such faith also dwells in Timothy.

Theology

'It is the same God of the Christians who was [also] of the Jews.' Thus commented Ambrosiaster on verse three of the text above.[4] It is one of the striking aspects of these verses that Paul links the God he serves with a clear conscience to the God his ancestors also served with a clear conscience. But how could this be, since clearly Paul serves the God and Father of the Lord Jesus Christ, who was not known as the incarnate Lord to his ancestors? In fact, behind this brief statement of 1:3 there stands the monumental theological thought that is the cornerstone of Paul and the rest of the New

---

2 But see Weiser, p. 93, who takes the participle as the *basis* for Paul's prayer.

3 See Bray, p. 319.

4 Ambrosiaster, *PL* 17, p. 512. I owe the quotation to Spicq, p. 702. The translation from the Latin is mine.

Testament. And that is that the God of Abraham, Isaac and Jacob is none other than the Father of Jesus Christ. Consequently, to serve Jesus Christ as Paul was doing was not a *discontinuation* of serving the God of his fathers but the only possible *continuation* of serving him. This means that serving Jesus Christ was not a contradiction of Jewish piety but the fulfilment of it.[5] If Timothy, then, for his part, is going to continue serving the God of his ancestors, he must guard the gospel of Jesus Christ, the fulfilment of the Sacred Scriptures that he had been taught since childhood (3:14–17).

B. The call to guard the gospel: duty, grounding and empowerment (1:6–14)

Context

The structure of this paragraph is twofold: (1) a call to follow certain commands and (2) reasons for following those commands. In keeping with the genre of 2 Timothy, namely that of a personal paraenetic letter (see Introduction under Genre), Paul gives Timothy numerous personal exhortations regarding his duty as a minister of the gospel. In verses 6–14 there are five verbal forms that are imperatival: 'rekindle', 'do not be ashamed', 'suffer', 'hold' and 'guard'. These commands are then grounded in essentially two realities. First, there is the fact that Timothy has received the empowering Holy Spirit (vv. 7–8, 12). Second, Paul mentions the wonderful salvation that believers have received through the appearing of Jesus Christ (vv. 9–10). The first reality we can call pneumatological; the second reality is both soteriological and Christological.

Comment

6. *For this reason.* With this phrase Paul looks back at what he has just said, namely the genuine faith that resides in Timothy. This, in part, serves as the basis for the personal commands that follow.

I remind you to rekindle the gift of God that is in you. The infinitive *to rekindle* has the function of an imperative, something Timothy must do in light of the pedigree of faith that is his. The verb *anazōpyreō*

---

5   This is also what the Paul of Acts protested in 24:4 and 26:6.

(a *hapax* in the NT, it is often used in Jewish-Hellenistic literature in both physical and metaphorical ways: e.g., 2 Kgs 8:1, 5; 1 Macc. 13.7). That which Timothy is to rekindle is *the gift (charisma) of God … in you*. More than likely, the thought here is the positive counterpart of what was said in 1 Timothy 4:14: 'Do not neglect the gift (*charisma*) that is in you.' The gift is a reference to the spiritual gifts that build the church, given by God. Often Paul points to the Holy Spirit as the giver of the gifts (see, e.g., 1 Cor. 12:4–11). The language of 'rekindling' is a metaphorical way of reminding Timothy to remain in step with the work of the Holy Spirit, who is the giver of the gifts (see below). The reason why the metaphor of rekindling is used stems from the biblical language that links the Holy Spirit with fire (see Luke. 3:16; Acts 2:3; 1 Thess. 5:19).

On the laying on of hands and spiritual gifts, see comments on 1 Timothy 4:14. Here, Paul focuses on his own hands instead of the council of elders. The most likely reason for this is the intimate, I-You nature of the personal paraenetic letter genre.

7. *For God did not give us a spirit of cowardice*. With the conjunction *gar* ('for') Paul provides a reason for why Timothy is to rekindle the gift. Verse 7 clarifies that we must not be afraid wherever the Spirit may lead us, even if it be a dangerous situation. For, in fact, God has not given us a 'spirit' that is cowardly (*deilia*, the opposite of *andreia*, the cardinal Greek virtue of *courage*). Rather, the Holy Spirit he has given us is characterized by *power … love … and self-discipline*.[6] *Power* and its cognates are linked in the Pastoral Epistles with the capacity to bear witness to the gospel (1:8; 4:17; 1 Tim. 1:12). Thus, power here is not primarily related to the ability to perform miracles or the capacity for pious living. Rather, it is God's enabling to bear witness to the gospel in intimidating circumstances. *Love* (see 1:13; 2:22; 3:10) is usually connected with virtue or piety. Love for God and neighbour is in fact the goal of Paul's instructions in 1 Timothy (1:5). The mention here may be to remind Timothy that love for other people is necessary when witnessing in a context of persecution (cf. 2:24–25). The Holy

---

6 Thus, I understand the genitives here as 'descriptive genitives'. See Wallace, *The Basics of New Testament Syntax*, pp. 45–46; Knight, pp. 371–372.

Spirit grants us the capacity to love (especially) in these circumstances. Lastly, *self-discipline* (or 'self-control', *sōphronismos*) and cognates are used in other ethical passages (see comments under 1 Tim. 2:9 and 15). In the setting of bearing witness in the face of opposition, this quality probably designates the capacity to refrain from exploding in vengeful attitude or abusive words towards the enemies of the gospel; rather, Timothy must endure under insults (cf. 1 Pet. 2:23). The Holy Spirit alone can give the capacity to endure in such circumstances.

8. With this verse Paul brings to summation (note the Greek *oun*, 'thus') the thoughts of verses 6–7, while at the same time clarifying the ultimate goal of this section. Negatively, Timothy must not be ashamed of bearing *testimony to our Lord or of me his prisoner*. In the ancient socio-economic Roman context, incarceration was a profoundly shameful situation, which affected not just the prisoner but also those related to the prisoner. Thus, it is likely that in part Paul had been abandoned in his first defence of the gospel because of his status as a prisoner (4:16). But to be ashamed of Paul the prisoner was a betrayal of both Paul *and* the gospel, for Paul had a unique relationship to the gospel as an apostle to the nations (see Rom. 1:1–6, 13–15; 15:14–21; Gal. 1:11–17; 2:7–8; 1 Tim. 2:7). Furthermore, the Christian love ethic includes the visiting of prisoners, a duty that goes back to Jesus himself (see Matt. 25:34–46). Rather than being ashamed, Timothy is to *join with me in suffering* (*syngkakopathēson*) *for the gospel*. The verb in both its compound and simple forms appears three times in this letter (2:9; 4:5). The dative of advantage *for the gospel* provides the context for which sake Timothy is to suffer: it is so that the good news of the death and resurrection of Christ be proclaimed and that the elect may experience the salvation of God's gospel.[7]

This capacity to suffer in the midst of gospel proclamation is possible by *relying on the power of God*. As we saw in vv. 6–7, it is the Holy Spirit who provides this power, for he himself is God's power.

9. *Who saved us and called us.* Mention of the gospel in the previous verse leads Paul to reflect on God's work of salvation. God is designated as the one *who saved us*, thereby expressing God's identity as Saviour, which is the most common appellation of God in the

---

7   The thought here is virtually identical to 1 Cor. 9:23.

Pastoral Epistles (see Introduction under Theological Emphases and comments on 1 Tim. 1:1; 2:4; Tit. 2:10). By way of hendiadys Paul specifies salvation as calling: *who saved us and called us*. This is an OT way of speaking of God's salvation.[8] Paul also employs this language in other letters (Rom. 8:28; 1 Cor. 1:9; Gal. 1:6). Paul is here highlighting God's *election* of a people to be his special possession. That is, God – in Jesus Christ – has freely chosen us to be his people (see below for further explanation of election). This salvific calling is termed in verse 9 as a *holy calling*. That is, the goal is for the chosen people to lead lives of complete dedication to God, which includes service to others (Gal. 5:13), purity (1 Thess. 4:7) and proclamation (1 Pet. 2:9–10).

Paul continues on the theme of salvation and election by now concentrating on its basis. He first speaks of it negatively: God chose us *not according to our works*. This assertion is central to Paul's proclamation of the gospel in that it explains that our present and final justification before God is not secured by obedience to the Jewish law or good works in general (see esp. Rom. 3:20; 23–30; Gal. 2:15–16; 3:7–14, 22; Tit. 3:5–7). Paul then states positively the basis of our salvation: God chose us *according to his own purpose and grace*. The term *purpose* (*prothesis*) is used by Paul to refer to God's eternal plan or *predestination* (e.g., Rom. 8:28; 9:11; Eph. 1:11; 3:11). In light of Romans 11:5, which uses the phrase 'election of grace' (*eklogē charitos*), it is likely that we should understand *purpose and grace* as a case of hendiadys. Election is thus presented as fundamentally a gracious act of God for salvation. It is important to underline this, for many Reformed interpreters automatically substitute Paul's language of election for the Calvinist concept of double predestination, as if election *as such* is double predestination.[9] By contrast, in this text election is essentially a salvific decree.

---

8 See esp. Gen. 21:12; Is. 41:8–9; 42:6; 43:1; 45:3; 48:12; 49:1, 6; 51:2; 54:6; 61:6; 62:12.

9 By double-predestination we refer to the doctrine of Calvin (*Inst.* 3.21–22), further developed by Reformed scholasticism, where a fundamental contrast exists: some are elected to salvation while others for damnation.

For Paul, Jesus Christ is the centre of the gospel. Thus, Paul concludes verse 9 by linking God's gracious election to Jesus Christ: *This grace was given to us in Christ Jesus before the ages began*. The two Greek prepositions, *in (en) Christ Jesus before (pro) the ages began*, clarify Paul's main thought. At the same time, the prepositions may lead us to ask what precisely *in Christ* and *before the ages* mean. Some understand this admittedly difficult clause as merely indicating that God planned our salvation before creation, and that, in time, Christ became the agent of God's election by his incarnation.[10] Thus, in this view, Christ himself played little or no part in the eternal decree of election: this was the work of the Father, who then in time sent the Son to make the election effective.

More exegetically and theologically satisfying for this verse are the explanations of Spicq and Johnson, who view election as fundamentally linked with the election of the *pre-incarnate Christ*. Spicq explains: 'Our predestination is a function of the Beloved's predestination; the incarnation and his death are themselves the first object of the election of the Father ... which is summed up in: "to gather up all things in him"' (p. 716). And Johnson: 'If the plan and gift were already given "before time," how could they be given "in Christ Jesus"? ... But if the phrase modifies both *prothesis* and *charis*—as it seems it must—then we see here the notion of Jesus as God's plan for the world from the beginning' (pp. 348–349). The significance of this line of interpretation is at least twofold. First, Jesus Christ would not just be the means of salvation in time, that is, the means of God accomplishing his eternal decree, which only *subsequently* includes the Son. The more likely interpretation is that Jesus Christ, the eternal Logos, is already himself the elect in whom humanity is by extension elect, since he came for all of humanity. Second, this would mean that God's eternal decision to create humanity was not that of an

---

10   Thus Guthrie, p. 142, speaks of Jesus as the 'medium' of grace. Towner, p. 470: 'It states simply the way in which God's grace was made available to people.' See also Weiser, p. 120.

abstract or hidden God, a *deus absconditus*, but that of the God and
Father of the Lord Jesus Christ.[11]

10–11. God's gracious election, determined in his eternal counsel
before creation, *has now been revealed*. The verb *phaneroō* ('to reveal'),
used here in the passive voice to explain that God is the one who
reveals, is often employed by Paul to speak of God's own disclosure
of his eternal salvific plan, which takes concrete form in time (e.g.,
Col. 1:26; 1 Tim. 3:16). The *now* of revelation is clarified with the following prepositional phrase: *through the appearing of our Saviour Christ
Jesus*. It is in the Christ-event, which begins with his incarnation
(1 Tim. 3:16), continues into the parousia (Col. 3:4) and concludes
in final judgment (1 Tim. 6:14; 2 Tim. 4:1, 8), that the eternal plan
is revealed. On the term *epiphaneia*, see comments on 1 Timothy
6:14 and 4:1, 8.

What it means for Christ Jesus to be the Saviour is explained
in the following clause with a negative/positive contrast (*men ...
de* in the Greek: 'on the one hand ... on the other hand'). On the
one hand, Christ *abolished death*. The verb *katargeō* is also employed
in a similar manner in 1 Corinthians 15:26: 'The last enemy to be
destroyed (*katargeitai*) is death.' By his own death and resurrection
Christ has brought death to an end; it can no longer have the victory
over those who have been saved. On the other hand – and serving
as the other side of death in the logic of the gospel – is resurrection.
And so in his work as Saviour, Christ has *brought life and immortality
to light*. Life (*zōē*) is used often to speak of *eternal* life, that is, the
glorious existence of the life to come of believers, which even now
is present (1:1; 1 Tim. 1:16; 4:8; 6:12, 19; Tit. 1:2; 3:7). This life is not
simply eternal in quantity but also in quality, as it is a sharing in the
life of the exalted Christ, who is himself our very life (cf. Col. 3:4). It
is therefore not surprising that in his death and resurrection Christ
not only brought to light[12] life, but also *immortality*, that is, the life
of God himself (cf. 1 Tim. 1:17).

---

11   See further Barth, *CD* II.2 pp. 3–203. It should be noted that we
     do not follow Barth in some of his apparent universalist tendencies.

12   The verb *phōtizein* speaks of revealing something that was previously
     hidden and in darkness. In this context, the emphasis falls on the

This new, wonderful reality of the destruction of death and the appearance of eternal life is proclaimed *through the gospel*. It is no wonder that Paul is willing to suffer for this gospel! It is thus a reason to rejoice – not be ashamed – that he was *appointed a herald and an apostle and a teacher* of this gospel (for the terminology used here, see on 1 Tim. 2:7).

12. *And for this reason* refers to the previous verse, namely Paul's appointment as a minister of the gospel, a glorious gospel, that brings life and immortality. *I suffer as I do,* namely in his imprisonment and the accompanying shame. *But I am not ashamed, for I know in whom I have put my trust.* This statement is similar to Romans 1:16. The emphasis here is more on Paul's relationship to the gospel as an individual.[13] What is it about the God in whom Paul has trusted that leads him not to be ashamed? *I am sure that he is able to guard until that day what I have entrusted to him.* The two key words in this sentence are: *able* (*dynatos*) and *what I have entrusted* (*parathēkēn*). The adjective *dynatos* is used in Romans 4:21 and 11:23 in the context of salvation history to speak of God's capacity to bring to being that which is not. In Luke 1:49 God is called *the Mighty One* (*ho dynatos*) because he is able to save his people. Paul asserts that God is able to 'guard my deposit' (i.e., the gospel). The word *parathēkē* was used in 1 Timothy 6:20 where Timothy was commanded to 'guard the deposit'. As we argued there, the reference is to the gospel. *Until that day* refers to the parousia when God will judge the living and the dead (4:1, 8).

To sum up, Paul's situation as a prisoner of a crucified man, executed as a criminal, would doubtless have been a reason for shame in his Greco-Roman culture. Yet, he boldly affirms that he is not ashamed. In Romans 1:16–17 he tells us that he is not ashamed of the gospel because it is God's power for salvation. One expects the same reasoning in 2 Timothy, especially after the statement

---

(note 12 *cont.*) resurrection of Christ Jesus piercing the darkness of death with his magnificent light. The language here is likely meant to take the reader to God's creation in Genesis 1:1–5.

13 The emphatic perfect tense *pepisteuka* ('I have put my trust') is probably an intensive perfect, highlighting Paul's continued allegiance to the gospel to the present period, despite all his sufferings.

concerning salvation in verses 9–10. But that does not happen. Instead, lack of shame is now linked to God's capacity to maintain 'the deposit' until the end. In light of 4:6–8 we should understand Paul's logic as meaning that at the parousia God will vindicate his gospel – and by implication the servant of the gospel, Paul – because the final judge will be no other than *ho kyrios*, the Lord, who had been crucified and who is himself the content of the gospel (1 Tim. 3:16).

13–14. *Hold to the standard of sound teaching that you have heard from me.* The two verses bringing this section to a close are expressed in the form of two imperatives. The first (*eche*, 'hold') is in the present tense, which implies that the holding to the standard should be a continuous activity. The *standard* or 'pattern' (cf. 1 Tim. 1:16) that Timothy is to hold is the *sound teaching* (genitive of apposition). As indicated earlier (cf. 1 Tim. 1:10), sound teaching refers to the genuine apostolic doctrine that brings healing to those who receive it (see also 4:3; 1 Tim. 6:3; Tit. 1:9; 2:8). It is also a requirement of deacons to 'hold fast' (*echontes*) to the 'mystery of the faith', which is a different way of expressing the concept of sound doctrine. Paul clarifies with a dependent clause that Timothy heard the sound doctrine from Paul himself (see also 2:2). On the meaning of *faith* and *love* in the Pastoral Epistles, see comments under 1 Timothy 1:5.

In a second imperative clause Paul exhorts Timothy to *guard the good treasure entrusted to you.* In 1:12 Paul stated that *God* is able to preserve the treasure or deposit (*parathēkē*). Here we see that Paul's words imply human responsibility in the preservation of sound doctrine. Lest Timothy feel confused or overwhelmed by this charge, Paul clarifies that this guarding is carried out *with the help of the Holy Spirit living in us.* We thus have an *inclusio* with 1:7, by which Paul puts the stress on the work of the Spirit.

Theology
The shadow of Paul's imminent death hovers over the entire letter that we call 2 Timothy. It is thus crucial that his co-worker understands his obligation in light of Paul's imminent death. Verses 6–14 constitute Paul's first instructions to Timothy in this letter. We can think of this section as containing three aspects: duty, grounding and empowerment.

First, Paul makes clear Timothy's *duty*. The section is dominated by three imperatives: 'join with me in suffering' (v. 8), 'hold' (v. 13) and 'guard' (v. 14). These imperatives make it clear that the ministerial work of preserving the gospel of God is demanding and painful. In 2:4 Paul will use the soldier metaphor to express the difficult demands of this call.

Second, there is the *grounding* of these commands. The grounding is twofold. First, we should labour to preserve the gospel because it is God's wonderful salvific act through Jesus Christ, who in his death and resurrection has annihilated death and given us a share in the blessed life of God (vv. 9–10). Second, in the future judgment the Lord will vindicate his name and crown his servants (4:8), thereby removing any vestige of shame.

Third, there is *empowerment*. In light of what he is to guard (the gospel) as well as the great difficulties in guarding it, Timothy may well have wondered if he was capable of completing the task. Twice in this section Paul mentions the Holy Spirit. Paul has no illusions that pure human determination will be sufficient to guard the gospel. Only by relying totally on God's Spirit will Timothy be able to endure and guard the good deposit.

C. Onesiphorus as an example for Timothy (1:15–18)

Context

In the previous section Paul equated, for the purpose of this letter, faithfulness to him with faithfulness to the sound doctrine. Thus, he exhorted Timothy not to be ashamed of bearing testimony for the Lord 'or of me his prisoner' (1:8). This new section is linked to the previous by means of the following phrase: 'and was not ashamed of my chain' (1:16), which is used of Onesiphorus. Paul is thus using the example of Onesiphorus to encourage Timothy to remain faithful to Paul – and thus to the gospel. But first Paul mentions two examples that Timothy must not emulate.

Comment

15. *You are aware that all who are in Asia have turned away from me*. To express his painful feeling Paul uses hyperbole in stating that *all who are in Asia* have abandoned him. This is his way of saying that the

Christians in the province of Asia, who should have been present during his arrest and trial, were absent (cf. Guthrie, p. 147). Despite Paul's long period of service – often accompanied by hardship – in the province of Asia (e.g., Ephesus), his brothers and sisters from there turned their backs on him.

Paul mentions two in particular: *Phygelus and Hermogenes.* While the former name is uncommon, LGPN provides 721 references to *Hermogenes.* Hermogenes is also one of the characters in the fictitious *Acts of Paul and Thecla.* Why Paul mentions these two men in particular is not clear. Perhaps Timothy knew them personally.

16. *May the Lord grant mercy to the household of Onesiphorus* (135 references to this name in LGPN). In contrast to the sadness expressed about the deserters Phygelus and Hermogenes, Paul offers a heartfelt prayer request for Onesiphorus. The great joy of Paul's prayer is observed in the fact that he begins the sentence with the prayer request rather than with Onesiphorus' name. The statement just erupts out of Paul: *May the Lord grant mercy!* The phrase, which is a stereotypical formula from the Old Testament (hence the use of the optative *dōē* ['may he grant']), asks for God to remember his faithful love to individuals when they are most in need.[14] On *mercy*, see comments under 1 Timothy 1:13. The prayer for Onesiphorus includes his entire household, which would have included slaves and extended family members living with him.

The reason for Paul's prayer is given in the causal clause that follows: *because he often refreshed me and was not ashamed of my chain.* What Onesiphorus did for the imprisoned Paul 'time after time' was to *refresh (anapsychō)* him. This verb could have a material sense, in which case Paul would be saying that Onesiphorus often provided for him during his imprisonment: food, clothing, etc.[15] This would be similar to what the Philippians had done for Paul in an earlier imprisonment (Phil. 4:10–20). It is better, however, to understand the verb in conjunction with the cognate *anapauō*, which has been shown to have more of a subjective sense in Paul's usage. Concerning this cognate, A. D. Clarke states: 'This refreshment would

---

14 See Gen. 39:21; Deut. 13:18; Is. 47:6; Jer. 49:12; Mic. 7:20.

15 So Rapske, *Paul in Roman Custody*, pp. 196–199.

appear to be subjective in that it relates to the feelings or emotions of the subject … It refers to the resulting effect of an action on one person's spirit by another.'[16] These repeated visits took place because Onesiphorus *was not ashamed of my chain*, that is, the profound shame that came with Paul's imprisonment.[17] This is exactly the attitude that Timothy is to adopt (1:8).

17. Paul further comments on on Onesiphorus' kind actions. Rather than being ashamed of Paul, when Onesiphorus *arrived in Rome, he eagerly searched for me and found me*. Again, this statement should be read with the Greco-Roman honour/shame attitudes in mind, particularly those of prison culture, where those accused awaited for trial. To care for a friend in prison by being present was considered one the greatest demonstrations of friendship in antiquity, precisely because of the horrendous conditions of prison and the shame that went along with being a prisoner.[18] Onesiphorus is portrayed as searching for Paul in a Rome which was a large city (with approximately one million inhabitants) and densely populated. Yet, at last he found Paul and refreshed him (v. 16).

---

16 Clarke, 'Refresh the Hearts of the Saints', pp. 277–300, at 299–300.

17 On the shame that accrued to the prisoner and friends because of jail and bonds, see Rapske, pp. 283–312.

18 The modern reader may glean a sense of this by reading the second-century AD author Lucian of Samosata's *Toxaris*, or *Friendship*, especially sections 18 and 29–31. Lucian describes the great love of Agathocles for his friend Deinias. The latter had committed a crime and was apprehended for trial: 'Agathocles alone of all his [Deinias] friends kept with him, sailed with him to Italy, went to trial with him and failed him in nothing. Moreover, when at length Deinias went into exile, he did not desert his comrade even then, but of his own accord sentenced himself to live in Gyaros and share his exile; and when they were completely in want of necessities, he joined the purple-fishers, dived with them, brought home what he earned by this, and so supported Deinias. [W]hen the latter fell ill, he took care of him for a very long time, and when he died, did not care to return again to his own country, but remained there in the island, ashamed to desert his friend even after his death' (*Toxaris* 18).

18. Paul's great appreciation – as it had been earlier for the Philippians – is made all the more clear as once again he prays for Onesiphorus *to find mercy from the Lord on that day*. With the prepositional phrase *on that day*, Paul refers to final judgment. There is surely also a play on words with the Greek *euriskō*, 'to find'. It is used in both verses 17 and 18: the idea is that just as Onesiphorus was able to *find* Paul in Rome, so Paul prays that the former may *find* mercy from the Lord on judgment day. The thought is similar to Matthew 25:31–46, where prison visits for 'the little ones' (believers who have been imprisoned because of their testimony for the Messiah Jesus) are positively linked to final judgment. Paul closes by reminding Timothy of Onesiphorus' previous service (*diēkonēsen*) in Ephesus.

Theology
One of the qualities necessary for the overseer is that of hospitality (1 Tim. 3:2). In what is surely an irony, Onesiphorus, by visiting Paul and refreshing his heart, has demonstrated life-saving hospitality, even though he was not Paul's host! Thus, hospitality is not just a matter of providing a comfortable space for others, or of 'entertaining'. Hospitality is ultimately about seeking those in misery and 'reviving' their hearts. This is what Jesus spoke of in Matthew 25:31–46. Such hospitality is a mark of belonging to the Lord and hence his gospel. Such hospitality – ultimately the fruit of faith – leads to vindication at final judgment. With the example of Onesiphorus, Paul encourages Timothy to make room in his heart for the battered apostle – and consequently for the gospel of the apostle.

D. Renewed call for perseverance: wisdom from life and the example of Jesus Christ (2:1–13)

Context
With the rhetorical use (*exemplum*) of Onesiphorus' care for Paul, he stopped momentarily from his use of direct imperatives. In addition, cognates of *dynamis*, which abounded in 1:6–14, were not present. In 2:1–13, however, Paul returns to direct exhortation. Consequently, verse 1 opens with the second-person, singular imperative *endynamoō*

('be strong'), followed by other imperatives. Thus, the structure of this section is more or less straightforward: commands are given, which are followed by metaphors that provide clarity – and thereby motivation – for the carrying out of the commands.

Two contextual observations are important to help us grasp this section. First, we note that Paul employs three metaphors: soldier, athlete and farmer. Descriptions of each of these ways of life were used widely by philosophers to clarify the reality of hardship and the necessity of perseverance that were needed to lead a virtuous life.[19] As we have noted in the Introduction and throughout 1 Timothy, Paul deftly uses the moral discourse of his period to help him communicate the moral obligations of Timothy and the believers. As an apostle, he equally employs the OT and the words of Jesus.

Second, it is likely that with the formal phrase in verse 11, 'the saying is sure', Paul introduces traditional, liturgical material of the early church that at the same time bears his own theological emphasis. Just as in 1:6–14 Paul provided the foundation for his commands on a tradition-based Christology, so he does again in 2:1–13.

Comment

1. *You then … be strong in the grace that is in Christ Jesus.* With the inferential conjunction *oun* ('then'), Paul signals that he returns to the commands that were paused in verses 15–18 (cf. Marshall, p. 723). The imperative, *be strong*, comes from the verb *endynamoō*, which was used in 1 Timothy 1:12 and will be used again in 2 Timothy 4:17. Note that in those verses as well as here, Paul asserts that union with the Lord Jesus Christ results in strength for the believer. Furthermore, the strengthening or empowering takes place for the purpose of ministering. Indeed, in 4:17 the Lord is said to have stood by Paul in court, and there gave him strength 'so that through me the message (*to kerygma*) might be fully proclaimed'. The language in 2:1, therefore, harks back to 1:6–8, where Paul exhorted Timothy not to be ashamed to witness for the Lord, since God has given believers

---

19   See, e.g., Plato, *Ap.* 28; Ps. Isocrates, *Demon.* 9; Dio Chrysostom, *Or.* 8.9–16; Epictetus, *Diatr.* 3.24.34–36; 3.26.27; 4.8.35.

'a Spirit of power (*dynamis*)'. Timothy is commanded to allow the Holy Spirit, sent by God and experienced in union with Christ, to empower him (cf. Eph. 6:10).

Paul completes the thought of verse 1 with the prepositional phrase *in the grace that is in Christ Jesus*. *Grace* was just employed in the powerful doctrinal statement of 1:9–10: '[He] saved us ... not according to our works but according to his own purpose and *grace* ... given to us in Christ Jesus.' We suggest that the inclusion of the term in 2:1 highlights the fact that the empowerment Timothy needs for ministry is not self-generated but is freely provided by the Holy Spirit for those who belong to Messiah Jesus. In theological language, the idea is that grace is not only active in the realm of soteriology (1:9–10) but also in ecclesiology, which includes the work of the ministry.

2. *And what you have heard from me through many witnesses entrust to faithful people.* Paul connects verse 2 with the preceding sentence with 'and' (*kai*), which means that the imperative 'entrust to faithful people' is probably based on the reality of the gracious empowerment of the Holy Spirit mentioned in verse 1.

The prepositional phrase *dia pollōn martyrōn* is rendered by the NRSV as *through many witnesses*. However, the preposition with the genitive has been recognized to mean something like 'in the presence of many witnesses' (thus NIV, ESV). The point is probably that what Paul has handed down to Timothy is not some secret, tantalizing information; rather, there are many witnesses who can testify to the truthfulness that what Timothy has received and is to pass down is sound, apostolic tradition. It is likely that Paul mentioning *witnesses* represents a warning to any who wished to falsify his words. The witnesses were probably leaders in the church, perhaps overseers and elders. This helps further to corroborate Timothy's identity as an orthodox and legitimate teacher of the gospel.

What, then, is Timothy to do with that which he has heard from Paul? He is to *entrust* it. The imperative of *paratithēmi* used here has the meaning 'to entrust, commend' (BDAG, p. 772). Clearly the choice of the verb is used to create a link with the noun *parathēkē* ('deposit'), which Paul has employed a number of times to refer to the apostolic gospel (1:12, 14; 1 Tim. 6:20). Timothy's task, therefore, is to entrust this very gospel to others. These are described as *faithful people* (*pistois anthrōpois*).²⁰

Using a relative pronoun Paul adds a qualification that the faithful people must possess, namely, *who will be able to teach others as well*. While it is likely that Paul did not mean that only a select few could teach the gospel (hence the use of the very unspecific *hikanoi* ('sufficient, able'), the choice of the infinitive *didachsai* ('to teach, instruct'; cf. 1 Tim. 3:2) more than likely implies that in view here are those who are gifted by God to teach. On the other hand, it would be straining the text to limit this verse to the office of overseer or to elders. The logic for this conclusion is that because the task of teaching is connected to the overseers in 1 Timothy, therefore the reference here must *also* be to these, since teaching is also mentioned. But this is fallacious for at least two reasons. First, Paul does say *people*, not overseers or elders. Second, this would be like saying that since the qualification, say, 'not given to much wine' (1 Tim. 3:3) is required of overseers and deacons, anywhere else it is used in the Pastoral Epistles it must also refer to overseers and deacons. But, in fact, this is a quality that every Christian should possess, not only the leaders of the church.

3–7. Verses 3–6 have as their main verb the imperative 'share in suffering' (*synkakopathēson*, see also v. 8).²¹ What this means is clarified with three analogies. First, Timothy is to suffer *like a good soldier of Jesus Christ*. Paul seems to have in mind not a temporary soldier but a professional soldier (Spicq, p. 740). This is the reason why Paul adds in verse 4: *no one serving in the army gets entangled in everyday affairs*. If the soldier were to do this, he could not please the

---

20 The ESV translates *anthrōpos* as 'men'. However, if Paul had wanted to limit the task to males only, he could easily have used the plural *andres*, which refers exclusively to males. The NIV translates *anthrōpos* as 'people', thus agreeing with the NRSV. Differently Knight (p. 391) and Marshall (p. 726) who view these as 'only males'.

21 Note that C3 D1 as well as the Majority Text include the conjunction *oun* ('therefore'), so as to create continuity with the preceding material. The shorter text, without the conjunction, is to be preferred: ℵ A C* D*, etc.

superior who enlisted him, which is a crucial goal: *the soldier's aim is to please the enlisting officer* [*tō stratologēsanti*]. Paul probably uses the analogy of the soldier who must not leave his assigned post, even if the circumstances were unpleasant. Moral philosophers, particularly Stoics, also used the soldier's commitment to his post as an analogy for spiritual loyalty to the divine.[22]

Second, Paul uses the analogy of the athlete (see also 1 Cor. 9:25; Phil. 3:14), common in the moral discourse of the period (see above under Context). Given the language used in this analogy, it appears that the point being driven home is the necessity of the athlete to prepare legitimately for the games. The combination of *athleō* ('to compete in a contest') and *nomimōs* ('being in accordance with the rules') is used in the context of the athlete eating the correct food to prepare his body for his particular sport.[23] In fact, professional athletes had to swear before Zeus that they had trained lawfully in preparation for their contests (*OCD*, p. 198). A modern analogy is the athlete who in preparation for the Olympic Games has used banned substances to become stronger. Such an athlete, upon discovery, is disqualified. Thus, Paul's point is primarily about the proper, arduous preparation to which the professional athlete had to submit if he was to win the crown.[24]

Finally, Paul uses the analogy of the farmer, stressing by word order that it is the farmer *who does the work*, who should be the first to eat of the crops. That the life of the farmer was one of hard labour was recognized in antiquity, both in the biblical and Gentile tradition (see Johnson, pp. 366–367). The idea is that without hard work ministry will not be fruitful (cf. Prov. 20:4; 27:18).

Metaphorical language can give rise to innumerable interpretations. However, we can be certain that at least the following is being communicated to Timothy: the ministry before him requires

---

22   See Epictetus, *Diatr.* 1.9.24. Cf. Malherbe, *Light from the Gentiles*, 1:146–8.

23   See Galen, *De alimentorum facultatibus* 6.488.4; *De victu acutorum* 15.464.3; Epictetus, *Diatr.* 3.10.8; *Ench.* 29.

24   On this theme, see Lucian, *Anach.* 1–6, 15, 24–30, where arduous exercises are explained by 'Solon' as necessary to make the Athenians the best citizens during war or peace.

total dedication, which includes hard work, suffering and singleness of mind. Only in this way will Timothy's ministry receive God's reward. Of course, these verses cannot be read in isolation from 1:6–14 where Paul made clear that it is the Holy Spirit who is the source of strength for the minister of the gospel.

8–9. In the previous verses Paul based his exhortation to 'share in suffering' on common analogies observable to all. In these verses the exhortation will be based on the church's tradition of Jesus Christ, a tradition which in Pauline literature already also appears in very similar language in Romans 1:3–4.

Remember Jesus Christ. Paul continues to use the language of memory to exhort Timothy (see 1:4, 6; 2:14). Timothy is to remember *Jesus Christ,* the Messiah who has been *raised from the dead.* With the use of the perfect participle (*egēgermenon*), which can communicate actions whose results continue into the present, Paul stresses the fact that this is the current (and eternal) state of Jesus Christ: he is the risen Lord! (cf. Marshall, p. 734).

A descendant of David. Just as the resurrection is a central statement of Christology in the New Testament, so is the belief that Jesus is the son of David, who in his humanity fulfilled the Old Testament promises that the redeemer would be a descendant of David, and therefore the King of all the nations. *This is my gospel.* With this statement Paul stresses the fact that not only is this the gospel that God revealed to him in particular as an apostle to the Gentiles, but also that 'his' gospel is the same as that which all the apostles also proclaimed (cf. Gal. 1:11–2:10).

Paul mentions the Davidic descent of Jesus in order to stress the humanity of the Lord. The Davidic root assures the ministers that Jesus Messiah can sympathize with their pain. The inclusion of the resurrection is probably present to highlight the fact that Jesus is the risen – and therefore *vindicated* – king, who as such is demonstrated to be the *kyrios.* He will therefore vindicate Paul and Timothy in the judgment that matters most – the final judgment (see further 4:6–8; Marshall, p. 735).

Despite this comforting Christological and eschatological reality, Paul presently suffers *hardship, even to the point of being chained like a criminal.* While it is probable that Paul did not always wear chains under house arrest, his condition of being a prisoner can thus be described. The term for *criminal* (*kakourgos*) highlights the irony that despite Paul's true vocation and identity, he is viewed as no more than a base person bent on doing evil. Yet, because he serves the risen king, *the word of God is not chained.*

10. *Therefore I endure everything for the sake of the elect.* The prepositional phrase *dia touto* (*therefore*), although in a sense looking backwards, primarily looks forward, as *hina* ('so that') in the next clause shows. For the moment Paul speaks of *the elect* (*eklektoi*). He uses the adjective in 1 Timothy 5:21 of the 'elect angels'. Here, however, as in Titus 1:1, it refers to believers. In the Septuagint, 'elect' can refer to men of God, the land, Jerusalem and people. In apocalyptic literature (e.g., 1 Enoch) the emphasis falls on Israel and her messiah as the elect (cf. *TDNT* IV: 182–188). Jesus uses the term in eschatological and polemical contexts where the elect are those who respond to him (see Matt. 22:14; Mark 13:20, 27). In the transfiguration Jesus is himself 'the elect' (Luke 9:35; 23:35). More than likely building on the Jesus tradition itself, Paul uses the adjective *elect* in order to highlight how precious in the eyes of God are these believers (e.g., Rom. 8:33; Col. 3:12). They are so precious to God that Paul is willing to *endure everything* for them.

So that they may also obtain the salvation that is in Christ Jesus. One of the important questions regarding this phrase is whether Paul speaks about *current* believers for whom he is willing to suffer so that they may persevere in their vocation as Christians, or whether it is a reference to future Christians who have not yet come to faith but need to hear the preaching of the gospel in order to be saved, since they are elect of God. The language used, while pointing to the future, final redemption of believers, does not clarify if Paul refers to those who already are Christians or those who will be so but have yet to experience the 'effectual calling'. It appears that Paul's use of 'elect' is meant to highlight their belonging to God, which demands the labour of Paul (and Timothy) in the context of eschatological salvation history. Hence, Paul concludes the thought by linking salvation to *eternal glory*, an eschatological phrase that highlights the current state of Christ, which will also be the believers' future state when they share in Christ's eternal glory (cf. Col. 3:4).

11–13. *The saying is true.* For this phrase see the comments on 1 Timothy 1:15. By using this phrase, Paul links the statements that follow with the sound apostolic doctrine that false teachers seek to corrupt but which the believers must accept as authoritative. For this section Paul uses the phrase to bring his thoughts to a close. He speaks of the necessity of persevering, even onto death, in order to share with the Lord in the life to come.

If we have died with him, we will also live with him. The language is almost identical to Romans 6:8, where Paul explains conversion by means of baptism. This verse, as well as the others comprising this section, is constructed as a conditional sentence. The completion of an obligation set out in the protasis (the 'if' part of the sentence) is the requirement for the fulfilment of the apodosis (the 'then' part of the sentence). Thus, in order to share in the life to come (cf. 1:1, 10; 1 Tim. 1:16; 4:8; 6:12, 19; Tit. 1:2; 3:7) we must die with him. In Paul, the concept of dying with Christ is a dialectical one based on the already/not yet eschatology of the apostle.[25] On the one hand, at conversion the Holy Spirit joined us to Christ in his death and resurrection (see esp. Rom. 6:6–11; Gal. 2:19–20; Col. 3:3): we are in fact one with Christ, and thus a new creation (2 Cor. 5:17), a reality which ineluctably leads to transformed existence. And yet, on the other hand, we are commanded to put to death the 'old man' (Rom. 6:12–22; 12:1–2; Col. 3:5–11). Given the context of verses 11–13, Paul is both affirming the reality of our death with Christ and simultaneously calling us to die with him by living into that reality.

If we endure, we will also reign with him. The second line, with the protasis in the present tense highlighting continuous action, speaks of enduring (*hypomenō*), a verb Paul just used in 2:10. Of course, the metaphors of verses 3–6 also all pointed to the necessity of endurance. Such endurance, namely faithfulness to the task of gospel proclamation whatever the circumstances (cf. 1:8), will result in our reigning with Christ. This astonishing thought of being co-regents with the Lord goes back to Jesus himself (Matt. 19:28) and is found in other places in Paul and the New Testament (e.g., Rom. 5:17; 1 Cor. 6:2; Rev. 1:5–6).[26]

---

25 See e.g., Dunn, *Theology of Paul the Apostle*, pp. 401–404, who also calls attention to the irreducibly collective reality of dying with Christ.

26 Cf. Jipp, *Christ Is King*, esp. pp. 139–210.

If we deny him, he will also deny us. This difficult statement, which is ultimately about apostasy in the face of trials, is entrenched in the Synoptic tradition (see Matt. 10:33; 24:13; Mark 8:38; Luke 9:26).[27]

If we are faithless, he remains faithful. In a series of statements implicitly demanding fidelity to Christ and declaring the consequences of unfaithfulness, this verse emerges, as one scholar puts it, 'totally unexpected'.[28] The use of *pistis* ('faith') language, especially as predicated of the Lord in the apodosis, suggests that we think of words such as 'faithful' or 'loyal' to translate the protasis, instead of *faithless*, which carries overly intellectual connotations. We may translate the clause with the following slight change: 'If we are unfaithful, he remains faithful' (NET, similarly GNB). Probably in view are episodes of denial of the gospel or failures in following the Lord. With the denial of Peter reported in all four Gospels, the early Christians were keenly aware of the potential for apostasy, however brief. But the good news is that *his* faithfulness is not dependent on that of the believer! Rather, it is in God's inmost character to be faithful and loyal to those he takes as his own.

He remains faithful. This statement courses through the Holy Scriptures: 'God is not a man, that he should lie; neither the son of man, that he should repent: hath he said, and shall he not do it? Or hath he spoken, and shall he not make it good?' (Num. 23:19 KJV; cf. Deut. 7:9; Mal. 3:6; 1 Thess. 5:24; Tit. 1:2). Why does God remain faithful despite human unfaithfulness? Paul concludes with a positive statement: *For he cannot deny himself.* The emphasis falls on the sheer impossibility of God 'denying' (surely a play on words with verse 12) his own nature. This is shown by the word order in Greek, where it reads like this: 'For to deny himself he cannot.'

Theology

Paul has put an overwhelming task before Timothy. In the context of persecution and false teaching, Timothy must remain faithful to 'the deposit', the apostolic sound doctrine that Paul has passed

---

27   The statement is 'difficult' because it is forthright in the possibility that Christians may turn their backs on their Lord and face judgment.

28   Wilckens, *Theologie*, I.3.289: 'völlig überraschend'.

down to him. Timothy must preserve it by embodying it and passing it down to faithful believers. The assignment is so demanding that Paul compares it to the proverbial hardships of soldiers, athletes and farmers. In fact, if Timothy is to be successful he must ultimately die to himself. Has Paul given his son in the faith an impossible assignment? If human capacity is all he has to go on, then the answer is yes.

This is precisely why Paul tells Timothy to rest on the power of the Holy Spirit given by the grace of Christ Jesus. Furthermore, Timothy is to remember Jesus Christ: he is the incarnate and risen Lord who will vindicate him on the last day and who keeps the gospel moving by his sovereignty. And what about those times when, in human weakness and fickleness, he fails in his loyalty to Christ? Will the gospel also fail? Will Timothy then be abandoned? Paul reminds us that God will not abandon us even when we are disloyal to him: he is the loving and faithful Lord who will not turn his back on us.

3. FURTHER INSTRUCTIONS – A CALL FOR PERSEVERANCE IN DOCTRINE AND LIFE IN LIGHT OF FALSE TEACHERS AND PAUL'S DEATH (2:14 – 4:8)

This is the second part of 2 Timothy. In many ways the format and style are similar to the first. There are commands, support for those commands, and metaphors. In a word, exhortation continues to dominate the material; and this is to be expected in light of the letter's genre as a paraenetic letter. What, then, is different in this section, which justifies calling it the second main part of the letter? The differences, as I see them, are at least two. First, there are new themes introduced, or at least *variations* of former themes: the character of the last days, the importance of Holy Scripture, the necessity of proclamation. Second, the *framing* of the composition is slightly different. While in the first part the danger of false teaching was *implied* in the injunctions to hold on and communicate 'the deposit', in this section the danger of false teaching will come to the foreground. Hence, the warnings, prescriptions and analogies given to Timothy are given *vis-à-vis* the reality of both present and future false teaching.

A. How Timothy can be an approved worker (2:14–26)

Context
With respect to the function of this letter's genre in this section, Johnson has shown how Paul shifts 'from memory and imitation of models to a more direct form of moral instruction through maxims' (p. 389; see also pp. 389–398). This is in keeping with the protreptic form of moral discourse that Paul has adopted as his communicative channel in 2 Timothy (see Introduction). This helps explain at least two aspects of this second part. First, Paul constantly charges the opponents. Second, Paul uses medical metaphors to facilitate speaking of the spiritual maladies of the false teachers (cf. also 1 Tim. 6:3–10).

Comment
14. *Remind them of this, and warn them before God that they are to avoid wrangling over words.* Just as Timothy himself is to 'remember', so is he also responsible for continually reminding the believers both what precedes and what follows in the letter (present tense imperative *hypomimnēske, remember,* suggesting that the reminding should be constant). In particular, Timothy is to warn them *before God* (see on 4:1 and 1 Tim. 6:13), that is, with the awareness that God is present as witness when Timothy exhorts them. Here he is to order them not to war about words or arguments. As we saw previously (1 Tim. 6:4), it is a trait of the false teachers that they are obsessed with arguments and disputes that have nothing to do with the truth.

They should not be quarrelling about words because it *does no good but only ruins those who are listening.* The second clause of the sentence explains why such quarrelling is not *good* (*chrēsimos*): it leads to *ruin* (*katastrophē*), that is, to the total destruction of the listeners. It should be noted that similar language was used of the effect that Sophists had on their listeners.[1] Paul thus compares the false teachers to public speakers who cared more about the striking style of their speech than about content that would aid the listeners. This was a typical target of moral philosophers (see Johnson, p. 384).

---

1   See Stobaeus 2.2.18, 22 (citing Ariston of Chios; NW II.2, pp. 982–983).

15–18. With these verses Paul moves to contrast Timothy's behaviour to that of the false teachers (Marshall, p. 747). Focusing on the vertical aspect of Timothy's life (*present yourself to God*), he is called to be *approved by him*, that is, *a worker who has no need to be ashamed*. One of the activities that will lead to Timothy not being ashamed before God (cf. 1 Tim. 3:13) is the following: *Rightly explaining the word of truth*. The expression *rightly explaining* translates the compound Greek verb *orthotomeō* (cf. Prov. 3:6; 11:5). Malherbe suggests as a possibility that the verb might evoke a medical metaphor from moral philosophers, where the 'rational word' was likened to a scalpel which cuts with precision.[2] The metaphor may thus be one of 'carefully cutting', as in surgery. Paul's point would therefore have to do with precision and care in understanding and explaining the sound apostolic doctrine, which he calls *the word of truth*.[3]

Paul then tells Timothy what he is to *avoid* (*peristēmi*, cf. Tit. 3:9), namely *profane chatter*. The adjective *bebēlos* ('profane') was used in 1 Timothy 1:9; 4:7 and 6:20. In 4:7 Paul associated it with 'myths and old wives' tales' (see also 1 Tim. 1:4; Tit. 3:9). It is probable that this is a polemical way of labelling the content of the false teaching; of course, this does not mean that the false teaching was not really false. What makes the false teaching *profane* is the fact that it is not the sound apostolic doctrine (cf. 1 Tim. 1:10). The reason Timothy is to avoid empty chatter is the following: *For it will lead people into more and more impiety*. This clause contrasts nicely with 1 Timothy 4:7, where instead of engaging in 'profane and old wives' tales', Timothy is to work towards 'godliness' (*eusebeia*). Here, by contrast, engagement in profane chatter will lead to ungodliness or *impiety* (*asebeia*). As indicated in the Introduction, the term *eusebeia* contains both a doctrinal and an ethical aspect. The message here is that departure from the truth leads to further and further corruption in thought and behaviour.

---

2   Malherbe, *Light from the Gentiles*, 1:124, n. 16. Cf. Spicq, *TLNT* II, 595.

3   The genitive 'of truth' is more than probably a descriptive genitive, so that we can translate 'the truthful word'. Cf. also Col. 1:5–6.

And their talk will spread like gangrene. Paul is not yet done speaking of the destiny of the false teachers and their hearers. With a simple *and* he adds a metaphor to describe their future state. *Gangrene* (Greek *gangkraina*) was defined by the Greek physician Galen as 'a death of infested tissue' (*Tum. Pr. Nat.* 720.8). As we have seen earlier (1 Tim. 4:2; 6:4–5), Paul uses the medical language of disease to describe the state of the opponents of the gospel. This was a common strategy of moral philosophers who in attacking their opponents spoke of them as diseased. The repulsive metaphor of gangrene is meant to highlight the deadly results of false teaching.

Paul usually does not name the false teachers he writes about; but here we have an exception with the singling out of *Hymenaeus and Philetus.* The first person is probably the same man mentioned in 1 Timothy 1:20. The second name is often attested in Greek sources and was popular.[4] Paul says of these men that they *have swerved from the truth by claiming that the resurrection has already taken place.* Naturally, there is debate on the meaning of this clause.[5] It seems likely that the false teachers have corrupted the bodily resurrection of the dead as taught by Peter, Paul and the apostles by either spiritualizing it or by saying that after the resurrection of Jesus there was no other bodily resurrection (see 1 Thess. 4:13–18). The problem with either view is that it denies the biblical teaching that the resurrection of Jesus was the first fruit that set in motion the eschatological fulfilment of a future, resurrection in glory of the saints (1 Cor. 15:20–57). A denial of this future bodily resurrection inevitably leads to hopelessness in the face of death; or to hedonism (i.e., if there is nothing more than this present life, we should live purely for enjoyment). It is to be expected, therefore, that this false teaching has led to the *upsetting of the faith of some.*

19–20. *But God's firm foundation stands.* With a strong contrasting particle that is not common in the New Testament (*mentoi*, 'nevertheless', cf. NIV, NASB, CSB; the NRSV 'but' is too soft), Paul shifts to speak of the destiny of those who are true believers. The use of

4 LGPN cites 14 references of the name in Greek sources. I thank the editor of this series for the statistic.
5 See the different interpretations in Marshall, pp. 752–754.

the *foundation* metaphor probably goes back to 1 Timothy 3:15, where it referred to the church. Here the church more clearly refers to the believers, who must not allow their faith to be upset: they rest on God's promise, which stands.[6] The foundation has a 'seal' (*sphragis*), which is used here metaphorically for an inscription that shows ownership: '*The Lord knows those who are his*', and, '*Let everyone who calls on the name of the Lord turn away from wickedness.*' The first sentence is a quotation from Numbers 16:5, where the revolt of Korah, Dathan and Abiram against Moses is reported. The rest of the story tells how God annihilated Korah and his household but spared the rest of the Israelites as a result of Moses' intercession. In this way God demonstrated that he *knows those who are his*. In the same way, those who have followed the truthful apostolic doctrine need not fear a hopeless ending, for they belong to the Lord, since he has chosen them (cf. 1:9). The second quotation is a mixture of Old Testament texts, including Numbers 16:5; Isaiah 26:13 and Psalm 119:26/118:29 (LXX). The command in the quotation stands in relation to the indicative of the previous quotation. This is common in the New Testament, where the declarations of believers' being secure in the Lord are followed by imperatives to stay away from sin. Timothy will encourage those whose faith has been troubled by the false teachers when he reminds them that the Lord, who 'remains faithful' (2:13), is their God. At the same time, precisely because they belong to this Lord, they must stay away from wickedness.

Paul continues contrasting the false teachers with the true believers. In these verses he employs the analogy of vessels in a household. The analogy of the household is the dominant one for church in the Pastoral Epistles. Therefore, it is not strange that Paul would shift from the 'temple' analogy of the previous verse to the household analogy. The phrase *in a large house* refers to a wealthy home where there is the possibility of having *utensils … of gold and silver*. The more menial utensils of *wood and clay* (*ostrakina*) were not very valuable; archaeological excavations have unearthed myriads of fragments of shattered clay pots. Paul says of these last utensils that they are for

---

6 The perfect form of *histēmi* underscores the present (and continuous) state of God's foundation: it will *not* be moved.

ordinary use. The phrase translates the Greek prepositional phrase *eis atimian*, which is also found in Romans 1:26 and 9:21. There, God is the subject who has the authority to make the lump of clay for honour or for destruction. Outside the New Testament the phrase *eis atimian* is used of the destruction of a city (Dionysius of Halicarnassus, *Roman Antiquities* 4.58.3). In the *Testament of the Twelve Patriarchs* 12.10 there is a contrast between those who, after death, go 'to glory', and those who go 'for destruction' (*eis atimian*). In view of verse 21, it is probable that the metaphor refers to those who, on the one hand, follow the apostolic truth and therefore will be honoured by God; on the other hand are those, like the false teachers and their followers, who reject the apostolic doctrine and therefore end in destruction. As we have already seen (1 Tim. 1:20) and will see below (2:24–26), this does not mean that the 'ordinary vessels' are beyond the possibility of repentance.

21. *All who cleanse themselves of the things I have mentioned will become special utensils, dedicated and useful to the owner of the house, ready for every good work.* The Greek text links the previous sentence with this one by means of the inferential conjunction *oun* ('therefore' NASB, ESV; left untranslated in NRSV, NIV). Paul brings the lesson of the previous verses to its conclusion. In fact, we discover that the material has as its aim a hortatory function. The goal is for Timothy to exhort all (including the false teachers) to *cleanse themselves*. The verb translated as *cleanse* (*engathairō*) is not very common in the Greek Bible (Deut. 26:13; Josh. 17:15; Judg. 7:4). However, it is found in 1 Corinthians 5:7, where the church is encouraged to 'clean out the old yeast', referring to sexual immorality. More than likely, then, the exhortation is to stay away from immorality, which is of course the result of following false teaching (see also Weiser, p. 206).

The one who cleanses himself (a work that God alone can do) will be like the gold and silver utensils mentioned in verse 20. What this means is fleshed out with three terms used adjectivally. First, there is *hegiasmenon*, which speaks of someone 'purified' and 'set aside' for God's purposes. Second, and put yet another way, the person will be *useful to the owner of the house* (*despotes*). And lastly, this means that the person will be *ready for every good work*. This last phrase is similar to 3:17; Titus 1:6 and 3:1. This is the theme of 'good works' which runs through the entirety of the Pastoral Epistles (see Introduction). It highlights the basic Christian doctrine that knowledge of the gospel ineluctably results in good works in the lives of the believers (cf. Eph. 2:8–10).

22–23. In the last verses of chapter 2 Paul speaks again more directly to Timothy. In particular, Timothy's character and attitude towards others – especially the opponents of the gospel – is highlighted.

Shun youthful passions. With a vivid verb in the present tense imperative (*pheuge*, 'flee'; see 1 Tim. 6:11), Paul commands Timothy to continually run away from *neōterikos epithymia*. Similar phrases are found in ancient authors to speak of those desires that are most active during youth.[7] Although lustful sexuality was probably viewed as the foremost youthful passion, the phrase is not restricted to this area.[8]

Instead, Timothy must continually *pursue righteousness, faith, love, and peace.* On *righteousness* see comments on 1 Timothy 6:11, where it is linked with 'faith' and 'love'. See also under Titus 2:12. On *faith* and *love* see on 1 Timothy 1:5. On *peace* see on 1 Timothy 1:1. Paul adds the prepositional phrase *along with those who call on the Lord from a pure heart.* The first part of the phrase harks back to 2:19. *Pure heart* was used in 1:5 as related to the ultimate goal of Paul's instruction, namely love. That is, love cannot emerge if the heart has not been purified on the basis of the vicarious death of Jesus: 'But the aim of such instruction is love that comes from a pure heart.' Paul instructs Timothy to practise those virtues that stem from obedience to the truth together, that is, with the community of believers.

In verse 23 Paul returns to the negative exhortations of the first part of verse 22. *Have nothing to do* translates the same verb used in 1 Timothy 4:7 (*paraiteomai*). The same urgency of that text is found here as well. Timothy must turn his back on *stupid and senseless controversies.* Paul spoke of *controversies* (*zēteseis*) in 1 Timothy 6:4 (cf. also 1:4) to describe the morally sick and morose false teachers

---

7 See, e.g., Aristotle, *Eth. nic.* 7.4. The corresponding Latin phrase, *cupiditates adulescentiae*, is found in Cicero, *Cael.* 42–43; Tacitus, *Hist.* 15.3. See further comments under Titus 2:6.

8 See Kelly, p. 189.

who, having abandoned the sound doctrine, were obsessed with 'controversies and for dispute about words (*logomachia*)'. There is a striking similarity between 1 Timothy 6:4, Titus 3:9 and the current text. Here Paul labels such controversies as *stupid and senseless*. The first adjective (*mōros*) is also linked with controversies in Titus 3:9, where the context has to do with false teaching that appears to be Jewish in some sense. Because it is not Christologically centred in its content or hermeneutic, it is stupid and *senseless* (*apaideutos*; the word is used only here in the New Testament). It is the opposite of someone who is educated and intelligent. The term is probably borrowed from the language of the moral philosophers who used medical terminology to speak of the intellectual errors of their opponents. Paul may hint at the fact that the teaching of the opponents demonstrates that they are 'cognitively deficient'.[9] Their false doctrine does not allow them to think straight! In fact, as Timothy knows (taking the participle *eidōs* as causal), all these false teachings do is to *breed quarrels* (*machē*): this is precisely the opposite of what the gospel produces (1 Tim. 6:4 and Tit. 3:9), which is 'faith, love and peace' (2:22).

24. *The servant of the Lord*, however, must be different. He must not be like the false teachers, who are always looking for a doctrinal or philosophical fight. He *must not be quarrelsome but kindly to everyone, an apt teacher, patient*. This statement is somewhat ironic in light of the fact that Paul himself has used the sharp vocabulary and arguments of moral philosophers. Some philosophers, especially some of a Cynic stripe, were known to be vicious to the public.[10] Paul's polemic statements against the false teachers mentioned in the Pastoral Epistles are not nearly as vicious as those found in some of the quarrelling philosophers of the period.[11] Furthermore, Paul's strong language, like strong medicine, has as its purpose the healing of the opponents.

The Christian pastor must not be *quarrelsome* (*machomai*, see previous verse and 1 Tim. 3:3). Instead, Paul gives three virtues that the

---

9 The phrase is Malherbe's, *Light from the Gentiles*, 1:429.
10 See M.-O. Goulet-Cazé, 'Cynicism', *BNP* III. pp. 1052–1060.
11 Ibid.

minister must possess. These virtues are usually exhibited in the act of instruction. First, he is to be *kindly*. Second, he must be an *apt teacher* (*didaktikos*, see 1 Tim. 3:2). Third, he must be *patient*, that is, 'bearing evil without resentment' (Marshall, p. 766).

How this works out in practice is somewhat surprisingly described *vis-à-vis* the opponents. One would have thought, especially in light of Paul's strong language from 2:14 forward, that there was no hope for those who opposed the gospel. Yet once again, as we also saw on 1 Timothy 1:18–20, Paul leaves the door open for a possible return to the truth, as verse 25 makes clear (see below). This is a reminder that Paul's strong polemical language in the Pastoral Epistles is highly stylized to fit with the rhetoric of the period, particularly that of moral philosophers. This does not mean that his words are just 'empty threats'. The language demonstrates the utter seriousness of the situation; but we must read them contextually if we are to comprehend and apply them properly.

25. God's servant must be an apt teacher towards outsiders, *correcting opponents with gentleness*. The prepositional phrase that concludes the clause is placed at the beginning in the Greek text, thereby highlighting the importance of *gentleness*. The word translated *correcting* is not the expected *didaskō* ('to teach') but *paideuō*, which was also used with respect to the 'correcting' of false teachers in 1 Timothy 1:20. The term conveys the sense of instructing someone as one would a child who needs to be educated. The verb can be found in moral philosophy to refer to education in the Stoic way of life.[12] The people Timothy is to correct are those who are 'opposing' (*antidiatithēmi*), expressed without a direct object, which is most plausibly 'the truth' or a synonym.

God may perhaps grant that they will repent and come to know the truth. The purpose of correction is now stated directly. However, by using the optative mood of the verb *didōmi* ('to give'), Paul speaks with a 'tentative tone' (Johnson, p. 402) about the possibility of return from apostasy. Note that God alone can grant repentance (cf. Acts 5:24), which by hendiadys is clarified as knowledge of the truth (see also 1 Tim. 2:4).

---

12 E.g., Epictetus, *Ench.* 5.

26. Verse 26, the end of the section, provides an analysis of the situation from the perspective of spiritual warfare. With *kai* ('and') expressing result, Paul adds: *And that they may escape from the snare of the devil*. The verb translated as *escape* (*ananēphō*) is best understood as 'to return to sobriety' (LSJ, s.v.) or 'to come to one's senses' (BDAG, p. 68; cf. NIV). The opponents are thus presented as being in an intellectual and moral fog.[13] Paul clarifies that the source of this spiritual malady is *the devil*, who has the false teachers in a *snare* (*pagis*). This phrase is the same used in 1 Timothy 3:7 to describe the overseer who, because of conceit and a bad reputation with outsiders, has been trapped by the devil. The similarity of language gives further weight to the likelihood that the false teachers were once teachers in the churches (see Introduction).

The final clause highlights the current state of the false teachers by using a perfect passive participle (*ezōgrēmenoi*): they *have been held captive to do his will*, that is, the will of the devil.

Theology

In concluding this section we return to the title of the subheading: How can Timothy be an approved worker? Paul has given Timothy a number of responsibilities that, if fulfilled, will make Timothy an approved worker. These responsibilities, which can only be carried out in the power of God, are the following: (1) Timothy must avoid false teaching; (2) Timothy must demonstrate character that is in step with godliness; (3) Timothy must be merciful even to the opponents, for God may grant them repentance through the teaching of sound doctrine.

In order to fulfil these responsibilities the minister must understand that there are deceiving, invisible powers at work in the church. The devil is at work taking captive and using for his purposes those who oppose the gospel. The minister needs God's wisdom in order to know how to navigate the irreducibly complex

---

13   Johnson, p. 402, cites moral philosophers thus using the verb: Dio
      Chrysostom, *Or.* 4.77; Josephus, *Ant.* 6.241. According to Philo, *Leg.*
      2.60, to come to one's senses means repentance (*metanoia*; see above
      v. 25).

realities that are part of the church's life. This wisdom is only possible when ministers submit their entire being to the sound, apostolic doctrine.

B. The last days that are already present (3:1-9)

Context

The one main verb of the entire section of vv. 1–9 is the present tense imperative *ginōske, You must understand* (NRSV). The second clause has a future verb, *will come*, used to speak of the *last days*. The remainder of the section consists of a catalogue of vices (18 in total) that describes the character of the people whom Timothy must guard against. This section, then, is a continuation of Paul's exhortation to Timothy. However, it is now framed from an eschatological perspective. And yet, we know that in Pauline thought the future is already breaking into the present, although greater intensification is to follow in the end.

Our exegesis of 2 Timothy 3:6–7 would be incomplete if we did not note that it more than likely provides us with a window into church problems that Paul was addressing. Of particular importance is observing that the portrait of the false teachers painted by Paul bears a striking resemblance to that painted by moral (mostly Stoic) philosophers of the early Roman empire. These philosophers complained that many men took up philosophy who really did not care for the upright and virtuous life, which was the aim of the discipline. The criticism was primarily aimed at certain Cynics. Their goal, complained opposing philosophers, was personal glory, an easy life and the acquisition of easy money. Thus, Lucian of Samosata (c. AD 120–190) writes about 'philosophers' who sought permanent posts in the homes of the wealthy in order to gain money without making much sacrifice, and for personal pleasure (*De mercede conductis* 6–7, 8–9). These false philosophers behaved more like beasts than humans (*Fugitivi* 5). In addition, 'they collect tribute, going from house to house. ... And they expect many to give, either out of respect for their cloth or for fear of their abusive language' (14). They love money (*phylargyria*) and are 'boasters' (*alazones*) (19–20, 22). The following statement is worth quoting in full:

But although outwardly and in public they appear very reverend and
stern, if they get a handsome boy or a pretty woman in their clutches or
hope to, it is best to veil their conduct in silence. Some even carry off
the wives of their hosts, to seduce them after the pattern of that young
Trojan [Paris!], pretending that the women are going to become
philosophers; then they tender them, as common property, to all their
associates.
(verse 18)

One husband, who apparently hired a philosopher to teach in his
home, complains that the philosopher took his wife away: 'He went
off with my wife because I took him in' (30).

It is possible to deduce that Paul is warning against a similar
situation. False teachers, using Christianity and/or Judaism as a philosophy,[14] became the teachers of wealthy women. They were teaching
them – not the sound apostolic doctrine that was common to the
ekklesia (1 Tim. 3:15) – but false teaching that had more to do with
the law, food abstentions and the resurrection (as already having
occurred). Naturally, as often happens when discovering a new teaching, the fresh excitement propels one to sharing it with those who
would listen. And so it is likely that Paul's statements about widows
who 'speak what they should not' (1 Tim. 5:13) is generally targeting
those women who have fallen prey to wandering philosophers.

Comment

1. *In the last days distressing times will come.* For Paul the last days
have already emerged (see on 1 Tim. 4:1). He describes this period
as *distressing* (*chalepoi*). The adjective is found elsewhere in the New
Testament only in Matthew 8:28 to describe two demoniacs from
the Gadarenes who came out to meet Jesus. Matthew describes
them as 'so fierce [*chalepoi*] that no one could pass that way'. The

---

14   Both Judaism and Christianity, because of their concentration on
     ethics and monotheism, were viewed by Gentiles as a new philosophy.
     See Malherbe, *Light from the Gentiles*, 1:100–102, for some helpful
     examples. See also Alexander, drawing on Galen's writings: 'Paul and
     the Hellenistic Schools', pp. 60–83.

phrase *distressing times* also appears in authors contemporary with Paul[15] who use the phrase to speak of times of war, specifically to the horror of a city being besieged.

2–5. With a causal *gar* ('for', 'because') Paul explains why this period will be distressing. A catalogue of vices follows: *For people will be lovers of themselves, lovers of money.* The first trait, *philautoi*, 'lovers of themselves', appears often in philosophers who were preoccupied with ethical subjects.[16] Philo (*Leg.* 1.49) equates love of self with a desire to be like God. It is probable, as Marshall suggests (p. 772), that this vice serves as the controlling one for the remaining vices: 'On this assumption the dominant motif is that people will be self-centered, and this affects their relationships with other people so that they think only of their own interests and behave violently to gain their own ends.' The next vice is love of money, for which see under 1 Timothy 6:6–10.

People will be *boasters, arrogant.* The *alazōn* ('boaster') in classical Greek literature is the person who always brags, without realizing that, ironically, he and she have nothing to boast about.[17] *Arrogant* (*hyperēphanos*) is found in the catalogue of vices in Romans 1:30. God 'scatters' and 'opposes' the arrogant (Luke 1:51; Jas 4:6; 1 Pet. 5:5, the last two examples coming from Prov. 3:34). *Abusive* translates *blasphēmos*, 'defaming, denigrating, demeaning' (BDAG, p. 178), on which see on 1 Timothy 1:13, where Paul described himself as a blasphemer prior to his conversion. *Disobedient to parents* (cf. Rom. 1:30) is the breaking of the fifth commandment (Exod. 20:12; cf. Deut. 21:18). *Ungrateful*, that is, not thanking God. Giving thanks to God is viewed by Paul as an essential virtue of the saints.[18] In Romans 1:21 being ungrateful goes along with not glorifying God as a cardinal vice. *Unholy* is also used

---

15   See, e.g., Josephus, *Ant.* 15.305; Dio Chrysostom, *Or.* 73.4; Diogenes Laertius, *Lives of Philosophers* 10.108; Galen, *ad Glauconem* 11.2.3.

16   See Aristotle, *Pol.* 2.25–40; *Eth. nic.* 9.8.1.

17   See Herodotus, 6.12; Dio Chrysostom, *Or.* 4.33; 55.7; Josephus, *Ant.* 8.264. See also Johnson, p. 404.

18   See esp. Col. 1:3, 12; 2:7; 3:15, 17; 4:2. See Pao, *Thanksgiving.*

in 1 Timothy 1:9, where Paul describes those who are essentially
lawless.

3. *Inhuman, implacable, slanderers, profligates, brutes, haters of good.* The
term *astorgos* gives the sense of someone who lacks natural affection
or is inhuman. The second vice translates *aspondos*, which is better
rendered as 'irreconcilable' (BDAG, p. 144). The word often accompanies *akēryktos*, which refers to a person who would rather wage
war than make a truce.[19] This attitude is in contrast to the 'kindly'
servant of the Lord of 2:24. On *slanderers* see under 1 Timothy 3:11.
Profligates (*akrastēs*) refers to people who lack self-control. Paul uses
the noun form in 1 Corinthians 7:5 in the context of sexuality. The
word is the opposite of *enkratēs* ('self-control'), a characteristic of
the overseer in Titus 1:8. *Brutes* (*anēmeroi*) can also be translated
as 'wild' or 'savage' (see LSJ, s.v.) and can refer to humans acting
like untamed beasts (see Epictetus, *Discourses* 1.3). The *haters of good*
stands in contrast to Titus 1:8, where the overseer is to be 'a lover
of goodness'.

4. *Treacherous* refers to a 'traitor, betrayer' (BDAG, p. 867); the
term is also found in Luke 6:16 to refer to Judas Iscariot (cf. also Acts
7:52). *Reckless* is often employed negatively of those who are overly
bold, even arrogant.[20] *Swollen with conceit* translates *tetyphomenoi*, which
Paul used in 1 Timothy 6:4 of the false teacher who does not follow
'the sound words of our Lord Jesus Christ and the teaching that is
in accordance with godliness'. The grammatical construction suggests that this is the state in which they are existing. As noted there,
the term was used in the world of medicine to describe someone
who was mentally ill. The moral philosophers used it pejoratively
to speak of their enemies (usually philosophers of other schools).
The last vice speaks of *lovers of pleasure rather than lovers of God.* The
Jewish philosopher/exegete Philo used the phrase to refer to that
soul that prefers bodily pleasures over love and service of God

---

19 See, e.g., Philo, *Sacr.* 18.1; Lucian, *Alex.* 25.17; Plutarch, *Per.* 30.3. The
    term, often translated 'implacable', is also found in a catalogue of vices
    in Philo, *Sacr.* 32.4.

20 See Plato, *Leg.* 630B, where it is used with 'boasters'; Aristotle, *Eth. nic.*
    3.6.

(*Agr.* 88; cf. NW II.2: 997–998). As Johnson (pp. 405–406) notes, the charge of being a lover of pleasure was common in polemical contexts of philosophical writings, where the moral philosopher accuses another of preferring vice over virtue.

5. *Holding to the outward form of godliness but denying its power.* Syntactically it is likely that the participle starting this verse (*echontes*, 'holding') is concessive; and so we could translate the sentence, '*although* they hold to the outward form of godliness, *yet* they deny its power'. *Morphōsis,* or *outward form,* is used in a similar way in Romans 2:20, where Paul speaks of the Jewish person who has 'in the law the embodiment (*morphōsin*) of knowledge and truth'. Paul does not deny that in the Torah there is 'knowledge and truth'. The problem is that while the Jews he describes pay lip service to the truth of the Torah, their conduct contradicts knowledge of God. So here in 2 Timothy 3:5 (and later in Tit. 1:16, also with Jewish false teachers as the object) Paul paints a scenario where the false teachers pay lip service to the sound doctrine but do not follow up with conduct commensurate to that sound doctrine. It is probable that they use similar language of godliness as Paul; yet they are *denying its power.* Paul's underlying theological assumption, which serves as the basis for his criticism, is that knowledge of God ineluctably leads to a holy life. In fact, if there is no holy life then there is no true knowledge of God. This is a truth that is found in the entire Bible, and was a particular topic of Jesus' proclamation: 'by their fruits you shall know them' (Matt. 7:16). The fruit of true knowledge of God, Paul has told us, 'is love from a pure heart and good conscience and sincere faith' (1 Tim. 1:5). The false teachers, by contrast, are characterized by being first and foremost 'lovers of themselves' (3:2). Thus, they show themselves to be lacking the Holy Spirit, who is given by God's grace in order to empower believers to leave behind godlessness (Tit. 2:11–12; 3:4–7). Timothy is to make a conscious effort to *avoid these* (see BDAG, p. 124 s.v. *apotrepō*).

6–7. Paul now provides a specific example of how these false teachers operate. These verses, which pinpoint the behaviour of women, should probably be read in conjunction with 1 Timothy 2:9–15 and 5:3–16 (cf. Weiser, p. 252). The reason Timothy is to stay clear of these false teachers is the following: *For among them are those who make their way into households and captivate silly women.* The verb *endyō*, translated here as 'make their way in', is a *hapax* in the New Testament and extremely rare in the contemporary literature. More common is the compound form *pareisdynō*, which basically has the same meaning, and is found in Jude 4 ('intruders'). This verb can also be translated as 'sneak in, creep in', always with a negative connotation.[21]

The false teachers, then, creep *into households* (*oikias*), which, as we will see below, more than likely refer to wealthy estates. To describe what they do once in the households, Paul uses the verb *aichmalōtizō*, which the NRSV translates as 'captivate'. It should also be noted that a number of Greek texts from the period use this verb to give the sense of 'to take captive', with the connotation of taking someone away as plunder.[22] Thus, verse 6 may be intimating not only that the false teachers 'brainwash' the women, but also that they may literally carry them away with them.[23] Whether literal or metaphorical, the false teachers are able to seduce certain women who profess knowledge of the truth.

In order to describe the character of these women, Paul uses the diminutive *gynaikarion*, translated as *silly women* (NRSV; NIV: 'gullible women', RSV, ESV: 'weak women'). This is a pejorative term found in Greek literature when the author is referring to women who are sensually corrupt.[24] Paul continues describing the women who are the targets of the false teachers by saying that they are *overwhelmed by their sins*. This continues the powerful language of the verse, conveying the idea of multiple sins piling on the women because of their refusal to repent and follow sound doctrine. The

---

21 See, e.g., Plutarch, *Ag. Cleom.* 3.1 (love of silver and gold 'creeps' into a city); *Apoph. lac.* 216B, 239F.

22 The verb is often used in the description of plundering during war: 1 Macc. 5:13; 8:10; Alexander Polyhistor, *Fragments* 3.26; Josephus, *J.W.* 10.172; Arrian, *Anab.* 3.22; Epictetus, *Diatr.* 1.28.26.

23 Cf. BDAG, p. 31. The Spanish Reina-Valera translates the verb as 'llevan cautivas' ('they carry away as captives').

24 See esp. Epictetus, *Diatr.* 2.22.24 (of Helen); 3.1.32, 3.22.36 (of an adulterer); 4.1.86. The Spanish diminutive *mujercitas* almost completely captures the sense of *gynaikarion*.

next negative characteristic is that they are *swayed by all kinds of desires.* The present tense with the participle *swayed* suggests that this is a continuous state of affairs. *Desires (epithymia)* refer to any disordered passion.

With verse 7 Paul adds one final descriptor of the deceived women. The language suggests a teaching-learning context. The women *are always being instructed and can never arrive at the knowledge of the truth.* The construction of the syntax is in the form of a chiasm ABA'B': A) always; B) learning; A') never; B') arriving. The chiasm has the ring of a proverb (Marshall, p. 777: 'a memorable epigram').

With some exceptions (most notable Musonius Rufus), the elite men and philosophers of the Greco-Roman period, including Jews like Philo and Josephus, viewed women as being incapable of learning philosophy. Commentators who dispute that Paul wrote 2 Timothy suggest that the anonymous author agreed with this view of women. They suggest that the author was attempting to return Christian communities to the patriarchal order that the more egalitarian historical Paul had relativized.[25] This is one of the main reasons why women are (in their view) portrayed so negatively in the Pastoral Epistles, including the belief that they lack the capacity to learn. Yet, we should note that verse 7 does not convey the sense that women could not learn *because* they were women. Rather, *certain* women could not learn because they were loaded with sinful passions. The problem is not one of gender but rather human sinfulness.

8. *As Jannes and Jambres opposed Moses.* Paul shifts back to the false teachers. He employs a tradition about the sorcerers of Egypt who responded to the wonders performed by Moses and Aaron. In Exodus 7:8–13 Aaron casts down his staff, which turns into a serpent. Then Pharaoh calls his own miracle workers to respond. The Septuagint calls these men *sophistas … pharmakous … epaoidoi,* all negative terms referring to magicians. The OT text provides no names for these Egyptian miracle workers. However, tradition subsequent to the writing of Exodus 7 gives these magicians names.

---

25 See Fiorenza, *Memory,* pp. 230–233, 288–291; Merz, *Selbstauslegung* pp. 344–375 (the author of the Pastoral Epistles interprets 2 Cor. 11:2–3); Hoklotubbe, *Civilized Piety,* pp. 89–90.

For example, the Targum Pseudo-Jonathan, a translation of Hebrew text of the OT into Aramaic, adds the following after 'sorcerers': 'and Jannes and Jambres'. This tradition is found in Greco-Roman literature. Pliny the Elder (first century AD) writes, 'There is yet another branch of magic, derived from Moses, Jannes, Lotaper and the Jews' (*Natural History* 30.11). Another Roman, Apuleius (second century AD), writes, 'call me the famous Carmendas or Damogeron, or their predecessors Moses, Iohannes [i.e., Jannes], Apollobex' (*Apologia* 90.6). The tradition outside Judaism has wrongly placed Moses in the same team as the Egyptians!

Paul probably included Jannes and Jambres because Jannes, in particular, had the reputation of being a magician: and in many sectors of the Greco-Roman world the practice of magic was the realm of charlatans and deceivers. Paul thus implicitly categorizes the false teachers as being no better than corrupt magicians who oppose the gospel for the sake of money.

In the following clause Paul brings out the spiritual condition of the false teachers. They are men *of corrupt mind and counterfeit faith*. The first trait was already used in 1 Timothy 6:5. We noted there that the language evokes medical imagery. Paul portrays the mind (*noos*) as broken. Furthermore, concerning their faith – here referring to both objective and subjective aspects – they are found to be 'reprobate' (LSJ, s.v. *adokimos*; cf. Tit. 1:16). What renders them corrupt and reprobate is the fact that they, like Jannes and Jambres, *also oppose the truth*. The *reason* they oppose the truth is that they are corrupt and reprobate. They are therefore in a vicious circle, standing against the gospel because they are corrupt and reprobate; and being corrupt and reprobate *because* they stand against the gospel. Only God's power can pull them out of such spiritual vortex.

9. Despite all the activity and occasional 'success' of false teachers (vv. 6–7), Paul is confident that they *will not make much progress*. How can Paul be so optimistic? The next clause provides the reason: *Because their folly will become evident to all, as also happened with those*. This is an unexpected cause for the future fall of the false teachers. One would have expected language that more directly involved God's action against the false teachers: perhaps something like, 'God will put away the false teachers.' Instead, the halting of their progress is directly tied to the perception of *all*, a hyperbole that speaks of the majority of believers in the Ephesian churches. The word that is used for this perception is *ekdēlos* ('quite evident, plain', BDAG, p. 300). This is a *hapax* in the New Testament. However, the simpler form in both adjectives and verbs (*dēlos* and *dēloō*, respectively) is used in other parts of the New Testament to speak of divine revelation given to God's people.[26] It is likely, then, that the Holy Spirit will work in the congregations to reveal the false teachers for who they truly are (cf. 1 Tim. 5:24–25). And this revelation will spur the believers to stop them.

A question remains, however: what is it about the false teachers that will be made plain (by the Holy Spirit) and which will bring their progress to an end? Paul says that it is their *folly* that will become manifest to all. The noun *anoia* appears only here and in Luke 6:11 in the New Testament. The Hellenistic moral philosophers use the word as a contrast to reason, which, they believe, leads to a life of virtue. *Anoia*, by contrast, is irrational and foolish, leading to trouble and a life of immorality.[27] The folly of the false teachers will be manifested in their immorality, which results from their resistance to the gospel.

Theology

There is in this passage arguably the most extensive description of the false teachers and their activities that we find in the Pastoral Epistles. Here we find an implicit challenge for the contemporary church. On the basis of the help of the Holy Spirit, the church is responsible for halting the activity of false teachers who speak in the name of the church of Jesus Christ. By both their teaching and ethics, which are inseparable in the Pastoral Epistles, it will become evident to the entire congregation (not just the leaders) that certain teachers are actually opposing the truth of the gospel. When this happens, it is our pastoral duty to unmask the false teachers after

---

26 See, e.g., Heb. 9:8 (the Holy Spirit reveals); 1 Pet. 1:11 (the Spirit of Christ reveals); 2 Pet. 1:14 (the Lord Jesus Christ reveals).

27 See particularly Dio Chrysostom, *Or.* 32.15–16. In *The Wisdom of Solomon anoia* is part of idolatry (16:18; 19:3).

warning them. This is to be done with gentleness, for perhaps God might grant them repentance (2:25).

This scenario implies that there is truth (*alētheia*, used twice in 3:1–10), which stems from God, who speaks through the Holy Scriptures (3:14–17) and which is the norm for the church. Transgression of the truth, namely the gospel of Jesus Christ, is not permitted in the church. Without the gospel of Jesus Christ, which is proclaimed and explained in the Bible, the church ceases to exist, even if it wants to call itself church and continue with all the external trappings. It is the duty of church leaders to teach the believers the gospel so that together they may perceive those who are enemies of the gospel. This requires constant instruction from the Scriptures, which is Paul's next topic in 2 Timothy.

C. Timothy's hope for distressing times (3:10–17)

Context
Apart from the second-person singular imperative of 3:1 ('you must understand'), the remaining verses of 3:1–9 only spoke in the *plural*, of others: 'people' (v. 2), 'among them' (v. 6), 'those' (v. 6), 'these people' (v. 8), 'those two men' (v. 9), 'their folly' (v. 9). This shows that 3:1–9 was dominated by a *description* of the false teachers. By contrast, the syntax of 3:10–17 is dominated by the second and first person *singular*. The thrust of the section now has to do with Timothy's individual response to the false teachers, which is largely based on his following of Paul's example and teaching. We can thus see that 3:10–17 is primarily about *prescription* to help Timothy remain faithful in the distressing future that has already arrived. Timothy will be able to remain faithful if he follows the example and teaching of Paul and his grandmother and mother, all of whom based their existence on the sacred Scriptures.

Another way of viewing the structure of this section, particularly verses 14–17, has been suggested by Weiser (pp. 268–270). He sees as the centre of the section the command of verse 14: 'continue'. This continuation of Timothy is based on two 'foundational thoughts'. The first foundation refers to *persons* (i.e., Paul and Timothy's grandmother and mother). The second foundation is of an *objective nature* and refers to the Holy Scriptures.

Comment

10. *Now you have observed …* Paul begins with a contrast. As opposed to the false teachers, who have rejected the truth, Timothy for his part has followed the way of godliness. The verb *parakoloutheō*, translated as *observed* (NRSV), can also be translated as 'follow' (NASB).[28] As is the case in all the Pastoral Epistles but especially in 2 Timothy, to follow Paul is to follow the truth, for Paul himself has been appointed an apostle and thus an authoritative carrier of the apostolic tradition, which goes back to the teaching of Christ himself (cf. 1 Cor. 4:14–16; 15:3–10).

Timothy has followed *my teaching, my conduct, my aim in life, my faith, my patience, my love, my steadfastness.* On 'teaching' (*didaskalia*), see on 1 Timothy 4:6 and Introduction. *Conduct* translates *agōgē*, which is often found in combination with *bios* ('life').[29] The word can thus refer to a 'way of life' (BDAG, p. 17). The philosopher and priest Plutarch, in quoting a speech from Lycurgus, links together 'teaching' and 'way of life' (*Lib. ed.* 4.3). As Johnson notes (p. 417), in antiquity it was the mark of a genuine philosopher that his life matched his teaching. This is exactly what Paul says the false teachers are not able to do (3:5). The next phrase, *aim in life*, translates *prothesis*, which was used of God's election in 1:9. Here it is used to refer to Timothy's 'purpose' or 'plan' for life, which is in imitation of Paul. *My faith* probably has both an objective and a subjective sense: body of doctrine and trust in God. *My patience, my love, my steadfastness.* The last two of these three virtues are also found in the 'fruit of the Spirit' text in Galatians 5:22. The first virtue can also be translated as 'forbearance' (see LSJ, s.v. and BDAG, pp. 612–613).

11. Paul makes a slight shift to speak of the hard circumstances of life which he, as well as Timothy, have experienced. The nouns change from the singular of verse 10 to the plural. It should also

---

28 An excellent example is found in Diogenes Laertius, *Lives of Eminent Philosophers* 7.1.3, where someone points out Crates to Zeno and tells him, 'follow this man' (*toutō parakolouthēson*).

29 See, e.g., Polybius 4.74.1, 4; 23.5.9; Josephus, *J.W.* 462.2, used in combination with *eusebeia*.

be noted that this text resembles the catalogue of sufferings in
2 Corinthians 4:7–12; 11:23–29 and 12:10. Here Paul speaks of *my
persecutions, and my suffering the things that happened to me in Antioch,
Iconium, and Lystra.* Luke describes these sufferings in Acts 13:44–52;
14:1–7, 19–23. From the first city Paul was kicked out; in the second
city there was an attempt by both Jews and Gentiles to stone him;
in the third city he was stoned, dragged outside the city and left
for dead. In mentioning these persecutions Paul probably wants
Timothy to view his sufferings through the lens of the ideal moral
philosopher.[30] In the Greco-Roman period many men boasted of
being virtuous philosophers. However, very few lived out their
philosophy during distressing circumstances. The true philosopher,
by contrast, endured hardships without complaining or quitting.[31]
Paul – and Timothy – demonstrate their genuineness of character
by lives of endurance in the face of persecution and hardship. As
we will see in 4:12, suffering in the Christian life is ultimately tied
to the suffering Saviour.

Yet the Lord rescued me from all of them. It is not clear if the identity
of *the Lord* here is that of the Father or the Son. In light of the
context, it seems to be a reference to Jesus Christ (3:12, 15; cf.
Marshall, p. 385). This would be significant, for this verse is very
nearly a quotation of Psalm 34:4 (LXX 33:5): 'I sought the Lord,
and he answered me, and delivered me from all my fears.' Paul

---

30 Ultimately, Paul's sufferings are in imitation of Jesus (2 Cor. 4:7–18;
    Gal. 6:7; Phil. 3:7–10). But it is probable that the sufferings of Jesus
    were themselves partly viewed as the sufferings of the noble
    philosopher, particularly Socrates. This has been well argued, at least
    as pertaining to the Gospel of Luke and Acts, by Alexander, 'Acts
    and Ancient Intellectual Biography', pp. 31–63; Sterling, '*Mors
    Philosophi*', pp. 383–402. This in no way minimizes the dominant NT
    portrayal of Jesus' suffering and death as that of the Suffering Servant
    of Isa. 40–66.

31 See, e.g., Seneca, *Ep.* 13.1; 24.18–20; Dio Chrysostom, *Or.* 8.11–16;
    Epictetus, *Diatr.* 2.19.24–28. On Paul and the ancient suffering
    philosopher, see Fitzgerald, *Cracks in an Earthen Vessel*; Malherbe,
    Light from the Gentiles, 2:710–711, 742.

would thus be identifying the Lord who answered David with Jesus Christ.[32]

The reason why Paul adds the last phrase is implicitly hortatory, nudging his hearers to bless the Lord – not very different from what the psalmist intended in Psalm 34. It is unlikely that Paul makes the statement in order to provoke a triumphalistic expectation for Timothy and his audience. Paul is not saying that all Christians will be spared death when they are persecuted. In fact, Paul uses the verb *rhyomai* at 4:18 ('The Lord will *rescue* me from every evil attack'), even though he is clear at 4:6 that his time of death is at hand. It is more likely that while Paul hints that God may rescue Timothy from death in upcoming persecutions (just as he rescued a younger Paul in the past), his statement is meant to remind Timothy that the Lord will *ultimately* deliver him from the greatest of afflictions, that is, eternal death. The thought would thus be very similar to 2 Corinthians 1:8–11, where rescue from the severe affliction in Asia was a foretaste of the ultimate rescue from eternal death, which is brought about by the resurrection of Jesus Christ (cf. also Rom. 7:24).

12. Paul concludes the first part of verses 10–17 by adding a statement about the reality of suffering for every Christian: *Indeed, all who want to live a godly life in Christ Jesus will be persecuted*. The Greek syntax highlights the word *all* by placing it at the beginning of the sentence. The implication may be that it is not only leaders of the church who will suffer but *all* believers. The statement is clarified by the phrase, *who want to live a godly life*. In a sense this statement is redundant, for the only way to live the Christian life is in a godly manner; otherwise it simply is not a Christian life. Paul adds the phrase to press the truth that *godly* (*eusebōs*) existence is not foreign to suffering. The reason for this can be explained in different ways, but for this text the prepositional phrase *in Christ Jesus* may provide one of the answers. The Christians suffer persecution because they exist in the sphere of Jesus Christ. They are one with the Saviour who 'came not to be served but to serve, and to give his life a ransom

---

32 See also 1 Thess. 1:10, where Jesus is identified as the one who 'rescues us from the wrath to come' (my translation).

for many' (Mark 10:45). They are one with the Saviour who 'being found in human form … humbled himself and became obedient to the point of death—even death on a cross' (Phil. 2:7–8). They are one with the Saviour who said, "'A servant is not greater than his master." If they persecute me, they will also persecute you' (John 15:20). The Christian identity, not least that of its leaders, is one of suffering (see also 1 Cor. 4:8–13; Col. 1:24).

13. *But wicked people and impostors will go from bad to worse.* In verses 10–17 Paul returns to the false teachers of whom he spoke about in verses 1–10. He calls them *wicked (ponēros)* and *impostors*, the latter an excellent translation of the Greek term *goēs*. This word was used of a 'sorcerer' or 'wizard'.[33] We may use the word 'trickster' to convey the sense of *goēs*. The word was also often used of false philosophers who performed 'rhetorical tricks' in order to deceive and gain money (Dio Chrysostom, *Or.* 32.11). An example is found in Philo, *Spec.* 1.315, where he speaks of the false prophet of Deuteronomy 13:1–11.

> Further if anyone cloaking himself under the name and guise of a prophet and claiming to be possessed by inspiration lead us on to worship of the gods recognized in the different cities, we ought not to listen to him and be deceived by the name of prophet. For such a one is no prophet, but an impostor [*goēs*], since his oracles and pronouncements are falsehoods invented by himself.

These imposters, Paul tells us, *will make progress for the worse.* Clearly Paul is using irony here, for the imposters are actually regressing. Perhaps further describing the 'worse' or adding a new element, Paul inserts another ironic aspect of the fate of the false teachers: *deceiving others and being deceived.* Because the minds of the false teachers are so corrupt, they do not realize that in deceiving others they are also deceiving and ruining themselves (see Johnson, pp. 418–419).

14–17. With this third section of verses 14–17 Paul returns to command Timothy directly. The implicit question, which gives rise

---

33 See LSJ, s.v. In Plato, *Symp.* 203D, it is used together with *pharmakeus* ('sorcerer') and *sophistēs* ('Sophist'). See our comments under Jannes and Jambres in 3:8, who were so considered.

to the command, is the following: how will Timothy be able to keep himself from being deceived by the false teachers?

14. *But as for you, continue in what you have learned and firmly believed.* The present tense imperative *mene* can also be translated as 'remain'. What must Timothy continually remain in so as to avoid deception? The next section of the clause provides the answer. The things Timothy has *learned* (*emathes*) refer to the sound, apostolic tradition, the 'deposit' which he has received (Marshall, p. 787; Towner, p. 580). Not only has Timothy learned the sound doctrine but he has also *firmly believed* it. This phrase translates the verb *pistoō*. The verb conveys the sense of persuasion and confirmation.[34] It will become clear in what follows that the Holy Scriptures are the source of Timothy's confidence in the apostolic doctrine.

Knowing from whom you learned. The participle *eidōs* ('knowing') at the beginning the clause is causal. Paul gives the reason why Timothy must continue in the sound doctrine. It is related to the persons who taught him the Scriptures. Some manuscripts read the singular (C³ D Maj.), which probably has only Paul in mind. However, the plural is better attested (א A 33 81). Paul probably refers both to himself and to Timothy's grandmother and mother, who taught him the Scriptures since he was a child (1:5 and 3:15).

15. *And how from childhood you have known the sacred writings.* The conjunction *and* provides a second reason for Timothy's remaining in the apostolic doctrine: it is not just *who* taught him but also the *source* from which he was taught, viz., the Scriptures. It is the combination of godly teachers basing their instruction on Holy Scripture that leads to permanence in the sound doctrine. From Acts 16:1–5 we learn that Timothy's father was a Gentile, and probably not a Christian. His mother, on the other hand, was Jewish and a believer in Jesus the Messiah. Since Timothy has known the Holy Scriptures from *childhood*, it is probable that his mother and grandmother (2 Tim. 1:1–5) instructed him, at least in his early years.

---

34 See, e.g., Dionysius of Halicarnassus, *Is.* 16.39; Polybius 8.15; 3 Macc. 4.19; Philo, *Alleg. Interp.* 3.208; *Legat.* 311.1; QE 2.9.2; Josephus, *Ag. Ap.* 2.1.3.

The phrase declaring Timothy's knowledge of the Holy Scriptures since childhood is similar to the statements of two other Jewish writers of the period. I quote their statements to give the reader a flavour of the Jewish commitment to the Scriptures, which is also found in Paul and Timothy. First is the statement of Philo: 'For all men guard their own customs, but this is especially true of the Jewish nation. Holding that the laws are oracles vouchsafed by God and having been trained in this doctrine from their earliest years, they carry the likenesses of the commandments enshrined in their souls' (*Legat.* 211). The second statement is from Josephus' apologetic work *Against Apion* 2.178: 'But, should anyone of our nation be questioned about the laws, he would repeat them all more readily than his own name. The result, then, of our thorough grounding in the laws from the first dawn of intelligence is that we have them, as it were, engraven on our souls.' The phrase *sacred writings* translates *hiera grammata*. This phrase was used in Greek literature to designate the 'holy records', often deposited in temples, which told the story of a particular civilization.[35] Philo and Josephus use the phrase to refer to the Old Testament.[36]

These sacred writings, Paul continues, *are able to instruct you*. The use of *able*, with its lexical form *dynamai*, takes the reader back to 1:7, 12 and 2:1 where 'ability' was predicated of the Holy Spirit. We should thus not think of 3:15 as saying that the written words of the Bible have some inherent magical power to instruct: as if the signs of ink on the paper have inherent power. That would be a pagan idea! Rather, it is the Holy Spirit, who inspired the Bible and commits to help believers understand it (illumination), who empowers God's Word to transform us. We should think of God himself speaking through the Scriptures. Calvin helps us understand this when, in speaking of Scripture, he says that 'God opens his own most hollowed lips' to speak to us (*Inst.* I.6.1). Further, Calvin understood

---

35 See, e.g., Plato, *Tim.* 23F; 27B; Hecataeus of Abdera, *Fragments* 3a, 264, F. 5 (Jacoby); Strabo, *Geogr.* 16.4; 17.1.

36 Philo, *Mos.* 1.23; 2.90; *Contempl.* 28.2; Josephus, *J.W.* 2.159 (with *biblos*); *Ant.* 1.13; 2.210.

Scriptures in the following way: 'God in person speaks in it' (*Inst.* I.7.4). Lastly, Barth speaks of the Word of God as 'God's speaking in person' (*CD* I.1 p. 134); or: 'God's Word is God Himself in His revelation' (*CD* I.1 p. 295).

With two prepositional phrases, one expressing purpose and the other means, Paul speaks of what the Scriptures are able to do: *To instruct you for salvation through faith in Christ Jesus.* The first item refers to all the aspects of salvation found in the Pastoral Epistles: redemption, justification, reconciliation, regeneration. The means of appropriating this salvation is *through faith*, that is, trust/belief *in* and commitment *to* the sound apostolic doctrine, which is ultimately about *Christ Jesus.* Thus, faith is not faith 'in faith' but on a person: Christ Jesus as known through the prophets and apostles.

16. *All scripture is inspired by God.* Paul begins verse 16 with asyndeton (that is, no connective particle), thereby giving the initial phrase a deep sense of solemnity and gravitas, almost like a proverb. With *scripture (graphē)* Paul refers primarily to Israel's Scriptures, what we call the Old Testament; possibly he also refers to his letters (cf. 2 Pet. 3:16). All these Scriptures, Paul declares, are *inspired by God. Theopneustos* is 'breathed-out by God'. Language similar to the one used by Paul here was used by Jewish writers to point to 'God's activity in inspiring Scripture' (Marshall, p. 794, pointing to: Philo, *Decal.* 35; *Conf.* 44; Josephus, *C. Ap.* 1.37). The Scriptures come from God and 'speak' with God's authority. Of course, since humans put the words of God into written language (*grammata*, v. 15), there is a human aspect to the Scriptures which, however, does not negate or in any way qualify the divine authority of the Scriptures.

We should understand the word *and* at the beginning of the second part of verse 16 in a consecutive manner: 'and as a result.' (So also Spicq, p. 788, who paraphrases: 'And in consequence'; cf. also Marshall, p. 791). Because Scripture is inspired by God, it is *useful for teaching, for reproof, for correction, and for training in righteousness.* On *didaskalia* ('teaching') see on 1 Timothy 1:10. *Elegmos* ('reproof'), which occurs only here in the New Testament, conveys an 'expression of strong disapproval, *reproach, rebuke, reproof*' (BDAG, p. 314). *Epanorthōsis* ('correction') is another New Testament *hapax* that is found in moralistic literature to speak of 'amendment' of life.[37] To express the last goal Paul uses the term *paideia* ('training'; for the verbal form see on 2:25 and 1 Timothy 1:20; see further on Titus 2:12). This training, which implies that time and effort will be necessary, is in the sphere of *righteousness*. The emphasis thus falls on behaviour that follows the commandments of God because of having been previously made right with God.

17. Since the Scriptures serve as the basis and standard of Christian existence, Timothy is to teach them; but first he must apply them to himself in order to avoid the deception of the false teachers. *So that everyone who belongs to God may be proficient, equipped for every good work*. Paul concludes with a statement of purpose about the ultimate aim of the teaching, reproof, correction and training that stems from the Scriptures. The syntax of the Greek text highlights the term *artios* ('proficient') by its placement at the front of the clause. The word conveys the sense of being thoroughly prepared to face any situation. Paul then explains in more detail with the following phrase (cf. Towner, pp. 513–514). *Equipped for every good work*. Proficiency as a result of submitting to Scripture means that the minister of the gospel will be ready to perform the kind of loving, good works that are the hallmark of genuine faith. On 'good works' in the Pastoral Epistles, see Introduction and on 2:21; 1 Timothy 5:10; 6:18; Titus 1:16; 2:7, 14; 3:1.

The expression *everyone who belongs to God*, which could be translated, closer to the Greek text, as 'the man of God' (*ho tou theou anthrōpos*; RSV, ESV), must refer to all believers, since the performance of good works is the duty of every Christian in the Pastoral Epistles. However, since the immediate context has to do with Timothy, the initial reference may be to Christian leaders (thus NIV: 'the servant of God'; cf. Köstenberger, pp. 268–269).

Theology
Second Timothy 3:16–17 is a definite statement of the nature of Scripture and how God uses the Scriptures in the church. Sadly,

---

37 See Timaeus, *Fragments* 224.2; Hierocles, *Elements of Ethics* 4.25.53; Philo, *Moses* 2.36; Epictetus, *Diatr.* 3.26.15, used with *paideia*.

some scholars who reject the orthodox and evangelical understanding of inspiration tend to concentrate on verse 17, to the detriment of the previous verse, which tells us what Scripture is. This is because a liberal view of the Bible wants to continue to use the Bible while (mis)translating the ontology of the Bible into something much more immanent and this-worldly. But to manoeuvre in this fashion is to destroy the integrity of the Bible as a whole and of this text in particular. For the usefulness of the Bible for morality ('every good work') is entirely dependent on its nature. Only because Scripture is God-breathed – that is, it comes from God through the Holy Spirit and not from ourselves – can it both determine what constitutes good works and give the strength, through God's Spirit, to perform those good works.

D. Proclaim the word in season and out of season (4:1-8)

Context
Paul continues and finalizes his exhortation to Timothy. The word *kairos* ('time, day, season') holds together 3:1–4:8, being used three times (3:1; 4:2, 6). In 3:1–17 Paul warned Timothy of the difficult times (*kairos*) that would come – and were in fact present – and which required him to follow the example of Paul and the Holy Scriptures. In 4:1–8 Paul again anchors his command to Timothy in the fact that a time (*kairos*) is coming when sound doctrine will not be accepted. Now Paul adds another layer to the element of *kairos* – and that is that Paul's own *kairos* for departure from this life has come. All the more reason, therefore, for Timothy to be bold in the preaching of the word. We could thus summarize this section as follows: in light of future rejection of sound doctrine on the one hand, and of Paul's departure on the other, Timothy must preach boldly.

Paul employs two common themes from the domain of moral philosophy in order to communicate clearly to Timothy. First, there is the theme of the proper time to teach: *favorable or unfavorable* (4:2). This was a common theme in moral philosophy. Given that the teacher must use frankness of speech (*parrēsia*) to help his pupil advance in virtue, the question of when to use *parrēsia* was common. The ideal philosopher should always use *parresia*. Paul picks up this theme to tell Timothy that – given the *kairos* – he must preach with all frankness in *favorable or unfavorable* times.

The second motif that Paul picks up is the 'itching ears'. The metaphor is used in a negative fashion by moral philosophers who contrast an itchy ear with the ear that wants only to hear the truth.[38]

Comment

1. *In the presence of God and of Christ Jesus ... and in view of his appearing and his kingdom, I solemnly urge you.* The construction of this verse is of a piece with that of 1 Timothy 5:21. Paul is about to give a command to Timothy for which he summons two witnesses: God and Jesus Christ. Paul perhaps invokes the two-witness motif of Deuteronomy 17:6 and 19:15. It is significant that we have God and Jesus Christ united, just as was the case in the salutations of both letters to Timothy.

As if the calling of the two witnesses was not sufficient to catch Timothy's attention, Paul adds even more gravity by saying that the adjuration made is also in light of Christ's *appearance* (*epiphaneia*) and his kingdom. On *epiphaneia* see on 1 Timothy 6:14; Titus 2:11; 3:4. The word refers to Christ's kingly appearance to vanquish his enemies and save his people. Since this is parousia language, it makes sense that the final clause mentions Christ's *kingdom*, which comes to full fruition at his return.

Who is to judge the living and the dead. This clause tells us something about Christ Jesus. He is designated as the one who will judge all. This powerful act, which is the prerogative of God alone, is also mentioned of Jesus Christ in other New Testament texts (Acts 10:42; 17:31; Rom. 2:16; 1 Pet. 4:5).

Paul views the commands that he is about to give as so vital that he calls on God and the Messiah as witnesses. The adjuration includes references to the return and judgment of Christ. It is important to observe that the theological logic implies that these future events are to have a profound effect on Timothy's activity in the here and now (cf. Oberlinner, 1996, p. 154; Marshall, p. 799).

---

38 See Philo, *Agr.* 136; Lucian, *Cal.* 21; *Salt.* 2; Seneca, *Ep.* 75.6–7; 108.6. For other examples see NW II.2:1008–1009.

2. What is this work for which Paul summons God and Christ and which is Timothy's task? *Proclaim the message.* The term *proclaim* (*kēryssō*) is traditional language of the early church for the preaching of the gospel.[39] *Kēryssō* takes a number of objects: 'word', 'Christ', 'gospel'. Furthermore, the language goes back to Jesus' own proclamation of the arrival of the kingdom of God (Mark 1:14, 38–39; 13:10; 14:9), which itself goes back to Isaiah 40:3. The NRSV renders the object of the proclamation as *the message.* The Greek text has *logos*, 'word', which goes back to 2:9 and refers to the Christian message of salvation as the truth (cf. also Eph. 1:13; Col. 1:5). As 4:5 clarifies, in view is not only preaching to believers but also missionary proclamation.

Paul follows this injunction with four more imperatives: *Be persistent whether the time is favorable or unfavorable; convince, rebuke, and encourage with the utmost patience in teaching.* The relationship of the first imperative *proclaim the message* to the others has been debated. Knight (p. 453) holds that the four imperatives modify the first, while others view each imperative standing independently.

The first imperative conveys the sense of alertness or readiness (BDAG, p. 418). By adding the phrase *whether the time is favorable or unfavorable* (*eukairōs akairōs*), Paul may be playing off the old philosophical question of when it is appropriate for an audience to receive frank speech. In light of the times they were living in, Paul seems to swat aside the question: *any* time is acceptable for proclamation! Of course, this does not mean that Paul was encouraging tactlessness, or that we should be overbearing in evangelization (see end of v. 2!).

The next imperative, *elenchō*, was used in 1 Timothy 5:20 to explain what Timothy must do with elders who 'persist in sin'. The verb was translated as 'rebuke' by the NRSV. Here, however, the verb is translated with *convince.* Although this is possible, we should note that the way the verb 'to convince' is employed in contemporary English language has more intellectual connotations than the Greek *elenchō.* As used in the New Testament, the verb gives the

---

39 See esp. Rom. 10:8–9; 1 Cor. 1:23; 15:11–12; 2 Cor. 4:5; Gal. 2:2; Phil. 1:15; 1 Thess. 2:9.

sense of 'convicting' or 'unmasking' that which is wrong.[40] Thus,
Timothy's activity here is that of showing his listeners their spiritual
shortcomings, doubtless with the help of the Holy Spirit. In light
of Titus 1:9, it is likely that false teachers are in view.

The verb, *epitimaō* 'rebuke', carries the sense of strong censuring
(it is used, for example, for Jesus 'rebuking' demons: Matt. 17:18;
Mark 1:25; 9:25). It is likely that false teachers are in view.

The last imperative, *encourage*, has believers in mind (see
1 Tim. 1:3 and 5:1). The prepositional phrase *with the utmost patience
in teaching*, modifies the last imperative. *Makrothymia* ('patience')
and *didachē* ('teaching') were used by Paul in 3:10 to speak of those
qualities exemplified by him, which Timothy imitated. As for the
second term, it is probable that Paul has used a word that is usually
employed for the *content* of teaching to speak now of the *manner*
of teaching. He wants to highlight 'that Christian exhortation is
… to have its basis in sound teaching of the gospel' (Marshall,
p. 801). Paul is stressing that there is only *one* teaching, that of sound
doctrine.

3. It is precisely the sound doctrine that will be rejected in the
future, part of which is now present: *For the time is coming when people
will not put up with sound doctrine.* Paul speaks of Christian teaching
as *sound doctrine* (cf. 1 Tim. 1:10). We noted that moral philosophers
often portrayed themselves as physicians of the soul who through
their rational teaching could bring back to soundness or health
those who were spiritually diseased because of their slavery to
passions and desires. A good example of this is found in the moral
philosopher Apollonius of Tyana (first century AD). Someone
asked him to turn his older brother from the immoral life he was
leading. After some protest, Apollonius agreed and said: 'So far as
I can do anything, I will heal (*iasomai*) him of these bad passions
(*pathōn*)' (Philostratus, *Vit. Apoll.* 1.13). Paul views the Christian
sound doctrine as that which, through its proclamation, can heal us
of our disordered passions. The sad irony found in this text is that
individuals who are spiritually ill will not receive the very thing

---

40 See, e.g., Matt. 18:15; Luke 3:19; John 16:8; 1 Cor. 14:24–25; Eph. 5:11,
       13; Tit. 2:15.

that will make them well. This in itself demonstrates that they are not well.

Rather than receiving sound doctrine, these individuals, *in accordance with their own desires, will accumulate for themselves teachers who will scratch their ears.* I have substantially altered both the order and language of the NRSV in order to bring out more clearly the logic of the sentence. In the first part of this clause Paul answers the question that one may be asking in light of the first part of verse 3: why would they not receive that teaching that will bring them healing of the soul? With a prepositional phrase placed early in the clause for emphasis, Paul says it is a matter of *their own desires (epithymia)*. This is the reason why they reject the good 'medicine' and instead acquire for themselves that which will only make them more ill. *Epithymia* is not of itself a bad thing: the term describes a desire or passion. However, in the New Testament it is often used of desires that are in a state of disorder. In the Pastoral Epistles this is usually the sense (see on 2:22 and 3:6). The term was very common in the vocabulary of moral philosophers to explain the diseased soul (see on 1 Tim. 6:9; cf. Malherbe, *Light from the Gentiles*, 1:124–6).

The sick soul not only rejects sound doctrine but also seeks numerous (*accumulate*) teachers who will scratch their ears. The metaphor was common to polemicize against people who, instead of wanting to hear that which is true, would rather only listen to speakers and teachers who said what was pleasing (see Context).[41] This was often linked with wanting to hear the latest fad or novelty (see Lucian, *Slander* 21; cf. Johnson, p. 429).

4. This verse brings to conclusion the thought begun in verse 3 by recapitulation; at the same time a crescendo is reached by means of a powerful literary contrast. This juxtaposition is expressed by means of a chiasmus: A B C A' B' C'. I rearrange the wording of the NRSV to bring out this contrast for the reader: *From* (A) *the truth* (B) *they will depart* (C) ... *to* (A') *myths* (B') *they will turn* (C'). The contrast is between the *truth (alētheia*; see 1 Tim. 2:4) and *myths*. This last term is used in the context of the Pastoral Epistles to speak of Jewish stories woven out of Old Testament genealogical trees (see on

---

41 Seneca, *Ep.* 75.6–7; Quintilian, *Inst.* 11.3.60.

1 Tim. 1:4; Tit. 1:4). Evidently, these myths proved to be tantalizing to the hearers, sweeping them away from the truth.

5. In typical paraenetic style, Paul moves back to commanding Timothy directly after explaining how things will be in the 'future'. *As for you, always be sober, endure suffering, do the work of an evangelist, carry out your ministry fully.* The first imperative (*nēphō*, 'be sober, self-controlled') is often found in eschatological contexts in the Christian tradition (e.g., 1 Thess. 5:6–8; 1 Pet. 1:13; 4:7). Since believers belong to the eschatological light and not the darkness, which is 'passing away' (Rom. 13:11–14), they must be alert, with thoughts clear as light. Since verses 1–8 are set in the end times (when deception is particularly rampant) it makes sense that Timothy is called to be sober. The call to be sober or self-controlled also appears as a necessary trait of the good philosopher, particularly in the context of his teaching. A neat example is found in the emperor and philosopher Marcus Aurelius, who is thankful for his father, because the latter rejected any type of adulation or pandering. Instead, he was always on the alert in his governing of the empire: 'yea, his soberness in all things' [*nēphon en pasin*].[42] This language is virtually identical to verse 5. The idea is that Timothy must always be on the alert against false teachers.

Paul again instructs Timothy to *endure suffering* (see 1:8; 2:3). Timothy must also take care to *do the work of an evangelist.* The term 'evangelist' (*euangelistēs*) is scarce in the New Testament (Acts 21:8; Eph. 4:11). In Acts 21:8 Philip, one of the Seven, is called 'the evangelist'. Philip had 'proclaimed (*ekēryssen*) Christ' to the Samaritans (8:5); he then met the Ethiopian eunuch and 'evangelized (*euēngelisato*) Jesus to him' (8:35, my translation). To do the work of an evangelist is to proclaim the identity and work of Jesus Christ to unbelievers. Oberlinner (1995, p. 158) indicates that the phraseology ('do the work ...') points not to an office in the church but to a task waiting to be completed by church leaders. I would add that the work of evangelizing is not the sole property of church *leaders* but of all Christians (see Acts 8:4).

The final command, *carry out your ministry fully,* expresses a sense of finality by the use of the verb *plērophoreō* ('bring to fulfilment'). The

42 Aurelius, *Med.* 1.16.3.

sense is that Timothy must complete the ministry for which God has called him (see further 4:17). As such, this command represents a fitting summary to the paraenetic section. To be noted is also the possessive pronoun *your*, which points to the fact that God had a very specific call/task for Timothy's life (see 2:2; and 1 Tim. 4:14).

6. *As for me, I am already being poured out as a libation, and the time of my departure has come.* It is clear that Paul wants to connect vv. 1–5 to the current verses. In the Greek text this is confirmed by the conjunction *gar* ('for', left untranslated by the NRSV). We can express the connection in the following way: 'Timothy, in light of the attraction to false doctrine of the later times, *and* in light of my imminent death, you must proclaim the message, be persistent.' Rhetorically speaking, it is likely that Paul employs in verses 6–8 the 'Last Will and Testament' genre.[43] One of the purposes for using this genre is to encourage the younger disciple to pick up the task that the older – and dying – teacher is leaving behind (cf. Towner, p. 609).

In this section Paul describes his death in moving fashion. He highlights the following. First, he presents his death as coming soon, indeed as already in the process of happening. He brings this out in three ways: (1) the adverb *already*; (2) the use of the present tense in *being poured out*; (3) the use of the perfect tense with *has come*, which suggests that the moment of death is at hand. Second, Paul describes his death metaphorically by using the language of a libation offering (*spendō*, 'offer a libation/drink offering' BDAG, p. 937). He also used this language to speak of his death in Philippians 2:17. The question is what he wants to communicate by describing his death in such a way. It is likely that the metaphor conveys the meaning of sacrifice. This would mean that Paul views his upcoming death as an offering. But what would *this* mean? For Towner, the sacrificial imagery suggests that Paul did not view his death as meaningless (p. 611). We can go further by saying that this represents Paul's total dedication to God for the sake of the church in imitation of Christ, who shed his blood for her. Given the 'Last Will and Testament' genre encoded in 4:6–8, there may be a not-so-subtle nudge for Timothy and his readers to be willing to offer

---

43 See Martin, *Pauli testamentum*.

their lives in martyrdom should God so call them. Third, Paul describes his death with another metaphor, namely *departure* (Greek *analysis*), which always has a positive connotation as a metaphor.

7. *I have fought the good fight, I have finished the race, I have kept the faith.* Paul describes his imminent death with an athletic metaphor. Paul's succinct formulations, along with the present tense of the three verbs fill the verse with a powerful sense of solemnity and finality, which moves the reader: the life of the beleaguered apostle has come to an end.

The use of athletic imagery to speak of life as a long, hard endeavour was common in the Greco-Roman world, especially among Cynic and Stoic philosophers.[44] Although more than one sport may be in view in verse 7, it is likely that the metaphor is primarily from running (see Pfitzner, p. 183). What is Paul communicating by employing the athletic metaphor? Towner, thinking of the metaphor as also including wrestling, provides an excellent summary: 'Keeping Pauline usage in mind, the application here is necessarily broad, viewing the whole of life as an intense struggle against an opposition in which spiritual power must be matched by personal commitment and resolve to endure to the end of the contest' (p. 612).

The third metaphor, *I have kept the faith*, has been the most disputed (see Marshall, pp. 807–808 for the different possibilities). It is likely that *pistis* ('faith') here has both a subjective and objective meaning. Subjectively, Paul has kept the commitment to his calling intact; he has not broken trust. Objectively, *pistis* refers to the 'deposit' of the Christian faith (see 1:12, 14; 1 Tim. 6:20): Paul has kept his commitment to guarding the gospel. Thus, the idea is not just unbendable commitment for commitment's sake, as if this were an end in itself (this would be more like a Stoic philosopher). Rather, it is commitment *for* the preserving of the gospel. This is the task that now Timothy must pick up.

8. Paul could have closed this section with verse 7. However, he adds another thought to highlight the Lord's just judgment, which will yield rewards to Paul and those like him. *From now on there is reserved for me the crown of righteousness, which the Lord, the righteous judge, will give*

---

44 Cf. Pfitzner, *Paul and the Agon Motif*, pp. 28–35.

me on that day. Paul continues the athletic metaphor. The image of athletes receiving victory crowns (Greek: *stephanos,* crowns made of a wreath of ivy branches or celery leaves) was used commonly in a metaphorical way to speak of virtuous individuals who lived righteously until the end. In Hellenistic Judaism the metaphor was used for the praise of martyrs who had given their lives for the Torah. We find an example in *The Wisdom of Solomon* 4:2: 'When it [virtue] is present, people imitate it, and they long for it when it has gone; throughout all time it marches, crowned in triumph [*stephanēphorousa*], victor in the contest [*athlōn agōna nikēsasa*] for prizes that are undefiled' (NRSV). More pointed is the following text which memorializes the martyrdoms of Eleazar the priest and the mother with her seven sons (see 2 Macc. 7:1–41 for this moving story):

> Truly the contest [*agōn*] in which they were engaged was divine, for on that day virtue gave the awards and tested them for their endurance. The prize was immortality in endless life. Eleazar was the first contestant, the mother of the seven sons entered the competition, and the brothers contended. The tyrant was the antagonist, and the world and the human race the spectators. Reverence for God [*theosebeia*] was the victor and gave the crown [*stephanousa*] to its own athletes. ... Because of which now they stand before the divine throne and live the life eternal of eternal blessedness.
> (4 Macc. 17:11–15, 18, NRSV)

Paul speaks of *the crown of righteousness,* which the Lord will award him on final judgment. Commentators are divided on the meaning of the genitive 'of righteousness'. The two most common interpretations are the following: (1) The genitive is appositional, which would be rendered as 'the crown *which is* righteousness'. Since righteousness, in this context, would mean God's gift of standing in right relationship with him, the metaphor would thus stand for salvation. (2) The genitive has the sense of 'righteousness which is the reward of someone who does righteousness' (see Marshall, pp. 808–809). It is likely that the two types of genitives converge. Paul would thus be affirming that he will receive God's final justification on the day of judgment. At the same time, this crowning is viewed as reward (v. 7). These two concepts are certainly dialectical but not antithetical:

in the New Testament and Paul, justifying faith is not real if it is not worked out in a life of righteousness. But the righteous life is empowered by God: 'not *propter opera sed secundum opera*': 'not on the basis of works but in accordance with works' (Simpson, p. 157).

Since this material is paraenetic, Paul also employs it for encouraging Timothy. Thus, in the remainder of verse 8 he looks away from himself to others. The crown of righteousness will not only be given to Paul *but also to all who have longed for his appearing*. The language is emphatic, as shown by the use of the verb *agapaō* in the perfect tense. The NRSV translation, *who have longed for*, captures the sense. The noun *epiphaneia* ('appearing') was used in verse 2, and as there it refers to Christ's return. The reward is for those whose existence is turned heavenward to please and await their Lord (cf. 1 Cor. 16:22; Rev. 22:20).

Theology

Verses 6–8 provide us with a rare, concentrated thought on Paul's attitude towards his approaching death. We have here, however briefly and implied, Paul's thoughts on facing death, from which we can learn. When facing death, there is a sense of looking backwards and looking forward. When we look back, it must be done through the lens of the gospel; more precisely, obedience to the type of life demanded by the gospel. There is reflection when we look back in this manner, and this reflection can bring contentment even during the valley of death. But contentment is tied both to the direction and intensity of existence. If life was spent in selfish ambition, in idolatry under the cloak of a passion for power, money, sensuality and control, then guilt – not contentment – will dominate the final reflections, unless we lie to ourselves. Paul's reflection in looking back undoubtedly communicates joy and contentment: the type of contentment that an athlete may feel when winning the crown after months, perhaps years, of dedication. Yet, because the biblical pattern of existence is one in which death is followed by resurrection and judgment, the time of dying can also involve looking to the future. Paul looks forward to meeting the Lord and receiving the unfading crown because, through the empowerment of the Spirit, he has been a faithful servant to his Lord until the end.

4. FINAL INSTRUCTIONS AND GREETINGS (4:9–22)

A. Personal requests, news of the judicial hearing and letter closure (4:9–22)

This section has to do chiefly with news of Paul, requests for Timothy and a short list of salutations. Yet, even in such an apparently prosaic context one can discover a theological substructure, especially in verses 9–18.

Context

The language and concepts in these verses point to what may be called a language of martyrdom, particularly vv. 10, 14 and 16–18. That is, Paul's portrayal of himself may be viewed as that of the martyr, one who accepts death for the sake of bearing witness for his Lord. Paul thereby also seeks to encourage Timothy to accept this world view.

The main evidence for this language of martyrdom is intertextual, namely the echoes of Psalm 22 that can be heard in verses 9–18 (see also Spicq, p. 390). Psalm 22 constitutes one of the primary

Scriptures in the framing of the narration of Jesus' suffering and crucifixion, especially in the Gospel of Mark.[1] Jesus is viewed as the righteous sufferer who is abandoned by God and given into the hands of unrighteous men. Nevertheless, the righteous sufferer expresses confidence that God will ultimately deliver him from his enemies. There are aspects of this in 2 Timothy 4:14–18,

It is clear that the New Testament views the crucifixion of Jesus not only as a sacrificial offering for our sins but also as a picture of martyrdom, indeed the martyr *par excellence* (see esp. 1 Pet. 2:21–25).[2] Paul presents his upcoming death as a martyrdom that follows the example of Jesus. The language of martyrdom includes the following elements: (1) the martyr expresses a sense of abandonment by all; (2) the martyr prays for his enemies, at times asking for God's retribution; (3) the martyr expresses confidence that God will judge his enemies; (4) the martyr expresses confidence that God will deliver him. It should be noted that in perhaps the earliest reception of 2 Timothy 4, namely Polycarp's letter to the Philippians (2:1–3; written c. AD 117), Polycarp uses this text to encourage the believers to be willing to accept martyrdom.

Comment

9–10. Paul feels the darkness of loneliness in his imprisonment at Rome. Twice in this last section he entreats Timothy to come to him *soon* (4:21; cf. also 1:4). With the conjunction *gar* ('for', 'because') at the beginning of verse 10, it becomes clear why Paul wants Timothy to come soon: he feels abandoned.[3] Paul names three people who are no longer with him.

The first is *Demas*, also mentioned in Colossians 4:14 and Philemon 24. In this last text Paul describes Demas positively,

---

1   Particularly helpful is Stuhlmacher, *Biblical Theology*, pp. 171–177.

2   This is most pronounced in the Gospel of Luke. See Stuhlmacher, ibid., p. 171.

3   It is true that at 4:21 Paul mentions a number of fellow believers who send their greetings to Timothy. So Paul was not completely alone. I would note that it is part of the language of martyrdom to express aloneness with hyperbole.

designating him a 'fellow worker'. By contrast, here Demas is said to have *deserted* (*engkatelipen*), i.e., abandoned, the apostle. The reason is given with the causal participle *agapēsas*, translated by the NRSV as *in love*. The choice of this verb serves to highlight a contrast with verse 8 where Paul spoke of 'all who have loved (*ēngapēkosin*) his [Jesus] appearing'. Thus, Demas is not someone who 'loves' the Lord's return and the coming kingdom. Instead, he is someone who loves *this present world* (cf. 1 John 2:15–17). Thus, Demas could not sincerely pray the second and third petitions of the Lord's Prayer: 'Thy kingdom come, thy will be done on earth as it is in heaven.' He loves the world as it is now, thus showing how far he has moved from his former commitment to Christ. In Paul's theology apostasy is a possibility. Demas went to *Thessalonica*, perhaps his place of birth or previous residence.

Although it is possible that the next two men also abandoned Paul (there is no verb supplied to describe their parting), it is likely that he himself sent them to other locations for missional reasons. *Crescens* (a Latin name) went to *Galatia*,[4] while Titus went to *Dalmatia*, during this time a Roman province in the region of Illyricum, east of the Adriatic (cf. Rom. 15:19). On Titus' movements and their historical plausibility, see Towner (p. 624).

11–12. *Only Luke is with me.* The reference is to Luke 'the beloved physician' (Col. 4:14) and probably the author of the two-volume work Luke and Acts.[5] *Get Mark and bring him with you.* Paul speaks of John Mark, the cousin of Barnabas (Col. 4:10). Earlier in Paul's career he did not want to bring Mark along for his so-called second missionary journey. The reason for this was the fact that Mark had left Paul and Barnabas in Pamphylia to return to Jerusalem before the Galatia mission (Acts 13:13). Evidently Paul viewed Mark's action as incongruent with missionary faithfulness. This led to a missionary separation between Paul and Barnabas that was probably

---

4   Some manuscripts (א C 81) support the reading 'Gallia', probably because 'Galatia' could refer both to the Roman province in Asia and to Gaul (i.e., Gallia). Most scholars (with the notable exception of Spicq) prefer the reading 'Galatia'.

5   For a defence of this view, see Padilla, *Acts of the Apostles*, pp. 21–37.

painful (see Acts 15:37–39). It appears that as time passed, Mark became a serious missionary, thus being rehabilitated in the eyes of Paul. At some point, Paul and Mark were reconciled. And so now he asks Luke to bring Mark with him *because he is helpful to me in my ministry* (NIV). The key term is *helpful (euchrēstos)*, which conveys the sense of someone who is committed to serving others. It is likely that Paul views Mark as someone who can assist him in the completion of his ministry in Rome. This, then, is a beautiful example of reconciliation between Paul and Mark, as well as an example of someone growing in courage as a missionary. Paul no longer views Mark as unreliable but as someone who is helpful in ministry.

The next person mentioned is *Tychicus*. He was a dear brother to Paul, made evident by Paul's reference in Ephesians 6:21–22 and Colossians 4:7–8 as a 'beloved brother and faithful servant in the Lord'. In the Colossians text we discover that he was a 'fellow-prisoner' with Paul in the latter's first imprisonment. Just as he had done before (Eph. 6:22), Paul again *sent Tychicus to Ephesus*.

13. *When you come, bring the cloak that I left with Carpus at Troas.* Paul was preparing himself for winter (cf. v. 21). As a prisoner, his living accommodations must have been spartan (see Rapske, pp. 220–225 on the hardness of imprisonment during the Roman empire). He therefore asks for his *cloak*. The Greek term *phailonēs* refers to a poncho-like 'thick upper garment, cloak' (LSJ, s.v.). Paul also asks Timothy to bring *my scrolls, especially the parchments* (NIV). We do not know what was written on these materials, which likely were made of papyrus (the scrolls) and animal skin (*membrana*). The range of possibilities as to what was written on these materials is debated: books of Scripture, notes, copies of letters, etc. (see Marshall, pp. 819–821).

14–15. Paul mentions one individual who has caused him great harm during his imprisonment and trial: *Alexander the coppersmith.* It is likely that this is the Alexander of 1 Timothy 1:20 whom Paul had 'handed over to Satan'. The nature of the evil that Alexander did to Paul may be more precisely understood if we view the Greek verb *endeiknymi* as meaning 'to inform against', often used in a court setting (LSJ, s.v.). In light of the language of verse 16 (*apologia*), it is possible that Alexander bore false witness at Paul's trial. Others note that the verb can simply mean to do *harm*, without any more precision being expressed (e.g., Marshall, p. 822).

The Lord will pay him back for his deeds. The sentiment expressed in this last clause of the verse is common in the Old Testament and Hellenistic Jewish literature (e.g., Judg. 4:9; 2 Sam. 22:25; *Pss. Sol.* 2:16; cf. also 2 Sam. 3:39; Pss 28:4; 62:12; Prov. 24:12). We also find it in the New Testament (e.g., Matt. 7:21–27; 25:31–46; Rom. 2:6). Like the just martyr who is oppressed by evil persons yet trusts that God will judge the oppressor, Paul declares that *the Lord* (probably a reference to Jesus Christ; cf. 4:8) will bring retribution against Alexander because of his evil deeds. It is important that we interpret this verse Christologically, remembering that God's justice was accomplished in Christ bearing our punishment. Therefore, should Alexander repent by God's grace, God would acquit him, even in spite of his serious misdoings.

Paul returns to the present, warning Timothy to *beware of Alexander.* The reason is given in the next clause: *for he strongly opposed our message.* The term translated as *message* (NRSV) is *logois*, which has a very wide semantic range, making it difficult to pinpoint the exact meaning. Paul may refer to Alexander opposing his *argument* at court, or, more likely, to Alexander's opposition to apostolic doctrine, which has been labelled *logos* in other parts of the Pastoral Epistles (e.g., 1:13; 1 Tim. 4:6; 6:3). Furthermore, the fact that Paul speaks of *our* message makes it likely that he refers to Christian doctrine also shared by Timothy.

16–17. *At my first defense no one came to my support.* With asyndeton Paul continues directly from the previous verses, giving the sense that the harm caused by Alexander took place in a context described in vv. 16–18, namely a court setting. Paul speaks of his *first defense.* This implies that at least one more hearing is expected.[6] Judging from 4:6–8, 18, Paul is not optimistic about being freed as a result of the next hearing. In the Roman judicial system imprisonment was not a punishment for breaking the law. Depending on the severity of the crime, punishments usually consisted of fines, seizure of property, corporal punishments, exile, and the death penalty, and

---

6 As explained in the Introduction, I argue that 2 Timothy was written during Paul's second imprisonment in Rome, probably after he had been released for some time.

so on. Under *coercitio*, the person charged would be kept under arrest until a final verdict was reached (see *OCD*, pp. 809–815). In the first stage (*in iure*) the parties determined the accusations/charges, in the second stage (*apud iudicem*, before the judge) there was the examination of the facts of the case (cf. Marshall, pp. 822–823). It is likely that Paul was awaiting this second hearing. The term translated as *defense* (Greek *apologia*) was also used in Acts 22:1; 25:16 to describe Paul's speeches before the crowd at the Jerusalem temple and before Agrippa, respectively (none of which involved a court setting). His argument on those occasions was that his actions in Jerusalem and the diaspora were not aimed against the Jewish people, the temple or the Mosaic law. Instead, he was defending the Pharisaic belief of the resurrection from the dead, insisting that it had begun with the raising of Jesus – and this statement, he argued, should not be viewed as seditious. It is probable that this was also his defence before the emperor. We note that Paul's defence simultaneously becomes proclamation of the gospel.

Continuing the motif of the just martyr, Paul informs Timothy that no one stood by him during his first defence. That is, he had no one testify in his favour (e.g., friends or a professional advocate). Instead, *all deserted me*. The verb is the same one used in verse 10 of Demas' action. Paul was deeply wounded by the abandonment of his friends. Yet instead of being resentful, he prays for them: *May it not be counted against them*. This phrase continues the language of martyrdom. Paul would have remembered the example of Stephen, who prayed for his enemies as he was being stoned to death: 'Lord, do not hold this sin against them!' (Acts 7:60).

Even though Paul was abandoned by his friends, by contrast, he says *the Lord stood by me and gave me strength*. This is likely an example of hendiadys, where two phrases placed side by side provide a single meaning. The reference to the *Lord* is to Jesus Christ. It should also be noted that by stating that the Lord empowered him in the defence of the gospel, Paul is harking back to the promise of Jesus, namely, that when imprisoned and having to speak, the disciples would receive help (Matt. 10:17–20; Mark 13:9–11; Luke 21:12–15). In the majority of the Synoptic tradition we find that the Holy Spirit is the one who will empower; but in Luke 21:12–15 it is Jesus himself who will empower the disciples to bear witness. This leads to the second comment, which is actually more of a question: is the Lord Jesus still the subject of the second action performed on Paul (i.e., 'gave me strength')? Or, in light of 2 Timothy 1:6, and Matthew and Mark, should we think of the Holy Spirit as the one who empowered Paul? The former option appears to be more likely. This, then, would be an important example of the theologoumenon concerning the inseparable operations of the Trinity: the operations of the Trinity outside itself are indivisible. Whenever God works in creation or salvation, each person of the Trinity is involved.[7] In this case, both the Son and the Spirit perform the act of strengthening.

Paul continues by reflecting on the effects of his *apologia* from the perspective of gospel proclamation. With a clause that expresses results (*hina* 'so that'), Paul writes: *so that through me the message might be fully proclaimed and all the gentiles might hear it.* A number of comments are necessary. First, these two clauses are again united by hendiadys. The result is that *the message … fully proclaimed* just means *all the gentiles might hear it* (cf. Towner, pp. 642–643). Second, Paul asserts that, by the empowerment of the Lord, he has completed the task for which he was called back thirty years earlier on the road to Damascus, namely, to proclaim the gospel to the Gentiles (see Acts 9:15; 26:17–18; Rom. 1:5, 13–15; 15:15–18; Gal. 2:9; Eph. 3:1–8; Col. 1:24–28). He has already mentioned this in 1:11 and 1 Timothy 2:7. Indeed, we can say that Paul's missionary task was constitutive of his very identity.[8] Third, we should not miss the irony that it is as a prisoner that Paul fulfils the task of carrying the gospel to *all the gentiles* (*all* being representative). This reminds us of Paul's previous statement, 'But the word of God is not chained' (2:9).

Instead of completing his thought with the climactic statement about 'all the gentiles' hearing the gospel through his *apologia*, Paul

---

7 Latin: '*opera trinitatis ad extra sunt indivisa*.' This is a core teaching of orthodox Christianity. See the helpful work of Barrett, *Simply Trinity*, especially chapter 10.

8 See Schnabel, *Paul*, pp. 39–122, which has helpful maps, showing Paul's missionary movements. Apart from Schnabel and Sanders, *Paul: A Brief Insight*, among relatively recent major studies on Paul (e.g., Schnelle, Wolter), insufficient attention is paid to Paul the missionary.

adds another thought with a simple *and*, *And I was delivered from the lion's mouth* (NIV). Is there a relationship between Paul's previous sentences in verse 17 and this final statement? Or is the final statement just another item in the 'list'?

First, the statement about the *lion's mouth* is not to be taken in literal fashion, as if Paul had been rescued from a beast in the arena. Some scholars (e.g., Hutson, p. 205) understand the *lion* as a covert reference to Rome. While possible, it is more likely that, in keeping with the potential motif of the righteous martyr of this section, the lion is a metaphor for death brought about by vicious, lawless men. As we observed earlier (under *Context*), Psalm 22 (LXX 21) was one of the most important biblical texts casting the death of Jesus as a fulfilment of the righteous sufferer. In the Psalm we hear of beasts that attempt to kill the sufferer: 'Many bulls encircle me, strong bulls of Bashan surround me; they open wide their mouths at me, like a ravening and roaring lion' (vv. 12–13); 'for dogs are all around me; a company of evildoers encircles me' (v. 16); 'save me from the mouth of the lion! From the horns of the wild oxen you have rescued me' (vv. 20–21). Paul, in imitation of Jesus, is the righteous sufferer who faced death; but the Lord delivered him. If, as we argued above, the reference was to the first of his two-part trial, Paul declares in dramatic fashion that the Lord Jesus Christ rescued him, in the sense that he allowed him to make a second defence: *so that* he would preach the gospel to the Gentiles. Now we can explain the relationship between the third and the first two clauses of verse 17. We should take the *and* at the beginning of the third clause as expressing purpose: the Lord rescued Paul so that he would proclaim the gospel to the Gentiles.

18. In the previous verse Paul spoke about the temporal deliverance from physical death granted him so that he could fulfil his ministry. In this verse he confesses confidence that the Lord will also rescue him from eternal death: *The Lord will rescue me from every evil attack and save me for his heavenly kingdom*. We should observe that the tense of the verb 'to rescue' in this verse shifts to the future, in contrast to its use in the previous verse, where the aorist referred to the past. We also find another use of hendiadys in this verse, with *rescue me from every evil attack* meaning that the Lord will *save me for his heavenly kingdom*. Marshall (pp. 825–826) sees a possible allusion to the Lord's Prayer, explaining the phrase as expressing Paul's trust that the Lord would preserve him 'from falling into apostasy under the pressure of persecution'. The future rescue refers to the resurrection from the dead. The reason Paul speaks of *his heavenly kingdom* is not to mark some contrast between physical death and spiritual life (souls floating around in heaven). In Scripture, God's kingdom or realm is said to be 'in heaven' or 'above' (see Col. 3:1–5) not in the sense that it is literally in the sky. Rather, this analogical use of language is used to express God's *transcendence* and otherness.

The thought that the Lord will raise Paul from a lonely jail to eternal glory moves him to close with a doxology: *To him be the glory forever and ever. Amen.*

19–22. With these verses we reach the closure of the letter by means of greetings, something that is common in Paul's correspondence. *Greet Prisca and Aquila.* Priscilla is the diminutive of *Prisca*, who with her husband receives greetings from Paul. He met this Jewish–Christian couple in Corinth after they had been expelled from Rome during the reign of Claudius for being Jews. They and Paul practised the same *technē* or occupation, so Paul joined them in their shop and shared a home with them (Acts 18:1–3). It is no exaggeration to say that Priscilla and Aquila were two of the closest fellow Christians, friends and co-labourers of Paul (see also Rom. 16:3–5; 1 Cor. 16:19). Of *the household of Onesiphorus* we have already heard in 1:16–17: they cared for Paul in Rome and constantly refreshed his spirit.

Paul now gives Timothy news of some of their fellow-workers in the Lord. *Erastus* is mentioned in Acts 19:22 and Romans 16:23. In this last text we are told that he is 'the city treasurer' (at Corinth). Since Paul says that *Erastus remained in Corinth*, it is likely that the reference is to the same individual as in Romans 16:23 and perhaps of Acts 19:22. On *Trophimus*, whom Paul *left ill in Miletus* (south of Ephesus), see Acts 20:4; 21:29. The reference here is to a different journey from the one described in the Acts of the Apostles. These short news items about Trophimus remind us that although Paul was often able to heal, this was not always God's will, and so in these cases Paul could not heal, since ultimately healing is an act of God: being an apostle did not grant him powers to heal whenever he wished.

Do your best to come to me before winter. When the winter season arrived, sea travel in the Mediterranean became treacherous and was avoided, with only a few intrepid (or foolish) sailors going on journeys. Paul wanted to see Timothy soon, so he asks him to come before the delays caused by winter.

Paul now sends Timothy the greetings from believers of Rome.[9] *Eubulus sends greetings to you, as do Pudens and Linus and Claudia and all the brothers and sisters.* Of *Linus* we learn from Irenaeus (*A.H.* 3.3.3) that he became Peter's successor as bishop of Rome. Of the others we know nothing, although they likely were known to Timothy.

The Lord[10] *be with your spirit.* The pronoun is singular, so the prayer here is focused on Timothy. The final phrase includes all: *Grace be with you.*[11]

Theology

Although many of us will probably never be martyrs, all of us will have to face death, unless the Lord returns before that. We noted in our comments on 4:1–8 that from Paul's experience we could distil lessons when facing death. This continues here, although the focus on dying by martyrdom is more focused. What can we glean from these verses on dying?

First, notice that Paul expects God's judgment, when God will make all things right. Although we may think of this in a positive way concerning our final justification before the throne of God, Paul also talks about Alexander and the many evil things he did against Paul and by extension the gospel. I doubt that Paul would rejoice in thinking of Alexander being sent to perdition upon God's final judgment. Yet, Paul is encouraged in his dying moments when

---

9 This is not a contradiction of 4:10 and 16. We must keep in mind the hyperbolic nature of the language of martyrdom. In addition, the people mentioned in this verse were not necessarily close friends of Paul: note that they are not found in the rest of the NT.

10 Some manuscripts include 'Jesus Christ' after 'Lord'. The shorter reading is better supported by *א F G 33.

11 The shorter reading, which lacks 'amen', is almost certainly the correct one.

he thinks that God *will* bring Alexander to give an account. This rejoicing is of a piece with the attitude of the saints in the book of Revelation, where judgment of the wicked is a reminder of God's sovereignty and lordship and the fact that there will be ultimate justice. It is not morbid to think of the final judgment of the enemies of the Lord when we are nearing death. It can be encouraging, when facing the end, to remember that God will make all things right, which also includes *our* being made right on the basis of Jesus' life, death and resurrection.

The second reflection on dying is found in 4:18, where Paul expresses certainty that the Lord will raise him from the dead. Funerals without the expectation of future resurrection can be very sad, if not hopeless. But what joy, even though mixed with pain, when the funeral is Christian, where there is hope that the one(s) being remembered will be raised immortal to be together with the Lord and his saints for ever.

TITUS
COMMENTARY

1. SALUTATION (1:1–4)

A. Opening (1:1–4)

The salutation of Paul's letter to Titus is comparatively long. In fact, in the Pauline Corpus only Romans and Galatians have longer salutations. As we explained earlier (cf. 1 Tim. 1:1–2) Paul employs the standard aspects of Greco-Roman letter writing but enlarges them with theological themes that are then developed in the body of the letter. Titus is a good example of this. Below we comment on the rhetorical artistry of the salutation as well as the themes announced.

Context
The first feature that the reader of the Greek text observes is the use of alliteration. In particular, we note that many of the terms that are theologically significant begin with the Greek letter epsilon, transliterated into English with the letter *e*. Note the following words in verses 1–4: *eklektos* ('elect, chosen'), *epignōsis* ('knowledge'), *eusebeia* ('godliness'), *elpis* ('hope'), *epitagē* ('command') and *eirēnē* ('peace').

The alliteration here has a cumulative effect, drawing the reader's attention to these terms.

The second feature refers to the theological themes. First, there is an emphasis on Paul's apostleship, with particular attention to his being entrusted with the proclamation of the gospel. Second, Paul highlights the privileged status of the believer by using the term 'elect'. Lastly, there is stress on the gospel as God's truth, which is the shared belief of all genuine Christians.

Comment

1. *A servant of God and an apostle of Jesus Christ.* Paul's designation of himself as an apostle is common in his salutations. However, calling himself a *servant (doulos)*[1] only appears in Romans 1:1, Galatians 1:10 and Philippians 1:1. Furthermore, in all these examples the possessive genitive is 'Jesus Christ', whereas in Titus 1:1 it is 'God'. It is likely that the sense Paul is conveying is the OT sense of 'the servant of God', employed primarily of the prophets (Jer. 7:25; Amos 3:7; Mal. 4:6 LXX). We can thus understand Paul presenting himself in verse 1 as a man who totally belongs to God and who represents God by speaking his word. The concept is similar to 'man of God', a description Paul used of Timothy in 1 Timothy 4:11. On Paul as an *apostle*, see comments on 1 Timothy 1:1.

For the sake of the faith of God's elect. As in most of his letters, so here Paul enlarges on the nature of his apostleship by appending a prepositional phrase. The NRSV takes the Greek preposition *kata* as indicating a goal. If this is correct, we should interpret Paul as saying that his apostleship has as its goal the building-up of the faith of believers. The sense of *faith* would therefore be faith as *habitus* or orientation in life.[2] It is more likely, however, that *kata* should be understood in its common meaning: 'according to, in accordance with' (see BDAG, p. 512). We should thus understand Paul as saying that his apostleship *corresponds* with the faith of the believers. That is,

---

1   The word *doulos* means 'slave'. The reader is directed to the comments at 1 Timothy 6:1–2 for an explanation of slavery in the Greco-Roman world.

2   This is also the conclusion of Mutschler, *Glaube*, p. 204.

both the readers and Paul share the same common, objective body of belief as the rest of the church worldwide (cf. Oberlinner, 1996, p. 4).[3] In this case *faith* would refer to *fides quae*, namely the content of the faith. This understanding is further corroborated in verse 4.

Paul refers to believers as *God's elect*. Why does he use this designation instead of, say, 'brothers and sisters', or 'beloved', or another more common label? As we explained under 2 Timothy 1:9 and 2:10, election in the Pastoral Epistles is to be understood in its OT sense of a people called out by God (out of sheer love on God's part) to receive his revelation and to be a blessing to the nations. We now must add that this calling of a special people to himself is usually found in OT contexts where the chosen people of Israel is contrasted with the nations: the latter are also loved by God but they are not his special possession in the same way that Israel was (e.g., Deut. 7:6–9; Isa. 2:2; 25:6; 49:6). One of the purposes of calling Israel God's elect was thus to unite the nation in solidarity by providing it with an identity: God's elect, the people chosen by God in a holy covenant (Exod. 19:5–6). It is likely that this is the reason Paul calls the believers *God's elect*. He has just spoken of his apostleship as corresponding to their faith; and in verse 4 he will again speak of the faith they share. Paul thus wants the Christians in Crete to be united in the common faith in order to resist the false teachers. By calling them *elect* he nudges them into unity and solidarity under the faith of the church. Therefore, election here has primarily an ecclesiological rather than a soteriological function.

And the knowledge of the truth that is in accordance with godliness. It is probable that we have here a case of hendiadys, where the second clause shares the sense of the first but expands it. The idea communicated may thus be that the *faith* of the believers can also be spoken of as *the truth*.[4] The term *truth* in the phrase 'the knowledge of the truth' is an objective genitive, giving the phrase the sense of 'knowing the truth'. As we observed earlier (cf. 1 Tim. 2:4;

---

3   On this understanding of faith see further 1:13; 2:2; 1 Tim. 4:6; 6:2;
     2 Tim. 2:18; 3:8.

4   The strong evidence for this is found in 1 Tim. 2:7; 4:3; and 2 Tim. 3:8,
     where *faith* and *truth* are placed in parallel position.

2 Tim. 2:25, 37), *truth* is often used in the Pastoral Epistles in the context of polemics. That is, those who follow the apostolic tradition communicated by Paul and his co-workers know the truth (which ultimately is God himself in his revelation in Jesus Christ) while the false teachers are following a lie and thus deceive and are being deceived (Tit. 3:3; also 2 Tim. 3:13). This truth corresponds to *godliness (eusebeia)*, a key term in the Pastoral Epistles used to speak of salvation, knowledge of God and Christian living. In light of the context of verse 1, *eusebeia* here perhaps primarily has to do with the knowledge of God. However, since there is no such thing as a break between salvation and ethics in Paul (i.e., the saved demonstrate their identity by their works), it is likely that *eusebeia* denotes all three areas mentioned above.

To summarize: Paul presents himself as a servant-apostle of God. His service as an apostle corresponds to, or occurs in the domain of, the content of the faith shared by all Christians. This is the truth, which encompasses all aspects of Christian existence. Paul refers to the Christians as *the elect*. Thus, by calling them 'chosen' and at the same time highlighting the one truth they share, Paul implicitly summons them to unity. This is a theme that we will continue to hear throughout the rest of the epistle.

2. *In the hope of eternal life.* Holding to the faith of the elect, the truth that accords with the gospel, has an aim: it leads to *hope*. The philosophical Greco-Roman perspective on hope was generally rather pessimistic: it was believed that we should not put our hope on hope, for it would disappoint us. In fact, hope was viewed as one of those human passions that could seduce us. For the Stoic Seneca, hope (the companion of fear, according to him) is an ill because it constantly looks to the future instead of living in the present.[5] The Bible, by contrast, presents hope as a virtue (1 Cor. 13:13). But hope is not some abstract, wishful thinking about the future. Hope is God himself in Jesus Christ (see 1 Tim. 1:1). This is why Paul adds that the hope of eternal life was promised by *God, who never lies*. A more wooden translation of the Greek *ho apseudēs theos* is

_____

5 See Seneca, *Ep.* 5.7–8. Cf. also Thucydides, 5.102–103, 113; Plato, *Tim.* 69D.

'the-never-lying-God', which highlights his absolute trustworthiness. Thus, we can put our trust in the God of the gospel, even though the promise of eternal life was made *before the ages began* (see further on 2 Tim. 1:9).

3. *In due time he revealed his word through the proclamation.* In the previous verse Paul stated that the promise of eternal life was made before the ages began. That is, God committed himself to be God for us in Jesus Christ even before he had made all things, visible and invisible.[6] By making this statement Paul introduces us to one of his most common structures of salvation history, one which has a past and a present (e.g., Rom. 3:21—26; Eph. 3:1—13; Col. 1:24—27). Here Paul highlights the present/fulfilment aspect of salvation history. God has revealed the fulfilment of eternal life *in due time*, which highlights his own sovereignty – and thereby his freedom as God – in the advent of Jesus Christ (see 1 Tim. 2:6; 6:15; also Rom. 5:6; Gal. 4.4). The message currently revealed is his *word*, which underlines the proclamation (*kērygma*) of the gospel.

With which I have been entrusted by the command of God our Saviour. With this dependent clause, which goes back to the proclamation of the word, Paul returns to the theme of his ministry as servant and apostle. In this way Paul forms an *inclusio* or 'bookend' with verse 1. On the gospel being *entrusted* to Paul, see comment on 1 Timothy 1:11. On God as *Saviour*, one of the dominant soteriological concepts in the Pastoral Epistles, see on 1 Timothy 1:1; 2:3 and Introduction.

4. *To Titus, my loyal child in the faith we share.* The designation of Titus as *loyal* is the same Paul gave Timothy (1 Tim. 1:2). The sense of *gnēsios* (*loyal*) is that of a child who is legitimate as opposed to illegitimate (Marshall, p. 132). With the prepositional phrase *in the faith we share*, Paul clarifies the statement as being metaphorical: it is not that Titus is his *biological* child; rather, he is his child with respect to the 'common faith' (*kata koinēn pistin*; cf. Jude 3). As in 1:1, it is probable that *faith* here refers to the body of belief that united the

---

6 Since there were no humans 'before the ages began', the meaning is probably that God committed himself – as Father, Son and Holy Spirit – to share his life *ad extra* with his planned creation. See Barth, *CD* II.1 pp. 272—276.

early Christians. It may thus be that Titus was converted under Paul's ministry (Knight, pp. 63–64). Whatever the case, Malherbe notes that with the use of *child* to speak of Titus (instead of the more common 'brother' or 'co-worker') as well as the use of *loyal* and *share*, we have an example of the language of friendship, a common feature in paraenetic letters. This tone of friendship ('philophronetic tone'), which was common in the relationship between father and son, was employed to communicate confidence into the person receiving paraenesis.[7] And this is precisely what Paul wants to express in the opening of the letter. Quinn comments: 'The body of the letter (1:5–3:11) then articulates the apostle's commission to the colleague who shares in and carries out Paul's apostolate, *as a man's son carries on the name and work of the father*' (p. 50, emphasis added).

Theology

Paul likely pursues at least two goals with the lengthy salutation. First, it reminds the readers of the relationship between his apostleship and the gospel. To be an apostle is to be God's servant, one who exists for the proclamation of the genuine faith that true Christians all share. Paul does not mention God's entrusting the gospel to him in order to brag. Rather, the lengthy and weighty use of language is for the purpose of his second goal in the salutation. This second goal is to commend Titus to the congregations on the island of Crete. From one end we hear of Paul's credentials as a genuine apostle; from the other end, by his use of philophronetic language, we hear that Titus is a loyal and therefore genuine minister of the same gospel Paul proclaims. With the churches in Crete probably also reading this letter (cf. Col. 4:16) and thus 'overhearing' Paul's opinion of Titus, the apostle is stoking their confidence in Titus. This helps open the way for Titus' ministry in Crete.

Theologically, we can conclude that the confidence churches place on individuals to be their leaders should be proportional to those individuals' commitment to the genuine faith, the orthodox body of doctrine that the churches share, the *fides quae*. Deviation

---

7 Malherbe, *Light from the Gentiles*, 1:409–410.

from the 'faith we share' automatically dissolves any claim of leadership over the church – even if those leaders are 'nice' or experienced or charismatic or family members.

2. INSTRUCTIONS FOR THE LIFE OF THE CHURCH ON THE BASIS OF GOD'S MERCIFUL SALVATION (1:5 – 3:11)

A. Instructions concerning leaders in the churches of Crete (1:5–9)

Context

Three observations are important to begin this section. The first has to do with the structure of the section. In particular, we note a phenomenon that is common in the moral literature of the period, namely lists of vices and virtues. We have observed Paul employ such lists in the Pastoral Epistles: 1 Timothy 1:8–11; 3:1–13; 4:11–12; 6:3–10; 2 Timothy 2:22–23; 3:1–5. In this section we see one of the distinctive features of vice/virtue lists, namely the juxtaposition of the negative with the positive. In verses 6–8 we find the following particular syntax: 'not … not … *but*'. Paul uses *mē* ('not') six times in this short space to describe what the elder/overseer must *not* be. Then he switches to the positive qualities by introducing the adversative *alla* ('but'). This is further proof that the epistle to Titus is the type of literature called protreptic, which aided an author in communicating precepts to his audience and grounding them on a world view that was shared by author and reader. See Introduction.

The second observation has to do with the concurrence of 'elders' and 'overseer'. In verse 6 Paul orders Titus to appoint elders, which is followed with the virtues that an elder must demonstrate. Then, in the very middle of the list of virtues (v. 7), the subject changes from elders to 'overseer'. How do we explain this sudden shift? First, it is necessary to note the relationship between elders and overseers. In his recent work on Paul's theology of leadership, Clarke has explored this relationship in the NT as a whole and the Pastoral Epistles in particular, and reached conclusions which we find compelling.[1] First, the overseer and elder are not identical. The expression 'the elders' is a *collective* term for leaders in the church, not an office.[2] Second, although not all elders were to teach and lead, the overseer(s) necessarily had to lead and teach (see 3:2; 5:17–25).[3] Third, it is likely that the overseer(s) (as a person, not an office) was one of the community of elders (the 'council of elders' of 4:14) who had the desire (3:1) to lead his own family and possibly others. Furthermore, the overseer(s) would have possessed the necessary qualifications (3:2–7) required for the office. Thus, while an overseer could be an elder (and more than likely was) an elder was not necessarily an overseer, that is, did not necessarily hold the office of overseer. Out of this group of elders emerged the individual(s) who would take on the office of *episkopos* or 'overseer', whose primary task was to teach and care pastorally for a home (or homes). When viewed from this perspective, one can understand why Paul switched from elders to overseer so abruptly.

Third, it may be helpful to further comment on the background for church leadership. The Greek term for the concept of managing the household was *oikonomia*.[4] Moral philosophers from the classical

---

1 Clarke, *A Pauline Theology*, pp. 52–60.

2 Ibid., p. 56.

3 Ibid., pp. 57–58: 'Whereas not all elders are required to teach, preach or manage a house church, these duties are essential for the office of overseer.'

4 The most important primary sources on this subject are: Xenophon, *Oec.* 1.19–23; Aristotle, *Oec.* 1.1–10; Pol. 1.2.1.1253b; Philodemus, *Oec.*

period forward were preoccupied with the best management, not only of the state but also of the household. The household needed to be well managed because it was viewed as the basic unit of the city-state. Furthermore, unlike many nations in the West today, where the family unit consists of only parents and children, the Greco-Roman household was much larger, including grandparents and slaves. This made household management particularly challenging. The standard Greco-Roman view of the relations between the different units of the household was one of rigid hierarchy and government: at the top was the father (*paterfamilias*) and at the bottom the household slaves, if the family was wealthy enough to own slaves. Moral philosophers sought to teach the fathers how to govern their households, often using the *a minori ad maius* (lesser to the greater) argument: the man must be able to manage his household (the smaller domain) if he is to manage the state well (the larger domain).[5]

The language, syntax and concepts of 1 Timothy 3:1–13 and Titus 1:5–9 all point to the locus of *oikonomia* as the background for the instruction of leadership offices. This should not be surprising in light of the fact that one of the principal ecclesiological analogies in the Pastoral Epistles is the household. Paul's employment of *oikonomia* as a template for church leadership means that his conception of leadership was not alien to his culture; rather, he builds on it, at times stressing a particular virtue or command and at other times removing the stress that might not have been viewed as particularly important in the culture.

Comment

5. *I left you behind in Crete for this reason.* We know from both the Acts of the Apostles and his letters that Paul, after planting a church, moved on and left those churches in the hands of his co-workers (e.g., Acts 14:23; 19:22; 20:17–35; 1 Thess. 3:1–13). We are not certain if this was the case with Titus in Crete. For the verb translated as

---

(note 4 *cont.*) 1.6–10. Much of this section finds inspiration in Malherbe, *Light from the Gentiles*, 1:559–73. Cf. also Johnson, p. 223.

5   See, e.g., Philo, *Ios.* 38–39; Plutarch, *An virt. doc.* 2 (439 D).

I left you behind (apoleipein) need not imply that Paul was present in
Crete. The verb could mean to dispatch or assign someone to a
duty.[6] Verse 5 may simply mean that Paul assigned Titus to care
for the churches in Crete.

Because he is not mentioned in the Acts of the Apostles, we are
not sure when to place Paul's deployment of Titus to Crete. We do
hear of Titus in Paul's letters, especially in Galatians and 2 Corinthians (Gal. 2:1, 3; 2 Cor. 2:13; 7:6, 13–14; 8:6, 16, 23; 12:8; see also
2 Tim. 4:10). It is clear that Titus was a beloved co-worker of Paul,
entrusted in part with the delicate matter of the collection for the
poor churches in Judea.

The island of Crete sits in the eastern Mediterranean Sea with
the Peloponnese to the north and Africa to the south. Homer spoke
only slightly hyperbolically when he wrote of 'Crete of the hundred
cities' (*Il.* 2.649), for although there existed numerous cities in the
classical and Hellenistic period, there were probably no more than
forty (*OCD*, pp. 393–394). Well known is the Cretan claim that the
god Zeus was born on Mount Ida in central Crete.

During the Hellenistic period Crete developed a reputation as the
home of mercenaries and pirates. During the period of the Roman
republic Crete was defeated by Q. Caecilius Metellus (69–67 BC).
The island became a province that was joined with Cyrene. There
were Jews in Crete at least since the period of Herod (Josephus, *J.W.*
17.327) and possibly earlier (Philo, *Embassy* 282). It is likely that Titus
began his work in Knossos, the largest city, where there was also
a colony of Romans (Strabo, 10.4.9). For more on Crete see 2:12.

*So that you should put in order what remained to be done, and should
appoint elders in every town.* With this purpose clause Paul comments
on the aim he had for Titus when he left him in Crete. The clause
is composed in an ABB'A' pattern. Further, it is likely that we have
an example of hendiadys, where the clause before *and* is subordinate
to, and further explained by, the clause that follows. This would
mean that when Paul speaks of *what remained to be done*, he is primarily
referring to *appoint elders in every town* (Spicq, p. 601). In our comments
on verses 1–4 we spoke of the importance of leadership for the

---

6   Thus, Marshall, p. 150.

well-functioning of churches. This continues to be evident in this reminder, which more than likely required Titus to go to several towns and perform the task of discerning those men who possessed the right character to lead as elders. Of course, Titus would have to accomplish this with help from the church communities.

As I directed you. The aorist of *diatassō* ('to order, command') looks back to a previous time when Paul had given Titus the orders above. As indicated in verse 5, it does not necessarily mean that Paul was present in Crete when he dispatched his co-worker. The verb *diatassō* is often used in a formal context, as when a higher official commands one below him to complete an order (see BDAG, p. 237).

6. Paul now lists the qualifications for the elders/overseer. As we noted in our comments on 1 Timothy 3:1–8, it is likely that these leaders belonged to a higher socio-economic layer of Greco-Roman society (although only very few would have been elite) who could read and write; furthermore, they would have lived in a larger house that could accommodate a larger group of believers.[7] Yet, as in some other communities (e.g., voluntary associations), leaders also needed to possess the right character. And so, in verses 6–9 Paul provides a list of virtues that the elders/overseer must display. The list in Titus is almost identical to that in 1 Timothy 3.

Blameless translates *anegklētos*, which was also used of deacons in 1 Timothy 3:10. The word, which Malherbe helpfully glosses as 'unimpeachable' (*Light from the Gentiles*, 1:416), serves as an umbrella term for the rest of the virtues. It is similar to being 'above reproach' as demanded of the overseer in 1 Timothy 3:2. The NIV translates the next phrase as *faithful to his wife*, for which see comments on 1 Timothy 3:2. The next qualification is *whose children are believers.* This is similar to 1 Timothy 3:4 but goes further, as the previous passage only speaks of having children in submission. We must ask at least two questions

---

7   It is hazardous to generalize numbers, since Christians in the first three centuries met in numerous locations, including tiny tenement flats (*insulae*). For important studies see Adams, *The Earliest Christian Meeting Places*, and Oakes, *Reading Romans in Pompeii*. For those who met in houses, the possibility would have been anywhere between 20 and 100 people.

of this requirement. First, how do we explain the difference between Titus and 1 Timothy? Second, how should the Titus text be applied today? For the first question, we should remember that although virtue lists for community leaders in the Greco-Roman period were very similar, they were not identical. It is likely that the differences concerning children in the texts above stem from contextual variations. For the second question, see below under *Theology*.

7–8. These verses continue the list but apply them specifically to the overseer. Here Paul repeats the quality of being *blameless*, with which he began the list. Now he adds a reason why the overseer must be blameless: *since an overseer manages God's household, he must be blameless* (NIV). The virtue is necessary because the overseer acts *as God's steward* (*oikonomon*). That is, *precisely* because he is the *oikonomos* of God's house, he must be *blameless*. There is a correlation between his office of overseer and the character he must display as a steward of God's house (cf. 1 Tim. 3:15). Essentially, the idea is that God is the Lord over the household and the leaders are servants who have been given the task of managing it appropriately.

The remaining items in this list have been explained earlier (1 Tim. 3:1–13). However, there are six new items, which we now explain. *He must not be arrogant or quick-tempered.* These two words are related in their usage outside the NT, both having to do with the temperament of an individual. The first is *authadēs*, which is used to describe an individual who is selfish, bad-tempered and proud.[8] The second term is *orgilos*, related to the noun *orgē*, which refers to anger or wrath. This speaks of someone who quickly 'loses it' and explodes when others test his patience.[9] A person who is not longsuffering and understanding of others cannot be a leader in the church.

In verse 8 Paul moves to positive qualities that the leader must have, mentioning the remaining four virtues that are unique in this letter. The third, *a lover of goodness*, is common in virtue lists of the Greco-Roman period, especially among Hellenistic Jewish authors (e.g., *Letter of Aristeas* 124, 292; Philo, *Mos.* 2.9). It is a quality that

---

8 Cf. Gen. 49:7; Theophrastus, *Char.* 15.1–11; Plutarch, *Lyc.* 11.6.

9 A definition is found in Aristotle, *Eth. nic.* 4.5.8.

those who govern must possess in order that those under them might live in an environment of peace and justice fomented by the leader's love of all that is noble. It is not surprising, therefore, that *dikaios* (one of the Greek cardinal virtues) is also mentioned. The KJV simply translates the term as *just*. This is a helpful translation, since the present context has to do with the capacity of treating others with equality and fairness, an indispensable quality of those who are in leadership. Next in the list comes *devout* (*hosios*), denoting someone who is totally given to the things of God (cf. 1 Tim. 2:8). The word is often used together with *eusebeia* (godliness). The last virtue is *self-controlled*. The word *enkratēs* appears only here in the NT but is common in moral philosophers to speak of someone who is able to control his desires and emotions.[10]

9. The final qualification that the overseer must demonstrate is expressed with the phrase, *he must have a firm grasp of the word that is trustworthy in accordance with the teaching*. The language explaining the relationship between the overseer and *the word* is strong, since *antechō* can describe a person having a tight grip on an object. The concept is to be understood metaphorically, expressing total devotion or faithfulness to the gospel, here rendered as *the word that is trustworthy* (*pistou logou*). This use of language may be implicitly polemic, speaking of the gospel within the context of heretical threats (cf. also on 1 Tim. 6:6). Lastly, we are told that this trustworthy word is *in accordance with the teaching* (*didachē*, cf. 2 Tim. 4:2). The *teaching* here refers to the content of basic Christian doctrine. Spicq (p. 605) puts it this way: 'The "*logos* that conforms to the *didachē*" refers to an official and traditional teaching in the church ... normative because it is issued by Christ.'

There is an end-goal to the leader's devotion to the apostolic teaching, which is expressed in the final clause of verse 9: *so that he may be able both to preach with sound doctrine and to refute those who contradict it*. Two related activities are envisioned here, one geared to insiders and the other to outsiders. As to the first group, devotion to the apostolic teaching will enable the overseer to *preach with sound doctrine*. The NRSV translation of *parakaleō* as *to preach* is too broad, since

---

10 See Plato, *Def.* 415D; Dio Chrysostom, *Or.* 1.14; 3.10; 3.84.

this verb has the more specific nuance of *to exhort* and *to encourage* (NIV). The overseer, then, is presented as exhorting and encouraging the believers, and this happens *with* (dative of means) *sound doctrine*. As we indicated (cf. 1 Tim. 1:10), the use of the term *sound* or *healthy* to speak of Christian teaching is polemic in nature. That is, it was common for moral philosophers to speak of the teaching and existence of their opponents as sick or unhealthy, while presenting their own teaching as wholesome and thereby of benefit for those who would follow it. Paul borrows from this language in order to communicate clearly to Titus: it is ultimately God through Christian doctrine who makes us whole.

Related to the overseer's exhortation towards insiders is his concomitant rebuff of outsiders who sought to pervert the sound teaching. The overseer was to *refute those who contradict it*. The thought is very similar to that found in 2 Timothy 2:24–26 (cf. Merkel, p. 90), where Timothy was to instruct opponents 'gently', so that perhaps God might grant them repentance.

Theology

Paul does not tire of insisting that leaders be appointed to oversee the different churches, and that those leaders must possess qualities commensurate with the holy calling of the Lord. Again, contemporary readers may be surprised by how little is said of the professional skills of the elders/overseer. Of course, these leaders had to have an aptitude for teaching (1 Tim. 3:2). But nothing else is said about the leader's 'gifting'. Instead, what is presented as crucial is the *character* of the leader: above reproach, faithful husband, self-controlled, patient, devoted, just. Furthermore, these virtues are defined by the sound doctrine, making it essential that the leader hold to the truth of the gospel. Paul thus envisages a faithful, godly man who is in the ministry out of obedience to God's calling. What counts is constant faithfulness in caring for the flock with the sound teaching, which is able to heal. Pastorally speaking, then, leaders in the church today would do well to remember that the ethos of leadership in the church is more akin to caring for family members in the home than a CEO implacably running a company for profit.

A final comment to add to this section is on how the qualification concerning the phrase in verse 6 is to be applied today: *whose children are believers, not accused of debauchery and not rebellious.* This qualification is similar to 1 Timothy 3:4–5: 'Keeping his children submissive and respectful in every way.' To understand this qualification we must avoid the mistake of reading it through the lens of the modern Western world, where children are often given freedom to choose the religion of their preference. By contrast, Paul's Greco-Roman world was rooted in patriarchy. The children, even older ones, owed loyalty to their fathers, which was demonstrated in all aspects of life, including of course religion. It was expected as normal, therefore, especially among the younger children (but not totally excluding the older ones), that they would adopt the religion of the father. In this scenario, a father who wanted to be a leader in the early church but whose children did not even respect his religion (in fact, children who could be accused of 'debauchery and rebellion') would have demonstrated exceedingly low competence as a household leader, and as an extension would have been disqualified from church leadership. It is possible to apply this verse today in such a way that if the children of the overseer reject the faith, the overseer must step down from his position. But this conclusion is complicated by the fact that we no longer (at least in North America) follow the type of patriarchy practised in the Roman empire: for example, it may not be socially unacceptable if children in the home 'take their time' to think about the Christian faith, especially older ones. In Paul's culture, on the other hand, this would have been socially unacceptable. Therefore, Paul must place this condition on the overseers, since he has to think of the missional repercussions of children rejecting their fathers' religion. In contemporary culture, however (I repeat, at least in North America from where I write), this would not break the missional possibility with unbelievers. Thus, the application of verse 6 may be that the church leader needs to direct the home so well that his children 'are not accused of debauchery and not rebellious' (Tit. 1:6). And so it seems that the qualification is not that different in principle from that of 1 Timothy 3:4–5.

B. The reason for the appointment of leaders (1:10–16)

Context
To gain a clear understanding of the following verses it is necessary to address two issues, all pertaining to the Cretan proverb
of verses 12–13. First, there is the question of the source of the
proverb, which Paul designates as coming from *one of them, their very
own prophet*. We should note that by using the word *prophet* (*prophētēs*)
Paul is not lumping the pagan speaker with OT prophets who spoke
truthfully in the name of the Lord. Instead, Paul is using their own
language (especially of poets), where the term *prophētēs* was used of
a religious man who was thought to have a close association with
the gods and even speak for them.[11] The quotation itself originates
with the Cretan Epimenides (seventh century BC). Centuries later,
Callimachus of Cyrene (third century BC) built on Epimenides. The
Cretans had boasted of preparing a tomb for Zeus, who apparently
had died. Epimenides and Callimachus took offence at this, since
they believed Zeus was immortal. So they composed poetry to
refute this lie:

Epimenides:
> They fashioned a tomb for thee, O holy and high one
> The Cretans, always liars, evil beasts, idle bellies!
> But thou are not dead: thou livest and abidest forever,
> For in thee we move and live and have our being.[12]

Callimachus:
> 'Cretans are ever liars.' Yea, a tomb O Lord for thee
> The Cretans builded; but thou didst not die, for thou are forever.[13]

Thus, the reputation of the Cretans as liars goes back to the
seventh century BC and continued to the Hellenistic and Roman

---

11   See the following references: Aeschylus, *Sept.* 612; Euripides, *Orest.* 365;
     Herodotus, *Hist.* 8.37.
12   Epimenides, *Cretica* 1–4 (trans. J. Rendel Harris).
13   Callimachus, *Hymn.* Jov. 8–9. I owe this quotation and the one above to
     Hutson, p. 221.

period.[14] With time, the Cretans garnered the reputation of not only being liars but also of being greedy for money and therefore shameless in how they obtained it (Polybius, 6.45–47), faithless in how they treat others (Diodorus Siculus, 31.45) and wily (Plutarch, *Phil.* 13.9).[15]

Second, we must ask how Paul employs this popular Cretan proverb in his argument flow of 1:5–16. Most commentators agree that Paul uses the proverb as the basis of his argument. That is, the truth of his assessment of the false teachers at Crete is in part corroborated by the statement of one of their own poets, which statement Paul judges as truthful in this case (v. 13). It might seem like a flimsy argument to base a moral judgment on a generalizing, popular proverb. But we must remember the manner in which Paul argues. As we have indicated in the Introduction and in 1:5–9, Paul uses the rhetorical tool of paraenesis. And in paraenesis arguments tended to be short because the speaker and the hearers shared the same world view. We know from his other letters that Paul could mount a tight, long and logical argument (e.g., Rom. 9–11). But given the protreptic genre of this letter, where paraenesis is the principal feature, Paul follows the rhetorical tradition in the way he grounds his exhortations. Lastly, we should note that quoting from ancient poets to validate an argument was common in Greco-Roman literature. This is precisely what Paul is doing here.

Comment

10. Verse 10 provides the reason for the establishing of godly leaders who must remain firm in the gospel (vv. 5–9): *for there are many rebellious people* (NIV). Just as he has done previously, so here Paul provides a list of vices to describe the opponents of the gospel. The first vice, *rebellious people*, translates *anypotaktoi*, which was already used in Titus 1:6 and 1 Timothy 1:9. Here the context suggests that the rebellion is directed against the sound teaching. The adjective *mataiologoi* ('idle talker, windbag', BDAG) appears

---

14 See Lucian, *Philops.* 3; *Tim.* 6; *Greek Anthology* 7.275; Ovid, *Ars.* 1.295–300; *Am.* 3.10.17–23.

15 See NW II.2 pp. 1018–1023 for a list of examples.

only here in the NT, but the noun form is found in 1 Timothy 1:6 of those who have committed apostasy. The noun *phrenapatēs* ('deceiver, misleader') in the list appears in its verbal form in Galatians 6:3 of those who deceive themselves. Here, as the following verse will show, those deceived by the false teachers are entire households.

Paul qualifies the *many* of verse 10 by adding *especially those of the circumcision*. Clearly, he is referring to Jews (including, perhaps, proselytes, i.e., Gentiles who had converted to Judaism). The phrase translated as *those of the circumcision (hoi ek tēs peritomēs)* is found in the following NT texts: Acts 10:45; 11:2; Romans 4:12; Galatians 2:12 and Colossians 4:11.[16]

11. What is Titus (and the chosen leaders) to do with these false teachers? *They must be silenced.* The language is strong, since the verb *epistomizō* could be used of putting a bridle on a horse or muzzling an animal, and from there metaphorically to *silence* speakers or enemies (LSJ, s.v.). Certainly violence is not an option when silencing the opponents. Instead, as we have seen in a number of texts (see esp. 2 Tim. 2:24–26), the false teachers should be silenced by careful argument based on the apostolic tradition. At times the teacher must rebuke the false teachers 'sharply' (Tit. 1:13); at other times 'gently' (2 Tim. 2:25; cf. Towner, p. 696).

Since they are upsetting whole families. Here we are given one of the reasons why the false teachers must be silenced. The text is similar to 2 Timothy 3:6, where Paul spoke of those who 'creep' into households and carry away certain women who are filled with sins. Here, it is the entire household – fathers, mothers, children, slaves – who the false teachers are envisioned as 'upsetting' (cf. 2 Tim. 2:18). As noted in the Introduction and 2 Timothy 3:5–6, it is possible that the false teachers had been hired as philosophical instructors to educate the family (primarily the wives) and so to bring harmony into the household, which was supposed to be one of the fruits of adhering

---

16 A helpful comparative text outside the NT is Justyn Martyr's *Dialogue with Trypho* 1.3, where the Jew (and philosophy lover) Trypho designates himself a 'Hebrew of the circumcision'. At 41.3 Justyn speaks of the way some Gentile Christians view circumcision.

to moral philosophy.[17] Instead, because they do not adhere to the 'teaching', the false teachers are actually 'upsetting' or 'destroying' every group in the household.

In the final clause Paul states how the false teachers destroy the faith of households, and what their motive is in this enterprise: *by teaching for sordid gain what is not right to teach.* The false teachers do their damage by instruction. The language and context are strikingly similar to 1 Timothy 5:13, where widows are in view. Just like the false teachers here, the younger widows went around homes where they were 'saying what they should not say'. This is one of the reasons we have argued (see Introduction) that the false teachers were having a strong effect on female widows, which is why Paul was not allowing women to teach (cf. 1 Tim. 2:12).

Paul continues by laying out the motives of the false teachers, namely *sordid gain* (*aischrou kerdos*; see 1 Tim. 3:8). This was a common theme in the polemics against wandering moral philosophers, namely, that the reason they taught was purely for financial gain. In addition, it was a common critique of Cretans that they were filled with 'sordid love of gain (*aischrokerdeia*) and lust for wealth' (Polybius, 6.46; Loeb translation).

12. Some scholars find these verses problematic because of the apparent 'slandering' of Cretans. It would also appear that Paul seems to support the statement by appending 'that testimony is true' to verse 13. Paul objects to 'slandering' in 2:3; but is he himself engaging in it by quoting the popular proverb about the Cretans?! We must remember that polemic speech in the ancient world was often 'biting'. First, Paul says that the statement about the Cretans comes from one of their own. Second, the readers of the letter were aware of the polemical 'game' in paraenesis. They understood that Paul was not calling every Cretan a liar or that he was inciting hate against Cretans. This was the way of the rhetorical polemics of the period. Third, Paul refers primarily to the false teachers, who were attempting to destroy the gospel. He must speak polemically lest Titus fail to grasp the seriousness of the situation. Lastly, Paul

---

17   See also Malherbe, *Light from the Gentiles* 1:286–287. For primary sources on this scenario, see Lucian, *De mercede conductis* 13, 19–20, 36.

calls himself 'the foremost of sinners' (1 Tim. 1:15), indicating that his approval of the Cretan proverb did not come from an arrogant, hateful position. The truth was that some Cretans did lie; and as one commentator has put it: 'We might consider how we are all a little bit "Cretan" sometimes' (Hutson, p. 223).

13. *For this reason.* Given the truthfulness of the Cretan proverb cited in verse 12, which is being manifested in the Cretan (Jewish) false teachers in the present, Paul tells Titus: *Rebuke them sharply.* The verb is a present imperative, giving the sense of continuous rebuking. On the verb *rebuke* in the Pastoral Epistles, see the earlier remarks (Tit. 1:9; 1 Tim. 5:20; 2 Tim. 4:2). The manner in which Titus is to rebuke the false teachers is *sharply (apotomōs).* Paul concludes with the final aim of Titus' sharp reproof: *so that they may become sound in the faith.* It is somewhat surprising that Paul still holds out hope for the false teachers, given the very negative way he has described them. Yet, this clause makes clear that the rebuking has a positive aim in mind. On the language of *sound* teaching or faith, see on 1:9.

14. What it means to be 'sound in the faith' is explained negatively with the participle of means *prosechontes: not paying attention.* The syntax suggests that Paul speaks of the false teachers as those who are giving heed to myths and human commandments. However, the statement indirectly applies to the believers, lest they themselves become like the false teachers. Two items are mentioned to which they should not pay attention: *to Jewish myths or to commandments of those who reject the truth.* The first item was already mentioned in 1 Timothy 1:4 but without the adjective *Jewish.* Nevertheless, it was clear that the *myths* had a Jewish source and content. As explained there, moral philosophers often polemicized against those who used myths, which were fantastic old tales that could not be proved to be true or false and that were devoid of reason.[18] More than likely, Paul has in mind the type of tantalizing genealogies that one finds in Jewish pseudepigraphic literature (e.g., Jubilees 8.1–30; Ps. Philo 1–2).

---

18 Cf. Josephus, *A.J.* 1.16, where he praises Moses for rejecting *mythologias* (myths) in his composition of the law, even though it would have been easy to permit falsities to creep in, given the great antiquity of what he wrote about.

The second item to which they should not give heed is *command-ments of those who reject the truth*. These refer to purity laws which were used to interpret Scripture likely having to do with food (*halakah*), that is, rabbinic commandments. The disciples were taught by Jesus to reject these human-derived commands as a measure of piety (see Mark 7:3, 5; Col. 2:16, 21–22; cf. Isa. 29:13). With the final participial phrase, *of those who reject the truth*, Paul gets to the bottom of things: anything that does not find its source in the apostolic tradition, *the truth*, with its centre in the incarnation, death and resurrection of Jesus (cf. 1 Tim. 3:15–16), is unhealthy and destructive to the faith. On the language of the rejection of the faith (*apostrephō*), see comments on 2 Timothy 1:15 and 4:4.

15. *To the pure all things are pure.* Without any connecting words to the previous claim, Paul makes this statement, which has the ring of a proverb, and in fact is found as a maxim in the New Testament and in Greco-Roman literature.[19] In this verse the maxim is functioning as proof that the false teachers are deviating from the truth when they give commandments prohibiting certain foods. Since God created everything good and 'nothing is to be rejected' (1 Tim. 4:4), what actually matters is not the food but the person. If individuals have been cleansed on the basis of the atoning death of Jesus (cf. Eph. 5:26), ingesting certain foods will not corrupt them. On the other hand, *to the corrupt and unbelieving nothing is pure*. The language of purity continues in this clause, with *corrupt* standing in antithesis to *pure*. Yet Paul adds the adjective *unbelieving* to clarify that purity is ultimately a matter of belief in God as he has been revealed in Jesus Christ (see also 3:8).

Paul concludes by introducing the conjunction *alla*, which extends the previous thought (Knight, p. 303). *In fact, both their minds and consciences are corrupted* [NIV]. The first term, *nous* (*mind*; see also 1 Tim. 6:5; 2 Tim. 3:8), is anthropological language whose meaning is difficult to convey with just one word. Sand's explanation is helpful: 'The meaning is not univocal. Νοῦς can indicate the *understanding* of a matter, the individual *capacity to judge,* and human *views* and *convictions.* At times, νοῦς approximates σοφία or is a designation for

---

19 See Rom. 14:20; Philo, *Spec.* 3.209; Seneca, *Ep.* 98.3.

the proper disposition — in contrast to earthly-human, therefore false, conduct' (*TDNT* II, 478). By saying that the false teachers are corrupt in their minds, Paul speaks of the very core of their being as standing against the truth of the gospel. On *conscience* see discussion under 1 Timothy 1:5 and 1:19.

16. Paul continues speaking of the false teachers who 'reject the truth'. He completes their unmasking by calling attention to the contradiction that exists between their profession of faith and their actions, and then concludes with another short vice list. First, as he did in 1 Timothy 4:2 and 2 Timothy 3:5, Paul shows the incongruous existence of these false teachers who profess to know God (probably boasting that as Jews they know the Torah and thus God better than Gentiles) yet *deny him by their actions*. It is a central tenet of New Testament (and Old Testament) faith that true knowledge of God is demonstrated by good works (see Matt. 7:15–23; Eph. 2:10; Jas 2:14–26). Second, Paul brings the argument to a conclusion by citing the vices of the false teachers, which demonstrate that they do not know God: *They are detestable, disobedient, unfit for any good work*. The first term, *bdelyktos*, appears only here in the NT. A helpful example of its use outside the NT is Philo who uses it in a list that includes 'robbers and pirates and associations of abominable [*bdelyktōn*] and licentious women'.[20] *Disobedient* is also used of false teachers in 2 Timothy 3:2, referring to disobedience to parents. Here it probably refers to disobedience to parents and God. The last phrase is the adjective *unfit* which conveys the sense of 'unqualified' (BDAG, p. 172; see 1 Tim. 3:10). That is, none of their works qualifies as *good*.

Theology
Paul continues to instruct Titus on his work on the island of Crete. One of Titus' central tasks is to appoint godly and capable leaders to oversee the relatively new churches. The reason for this is that false teachers are already operating in such a way that they are deceiving entire households. Paul provides a detailed description of the false teachers that can also help us as we pray for discernment. First, he speaks of the motives of the enemies, saying in verse 14 that they

20 Philo, *Spec.* 1.323.

teach 'for sordid gain'. This means that they do not care for the health and well-being of the sheep (cf. John 10:10–13) but primarily use them to gain from them. Second, he speaks of non-biblical doctrine to which the false teachers pay heed. Rather than teaching sound doctrine, they give commands about ceremonial purity that are not in accord with the truth (v. 14). They probably boast about their superior purity. The problem, and this leads to the third point, is that, judged by the sound doctrine, they are not pure. They boast of knowing God and his ways, yet their actions – and lack of actions – demonstrate that they really do not know God. To know God is to obey his commandments – and these commandments stem from the ethics of the gospel, not man-made myths or teachings.

C. Instructions for the household (2:1–10)

Context
We noted earlier (1 Tim. 5:1–6:2) Paul's use of material that was similar to Greco-Roman household codes or *Haustafeln* but which upon closer inspection turned out to be a more general case of paraenesis or moral exhortation. This section of Titus more closely resembles the household code.

In Greco-Roman literature it is clear that the question of how fathers of households could relate virtuously to others in the household was vigorously discussed. Philosophers (going back at least to Aristotle but likely prior to him) produced a sort of code or template to address the question. Formally, the content of household codes was arranged in pairs, instructing the father how he must act towards the different members of his household: father–sons; father–wives; father–slaves.[21] During the Hellenistic and Roman period the format was altered (i.e., pairing was not always followed) but the goal remained the same: to provide a moral manual for fathers in their relationship with the different members of the household.[22] Since the dominant conception of the church in the Pastoral Epistles is the home, one can see how the use of the

---

21 See Aristotle, *Pol.* 1.2.1–1.5.12.
22 See helpfully Seneca, *Ep.* 94.1; Epictetus, *Diss.* 2.10.7–9.

household code would be helpful to communicate to Titus (the *oikonomos*, or 'steward' in this setting) the proper behaviour of the different members.

One use of the household code is found in Hellenistic Jews such as Philo and Josephus, who may provide a historical bridge to help us understand how the early Christians used the code, particularly Paul. Hellenistic Jewish authors used the code, although in a modified form, as a means to make an apologetic argument on behalf of Judaism. This was necessary since Gentile authors often denigrated Jews as enemies of Greek and Roman virtues. Tacitus, for example, states that when proselytes convert to Judaism, they are taught the following: 'The earliest lesson they receive is to despise the gods, to disown their country, and to regard their parents, children, and brothers as of little account.'[23] One can see how Tacitus uses the broad format of the code (particularly in the third clause) to denounce the Jews as a people fundamentally lacking *pietas* or godliness. Authors like Josephus and Philo responded by employing a form of the code where they describe the pious way in which Jewish family members treat one another.[24] It is therefore not surprising that Paul (e.g., Eph. 5:22–6:9; Col. 3:18–4:1) and Peter (e.g., 1 Pet. 2:13–3:7) use the household code, since the early Christians were often perceived as Jews or a sect of Judaism. The use of the code *itself* already sends signals to outsiders that the Christians were conversant in the ethics of the *polis*; they understood the importance of *pietas* in the household.

For the insiders, Paul is using this code to remind them of their relationship with one another and with outsiders. When each group within the churches displays the type of behaviour commanded by Paul, they will overcome the preconceptions of Gentiles and win them for the Lord. In fact, the purpose clause that is at the end of the section points in this direction: 'so that in every way they will make the teaching about God our Saviour attractive' (2:10, NIV).

---

23 Tacitus, *Hist.* 5.5. Cf. Malherbe, *Light from the Gentiles*, 1:100.
24 Philo, *Hypoth.* 7.3, 14; Josephus, *Ag. Ap.* 199–208.

Comment

1. *But as for you.* That is, in contrast to what the false teachers were instructing, as described in 1:10–16, Titus must continually teach that which corresponds to the *sound doctrine* (see 1 Tim. 1:10; 2 Tim. 4:3). The ethical list that follows is full of the language of virtues that good citizens were expected to exemplify. Since the congregation is a household (1 Tim. 3:15), Paul structures the commands by means of the different ages and gender of the members.

2. The first group to be addressed are *the older men.* In antiquity there was no consensus on what constituted old age.[25] The percentage of the population of early Rome aged 60 or above is estimated to have been only 7%.[26] More important than figuring out the specific age that counted as 'old' is the value attached to old age during this period. That is, what characteristics did society attach to old age, in particular older men? On the one hand, as reflected in the writings of Aristotle, Horace and Juvenal, there was an understanding that old age could be devastating to the individual. These authors could speak in a denigrating manner of old men: they are always hesitant, easily deceived, cowards, selfish, and so on. On the other hand, there is a long tradition, specially found in moral philosophers that venerates old age (e.g., Plato, *Resp.* 328D–330A; Cicero, *Sen.* 6–8). Old men and women should be respected, honoured and cared for. Paul, partly moulded by the insistent OT commands to honour parents and care for widows, would have appreciated this tradition. We have already seen in 1 Timothy 5:1 that his injunction to Timothy is to treat older men like fathers.

Nevertheless, Paul does not idealize older men, as if they were beyond the possibility of misbehaving. And so he provides exhortation for the older men. The goal is for them to behave in ways that Greco-Roman culture considered virtuous. Therefore, Paul instructs the older men to be *temperate, serious, prudent.* The first two terms in particular (*nēphalios, semnos*) convey the concept of *gravitas* and respectability that one comes to expect from godly, older men.

---

25 See Malherbe, *Light from the Gentiles*, 1:487. More cautious is Barclay, 'There Is Neither Old Nor Young', pp. 225–228.
26 Barclay, 'Neither Old Nor Young', p. 228.

Paul then adds three more virtues: *sound in faith, in love, and in endurance*. We should note that these virtues are identical to the fruit of the Spirit of Galatians 5:22. Furthermore, since Paul has previously linked *sound* with doctrine, we should understand the relationship with the final three virtues in the following way: sound doctrine irrevocably leads to virtues such as faith, love and endurance. This is why Paul, speaking of the false teachers in 1:16, said that although they confess to know God, 'they deny him by their actions … [they are] unfit for any good work'.

3–5. Just as older men could be denigrated in ancient culture, so also older women. There existed a stereotype, especially prevalent in art, where old women were represented as drunks, toothless and overall dirty and useless.[27] Paul's commands to *the older women*, while clearly not abusive, show us that he was aware of some of these stereotypes. Therefore, he orders them not to be *slaves to drink*.[28] Paul's emphasis is on their roles as instructors of younger wives. Thus, he commands the older women to *teach what is good*. More specifically, the goal is for the older women to 'recall to their senses' (cf. LSJ s.v. *sōphronizō*) the younger wives in their domestic domains. As we have seen (especially 1 Tim. 2:8–15), it appears that some wives in the Pauline congregations were not paying attention to homely virtues. Therefore, Paul wants the older women to remind the younger women of their duty. He mentions seven virtues that the younger wives were to practise. They are the following: *love their husbands … love their children … be self-controlled, chaste, good managers of the household, kind, being submissive to their husbands*. Each of these virtues is predicated of ideal young wives in literature and epitaphs of the period.[29] The general idea in

---

27 See the evidence in Parkin, *Old Age in the Roman World*, p. 86. On art, the evidence comes from Brandt, *Wird auch silbern mein Haar*, pp. 99–100, 109–110.

28 The stereotype of women as alcoholics is used of both old and young women in Greco-Roman literature: Dionysius of Halicarnassus *Ant. rom.* 2.25.6; Val. Max. 6.3.9 (see NW II:2, pp. 1031–1032).

29 For epitaphs, see Spicq, p. 252. Some primary sources include: Philo *Praem.* 139; *Spec.* 3.169; Plutarch *Conj. praec.* 9 (see NW II:2, 1033–1037).

the culture was that the woman's domain was her home; there she could take care of husband and children, doing all this with modesty and kindness, and deferring to her own husband. Paul appreciates these virtues, encouraging the more experienced, older women to teach the younger how to practise them.

Paul concludes the injunctions to the women with a purpose clause stated in negative fashion: *so that the word of God may not be discredited*. In his other letters, the respectful and loving attitude that the wife is to have to her husband is motivated by a different reason ('as is fitting in the Lord', Col. 3:18 [NIV]). In Titus the emphasis falls on the relationship between the young wives' virtues and the reputation of *the word of God*, that is, the sound teaching in its preached form. If the women of the churches, particularly those who were married, behaved in ways that were incongruous with virtues acceptable to both Gentiles and Christians, the result could be the discreditation of the gospel. This is similar to the thought of 1 Timothy 6:1 where the slaves were ordered to behave in such a way that 'the name of God and the teaching would not be blasphemed'. If the younger wives failed in their conduct, the gospel would be discredited. At stake, therefore, is the mission of the church. We can thus say that the grounding for the behaviour of the wives (see also the younger men and slaves) is essentially missional (cf. Towner, pp. 729–730; see below under Theology).

6–8. From the older men and older and younger women, Paul now moves to the younger men. As Greco-Roman culture could label older men and women positively and negatively, so also with younger men. The negative, dominant stereotype of the young man was of one who was mastered by his passions (*epithymiai*), particularly sexual passions.[30] In fact, in many ancient authors young men were contrasted with older men in that the latter, because of their late age, were supposed at last to attain self-control (but purely because of biology, it was added cf. Plato, *Resp.* 329C–329D), while the former lacked it (e.g., Plutarch, *Praec. ger. rei publ* 13.1; Philostratus, *Vit. Apoll.* 1.13). Paul calls the young men to be *self-controlled* (*sōphronizō*), and

---

30 See Aristotle, *Rhet.* 2.12.

not just in one area but *in everything*.³¹ This would have been viewed as a very difficult – if not impossible – imperative. As we will see in 2:11–14, it is only the heavenly, powerful and gracious Saviour who could empower the young men (and everyone else mentioned in this household code) to live a godly life even in the present.

From the instructions to the young men in general, Paul next addresses Titus specifically, himself a young man. This text is similar to 1 Timothy 4:12, where Timothy was encouraged to lead the congregations as an example in conduct and word. So also here, Titus is ordered to be *a model of good works* (on *good works*, see 1 Tim. 2:10; 3:1; 5:10; 6:18). In what follows Paul provides three concrete examples where Titus must be a model. First, Paul commands: *in your teaching show integrity*. This probably refers to the content of Titus' teaching. That is, in contrast to the false teachers (cf. 1:9, 13), who had abandoned the apostolic doctrine, Titus is to be an example in teaching only that which is truly apostolic. Second, Titus is to be an example in *seriousness* (NIV). The Greek word is derived from *semnos*, which was used in verse 2 as a virtue required by older men (see also 1 Tim. 3:4, 8, 11). Titus must not be a 'flippant' individual but someone who is taken seriously because of his conduct and speech. Third, he must be an example in *sound speech that cannot be censured*. In light of the clause that follows, it is likely that this is not primarily a reference to the proclamation of sound doctrine (*pace* Oberlinner, 1996, p. 118). The emphasis falls on Titus being a young man who is careful, reasonable and thoughtful in his speech with others, particularly outsiders.³²

Just as he provided a purpose for the women to behave in virtuous ways, so again Paul provides a purpose clause that expresses the aim of Titus' sound character, doctrine and speech. As in verse 5,

---

31 The phrase *peri panta*, 'in everything', most probably modifies the previous command in v. 6, as indicated in NA²⁸; among English translations, only CSB seems to follow this analysis.

32 On the combination of *logos hygiēs* ('sound/wise speech'), see Herodotus 1.8; Dionysius of Halicarnassus, *Din.* 4.12; Dio Chrysostom, *Or.* 77/78. 39. Hutson, p. 231, hits the mark when he says in this context that Titus 'must be circumspect'.

the thought is concerned with unbelievers; in fact, with those who are adversaries towards the new faith: *so that those who oppose you may be ashamed because they have nothing bad to say about us*. Paul is not here speaking of people who were neutral but about those who were enemies of the believers' faith. Titus' behaviour in action and word should be such that these adversaries may no longer attempt to oppose him, since they have *nothing bad to say about us* that will cause the type of shame that will stop them.

9–10. The final group that Titus is to address are the slaves. The slaves that Paul is referring to here would have been household slaves, who, while still under the terrible 'yoke' (1 Tim. 6:1) of slavery, were in less unfortunate positions than slaves who laboured in the mines or in brothels, for example (on slavery in the ancient world and in Paul's letters, see comments under 1 Tim. 6:1–2). Paul calls for these slaves *to be subject to their masters in everything* (NIV). He will provide a purpose for this attitude in verse 10; but we should also remember that, generally speaking, slaves who behaved well were rewarded, sometimes even with manumission.[33] Therefore, given the state of affairs in the Greco-Roman world, submission could often be in the best interest of the slave. It was possible for a slave to be submissive but at the same time quietly display a 'nasty' attitude towards the master; or *talk back*. Instead of this, Paul calls on slaves to go beyond submission to actually *please them*. That is, their presence should be a cause of enjoyment for the master.

Many trustworthy household slaves managed the monetary funds of their masters. This opened the opportunity for stealing, an action that became stereotyped in the description of slaves in the literature.[34] Thus, Paul commands them *not to pilfer* but to *show complete and perfect fidelity*. As he did in verses 5 and 8, Paul links the believer's conduct with a concrete purpose. Here, the goal of the slaves' virtuous conduct in speech and action is *so that in everything they may be an ornament to the doctrine of God our Saviour*. Given the

---

33 See Fitzgerald, 'The Stoics and the Early Christians on the Treatment of Slaves', p. 142.

34 Pliny the Elder *Nat.* 33.26; Diogenes Laertius *Vit. phil.* 7.23. See also Joshel, *Slavery*, pp. 154–158.

context of verses 1–10, it is likely that Paul refers to the response of unbelievers (some actually enemies, cf. v. 8) to Christian doctrine. God granted the Christian slaves a wonderful opportunity: by their conduct they could make the gospel more attractive, more desirable to unbelieving owners. Paul describes the doctrine as that of *God our Saviour*. In light of 2:13, the accent falls on Jesus Christ as *God our Saviour*. This is a powerful Christological statement, which we will revisit in the following section. Furthermore, by using the appellation *Saviour*, Paul prepares the way for 2:11–14, where God is so designated.

Theology

As Christian missionaries can amply attest, one of the great hurdles to the reception of the gospel in regions that have never been evangelized is the *suspicion* of the local population. They are naturally cautious when first hearing of a new, sometimes strange religion. Such suspicions may be relieved when the believers display the virtues that are common of good citizens in society. The espousal and demonstration of virtues such as seriousness, decency, love of one's spouse and children, and honesty can be instrumental in allaying the doubts and suspicions of unbelievers. Paul the missionary understood this.

The context of the Pastoral Epistles, as we have noted throughout this commentary, is one in which outsiders viewed the new religion as perhaps another strange, exotic mystery cult from the eastern part of the empire. Naturally, many would have questioned the validity of this new religion. And so Paul, through Titus, exhorts the new Christians in Crete to display those virtues that were respected in the Greco-Roman cities. The practice of those virtues could put suspicions to rest. Paul puts the exhortations of this section in the form of the household code both because the Christians viewed themselves as a family (going back to Jesus himself, cf. Mark 3:31–35) and because they would have better understood what Paul was asking of them.

Some dispute that Paul, in a passage having to do with ethics, grounds the motivation for ethics in what they think are purely pragmatic goals or 'bourgeois morality'. Instead of ethics motivated by the love of Christ or love for one another or by the Christians' new reality as the people of God, here the reason for ethics appears to be concern that outsiders may not speak negatively of Christian teaching. How do the precepts of Titus 2:1–10 fit with an overall Pauline ethic, when, as some assume, the motivation for obedience seems to lack Christological or soteriological grounding?[35]

The stated purposes in verses 5, 8, 10 are examples of *the ethics of mission*, which ultimately falls under the love-command: love for God and love for neighbour. Verses 1–10 should not be read in isolation from verses 11–14 that speak of God's gracious salvation, which has appeared for the sake of all humanity. The logic then works as follows. First, God has antecedently reached out to all humanity in order that they might experience his saving grace. Second, God has so empowered the Christian community that it has a role to play in God's mission. Third, the duty of every Christian is to reflect the type of conduct that will better show the beauty of the gospel, thereby attracting unbelievers so that they will be caught up in God's work of salvation history. These are the ethics of mission, which imitate God's antecedent love of humanity. By the Christians' *internal* treatment of one another in a way that is worthy of the sound doctrine, and also by their respectful treatment of non-Christians who may be socially superior, there is an *external* effect that wins the non-Christian to the gospel.[36]

D. Soteriology as the basis for Christian behaviour (2:11–15)

Context
We have already hinted at the relationship between the commands of 2:1–10 and the packed theological statement of 2:11–14. Simply put, verses 11–14 serve as the basis or grounding for the injunctions

---

35 Particularly critical of the ethics of the Pastoral Epistles is Schrage, *Ethics of the New Testament*, pp. 257–268, mostly following Dibelius and Conzelmann. Schrage misses the missional context and concerns of the Pastoral Epistles.

36 On the relationship of missions to the Pastoral Epistles' theology (and therefore Paul's ethics), see Schnabel, *Paul the Missionary*, pp. 149–154. Also helpful, it does not deal with the Pastoral Epistles directly, is Horrell, *Solidarity and Difference*, esp. pp. 271–299.

of verses 1–10. As is typical of Paul, the imperative is based on, and made possible by, the indicative of salvation.[37]

Within this overall framework it may be helpful to point out two more specific structural elements. First, we note that verses 11 and 14 form an *inclusio* or bookend: both verses speak of the work of Christ for our salvation. Verse 11 views the work of Christ from the perspective of his advent; verse 14 from the perspective of one aspect of his advent, namely his vicarious work. With this *inclusio* Paul leaves no doubt that salvation is only possible on the basis of the Christ-event. Second, we note that the reality of salvation in this section is presented through the lens of *time*. There is the past action of the advent of Christ highlighted by the past tense 'has appeared' (v. 11).[38] The present perspective of salvation is indicated by the virtues that the believer must display 'in the present age' (v. 12). Lastly, the future perspective is given with the statement that the believer awaits expectantly for the parousia of Jesus Christ (v. 13).

Comment

11. The subject of the initial sentence of this section is *grace*. Paul has used this term a number of times in the Pastoral Epistles to speak of salvation (see esp. 3:7; 1 Tim. 1:14; 2 Tim. 1:9; 2:1). Here Paul qualifies *grace* in four ways.

First, he says that grace *has appeared*, choosing the verb *epiphainō* to declare this truth. With the exception of 2 Thessalonians 2:8, the verb and its cognates are exclusive to the Pastoral Epistles in the Pauline Corpus (see 2:13; 3:5; 1 Tim. 6:14; 2 Tim. 1:10; 4:1, 8; sometimes Paul uses the verb *phaneroō*, 'to appear'; cf. Tit. 1:3 and Col. 3:4). This vocabulary was used especially in the Septuagint to speak of God's salvation of his people by his delivering them from their enemies (see on 2 Tim. 1:10). The language is often found in poetic statements to denote the glory of the Lord as he saves (see

---

37 Oberlinner (1996, p. 125) heads this section: 'The Salvation-Historical Foundation for the Life of the Christian Community'.

38 Siebenthal, *Ancient Greek Grammar*, p. 326, includes the aorist *epephanē* ('has appeared') among a group of aorist verbs that 'indicate the great facts of the history of salvation'.

Deut. 33:2; 1 Sam. 7:23; Ps. 30:17; 79:4; 2 Macc. 3:30; 3 Macc. 2:19; 6:4, 18, 39). Towner highlights the concept of God's transcendence implied in such language. In the Lord's *epiphaneia* there is 'a massive incursion of the invisible' into human history (p. 745). Thus, the use of the verb in this particular text is fitting, because Paul expresses in exalted language the inbreaking of 'the great God and Saviour, Jesus Christ' (v. 13).

The second qualifier of grace is the genitive phrase *of God*. This is probably a subjective genitive, thereby placing God as the subject, the one who brings grace. Theologically, it is important to grasp that when we speak of *the grace of God*, we are not referring to something that is foreign to God. The grace of God is God himself in his movement of love towards humanity. When we speak of grace, 'It is always God's turning to those who not only do not deserve his favour, but have deserved its opposite.'[39]

The third qualifier of grace is *sōtērios*, which the NRSV translates as *bringing salvation*. Paul clarifies that God's gracious move of love to humans is for the goal of their salvation, which will be described in verses 12–13. The fourth and final qualifier of grace is expressed with the dative of advantage phrase, *to all*, which goes with *bringing salvation* (cf. Marshall, p. 268). That is, when God drew near in love for salvation, he was not only being gracious to Jews but also to Gentiles, indeed to the whole world (cf. Rom. 1:16–17). This statement is of a piece with Paul's emphasis in the Pastoral Epistles that salvation has been made possible for all of humanity: God is the one who 'desires everyone to be saved' (1 Tim. 2:4; cf. 1 Tim. 2:1; 4:10).

12. In the previous verse Paul declared that God's grace, *which is bringing salvation to all*, has been made manifest. In the current verse he explains the meaning of this salvation from the perspective of present existence. In other words, God's grace empowers the recipients of his grace in such a way that they are able to display basic virtues in the here and now of salvation history.

In order better to explain these theologically condensed verses at least two preliminary comments are necessary. First, with respect to their structure, we have an example of chiasmus in the form of

---

39   Barth, *CD* II.1 p. 356.

an ABB'A' pattern. The pattern is present in the order of the Greek text, which I reproduce here: (A) *renounce*; (B) *impiety and world passions*; (B') *self-controlled, upright, and godly*; (A') *live lives*. The A and A' are the verbal forms that speak of the responsibility of the Christian. The B and B' express the vices to be renounced and the virtues to be lived out. This type of parallelism may indicate that Paul was working with a liturgical formula, perhaps used in baptism and/or catechism (see Jeremias, p. 72).

The second observation has to do with the vocabulary Paul uses to speak of the vices and virtues. The language stems from Hellenistic moral philosophy. In fact, two of the virtues, *sōphrōn* ('self-controlled') and *dikaios* ('upright'), are found in the cardinal virtues of Greek moral philosophy. In addition, the participle of the verb *paideuō*, translated as *training*, is used with the Hellenistic denotation of 'educating in virtue', a basic topos of moral philosophy. As we stated earlier (Tit. 2:1–10), Paul, like a good missionary, contextualizes his message by employing language understandable to his audience.

God's grace, then, is *training us* for the following purpose: that we might *renounce impiety and worldly passions*. The first vice is the opposite of *godliness (eusebeia)*, one of the key terms in the Pastoral Epistles to signify a world view and conduct that are fundamentally shaped by the 'sound teaching' and the gospel (see on 1 Tim. 1:9–11; 3:16; 6:3 and Introduction). The second vice to be renounced refers to all passions that are dominated by selfish desires and gratification (cf. under 2 Tim. 2:22).

On the one hand, salvation requires repentance, a renouncing of vices contrary to the gospel (*training us to renounce impiety*). On the other hand, salvation involves embracing an existence that is *self-controlled, upright, and godly*. On the terminology of *self-control* or 'prudent' (*sōphrōn*), see on 1 Timothy 2:9, 15; 3:2; Titus 1:8; 2:1–2; for *upright* or 'just' (*dikaios*), see on 1 Timothy 1:9; Titus 1:8; for *godly*, see paragraph above.

13. While verse 11 focused on the past of salvation and verse 12 on the present, verse 13 points to a future event which nonetheless has repercussions for the present. As believers, we wait expectantly (cf. 2 Tim. 4:8: 'all who have longed for his appearing') *for the blessed hope and manifestation of the glory of our great God and Saviour, Jesus Christ.*

This is a theologically loaded phrase to refer to the second coming of the Lord Jesus Christ. Paul uses two nouns with two qualifications to speak of the parousia. First, he speaks of the event as a *blessed hope* (cf. 1 Thess. 4:13). The virtue of hope in the Greco-Roman world was not particularly admired, since hope was viewed more as 'wishful thinking' than something trustworthy (see on 1:2). Not so with the early church, which based its hope on the resurrection of Jesus from the dead. Jesus' resurrection, like the first fruit that guarantees a harvest (1 Cor. 15:20), was the concrete and sure event that assured the Christians that just as he was raised immortal, so would they be raised from the dead at his return (1 Thess. 4:14). Belief in the resurrection and return of Jesus was ultimately the only way not to be engulfed by the bleakness of death. It was this hope of the resurrection that would occur at Christ's return that kept Paul joyful, even though he was a lonely prisoner expecting death (see on 2 Tim. 4:6–8, 16–18). It is fitting, therefore, that Paul uses the adjective *blessed* to describe this hope.

The second way of referring to the future return of Christ is with the term *epiphaneia* (*manifestation*), a cognate of *epiphainō*, which was the main verb of verse 11. To qualify this noun Paul uses the phrase *of the glory*, which should be understood as a descriptive genitive and therefore translated as *glorious*. Paul's language is selected carefully since the term *manifestation* was often employed of the gods' splendorous intervention to rescue the people they favoured (see under 2 Tim. 1:10). By speaking of the parousia of Jesus with these terms, Paul is already leading the reader to understand Jesus as more than a mere human. In the final clause of this verse this is done even more directly.

The parousia, then, is nothing less than the glorious manifestation *of our great God and Saviour, Jesus Christ*. Along with texts such as John 1:1, 18; 20:28; Rom. 9:5; Heb. 1:8 and 2 Pet. 1:1, this text from Titus is one of the most direct declarations of the divine nature of Jesus: Paul designates Jesus as *megas theos*, 'great God'. On the other hand, many scholars have argued that the subject of the clause is not just one person, namely Jesus Christ, but two, God (the Father) and Jesus Christ. Thus, the term *God* is viewed as a reference to the Father, while *Saviour* is related to the Son. The following reasons explain why the text should be taken to refer to one person, namely Jesus Christ, who is predicated as God. [40] First, the language used of the parousia is already heavily freighted with vocabulary and intertextuality that belong to God (e.g., 'manifestation', 'glory'). It would therefore not be a great theological leap for Paul to speak of Jesus directly as God. Second, the fact that there is only one article governing *great God and Saviour* points to one person (Granville Sharp Rule). [41] Third, it makes sense syntactically to take the genitive phrase *Jesus Christ* at the end of the verse as a genitive in apposition, which would mean that *our great God and Saviour* is identical to *Jesus Christ*.

14. Verse 13 ended by speaking of Jesus as *our great God and Saviour*. In verse 14 Paul draws from early church tradition (tradition he himself might have written) to expand on the meaning of Jesus as Saviour. There is a great paradox in this verse: while verse 13 speaks of Jesus in terms of exaltation, verse 14 infers the humiliation of Jesus as the one *who gave himself for us*, a reference to the crucifixion. Jesus' greatness as God, therefore, is not only to be found in his identity as creator and judge but is also found in his incarnation and in his self-humbling to the point of dying shamefully on a cross (cf. Phil. 2:6–11). And yet this humiliation does not negate or diminish his glory but makes it shine all the brighter. [42]

Paul uses a traditional formulation to explain the meaning of the death of Jesus. This goes back to Jesus himself (see Mark 10:45; Luke 22:19) and has been developed by Paul and Peter (e.g., Gal. 1:4; 2:20; 1 Pet. 2:21–23; 3:18). We have already seen this formula

---

40 For a fuller discussion of the matter cf. Knight, pp. 322–326; Marshall, pp. 276–282; Towner, pp. 755–758 accepts the equation of Jesus Christ with God as an exegetical possibility, but finds his equation with 'the glory of the great God and Saviour' more plausible.

41 See Wallace, *The Basics of New Testament Syntax*, pp. 120–122, which includes this text as a valid example of the rule.

42 This is especially jarring in the Gospel of John where Jesus' crucifixion is his glorification. See Frey, *Glory*, esp. pp. 237–258. See also Moltmann, *The Crucified God*, p. 295: 'When the crucified Jesus is called the "image of the invisible God", the meaning is that *this* is God, and God is like *this*. God is not greater than he is in his humiliation. God is not more glorious than he is in this self-surrender.'

in 1 Timothy 2:5–6. The formula has the following elements (cf. Marshall, pp. 282–283): (1) the use of the verb *didōmi* to speak of Jesus 'giving himself' on the cross; (2) the use of the preposition *hyper* or *anti* to express the vicarious nature of Jesus' death; (3) an object of the preposition: Jesus gave himself 'for our sins;' or, as here, 'for us'. What this giving of himself *for us* means is unpacked in the purpose clause that follows.

That he might redeem us from all iniquity and purify for himself a people of his own who are zealous for good deeds. There is a negative and a positive purpose of the self-giving of Jesus. Negatively, Jesus' death was to *redeem us*. The verb *lytroomai* here means 'to rescue' or 'free' (see GELS, p. 436). With a prepositional phrase Paul gives more precision as to what/who God is rescuing us from: it is from *all iniquity* (*anomia*; for this term, see on 1 Tim. 1:9). Paul uses language from the Septuagint (e.g., Exod. 34:8; Pss 58:2; 72:14). In fact, his statement is virtually a quotation from Psalm 130:8 (LXX 129:8): 'It is he [the LORD] who will redeem Israel from all its iniquities.' Crucially, what Yahweh has promised to do in the Psalm is what Jesus Christ now does for the believers.

The next phrase communicates the positive purpose of Jesus' death for us, which is: *to purify for himself a people of his own.* Just as the previous clause was based on the Septuagint, so also is this one. Particularly noteworthy is Ezekiel 37:23, where the Lord promises what he will do with Israel at the time of restoration: 'I will save them from all their apostasies into which they have fallen, and will cleanse them. Then they shall be my people and I will be their God' (see also Exod. 19:5; Deut. 4:20; 7:6; 14:2).

The verse concludes with a statement that highlights an important aspect of what it means to be the special people of God. They are to be *zealous for good deeds*. We should note the intensity of the language: the believers are not just to perform good works but are to be *zealous*, that is, eager and totally committed to the doing of *good deeds* (*kalōn ergon*; see 1:16; 2:7; 1 Tim. 2:10; 5:10; 6:18; 2 Tim. 2:21; cf. 1 Pet. 3:13). Salvation by grace does not allow for an immoral lifestyle; quite the opposite is the case. We have learned in the Pastoral Epistles that confession of faith bereft of good works is an illusion; in fact, it is the mark of false teachers (1:16).

Theology

As Paul explains the meaning of salvation he resorts to language that evokes God's salvation of Israel in the exodus from Egypt. The exodus was the paradigmatic story of salvation in the OT; and already in the later prophets of the OT we can see a spiritualizing of the main aspects of the original exodus event. Sin, rebellion and death, not Egypt, are those powers from which God promises to deliver the people (see Marshall, p. 284).

What is remarkable in Titus 2:11–14 is that Jesus of Nazareth becomes the subject of this salvation, the one who carries it out. Whereas Yahweh was the one who was the subject of the narrative of salvation in the exodus and the Old Testament, here Jesus is, as it were, inserted into the narrative as the subject of the new exodus, which includes Jews and Gentiles. *Jesus* is the deliverer; *Jesus* is the God and Saviour; *Jesus* is the one who redeems and cleanses a people for himself. These are actions that God alone can do.

The early Christian prophets and apostles, under the guidance of the Spirit, very early understood what this meant for the reality and identity of God. This did not mean that there were two Gods (cf. 1 Cor. 8:6), or that Jesus had replaced the Yahweh of the OT (Marcionism), or that the two were the same person simply appearing differently (Sabellianism). Instead, the new revelation of Jesus Christ as God had a decisive effect on their understanding of God. The fact that they include Jesus Messiah in the divine identity of Israel's God implies that the identity of Yahweh was complex, with Jesus as constitutive of that identity. But they also understood that the identity of Jesus was equally complex, because Yahweh was constitutive of the identity of Jesus. Thus, one could not know God without Jesus and Jesus without God. When it was understood that the Holy Spirit is also innate to the identity of God, we have the beginnings of a fundamental understanding of who God is: he is one God who eternally exists in three persons: the Father, the Son and the Holy Spirit (see Matt. 28:19; 2 Cor. 13:13). The Greek Fathers would develop this basic judgment in the centuries that followed.

E. The behaviour of the church towards society and the theological reason (3:1–11)

This section is structurally very similar to the previous one. Both 2:1–14 and 3:1–11 begin with: (1) commands for Titus to pass on to the churches; (2) a theological grounding, particularly by way of soteriology; and (3) further injunctions that work as bookends to the initial commands.[43]

It appears that the main difference between these two sections has to do with the context of the behaviour of the believers. While 2:1–14 concentrated on the household/insiders, 3:1–11 concentrates on the behaviour of the believers towards non-Christians/outsiders. The ethics of the Christians internally had a simultaneous external, missional purpose (2:1–10). The same is true in 3:1–11, the difference being that in this text the relationship with outsiders is presented in *more direct* fashion (see esp. vv. 1–2 and 8). As to why Paul includes in this letter commands towards outsiders, particularly the state, it is likely that such commands were part of early Christian teaching and discipleship (see Rom. 12:17–13:7; 1 Pet. 2:11–25).

A second observation pertains to the logic that holds together 3:1–11. Again, most commentators have noted that the internal logic is of a piece with 2:1–14. That is, virtuous behaviour is based on an antecedent theological reality that provides the ultimate reason for the good treatment of others. 'The reason is that baptism and the gift of the Holy Spirit have given a new interior life that must be made manifest in exterior conduct, which is a visible testimony of God's gift' (Spicq, p. 270).

This section can be divided into three parts (cf. Marshall, p. 298): (1) commands related to authorities and outsiders; (2) the theological basis for obeying the commands; 3) reinforcing of the commands.

---

43 Cf. Oberlinner (1996), pp. 160–161.

i. Commands towards authorities and outsiders (3:1–2)

Context

As indicated above, the early Christian leaders continuously taught the believers, especially new believers, how they should comport themselves regarding unbelievers, including the state authorities. Contextually, we should note that the posture towards outsiders, especially the state, that is urged here, was a matter that Judaism had already reflected upon carefully, which probably shaped the attitude of the Christians. The general belief in Judaism was that God had placed in power those who possessed authority, even when they were pagan kings and rulers (see esp. Dan. 2:21, 37; *Wis.* 6:1–3; *Letter of Aristeas* 219; Josephus, *J.W.* 1.390; *Ant.* 11.334. I owe some of these citations to Wolter, *Der Brief an die Römer*, 2:311). Therefore, one should submit to the authorities, unless asked to perform acts that go against Torah (e.g., idolatry). Jesus continued this tradition, thereby making the command more clearly obligatory for the church, when he commanded: 'Render to Caesar the things that are Caesar's, and to God the things that are God's' (KJV; Mark 12:17// Matt. 22:22//Luke 20:26). Paul does not thematize the matter here as he does in Romans 13:1–8: he gives *ad hoc* commands.

Comment

1. Connected with the imperative *remind*, Paul speaks of three obligations of the believers *vis-à-vis* the secular authorities: *to be subject … to be obedient … to be ready*. First, they are to submit *to rulers and authorities*. To submit to the authorities means to obey them, as the second infinitive, *to be obedient*, clarifies. The fundamental attitude is one of deference to the mandates of those in authority. In Romans 13:1–2 Paul provides a reason for such obedience, namely, that the authorities are in place because God established them. Here in Titus he will provide another reason, as we will see in verses 3–7. As to the sphere of obedience, the scope would be broad in a senatorial province such as Crete (together with Cyrene). At the top would be the emperor, who was represented at the province by a proconsul. This proconsul would have a 'team' (*apparitores*) of officials with him, which included clerks (*scribae*), bodyguards (*lictores*), errand-runners (*viatores*) as well as announcers (*praecones*). In addition, there would

be those immediate authorities who would have direct contact with
the population: tax collectors, officials supervising roads, streets,
aqueducts, and so on.[44] The proconsul would also have a *consilium*,
that is, an advisory board made up of his friends as well as members
of the local elites.[45] All of these people represented the *authorities*.

The final infinitive speaks of being 'ready for every good work'.
Paul often uses 'good work' in the Pastoral Epistles (see on 2:14;
2 Tim. 2:21), which can be directed towards fellow Christians and
non-Christians alike. Given the present context, he may be asking
Titus to remind the Christians at Crete to be cooperative with the
ruling authorities in performing acts of kindness to the populace.
Neudorfer reminds us that the concept here is similar to *philanthropia*
(see 3:4), which calls to mind the good works of patronage in the
ancient city-state.[46] Perhaps Paul calls the Christians to be engaged
in the type of city-sponsored benevolence that helped the poor.

2. With the addition of *no one*, Paul broadens the reminder beyond
the ruling authorities. The believers must *speak evil of no one*, or 'revile'
no one (see BDAG, p. 178). Instead of this, the believers should treat
everyone with the sense of kindness and courtesy that befits those
whose God is himself kind and loving. Paul expresses this thought
by employing terms that share the same semantic domain: *peaceable
and considerate … and always gentle*. To be noted is that the first two
virtues are also expected of the overseer (see 1 Tim. 3:2), while the
third is expected of 'the servant of the Lord' (2 Tim. 2:24). For Paul,
Christian virtues are not divided: one set for the clergy and another
(less demanding) for the rest of the Christians.

ii. The theological basis for obeying the commands (3:3–7)

Context
The structure of this text is a straightforward comparison of the
readers (and Paul's) existence before and after their salvation. First,

---

44 This helpful addition comes from the editor.
45 On the governance of the provinces, see particularly Fuhrmann,
    Policing the Roman Empire, chapter 8.
46 Neudorfer, *Titus*, p. 188.

with the word 'once' in combination to a list of vices, Paul describes their lives before conversion. They were spiritually 'sick', slaves to passions, and hating one another (v. 3). Second, beginning in the second half of verse 5, Paul speaks of their lives with the language of 'rebirth' and 'renewal', culminating in verse 7 with a look towards the future. He speaks of them as 'heirs' and describes their new existence as 'eternal life'. The middle or 'hinge' of this section is the phrase 'he saved us' (v. 5). The crafting of a text with a 'then/now' structure is also common in the other letters of Paul. One of the clearest is Ephesians 2:1–10. These texts serve as windows into Paul's theology of salvation. Humanity is in spiritual slavery due to its sin (and therefore also under God's wrath). But God, not on the basis of any merit of our own but completely on the basis of his mercy, has reached down to save us, the result being lives that are fundamentally different from those before conversion.

Comment

3. The logical connection between verses 1–2 and 3–11, as expressed by *for* at the beginning of verse 3, is the following: our treatment of other people (even enemies) with kindness and love stems out of the fact that God himself loved us when we led a depraved existence. The theological logic, then, is very similar to the love-command as expressed by Jesus: 'Love one another. As I have loved you, so you must love one another' (John 13:34; cf. 1 John 2:8; 3:23).

Paul continues with a list of vices describing behaviour prior to conversion: *For we ourselves were once.* We should note that Paul includes himself in this list, despite the fact that he was a scrupulously religious Pharisee (cf. Phil. 3:3–6). When Paul met the Lord Jesus Christ he had a new insight into his past life, an insight based on the fact that Jesus was the Messiah to which all the Scriptures pointed (see on 1 Tim. 1:12–16). The fact that Paul had violently rejected the Messiah demonstrated that, in the light of the advent of Jesus, his religious deeds could not transform his unrighteousness. *Foolish* (*anoētos*) is a general term found in many vice lists in moral philosophers.[47] It

---

47   See, e.g., Plato, *Gorg.* 505B; Dio Chrysostom, *Or.* 1.26; 3.33, 53; 4.126; 5.16 (with *epithymia* and *hēdonē*).

gives the sense of someone who is not able to reason morally and
therefore is ignorant, behaving like a child when they should be
mature. On *disobedient* see comments on 1:16 and 2 Timothy 3:2,
where the object of disobedience are parents, God and even the
state. The next vice is expressed with the passive voice, and is rightly
translated as *led astray* (see 2 Tim. 3:13). Deception, being *led astray*, by
false doctrine is a sign of spiritual blindness (see Matt. 15:14; 24:11).
Passions and pleasures are constitutive of humanity; God made us so
that we could experience these. However, passions and pleasures
– like a delight in beauty, wine, sexuality, sports, etc. – which are
good in themselves, can become enslaving when they turn into the
goals of our existence. This common human plight was clear to
Greco-Roman philosophers, with the result that the terms *epithymia*, *hēdonē* and (in Latin) *concupiscentia* often mean *evil* passions and
desires. Ultimately, our rejection of God with the aim of becoming
gods ourselves paradoxically leads to our being *slaves to various passions and pleasures*. Freedom is lost and we become addicted. It is only
logical, then, that in this state we should be *passing our days in malice
and envy* (contrast this phrase with 1 Tim. 2:2 where the same verb
is used). *Despicable* (*stygētos*) is a *hapax*, and not very common outside
the NT. It is not clear if the adjective has an active or passive sense
(despising or worthy of being despised); perhaps both are meant.
The final vice indicates reciprocity: *hating one another*. This is the
climax of the vices, since it is the opposite of the love-command
(see Matt. 22:34–40), which constitutes the central obligation and the
raison d'être of humanity: to love God and to love neighbour. *Hating
one another* simultaneously shows that we have no love for God.

4–7. Verse four is the hinge of the passage, with the adversative
but (*de*) introducing God's attitude and action towards a humanity
that does not love either God or human beings whom God created
to be loved. God's eternal response to humanity is love, a love that
reaches its climax[48] in the incarnation of Jesus Christ: *But when the
goodness and loving kindness of God our Saviour appeared.* The concept is

---

48 This is the case from the point of view of humanity: I take it that God's
love does not 'grow' in time. All his perfections (love, freedom, justice,
holiness, etc.) are complete from everlasting to everlasting: he is God.

the same as in the other great texts of God's love in the NT (e.g., John 3:16; Rom. 5:8; 1 John 4:8–9). The difference is that instead of using language and diction from the OT, Paul uses terminology that would have made sense to Greek ears: *chrēstotēs* and *philanthropia*. The meaning is the same: God has so loved humanity ('before the ages began', 2 Tim. 1:9) that he has *appeared*, that is, taken on human flesh for our redemption in the life, death and resurrection of Jesus Christ. In verse 5 Paul speaks of God's love in a different way, saying that God saves us *according to his mercy*.

5. Lest the readers misunderstand God's saving love as something that is congruous with their character, that is, that God *ought* to save them because they deserve it, the Greek of verse 5 begins with an emphatic negation: God saved us *not because any works of righteousness that we had done*. The thought is identical to Paul's statements in Romans and Galatians (e.g., Rom. 3:9–29; 5:8; Gal. 2:16; 3:11). And although some teachers from the Reformation might have decontextualized such statements at times, at the end of the day the Reformation teaching that any kind of good works cannot cause God to justify humanity is a biblical doctrine, based on passages such as these.

Verse 5 speaks of our salvation from the perspective of the Holy Spirit.[49] With a second prepositional phrase that correlates with the first one (*according to his mercy*), Paul expands on the meaning of salvation. Salvation is not only based on God's mercy; it is also *through the water of rebirth and renewal by the Holy Spirit*. This is a packed phrase, rich in theological meaning.

First, Paul describes the work of the Holy Spirit: *through the washing of rebirth and renewal* (NIV). The concept of washing referring to a spiritual cleansing is a core teaching of the Old Testament: 'Washing in the Bible is an outward physical action representing the desire for an inner spiritual cleansing.'[50] Key texts include Leviticus 17:11; Psalm 24:2; Isaiah 1:16; Ezekiel 36:25–27. Jesus takes this theme and applies it to himself as the one who is able to cleanse (e.g., his many

---

49 Thus, *pneumatos hagiou* at the end of verse five is a subjective genitive. See also Oberlinner (1996), p.175, n. 49.

50 Wenham, *Leviticus*, p. 139.

healing miracles; see also John 3:5–14; 13:6–10). The theme is developed into basic New Testament teaching in the context of baptism (see below and Eph. 5:26; Heb. 9:22; 1 Pet. 3:21). Thus, God's salvation of his people includes a washing and cleansing of all our iniquities. This leads the believer into thanksgiving and freedom.

The second comment has to do with the relationship between, on the one hand, *washing*, and on the other hand, *rebirth and renewal*. It seems that *washing*, *rebirth* and *renewal* are all variations of the same theme, namely the cleansing effected by the Holy Spirit. The act of salvation is presented as the work of the Holy Spirit, who cleanses us, causes us to be born again and renews us.

The third comment has to do with the relationship between *rebirth* and *renewal*, terms that are not common in the New Testament (cf. Eph. 5:26; John 3:5; 1 Pet. 1:3). We should note that both nouns are governed by the one preposition *through* (*dia*). It is likely, therefore, that two terms are used in order to highlight the *total* transformation performed by the Spirit. The language of *rebirth* in connection with the Holy Spirit is similar to Jesus' statements to Nicodemus in John 3:5, where he says to Nicodemus: 'Very truly I tell you, no one can see the kingdom of God unless they are born again.'

The fourth and final comment to be made about verse 5 is that *baptism* is the controlling image used to speak of salvation. The components of baptism in the New Testament include: water, cleansing, new existence by union with Christ and the work of the Holy Spirit (see Matt. 28:19; Acts 2:38; 9:17–18; 22:16; Rom. 6:2–11; 1 Cor. 6:11, 19; Eph. 4:4–5; 1 Pet. 3:21). Since baptism is the initiatory rite and act of obedience for all Christians, which serves as a picture of salvation, Paul uses it in order to help the Christians in Crete comprehend the meaning of salvation. It is not surprising, therefore, that many commentators see in these verses traditional, even liturgical, language of the early church.

Verse 6 continues the train of thought on salvation by speaking of a unified work of God, Messiah Jesus, and the Holy Spirit. The implied subject in the phrase *he poured out on us richly* is clearly God the Father. The thought reminds us of Luke 24:49 and especially of John 14:16–17: 'And I will ask the Father, and he will give you another Advocate, to be with you forever. This is the Spirit of truth, whom the world cannot receive … You know him, because he abides with you, and he will be in you.' The Father, then, pours out his Spirit on us. Paul then adds a concluding prepositional phrase: *through Jesus Christ our Saviour.* The point is not that Jesus is some necessary mediator between the Father and the Spirit: this would fragment the unity of the Triune God. Jesus is mentioned as the one *through* whom the Spirit was poured out in order to highlight the *unity* of the work of the one God in salvation. In both creation (Gen. 1:1–3; 2 Cor. 4:4; Col. 1:15–17) and new creation (John. 3:3–15; 14:16–17, 25–26; 16:12–15; Acts 2: 32–33; Gal. 3:13–14, 26–29), the Father, Son and Holy Spirit operate as the one God in three persons. The concept of salvation here is very similar to the speech of Peter at Pentecost, particularly Acts 2:32–34.

7. With verse 7 Paul expresses the ultimate aim of our salvation, which he has been explaining in the previous verses by means of baptism.[51] This aim is eschatological in nature, although we already experience eternal life, who is God himself: *so that we might become heirs according to the hope of eternal life.* The thought is similar to Romans 8:17; Galatians 3:29 and 1 Peter 1:4–9.

Paul qualifies the ultimate goal of eternal inheritance with the phrase *having been justified by his grace.* Teaching on justification, which is crucial in Romans and Galatians, is not as common in the Pastoral Epistles, perhaps because justification by grace was not a theme which was critical for the situations addressed in the Pastoral Epistles.

As in his other letters, the forensic analogy of justification highlights that, although we stood condemned before God on the basis of our sins, he, on the basis of the atoning life, death and resurrection of Jesus, no longer considers us guilty – we have been forgiven of all our sins! Since this is not by any merit of our own, Paul concludes the thought by saying that this is *by his grace* (see also Rom. 3:24; Eph. 2:5, 8). This is the positive counterpart to the phrase *not because of any works of righteousness we had done* (v. 5).

---

51   Of course, this does not in any way mean that the ritual of baptism saves us: this would be more like a magical operation than a Christian understanding of baptism. Paul uses the image of baptism to express a spiritual reality accomplished by God, not physical water (see Rom. 6:2–11).

We conclude by asking the question of why Paul has introduced teaching on justification in a section where he has primarily been employing baptism – and its constituent aspects of washing and regeneration. Justification does not seem to belong in this context. However, if one of the central aspects of baptism is union with Christ, then we could see why Paul would have included justification in this thought-unit. For justification is an aspect of our union with Christ. As John Calvin put it hundreds of years back, as long as we are separated from Christ, we cannot participate in any of his benefits; and we are united with Christ by the work of the Holy Spirit.[52] In fact, there is currently a wave of scholarship that views justification as emerging from our union with Christ.[53]

Theology

This is probably the richest theological section of Titus, if not of all the Pastoral Epistles. Verses 4–7 in particular speak of 'God our Saviour', 'the Holy Spirit', and 'Jesus Christ our Saviour'. Guthrie's statement is on target: 'There is in these verses a clear Trinitarian statement.'[54] The Father saves, the Son pours out the Spirit and the Holy Spirit causes us to be reborn and renewed. At the same time we must remember the wise *theologoumenon* (i.e., theological statement) of orthodoxy, namely, *opera trinitatis ad extra indivisa sunt*: the works of the Trinity beyond itself are indivisible. *Each* person of the Trinity is involved with one another in creation and redemption.

Some New Testament scholars, including evangelical biblical scholars, are hesitant to speak of the Trinity as the subject of explicit teaching in the canon of the New Testament. For these scholars, while we may speak of the Father, Son and Holy Spirit as the subjects of a New Testament text, the doctrine of the Trinity is said to *really* appear in the fourth century Nicene Creed. The key is what we mean by *doctrine*. If doctrine is densely, systematized thought that requires centuries to put together in specialized language and in the

---

52 *Inst.* 3.1.1, 4
53 See, e.g., Macaskill, *Living in Union with Christ*; Campbell, *Paul and Union with Christ*; Billings, *Union with Christ*.
54 Guthrie, p. 218.

face of doctrinal dangers against the universal church, then, indeed, the doctrine of the Trinity is not present in the New Testament. But why must we adopt *this* definition of doctrine? On the other hand, if we think of doctrine as simply a particular body of *teaching* (see Latin *doctrina*), or as a 'pattern of judgments', then I believe that we not only can but also must speak of the doctrine of the Trinity as already the fundamental Christian understanding of God in the New Testament.[55] This definition is as simple as the following: God is Father, Son and Holy Spirit – and this does not mean that there are three gods, but one God.

Titus 3:3–8 is one of those precious texts in the New Testament where we encounter an understanding of God as Father, Son and Holy Spirit.

iii. Closing, bookend exhortations (3:8-11)

Context
This final set of exhortations parallels those at the beginning (see Context for 3:1–2). This parallelism is seen in (1) the repetition of the motif of 'good works' *vis-à-vis* outsiders; (2) the repetition of terms (e.g., *amachos/machē*, vv. 2, 8; *pantas anthrōpous/tois anthrōpois*, vv. 2, 8). Once again we see that soteriology is related to ethics, particularly the ethics of missions (see 2:1–10, *Theology*).

Comment
8. *The saying is sure* refers back to the doctrinal statement of verses 3–7. For the meaning of this phrase, unique to the Pastoral Epistles in the New Testament, see on 1 Timothy 1:15. In light of the fundamental importance of what Paul has just taught (namely, that

---

55 In using the phrase 'pattern of judgments', I am leaning on Yeago's essay, 'The New Testament and the Nicene Dogma', pp.152–164. Yeago explains that while the Nicene concept of the *homoousion* is not present in the New Testament in the same *conceptual category*, nevertheless, the same 'pattern of judgments', namely, that Jesus and God are of 'one substance', is the same in the Nicene Creed as in the New Testament.

God saves us on the basis of grace), it is not surprising that he wants Titus to *insist on these things*. The gospel, in its many forms, must be taught constantly.

The purpose of the constant teaching of the gospel message is expressed in language that points to the ethical existence of the believers: *so that those who have come to believe in God may be careful to devote themselves to good works*. Proclamation of the gospel of grace does not lead to rebellious behaviour; rather, it is the foundation for a life dedicated to *good works*. As we have seen throughout the Pastoral Epistles, this repeated phrase envisions Christians in their relationship with both believers and unbelievers. Here, Paul refers to the latter: *these things are excellent and profitable to everyone*. The term translated *profitable* (*ōphelimos*) was often used by moral philosophers to speak of their own teaching, which they compared to medicine that was beneficial (*ōphelimos*) to sick patients. It is likely that the term *everyone* (*tois anthrōpois*, 'to people') refers to unbelievers (cf. 3:2). This should be understood in a *missional* sense. The good work of salvation from God received by the Christians is to be translated into good deeds for the benefit of unbelievers, always with a missional eye towards the knowledge of the Saviour.

9. This verse marks a contrast with verse 8. While one is to be devoted to good works, the vices listed are to be avoided. All of the terms used here have been used in 1 Timothy 1:3–7; 2 Timothy 2:23–26; Titus 1:10–16. As we have explained earlier, the types of vices mentioned by Paul probably stemmed from unhealthy curiosity about myths that had developed in Judaism. Devotion to these things results in the opposite of the good works of verse nine: *they are unprofitable and worthless*.

10–11. Now Paul provides Titus with a more precise example of what he is to avoid. He mentions the *divisive person* (*hairetikon anthrōpon*, NIV, CSB) as someone with whom he must *have nothing to do* (see 1 Tim. 4:7; 5:11). The situation that could be caused by the *divisive person* is similar to what we find in 1 Corinthians 1:10–17, where divisions were formed by people who were breaking up the congregation into different parties: 'I belong to Paul, I belong to Apollos, I belong to Cephas.' The *divisive person* is characterized by a delight in argumentation over even small doctrinal matters (Hutson, p. 245). The unity of the church is something they care little about.

Such a person, says Paul, *after a first and second admonition*, is to be avoided by Titus. Paul thinks of disciplining, or more likely the 'excommunication' of the individual (see similar texts in the Pastoral Epistles, e.g., 1 Tim. 1:18–20). However, we should note that with the use of the term *admonition* (*nouthesia*), the emphasis falls on the correction of the person so as to avoid a separation. Only in severe cases (after two admonitions) is some sort of separation the step.

Verse 11 provides the reason for the action described above. Paul uses two verbs, one in the perfect and the other in the present tense, to explain the problem with the person who causes division. The use of the perfect in the first verb communicates the idea that the divisive person finds himself (assuming that the divisive person is a male teacher) in such a state that he is *perverted*. The second verb is in the present, thereby pointing to the continuous sinning of the one who divides. The person is constantly sinning, in the sense of missing the mark. There is a strong sense of self-willingness in this individual: he has no one to blame but himself to arrive at this state of condemnation.

Theology

Titus 3:1–11, particularly 3:3–8, is the richest in theological content in the Pastoral Epistles. It is striking, therefore, that it is framed on both ends with exhortations that are ethical in nature. The logic is the following: our behaviour in everyday life is only possible on the foundation of God's antecedent gracious work on us. We can be gracious to the rest of humanity only when God has been gracious to us first. The reason for this is that God's gracious act of salvation is not some empty metaphor, at the end just human translation of what is really an immanent human potential. Biblical, Christian faith, by contrast, understands salvation as a genuine, transcendent act of the Father, Son and the Holy Spirit, who transforms us and thereby enables us to be gracious to all. This understanding of salvation then ineluctably leads to a life devoted to good works.

The gospel, then, as indicated above, must be taught in as many ways as possible. This can be done through preaching, teaching and singing; many denominations also take advantage of traditional liturgies that are rich in the gospel message.

3. FINAL INSTRUCTIONS AND CLOSURE
(3:12–15)

Context

The last section of the letter gives us a window into Paul the missionary administrator. He informs Titus of his own plans and directs him on how to proceed in the future. Lastly, Paul returns to the topic of good works, reminding Titus to encourage the churches in Crete to be fruitful.

Comment

12. *Do your best to come to me at Nicopolis.* As indicated in the Introduction, it is difficult to know with precision Paul's location when he wrote to Titus. The beginning of verse 12 does not mean that Paul is already at Nicopolis but that it is to be a future meeting place for Titus and him. It is possible that this took place during the first of Paul's two incarcerations at Rome (see Introduction). There were at least four cities named *Nicopolis* ('city of victory') during the Greco-Roman period. Here Paul refers to Nicopolis in Epirus, located across from Actium on the Preveza peninsula. The city was founded by Octavian (Caesar Augustus) near

31 BC after his defeat of Mark Anthony and Cleopatra at Actium (*OCD*, pp. 1015–1016). It became a free city of the province of Epirus. Although comparatively small, there was a lot of activity at Nicopolis, especially after Augustus made it the new site for the Actian games. Why Paul chose to spend the winter there he does not say.

Titus is to *do his best* to meet him in Nicopolis *when I send Artemas to you, or Tychicus*. Of the former nothing is known; the latter was a beloved co-worker of Paul and fellow missionary who also carried his letters to churches (see Acts 20:4; Eph. 6:21–22; Col. 4:7–8). According to 2 Timothy 4:12, Paul had sent him to Ephesus during the former's final Roman imprisonment.

13. *Make every effort to send Zenas the lawyer and Apollos on their way.* We have no other knowledge of Zenas except that he was a *lawyer* and a Christian. The term *nomikos* (*lawyer*; see Matt. 22:35) refers here probably to lawyer in Roman law (see LSJ, s.v.). Paul perhaps sends for him in order to obtain his advice. *Apollos* is probably the powerful preacher of the early church connected with Ephesus (Acts 18:24–28; cf. 1 Cor. 1:10–17; 3:1–23; 16:12). Titus is to 'assist' (*propempō*) these men *so that they lack nothing.* Clearly, then, Zenas and Apollos were with Titus at Crete. Titus is to make sure that they have whatever is needed for their journey.

14. Paul takes advantage of the letter closing for one last reminder for the believers in Crete *to devote themselves to good works.* Paul clarifies that this is something to be learned: *our people must learn to devote themselves to doing what is good* [NIV]. It is not contradictory to have experienced 'rebirth and renewal by the Holy Spirit' (3:5) and yet need time and effort to be engaged in Christian good works. The language of the following phrase, *in order to meet urgent needs* (*tas anankaias chreias*; see LSJ, s.v. for examples that corroborate the English translation), makes it clear that the *good works* are to help meet the basics of life of church members. Of course, in light of 3:1–2, 8, Christians should also help meet the needs of unbelievers. But the logic here is similar to Galatians 6:10.

15. Paul closes the letter by passing warm greetings from all the believers who are present with him. This must have been greatly encouraging to Titus. Paul then asks him to *greet those who love us in the faith*, where *faith* is shorthand for believers.

Grace be with you echoes the beginning of the letter (1:4), providing an *inclusio* for the entire correspondence, thereby showing the centrality of this concept for the letter.

Theology

The fact that Paul uses the closing of the letter, which was usually brief, to speak once more of the necessity of good works, demonstrates not only the need for the Cretan Christians to pay attention to this matter but also for all Christians to do the same. As in James 2:1–4 and 1 John 3:17, the church should prioritize providing for the basic needs of the Christian poor, without forgetting the poor outside her walls.